CREATION Cries Out!

the Heavenly Scroll

the book of the Mazzaroth

by Rav Sha'ul

Creation Cries Out! 3rd *Edition*
The book of the Mazzaroth

Creation Cries Out! 3rd Edition
The book of the Mazzaroth

by
Rav Sha'ul, author of
www.sabbathcovenant.com

To My Wife and Kids,
You Mean The World To Me.

Special thanks to Connie Sell for your labor of love editing this book you are a life saver! A special thank you to all who read this book, for trusting me with the most important knowledge in the Universe. I take that trust, and I guard it with my life.

Copyright © 2015 by Rav Sha'ul
All rights reserved. No part of this book may be reproduced, scanned, or distributed in any printed or electronic form without permission.
First Edition: 04/13 Third Edition 02/17
Printed in the United States of America
ISBN: **978-1511802673**

TABLE OF CONTENTS

Introduction 1
    Name corrections 2
    Context 4
    The beginning 5

The Scientific Dictatorship 12

The Battle of the Ages 16
    Yahuah declares that He authored the Zodiac… 16
    The Zodiac is His throne…................................. 16
    His message is securely written in the Zodiac and endures for all mankind to "see" … 16
    That message is understood by the Zodiac; which is the path the Sun takes through the constellations each year…17
    The Zodiac is the gospel message of the coming Messiah Yahusha….. 17
    It is Yahuah's will declared in the Zodiac that will be done on Earth….. 17
    We are forbidden to misuse the Zodiac by creating images of the Zodiac Signs to worship… 18
    We are forbidden from worshipping the signs of the Zodiac, they are not gods but a message to all mankind…
.... 18
    The Zodiac reveals Yahuah's wrath upon all those who abuse it… 18

Chapter 1

The Role of Myth and Science 24
    Mythology... 26
    Giants: Fact or Fiction?....................................... 26
    The Nephilim 28
    Vampires: Fact or Fiction?................................... 30

The Book of Enoch.................................. 35
    The Book of Enoch – an eye witness to our origins 38

Why the fallen angels hate YAHUAH?........................... 39
The Watchers taught humanity the heavenly secrets........ 40
Ancient Genetic Engineering..................... 42
Conclusion... 44

Chapter 2
Yahuah Created and Named the Stars!..... 46
Yahuah is the author of the Zodiac................................... 47
God's Sun a metaphor for God's Son............................... 53
The Plan of Salvation laid out in The Heavenly Scroll.. 56
The Blind Following the Blind.. 58
Creation is crying out the Plan of Salvation
.... 61
The Heavenly Scroll is the FOUNDATION of the Earthly Scroll.. 65
Amos... 65
King David.. 65
Moses.. 66
Job.. 66
Enoch.. 67
Ezekiel.. 68
Zechariah.. 69
Isaiah... 69
John the Revelator.. 71
Daniel.. 74
Yahusha... 77
Peter.. 78
Sha'ul... 78

Chapter 3

Sha'ul declared Faith comes the message proclaimed by The Heavenly Scroll! 81
"How Yahuah preached the Gospel to Abraham" 90

    Star names and languages by Barry Sutterfield 90
    Seasons and constellations by Barry Sutterfield 91
    The stars carry a gospel message by Barry Sutterfield 92
    The importance of the Sun by Barry Sutterfield 93
    The strong man constellation figures by Barry Sutterfield 94
    The origin of mythology and tradition by Barry Sutterfield
    94
    God's promise to Abraham by Barry Sutterfield 96
    The significance of the Sphinx by Barry Sutterfield 97

Chapter 4

A lamb that has been slain from the foundation of the world 99

Chapter 5

What is the Zodiac? 122
The 12 Signs of the Zodiac 126

Chapter 6

The Heavenly Scroll 131

    Faith comes from 'hearing' the message in the stars!..... 138
    The Heavenly Scroll is opened 144

Chapter 7
The Zodiac proclaims the Feast Cycle.... 148
The annual wedding portrait 153
The Physical Shadow of Greater Truths 154

Chapter 8
Righteous Astrology? 163
Daniel the Chief Astrologer.................... 165
Astrologers the only ones to find the King 166
Yahusha the Astrologer?.. 167
The Sign of the Son of Man..................... 170
The meaning of the Sphinx 172

Chapter 9
How to read the scroll in Heaven 175
Where did the images come from? 175
Constructing the images of the Signs of The Zodiac 178
Decans... 180
Virgo 182
Libra 186
Scorpio 189
Sagittarius... 193
Capricorn... 197
Aquarius 200
Pisces 204
Aries 208
Taurus.. 212

Gemini 215
Cancer 218
Leo 221
The Solar Messiah 225
    The Sun foretells the crucifixion and resurrection 229
    The Sun is a physical metaphor of the Son 230
The Messiah as 'The Son of Man' 233
The Messiah as the Bread of Heaven 236
The Mazzaroth 240
Enoch's Zodiac in detail 248
    John reveals the meaning of Enoch's Zodiac 250
    Ezekiel's vision of the Enoch Zodiac 252
    The 4 "wheels within a wheel" 255
    "Full of eyes all around" vs. 18 256
    The throne like a rainbow 257
Heaven – is the Mazzaroth? 259
    Exodus 20 – You shall have no other gods in my face! .. 260
    Deuteronomy 3 – gods in heaven 261
    Deuteronomy 3 – The whole heavenly creation given to all humanity 262
    Psalms 119 - Yahuah's instructions/plan preserved in heaven 263
    Psalms 11 – The Throne of Yahuah in heaven 264
Origin of the Book of the Mazzaroth 266

Chapter 10
Ages & Epochs of Mankind 270
    "The Great Year" 271
    Ages are approximately 2,000 years each 275
Yahuah's Celestial Clock 276
    The Plan of Salvation 277

The Sabbath Covenant 278
The Messiah's birth synchronized 280
Enoch's Timepiece – the Zodiac Ages 281
What does the Bible say about 'ages'? 283

Age Transitions 286
The Ages 288
The Age of Gemini 289
The Age of Taurus 289
The Age of Aries 294
The Age of Pisces 295
The Age of Aquarius 296
The Festival of Water Libation 300
Why 12 constellations? 304

Chapter 11
When was the Debar fulfilled in the flesh?
.... 307
What year was the birth of the King? 312
The Scriptural "clues"! 313
The Evidence 313

Chapter 12
The Bible and The Zodiac: Two scrolls, one message 319
"I will not yield my glory to another" … Yahuah Elohim 328
Divin'ation? Or Divine Revelation? 331
Divine Corrections 340
Prophet or a Soothsayer? 345
True Prophets of Yahuah 346

Astrologers called "wise men" by Yahuah 346
False Prophets, soothsayers, and star gazers 347

Does the Bible forbid the Zodiac, or the misuse of it? 348
Do the stars have influence 353
Humanity denies the Creator 363

Chapter 13
The Foundation of All Faiths 366
The Zodiac – Foundation from which all faith was established 368

Historical Evidence 375
The ruins of the Hammath-Tiberias synagogue 375
Mosaic of Zodiac on the floor of the synagogue at Zippori 379
Synagogue at Ein Gedi 382
Mosaic of Zodiac at the Synagogue at Ein Harod 383
Mosaic of Zodiac at Synagogue Floor at Beit Alpha 384
The Zodiac in the early Church 386

More abominations from the false prophet 391

Chapter 14
Messianic Solar Counterfeits 395
The Battle of the Ages 399
Attributes of all god-men throughout history 400
God's Sun or the Sun of God 401
Why the cross is the universal symbol of ancient religions 403
Solar Messiahs 406
The Sun foretells of the death and resurrection 408

Conclusion 411
The 'Battle of the Ages' continues… 419
   Book 1: Creation Cries Out! 420
   Book 2: Mystery Babylon the Religion of the Beast 421
   Book 3: 'Christianity and the Great Deception' 422
   Book 4: 'The Antichrist Revealed!' 423
   Book 5: 'The Kingdom' 424
   Book 6: 'The Yahushaic Covenant Volume 1 - The Mediator' 425
   Book 7: 'The Yahushaic Covenant Volume 2 - The Law and the Sha'uline Doctrine' 426
   Book 8: 'The Yahushaic Covenant Volume 3 - Melchizedek and the Passover Lamb' 427
   Book 9: 'The Narrow Gate' 428
   Book 10: The Mistranslated Book of Galatians 429
   Book 11: The Nazarene 430

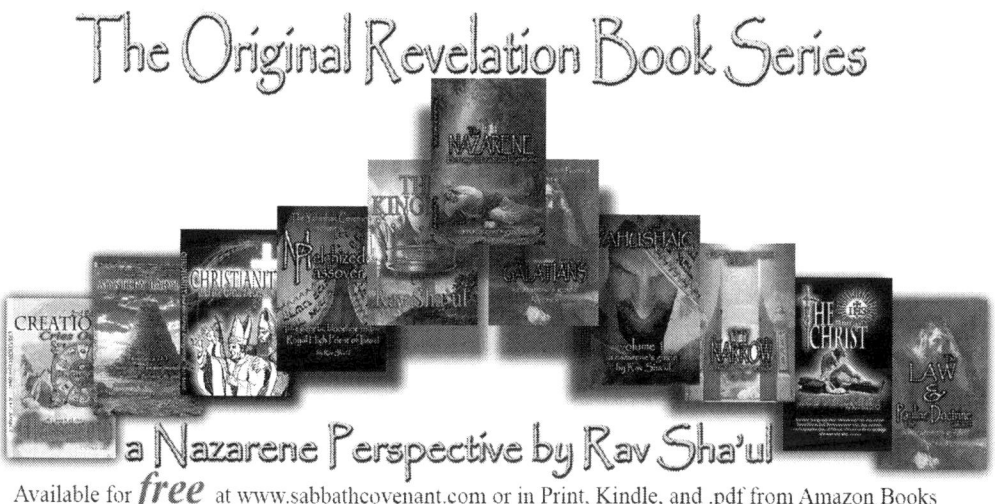

Available for *free* at www.sabbathcovenant.com or in Print, Kindle, and .pdf from Amazon Books

Introduction

You have just begun the journey of a lifetime! This is the first book in a 11-book series. Over the course of this book series, every question you could ever possible ask is answered in great detail. Those who finish this book series will have a foundation set so firmly in stone; nothing will ever be able to shake it again. However, your current foundation is about to be rocked to the very core. For that, I offer my sincere prayers; because it is going to be painful at times. In the end, however, it will be well worth the journey, and you too will look back and thank Yahuah for the day you made the decision to take this journey with me.

I am deeply humbled that you have trusted me with the most sacred knowledge in the Universe! I take that very seriously. Although at time, you will think I have completely lost my mind! You will want to just close the book and toss it in the nearest trash bin. Press through that inclination and, as you continue, you will come to realize that it is established religion and tradition that is the author of all the confusion. I am just helping you sort it all out.

Name corrections

First, let me say, that throughout all the books in this series '***Original Revelation***', I will replace the titles of *The LORD* and *God* (where used as a personal proper name) with the proper name of ***The Creator*** as given to Moses, which is ***Yahuah*** (which is the English transliteration of the Paleo Hebrew script 𐤉𐤄𐤅𐤄, YHWH or Yahweh in modern Hebrew).

I will replace the name *Jesus Christ* with the proper name of the Messiah, which is **Yahusha the Messiah**.

I will **most of the time** replace the word 'God' with 'Elohim' when used as a <u>common noun</u>. However, I may at times leave the word "God" when used as a <u>common noun</u>, because certain phrases such as "the son of God" embody a certain idea, and I will leave it that way <u>for effect</u>....

The word "God" is never to be used as a proper noun or name, and is only acceptable as a common noun. I realize there are teachers who have made the English language into a stumbling block, claiming the proper name of a pagan deity known as "Gad" is the same word in English "God". These are two separate words, two separate spellings, they are *Homonyms* (two words that sound the same, but have different spellings and meanings). We all must be more mature than that, the English language has words, and definition of words, and we cannot make a connection between two words <u>in two totally different languages</u> based solely on how they "sound".

"God", in English has no associated meaning related to a pagan god in Hebrew. There is no word trail to link them, and the English language is not based on the Hebrew language.

"God" is used in error, as a proper name in English in addressing the Creator. The use of God as a proper name is an abomination, and a violation of the 3rd Commandment.

> **Definition:** *Proper noun* - A proper noun is a noun that in its primary application refers to a unique entity by name.

"God" in English can also be used as a common noun, referring to the "class of entity"; for example, *deity*. This is how the Bible uses this term, *Elohim*, translated as *God*. For example, YHVH Elohim translated in English would be Yahuah (who is a) God (or deity). When used in that way, it is perfectly acceptable, we are not calling Yahuah by the name "Gad", we are using "God" as a common noun.

> **Definition:** *Common noun* - common noun, which usually refers to a class of entities (city, planet, person, corporation), or non-unique instances of a specific class (such as deity, human or animal)

I will explain in this book series how the Creator's name, ***Yahuah,*** was originally in the scriptures over 8,000 times. The true name was removed by human tradition and replaced with titles *The Lord* and *God* (which can be used as titles for pagan gods, not the proper name of the Creator). Adding to and removing from scripture is expressly forbidden.

In book 3, ***Christianity and the Great Deception***, I will prove the name *Jesus H. Christ* is not the name of the Messiah but the name of the Roman demi-god created at the Council of Nicaea by combining 3 pagan gods. Rome (Constantine) took the three most popular pagan gods in the Roman Empire: ***Hesus*** (the Druid god of the Western regions), ***Horus*** (the Middle Eastern god), and ***Krishna*** (the god of the Far Eastern regions) and combined them into one Greek appropriate demi-god named ***Hesus Horus Krishna***.

Over time the *J* was introduced into our languages (only a few hundred years ago) and *Hesus* became ***Jesus***. *Horus* was abbreviated to ***H.***, and *Krishna* is Sanskrit for *Christ*. Therefore, over time, *Hesus Horus Krishna* became *Jesus Horus Krishna* then *Jesus H. Krishna* and finally the name has evolved into ***Jesus H.***

Christ. I know this is shocking and hard to believe. This name has intentionally been placed in all our Bibles replacing the true name of the Messiah which is ***Yahusha***. We all have come to love and even worship this name Jesus. There was a time in my own life, when I would have literally cut out my own tongue, rather than defame that name. I simply request that the reader be patient, because in time I will prove everything with historical documents and Catholic Church records over the course of this book series.

For the sake of this first book in the series, I just wanted to explain the correction of *The LORD* and *God* (when used as a proper noun) with Yahuah; and Jesus with Yahusha.

Context

Throughout my book series, I will put each scripture I quote back into context using blue parenthesis if you are viewing this book in color or just parenthesis if in black and white.

In this books series, I will re-establish what the Bible truly teaches in context; and embed within New Testament scriptures references to OT scriptures and visa versa. I do this to show how the Bible fits together like a perfect puzzle. When context is added in this way, the verses literally jump off the page with meaning. The New Testament cannot be properly understood outside of this much needed context of the original scriptures; because the New Testament testifies to Yahusha the Messiah's fulfillment of all the covenants found in the original scriptures (what we in error call the Old Testament). All Scripture must be understood in context of The Heavenly Scroll which is the Original Revelation and foundation of the Earthly scrolls. All of this will be covered in great detail throughout this book series.

The beginning

Before we can understand why the Bible is true, we must first go back to the foundation of Truth; which is the original revelation given to all mankind. The Bible outright declares that Yahuah is the Creator of the Universe, and that His creation literally "cries out" His existence and His Plan of Salvation to all mankind written in the stars. Creation is the "***Original Revelation***" from Yahuah to all mankind. Yahuah literally designed into His Creation the very first Gospel of Yahusha the Messiah. It is Yahuah's witness of His first born son, and stamp over His Creation. It was first written in the stars, then written in stone, and finally written on our hearts. That is where this journey begins, and what this book brings to life. This is why I named this book ***Creation Cries Out!***:

> **Luke 19**
> 37 When he came near the place where the road goes down the Mount of Olives, the whole crowd of disciples began joyfully to praise Yahuah in loud voices for all the miracles they had seen: 38 "Blessed is the king who comes in the name of Yahuah!" "(bringing) Peace (foretold) in (the) heaven(nly scroll) and (fulfilling the) glory (promised) in the highest (realm i.e. The Heavenly Scroll Psalm 19)!" 39 Some of the Pharisees in the crowd said to Yahusha, "Teacher, rebuke your disciples!" 40 "I tell you," he replied, "if they keep quiet, the stones will cry out."

What Yahusha was saying was simple... creation cries out that he is the Messiah! We have stopped listening, however, and as Sha'ul the Apostle proclaimed in Romans Chapter 1; *we have begun to worship the creature over The Creator*. It is for this reason I titled this book ***Creation Cries Out!*** The question is: "How?" In what "way" does creation *cry out* and "what" exactly is it saying?

In this book, we will look into these questions further, and demonstrate that there is a pure Hebrew star chart (yes, the Zodiac) called the *Mazzaroth* in scripture. The *Mazzaroth* was intended for spiritual enlightenment that points to Yahusha as The Messiah in a divine plan of salvation for mankind.

Yes, Yahuah literally wrote the *Plan of Salvation* into the stars and used it to witness to Abraham, all the prophets, King David, the assembly in Galatia, Sha'ul the Apostle, John the Revelator, and many others in scripture as we will see. *The Mazzaroth/Zodiac* is mention and literally defined in the pages of the Bible! All references to 'heaven' are literally referring to the *Mazzaroth*. However, the false religion has conditioned us to believe the Mazzaroth/Zodiac is evil; and that we should not even seek out the message found within it. Much like we have been conditions to believe the Law (instructions in righteousness) is to be shunned and anyone who even looks at it will fall from grace!

The term "Zodiac" simply means "path or circuit" or "the way" that the sun follows as it journeys through the stars (as visible from Earth) over the course of a year. It is a scientifically accurate chart of the heavens showing the "cross" of the equinoxes and solstices. There is nothing inherently "evil" about it. In this book I will demonstrate that this original star chart was corrupted by the angelic realm. The angelic realm corrupted the message of creation as to hide the true messiah behind a false messiah. This was the very reason for the angel's fall from grace (among a few other things which we will discuss).

The existence of powerful counterfeits surrounding the Zodiac, such as astrology, mysticism, magic, fortune telling, palm reading, etc. <u>strongly suggests a real body of truth lies within the Zodiac that was lost when Adam fell</u>. This "truth", that Adam knew walking in close communion with Yahuah is known as "***Original Revelation***" and is found written in the stars. That is why the Mazzaroth/Zodiac is the focal point of the enemy's attack to corrupt it and convince us that it is evil. It is true that the Mazzaroth has been corrupted and used for evil. That must change. This ***Original Revelation*** that lived in the mind of Adam began to fade into confusion in the mind and memory of man after mankind fell, and was separated from His Creator. This ***Original Revelation*** of truth was further perverted by the angels (Watchers as they are called in the Book of Enoch) resulting today in an array of religions, myths, fables, legends, saviors, and gods.

The basic premise of this book is that a perfect revelation existed between Yahuah and man in the beginning. The first man, Adam, was one with Yahuah (in mind/will/purpose/spirit) and perceived divine knowledge from the mind of The Creator. Like angels; Adam was "in tune" with the mental processes of Yahuah, and understood, therefore, what Yahuah knew about science, astronomy, cosmology, eschatology, and so on.

After the fall, Adam was "detached" from the mind of Yahuah. He did, however, retain an imperfect memory of the *Original Revelation* including knowledge of Yahuah's Plan of Salvation written in the stars at creation. This point of view seems reasonable when one considers that the earliest historical and archeological records from civilizations around the world consistently point back to and repeat portions of a similar creation story.

Three things began to occur over time after the fall:

1. The *Original Revelation* began to fade, and became distorted as it was dispersed among the nations and was passed from generation to generation.

2. The realm of fallen angels seized upon this opportunity to receive worship, and to turn people away from Yahuah, by distorting and counterfeiting the *Original Revelation* with pagan ideas and "gods" based on worship of the Sun, Moon, Stars, and Constellations.

3. Mankind began inventing myths and legends of god-men to fulfill the prophecies in the Heavenly Scroll and religions were formed abound these myths and legends.

Instead of viewing the "heavens" (i.e. the stars) as a heavenly map or pictographs foretelling the Plan of Salvation, spread out by Yahuah for all mankind. We began celebrating the stars, the constellations, the Sun, and the moon, and worshiping the 'deities' believed to be represented by them. Mankind was led astray rebellious angels who desired our worship. Humanity began worshipping so-called "incarnate god/men" who were solar false messiahs based on the corrupted message of the Mazzaroth/Zodiac, and the Sun, moon, and stars, and the signs of the Zodiac (birds, four footed animals, and crawling creatures).

Sha'ul pointed out our error below very clearly as he condemned the Church in Rome" for corrupting the Zodiac through mythology:

> **Romans 1**
> The wrath of Yahuah is being revealed from heaven (H8064 shamayim - The place where the stars are located i.e. the Zodiac) against all the godlessness and wickedness of people, who suppress the truth (of its message) by their wickedness (and worship the signs of the Zodiac, Sun, Moon, and stars Deuteronomy 3:19), 19 since what may be known about Yahuah (the Plan of Salvation) is plain to them (proclaimed in The Zodiac), because Yahuah has made it plain to them (this message goes out unto all the Earth Psalms 19, given to all mankind Deuteronomy 3:19). 20 For since the creation of the world (written in the stars at creation Rev. 13:8, 1 Peter 1:20) Yahuah's invisible qualities—his eternal power and divine nature—have been clearly seen (in The Zodiac Galatians 3:1, as Yahuah witnessed the Gospel to Abraham Genesis 15:5), being understood (they are metaphors and analogies) from what has been made (in heaven: the Sun, Moon, stars, and constellations Psalms 119), so that people are without excuse. 21 For although they knew Yahuah (is The Creator), they neither glorified him as Elohim nor gave thanks to him (for the message proclaimed in the Zodiac), but their thinking became futile (understanding the Zodiac literally as gods) and their foolish hearts were darkened (to worship the creation over The Creator). 22 Although they claimed to be wise (through science, religion, tradition, philosophy and mythology), they became fools (1 Cor. 1:25) 23 and exchanged the glory of the immortal Elohim (the Glory of Yahuah is Yahusha 2 Corinthians 4:6! So they exchanged Yahusha) for images made to look like a mortal human being (solar demi-gods) and birds and animals and reptiles (the signs of The Zodiac).

> *Notice how I inserted CONTEXT into the letter above to demonstrate the true meaning. I do this throughout the entire book series.*

In his book, ***The Real Meaning of the Zodiac***, Dr. James Kennedy echoes such ideas, pointing out that the ancient signs of the Zodiac record a singular and original revelation -- a kind of Gospel in the stars--and that the message of the stars, although converted into astrology after the fall of man, originally recorded the Gospel of Yahuah that points to the Messiah Yahusha. He writes:

> *"There exists in the writings of virtually all civilized nations a description of the major stars in the heavens-- something which might be called their "Constellations of the Zodiac" or the "Signs of the Zodiac," of which there are twelve. If you go back in time to Rome, or beyond that to Greece, or before that to Egypt, Persia, Assyria, or Babylonia--regardless of how far back you go, there is a remarkable phenomenon: Nearly all nations had the same twelve signs, representing the same twelve things, placed in the same order....The book of Job, which is thought by many to be the oldest book of the Bible, goes back to approximately 2150 B.C., which is 650 years before Moses came upon the scene to write the Pentateuch; over 1,100 years before Homer wrote the Odyssey and the Iliad; and 1,500 years before Thales, the first of the philosophers, was born. In chapter 38, God finally breaks in and speaks to Job and to his false comforters. As He is questioning Job, showing him and his companions their*

> *ignorance, God says to them:* "**Canst thou bind the sweet influences of Pleiades, or loose the bands of Orion? Canst thou bring forth Mazzaroth in his season? or canst thou guide Arcturus with his sons?**" *(Job 38:31,32).*

We see here reference to the constellations of Orion and Pleiades, and the star Arcturus. Also in the book of Job there is reference to Cetus, the Sea Monster, and to Draco, the Great Dragon. Job refers to the Zodiac specifically (Hebrew Mazzaroth means Zodiac!)

Job 38:32
"Canst thou bring forth Mazzaroth in his" season?"

Mazzaroth is a Hebrew word which means "*The Constellations of the Zodiac.*" In what may be the oldest book in all of human history, we find that the constellations of the Zodiac were already clearly known and understood... Having made it clear that the Bible expressly, explicitly, and repeatedly condemns what is now known as astrology, the fact remains that there was a God-given Gospel [*universally acknowledged original revelation*] in the stars which lies beyond and behind that which has now been corrupted." That message is the Zodiac! We are going to sort through it all in this book, and get back to the ***Original Revelation*** that witnessed to Adam, Enoch, Noah, Abraham, King David, Sha'ul, and to all the inhabitants of Earth. How are we going to do that? By simply looking to the heavens just like Abraham did, like David did, like Daniel did, and like Yahusha did… to find what Yahuah had written in the stars for all humanity as uniquely viewed from Earth. The Zodiac.

There is a very real truth found "written in the stars". All ancient civilizations, every culture, across every language and throughout all time, has ended up with twelve constellations (signs) of the Zodiac, and many legends connected with these signs contain similar themes and stories. The names of stars and constellations and their meaning has remained constant over time throughout all cultures. However, the truth found written into the stars has been diluted over time through many cultures as the memory of Yahuah's ***Original Revelation*** faded. For this reason, we must study the history of man passed down from generation to generation through legend, myth, oral traditions, hieroglyphics, art, music, poetry, literature, ancient languages, and <u>even world religions</u> in order to understanding what this ***Original Revelation*** revealed. We must establish this ***Original Revelation*** because it is the foundation of the Plan of Salvation for mankind through a coming human Messiah. That plan was then revealed over many thousands of years to mankind through the covenants in the Bible from Genesis to Revelation and ultimately fulfilled in Yahusha the Messiah.

The Scientific Dictatorship

Our generation today relies almost completely on science as the final arbitrator in matters of human history. This scientific *illusion* that we *know more and are more advanced than our ancient ancestors* is simply untrue. In fact, we have been moving quickly (as a race) downhill in our quality of life, richness of our cultures, our social lives, and our families as we descend into a scientific dictatorship that controls every aspect of our lives. Tragically, we are moving further and further away from our Creator and the knowledge our ancient ancestors possessed.

Science, left unchecked, serves to separate us from our Creator. Science, alone outside of all other disciplines, tends to unite us with the physical world destroying the basic concepts of a "spiritual" humanity set apart by Yahuah (the Creator) for a purpose. Science also removes the supernatural aspect of Yahuah's creation! We are living at the end of history, and we are now very far removed from the profound realities men knew concerning our origins and our Creator before and just after the Flood of Noah.

In this book, we are going to look deep into what the Bible actually says concerning the stars and the message contained within them. We are going to compare what the Bible says… to what the Zodiac proclaims. We are going to look into "sun worship" and its origins. *We are going to leave no stone unturned.* My hope is that we can more fully understand how man fell into worshipping the creation over the Creator. The main concept I want to explore is *"what is the Gospel written in the stars for all mankind to see?"* Can we discern it? If so, can we then understand the confusion between Mystery Babylon and the Bible and resolve it? If we can do that, we can bring humanity out of idolatry and back to the Creator! After all, that is what His children are on this Earth to accomplish.

The battle for humanity has waged since man was created and Adam was separated from Yahuah. That battle rages even today as we struggle to clearly understand the "message" in the heavens; because that was corrupted into "sun worship". Sun worship has been passed on through tradition and religion and is the largest religion on Earth today... we call it Christianity! This is where we get Sunday worship (Dias Solis i.e. the day of the Invincible Sun) and rituals such as Christmas and Easter. None of these rituals of sun worship are ordained in scripture. These rituals are, in fact, condemned outright by Yahuah.

For example, we see this battle rage in 2 Kings:

> **2 Kings 23**
> 4 The king ordered Hilkiah the high priest, the priests next in rank and the doorkeepers to remove from the temple of Yahuah all the articles made for Baal (Babylonian Sun God Nimrod) and Asherah (Babylonian Queen of Heaven Ishtar/Easter) and all the starry hosts (they worshipped the constellation which 'host stars'). He burned them outside Jerusalem in the fields of the Kidron Valley and took the ashes to Bethel. 5 He did away with the idolatrous priests appointed by the kings of Judah to burn incense on the high places of the towns of Judah and on those around Jerusalem—those who burned incense to Baal (The LORD), to the sun and moon, to the constellations and to all the starry hosts.... He removed from the entrance to the temple of Yahuah the horses that the kings of Judah had dedicated to the sun. They were in the court near the room of an official named Nathan-Melek. Josiah then burned the chariots dedicated to the sun.

So we see in the Bible that even the children of Israel continually fell back to the corrupted message of the Zodiac and began worshipping the signs of the Zodiac, Sun, and moon. Later in the New Testament, as I have shown already, Rav Sha'ul the Apostle confronted this very same practice in Rome (***Romans 1***).

It is my goal with this book series, ***Original Revelation***, to restore back to Yahuah the message that He authored in His creation. This book, ***Creation Cries Out!*** is the first step in that journey. This book will demonstrate that the Bible and Apocryphal books such as the Book of Enoch clearly teach that the God of Creation (***whose name is Yahuah***) is the author of the Zodiac. He is the one who pre-determined the path the sun takes through the constellations (He named), and the stars (He named). Yahuah declares very strongly and clearly that He named the "signs" of the Zodiac (the Constellations) and gave them their meanings. He authored a "Gospel" message in them for all mankind, so Yahuah declares. The story the Zodiac reveals is that of Yahusha, the Messiah of Israel and by proxy… the savior of mankind. It was the fallen angelic realm that corrupted this message into astrology, magic, mysticism, and misled humanity to gain worship and control.

The main idea in this first book is to establish one simple very important truth. That truth is that at the beginning of mankind there were two revelations:

1. One revealed by Yahuah to Adam/Enoch/Noah/Abraham etc. and it is the "story of salvation through a messiah" written in the stars.

2. The other revealed by fallen angels to the Sumerians and Babylonians that the Zodiac contained solar demi-gods and the Sun, Moon, Stars, and Constellations were to be worshipped.

Since the beginning of modern man, the false revelation of mythology and Sun worship has competed with the Truth of Yahuah for the hearts and minds of man… and the lie is winning that battle. It is a battle that rages from Genesis to Revelation, when in the end Yahusha the Messiah returns to destroy the false image known as the False Messiah and puts an end to the Mystery Religion of Babylon.

What I will reveal in this book is not "Astrology" as we think of it today, that is the twisted use of the Zodiac, and an abomination to Yahuah. Abusing the Zodiac is strictly forbidden. There is only man's future foretold by the heavens, and that is the Messiah Yahusha's. The watchers twisted the revelation of Yahuah and taught women magic, spells, palm reading, horoscopes, and to use the signs of the Zodiac for the purpose of fortune telling. I will explain all of this in detail in this book.

The first to be attacked by the enemy was the revelation of the Messiah in the Plan of Salvation written in the stars. The Bible calls it the Mazzaroth and Heavenly Scroll. We, today, call it the Zodiac. It is time we reclaim His handiwork and restore back to The Creator the heavens, the stars, the constellations (which He named) and the revelation they conspire to keep a secret. There is a *"secret preserved in the heavens"* as Enoch proclaimed and we will reveal that eternal secret in this book:

Enoch Chapter 9

*6 things, and nothing can hide itself from Thee. Thou seest what Azazel hath done, who hath taught all unrighteousness on earth **and revealed the eternal secrets which were (preserved) in heaven**, which 7 men were striving to learn.*

The problem is, in striving to learn these secrets in the stars, we sought answers from angels, not Yahuah. A costly mistake.

The Battle of the Ages

This book lays the foundation for the sons of Yahuah to retake the Zodiac, and reclaim its message from the enemy. The *Battle of the Ages* is literally the battle for creation! This battle began with the very first Gospel of the Messiah written in the stars which was promptly corrupted. Now we have the Truth vs. the Lie and a 6000-year battle to reclaim the Heavenly Scroll.

Yahuah declares that He authored the Zodiac...

> **Isaiah 40:26**
> Lift up your eyes and look to the heavens (the Zodiac): Who created all these? He who brings out the starry host (constellations) one by one and calls forth each of them (the constellations) by name. Because of his great power and mighty strength, not one of them is missing (there are exactly 12 constellations in every culture dating back to the origin of man!).

The Zodiac is His throne...

> **Psalms 11**
> 4 Yahuah is in his holy temple; Yahuah's throne is in heaven (shamarym/Zodiac). His eyes watch; his eyes examine all people.

> **Isaiah 66:1**
> This is what Yahuah says: "Heaven (shamarym/Zodiac) is my throne, and the earth is my footstool. Where is the house you will build for me? Where will my resting place be?

His message is securely written in the Zodiac and endures for all mankind to "see"...

> **Psalms 119**
> O Yahuah, your instructions endure; they stand secure in heaven (originally written in the stars, untouched by human

hands).

That message is understood by the Zodiac; which is the path the Sun takes through the constellations each year...

Psalm 19
1 The heavens (stars and constellations) declare the glory of Yahuah; the skies proclaim the work of his hands. 2 Day after day they pour forth speech; night after night they reveal knowledge. 3 They have no speech, they use no words; no sound is heard from them. 4 Yet their voice goes out into all the earth, their words to the ends of the Age. In the heavens (among the Stars and Constellations) Yahuah has pitched a tent for the sun (the Zodiac). 5 It is like a bridegroom (Yahusha) coming out of his chamber (to wed the Bride, Remnant Israel), like a champion (Conquering King) rejoicing to run his course (through the ecliptic). 6 It rises at one end of the heavens and makes its circuit (Zodiac means circuit of circle or path) to the other; nothing is deprived of its warmth.

The Zodiac is the gospel message of the coming Messiah Yahusha...

Genesis 15
5 And he brought him forth abroad, and said, Look now toward heaven, and tell (what the) the stars (proclaim), if thou be able to discern the order of them (the Zodiac): and he said unto him, So shall thy seed be (the Messiah)

It is Yahuah's will declared in the Zodiac that will be done on Earth...

Matthew 6:10
"your kingdom come, your will be done, on earth as it is where the stars are visible in the sky (Mazzaroth)"

We are forbidden to misuse the Zodiac by creating images of the Zodiac Signs to worship...

Exodus 20
Yahuah spoke all these words: 2 "I, Yahuah, am your Elohim, who brought you from the land of Egypt, from the house of slavery. 3 "You shall have no other gods before me (in My face). "You shall not make for yourself a carved image or any likeness of anything that is in heaven (shamayim i.e. the Mazzaroth) above or that is on the earth beneath or that is in the water below.

We are forbidden from worshipping the signs of the Zodiac, they are not gods but a message to all mankind...

Deuteronomy 3:19
When you look up to the sky (sky is Hebrew shamayim/Zodiac) and see the sun, moon, and stars (speaking of the Zodiac) — the whole heavenly (Mazzaroth/Zodiac) creation — you must not be seduced to worship and serve them (signs of the Zodiac), for Yahuah your Elohim has assigned them (the signs of the Zodiac) to all the people of the world (they were created by Yahuah to proclaim the coming Messiah Yahusha, see Psalm 19, they are not gods).

The Zodiac reveals Yahuah's wrath upon all those who abuse it...

Romans 1
18 The wrath of Yahuah is being revealed from (the) heaven(ly scroll... Shamayim/Mazzaroth) against all the godlessness and wickedness of people, who suppress the truth (of its message) by their wickedness (turning The Heavenly Scroll into witchcraft **Galatians 3:6-8** and worship the signs of the Zodiac, Sun, Moon, and stars), 19 since what may be known about Yahuah (the Plan of Salvation) is plain to them (proclaimed in The Heavenly Scroll day after day, night after night Psalms 19), because Yahuah has made it plain to them (by authoring the life of Yahusha into the fabric of Creation on Day 4 this message goes out unto all the Earth Psalms 19, given to all mankind ***Deuteronomy 3:19***). 20 For since the

creation of the world (day 4 of Creation when Yahuah created the sun, moon, and stars) Yahuah's invisible qualities—his eternal power and divine nature—have been clearly seen (written in the stars at creation *Enoch 35:3* in The Zodiac), being understood from what has been made (in heaven), so that people are without excuse (for denying Yahusha). 21 For although they knew Yahuah (is The Creator), they neither glorified Him as Elohim nor gave thanks to Him (for the Plan of Salvation written in the stars), but their thinking became futile (twisting the Zodiac and signs into 'gods' and witchcraft) and their foolish hearts were darkened (to worship the creation over The Creator). 22 Although they claimed to be wise (through religion, tradition, philosophy and mythology), they became fools 23 and exchanged the glory of the immortal Elohim (the Glory of Yahuah is Yahusha *2 Corinthians 4:6*! So they exchanged *Yahusha*) for images made to look like a mortal human being (incarnated demi-gods) and birds and animals and reptiles (the signs of The Zodiac).

...

28 Furthermore, just as they did not think it worthwhile to retain the knowledge of God (that He is IMMMORTAL and INVISIBLE and SPIRIT found written in the stars *Enoch 35:3*), so Yahuah gave them over to a depraved mind (they do not understand the Scriptures OR The Heavenly Scroll), so that they do what ought not to be done (blaspheme the Holy Spirit which declares Yahuah is immortal invisible Spirit NOT a mortal man who died and worship the Sun)."

Sha'ul was telling the Greco-Roman people to look at the very Zodiac they corrupted into mythology. The Zodiac condemns all mankind, as it reveals from heaven (*shamayim*), for worshipping the creation over the Creator. We have failed to see the Spiritual message behind it. It is the Truth vs. Sun worship, the Battle of the Ages. Ba'al vs. The Creator... the false messiah based on Sun worshp vs. the true Messiah of Isra'el.

The watchers (fallen angels) perverted that message in the stars and revealed to mankind the "*secrets preserved in the heavens*" but in such a way as to cause mankind to worship the Sun, Moon,

Stars, and Constellations. The watchers taught the Sun as the supreme deity.

They then created for themselves 'Solar Christs' to fulfill the message in the Zodiac (pagan demi-god 'Christs' from Tammuz to Jesus). This Sun worshipping religion is the largest religion on Earth today.

This twisted version of the Zodiac was formulated into a religion in Babylon. This religion of sun worship was then dispersed throughout the Earth when the languages were confused at the Tower of Babel. Every pagan religion on Earth is an incarnation of sun worship in Babylon, which was based on the corrupt message of the Zodiac. The corrupted message in the Zodiac is universal (being dispersed at the Tower of Babel), that is why every pagan solar messiah or 'Christ' is a demi-god member of a Trinity with the same basic life story. These demi-gods, beginning with the Babylonian Tammuz, were all human attempts at fulfilling the Zodiac's story.

The true prophets of Yahuah understood the message in the stars as foretelling of a coming Messiah. The false prophets of Ba'al (the sun) said the message in the stars was speaking of their pagan kings and children of the kings. Every pagan king assumed the Zodiac was speaking of him directly and derived their authority to rule over the people from the Zodiac. The battle between the coming King and the reigning King was fought in the stars going all the way back to Babylon. That battle will continue to be fought in the stars until the Lion of the Tribe of Judah returns to fulfill the "circle of animals" known as the Zodiac, and then it will be completed with the Sign of Leo. When the conquering king vanquishes the dragon...

The Zodiac (the path the sun takes through the constellations), the names and meanings of each constellation, and the names and meanings of the stars that make them up are all divinely inspired and created by Yahuah. ==The images that are associated with the Zodiac are simply pictographs that represent the meaning of the constellation.== The signs of the Zodiac are not gods; they are not even images derived from "connecting the dots" i.e. the stars in each constellation! I will explain exactly where those images came from in this book and how they have remained the same across all cultures over 6,000 years.

The sons of Yahuah have passed down the proper meaning of the Zodiac from Seth to Enoch to Noah to Abraham to Daniel to Yahusha who fulfilled (in the process of fulfilling) its message. The pagans have passed down the twisted version of the Zodiac, which idolizes the Sun and the signs of the Zodiac.

This is *"The Battle of the Ages"* in scripture that rages even today, the battle for the message contained in the Zodiac, yes the Battle is for Creation...

- Jerusalem vs. Rome/Babylon
- Yahuah vs. Sol Invictus/Ba'al
- The Shema vs. The Cross/The Trinity
- Yahusha vs. Jesus/Tammuz
- The Sabbath vs. Dias Solis/Sunday
- The Passover Lamb vs. Easter/The Ishtar Pig
- The Holy Days vs. Holidays
- The Law vs. Lawlessness
- The Spirit of Truth vs. The Spirit of Error
- The Spirit of Yahuah vs. the Spirit of the False Messiah/Incarnation
- The Nazarene vs. Christianity

In this book, I refer to the message authored by Yahuah in the stars as the Mazzaroth, the Zodiac, Heaven, and the Heavenly Scroll.

These terms are all interchangeable. I use all 4 throughout this book, to firmly establish all 4 terms in the reader's mind.

Let us begin our journey… at the very beginning.

CHAPTER 1

THE ROLE OF MYTH AND SCIENCE

Chapter 1 - The Role of Myth and Science

For us to "see" through the cloud of myths and legends, it is necessary to understand the role they play in the story of humanity. All too often in our quest for "pure science", we discount and discard "myths" that have been handed down since the creation of man.

Legends, oral traditions, and myths... everything must be "proven scientifically" in our modern day scientific dictatorship. We demand everything fit nice and neatly into our scientific consciousness; or we relegate it to the trash bin of history as "worthless garb". Is there no function in our history for myths, legends, and oral traditions? Could they instead be a guiding light into our ancient past; even to the origin of mankind? Maybe we should not so readily dismiss ancient myths, legends, and oral traditions? Is there truth behind them? Historical realities of ancient times that can be understood in light of these myths and legends? When seeking out "truth", is it a matter of just science as we have come to believe today?

There is truth behind these myths, and it is not just a matter of science. Myth must take its rightful place in our understanding of the Ages past, because we were not there and our ancient ancestors did not keep a "history book". What we have are the remains of wall drawings, hieroglyphs, and ancient languages long deceased. It is "mythology" that is the very means used by the ancients to pass down historical events. In other words, in our search for our origins, we might do well to let myths, legends, and oral traditions *DRIVE* the direction we take in science and direct us in our quest for answers.

We now have "science", whereby we explain the world and make its phenomena intelligible, the ancients had "***mythology***". Both disciplines have the same goal: to understand the world around us and pass that understanding on to the next generations to come. In the introduction to ***Larousse World Mythology page 9*** we read:

> *[T]oday the myth is no longer considered a mode of thought reserved for primitive societies. If each one of us considers the matter carefully and honestly, he will be forced to recognize that myth is far from foreign to our daily thought, and, what is more, that it is far from opposed in essence to scientific thought. It is the object of the myth, as of science, to explain the world, to make its phenomena intelligible.*

Our ancient ancestors (*who were eye witnesses to our origins*) would take the world around them and try to explain that world to future generations using myths and legends. They did not have science or history books. So we must look at these myths with the understanding that they were created to help explain the world that was occurring around the ancient human societies. In other words, there is truth behind the myths and to ignore mythology is to lose the insight it brings into human history.

The danger we, as a modern society, have fallen into is this: *we scoff at myths and legends in such a way as to make us biased toward the underlying truth behind them.* As a result, we have lost the vast insight handed down to us from our ancient ancestors. We simply are not "listening" to the very ones (*our ancient ancestors*) who lived during the time humanity originated... while at the same time we are seeking to understand our origin! If we want to learn of the origin of mankind, we should listen to what those alive at the time have been telling us.

It is not the purpose of this book to explore mythology in depth, or to demonstrate through historical evidence that there is truth behind mythology. I am simply illustrating a point as it will relate directly to the Zodiac, which has existed in every culture dating back to the origin of mankind. The Zodiac is a prime example of writing off a very important truth that has been passed down through legends and myths. So the purpose of this book is to get to the bottom of this most fascinating chart that has served as the foundation of every religion known to man... Even Christianity and Judaism as I will show later in this book.

Therefore, I would like to quickly illustrate my point and then move on. We must come to understand that there is truth behind mythology, because we are going to dive deep inside ancient human myths across civilizations and cultures in the first 3 books in this book series. Our goal is to determine if there was **Original Revelation** from Yahuah to man that was lost and corrupted over time. The only real "link" to that **Original Revelation** is found in the myths, legends, and oral traditions across cultures dating back 5000 years, and the Zodiac.

Mythology

Mythology is full of genetic mutants (half human half beast), giants, gods, god-men, vampires and the like. Are these all just fantastic bed time stories made up from thin air? Or can they be shown to be based in scientific fact and Biblical evidence? Let's take a quick look at *some of the mythical figures* and quickly establish that instead of dismissing myths and legends, we should be listening to our ancestor more closely.

Giants: Fact or Fiction?

Giants are prevalent throughout mythology and legend both. Is there evidence of giants throughout human history that would justify their existence in myths and legends? Is there a Biblical explanation for such giants? If so, why is this not taught in our educational centers and churches? What is being hidden in plain sight and why?
We've all watched a special on the Discovery Channel or cable TV about giants or ancient aliens. And when we do we are all left with a huge question mark? Because the answer to the questions above is "yes". Yes, there is a wealth of scientific evidence of giants in

our past. We find clues of giants in archeological digs across the globe. There are "bricks" in ancient structures so large, modern machinery cannot move them. Again, this book isn't about giants, watch the Discovery Channel specials, they do a pretty good job.

We have ruins of massive structures (like the ancient pyramids) that even today modern man cannot duplicate. Who built these structures? Giants? What does the Bible have to say about this? Is there evidence of these giants in scripture? Yes, the Bible explains their origin too:

> **Genesis 6:1-4**
> And it came to pass, when men began to multiply on the face of the earth, and daughters were born unto them, 2 That the sons of Yahuah (angels) saw the daughters of men that they were fair; and they took them wives of all which they chose. 3 And Yahuah said, My spirit shall not always strive with man, for that he also is flesh: yet his days shall be an hundred and twenty years. 4 <u>There were giants in the earth in those days</u>; and also after that, when the sons of Yahuah (angels) came in unto the daughters of men, and they bare children to them, <u>the same became mighty men which were of old, men of renown</u>.

So giants did exist and they were "men of renown" or "legend"! The Bible clearly states that these legends were based on these giant Nephilim that had super human strength and size due to the genetic structure being corrupted by angels. I'm not talking about the modern "gigantism" gene that may produce at the most a 10-foot-tall human. These giants were so large; mankind were like "grasshoppers" in their site.

> **Numbers 13:33**
> "There also we saw the Nephilim (the sons of Anak are part of the Nephilim); and we became like grasshoppers in our own sight, and so we were in their sight."

The resulting race of half-breed (*half angel - half human descendants*) was called *Nephilim*. I will cover these more in detail later and explain their role in corrupting the message Yahuah had written in the stars.

The Nephilim

According to the most ancient human cultures, such as the Sumerians, giants literally ruled over mankind. This fact is also supported by the Bible's witness of them. We see these giants depicted clearly in cuneiform scripts, tablets, and wall drawings.

Following is a depiction of such a "giant ruler" of the Sumerians on wall reliefs dating back 5,000 years. You can see that humans scarcely come to the knees of this ruler of the Sumerians. Also note the blazing sun image on an altar that looks like a wheel. This is the Zodiac which they used as their authority to rule over man. Sun worship began with these early cultures.

Creation Cries Out!

The wall drawings above are depictions of "the Anakin", as they are known to the Sumerians, or "sons of Anak" in the Bible. Notice humans are depicted as almost "toy" figures to them and again we see them teaching men sun worship. We see the sun disk in both images with the Zodiac wheel in the left image.

There are archeological discoveries of giants in our past, massive footprints in stone and remains of massive giant humanoids. There is a lot of disinformation out there on this subject. It seems a deliberate effort to discredit the historical truth. What is commonly known as truth in the archeological and scientific circles is routinely hidden from the masses. The masses are dumbed down in public schools and universities. We are led to continue to treat these topics as childhood fairytales.

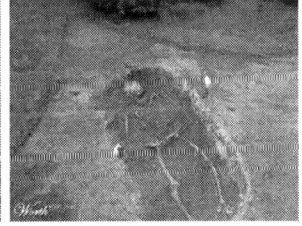

When doing just a little research we find… it is not "myth" at all, but rather humanity passing down stories of actual encounters with giant humanoid beings. What the Bible explains as "the offspring of the union between angels and human women".

Vampires: Fact or Fiction?

The legend of vampires has been passed down through many cultures as well. Vampires are mythological or folkloric beings who subsist by feeding on the life essence (generally in the form of blood) of living creatures; regardless of whether the vampires are undead or a living person/being. Vampires are said to have super-human strength, are nocturnal, and have an eternal seeking nature.

We all know the stories and how fascinated our society has become with vampires. You can hardly turn on the TV and browse through the channels without running across a vampire TV series or go to the movie without seeing a vampire billboard. But like giants (the result of a union between fallen angels and women), can we find a Biblical "source" to explain the legend of the vampire? Actually, yes there is. It is the exact same source... The Nephilim!

These giant half breeds that began to dominate the Earth eventually started eating humans and drinking their blood. These giant man eaters were, in fact, the main reason Yahuah destroyed the Earth in the days of Noah. Yahuah had to rid the Earth of these offspring of angels and women. The Book of Enoch, the oldest human record, tells us of these beings as well. These "giants" had super-human qualities and descended from eternal beings (angels). They were eternal seeking beings by nature.

To understand the evolution of the vampire myth, we need look no further than the Hebrew lore of a creature named "*Lilith*". The *Lilith* myths date back as far as 2,500 BC. We see *Lilith* mentioned by name in earlier manuscripts of Isaiah that later translated *Lilith* as "*night creature*" or vampire.

> **Isaiah 34:14**
> Desert creatures will meet with hyenas, and wild goats will bleat to each other; there the night creatures (or vampires originally written as Lilith) will also repose and find for themselves places of rest.

However, the Hebrew word translated as *"night creature"* is לילית *Lilith*. The Jewish oral tradition calls a she demon by this name *Lilith*. The oral tradition says she has a human face, has wings, and destroys children as soon as they are born. Mankind has recorded this *Lilith* for many centuries using legends and myths. Her features are what we would expect from a union between angels and humans… and it is *Lilith* that actually caused the fall of humanity in the Garden of Eden in some oral traditions.

Lilith is depicted with wings and clawed feet surrounded by owls that represent dark knowledge. She is depicted as a serpent with a female body and wings seen wrapped around a "tree" as Eve takes a bite of the apple.

Lilith embodies the very idea of a half-breed creature (part human part angel) leading mankind astray with "dark knowledge".

Many translations of the Bible are now corrected and read as follows in **The New Revised Standard** version:

Isaiah 34:14
Wildcats shall meet with hyenas, goat-demons shall call to each other; there too Lilith shall repose, and find a place to rest.

While Isaiah is the only direct mention of *Lilith* in the Bible, she is made mention of multiple times in the Jewish Talmud. For example: in the 13th Century writings of Rabbi Isaac ben Jacob ha-Cohen, *Lilith* left Adam after she refused to become subservient to him, and then would not return to the Garden of Eden after she mated with archangel Samael.

Lilith is also mentioned in the Dead Sea Scrolls which contains one indisputable reference to Lilith **in Songs of the Sage (4Q510-511)[43] fragment 1:**

> *And I, the Instructor, proclaim His glorious splendor so as to frighten and to te[rrify] all the spirits of the destroying angels, spirits of the bastards, demons,* **Lilith***, howlers, and [desert dwellers...] and those which fall upon men without warning to lead them astray from a spirit of understanding and to make their heart and their [...] desolate during the present dominion of wickedness and predetermined time of humiliations for the sons of lig[ht], by the guilt of the ages of [those] smitten by iniquity – not for eternal destruction, [bu]t for an era of humiliation for transgression.*

We see in this reference above the mention of the ***Age of Taurus*** which is known as the Age of Chaos that followed after the fall of man. It was an Age dominated by angelic deception that culminated in the flood of Noah. I will explain these ages later in this book. Once we again restore *Lilith* from the realm of "myth" we find she is mentioned not by name, but in reference in Proverbs 2, 5, 7, and 9

Proverbs 2:18-19
Her house sinks down to death, and her (*Lilith*) course leads to the shades. All who go to her cannot return. And find again the paths of life (because she cost humanity eternal life by misleading Adam and Eve).

For more on *Lilith* reference: http://en.wikipedia.org/wiki/Lilith. Again, *Lilith* embodies the reality of angels having sexual union with women. Their offspring having attributes of angels and women and were blood drinking nocturnal creatures damned by the Creator.
All of this is explained in detail in the Book of Enoch. It is these attributes embodied by *Lilith* that are the foundation of the vampire myth and legends of today. Many of the ancient vampires had "angelic wings" and were females (the wings later became a long cape extended behind the body 'like wings' when grasped by the arms and lifted up). When put into context of The Book of Enoch, the images of ancient vampires connected with "dark knowledge" and eternal life begin to come into focus. The "myths" do have an origin after all and can be traced right back to The Nephilim.

The Book of Enoch gives us that origin. Enoch explained the fall of the angelic realm and humanity in context of sexual union between angels and women. Then Enoch describes the future disclosure of "knowledge" from angels to their offspring. That "offspring" was a race of half-breed nocturnal blood drinking eternal seeking beings.

Enoch is listed in Genesis in the generations of Adam. Enoch is described as the great x 4 grandson of Adam (through Seth) (Genesis 5:3-18), the son of Jared, the father of Methuselah, and the great-grandfather of Noah. Enoch was so special that Yahuah assumed him to "heaven" (or the stars) while still living according to the Bible. After this assumption, Enoch wrote a book called ***The Book of Enoch*** that chronicled the fall of the angelic realm (the Watchers) and the creation of the Nephilim (giant vampires) who were the offspring of The Watchers and human women.

The Book of Enoch

The Book of Enoch picks up from Genesis chapter 1, verses 1-4. The Book of Enoch reveals that vampires originated from the offspring of the union between the Watchers (Fallen Angels) and human women. After consuming all the available food on Earth, the children of the Watchers **turned to mankind and began to eat their flesh and drink their blood seeking eternal life like their angelic fathers.**

The Book of Enoch is considered one of the books of the Apocrypha (books so sacred that the Catholic Church deemed them not suitable for the eyes of the common man). Books that were deliberately left out from the Bible by the Catholic Church but still considered "inspired" are called APOCRYPHA. Initially, only chosen priesthood and initiates had access to such writings. The Book of Enoch was declared apocryphal, and like the Book of Seth, and other ancient manuscripts, was denied entrance into the approved version of the original Bible (by the Nicene Council of 325 A.D.)

By the time I finish this book series, the abominations that took place at the Nicene Council will be evident. One of which was restricting access to VERY important books of scripture. In the canonization criteria, Yahuah and his message of salvation must be the central theme and therefore very important books such as The Book of Enoch were left out.

The Book of Enoch mainly emphasizes the fallen Watchers and their judgments and therefore was not canonized. This omission of books such as Enoch from our consciousness has left humanity with a void of knowledge about our origins. If Enoch was cherished by Yahuah to the extent that he was and wrote a book… <u>maybe, we should read it</u>? Yahuah didn't show these things to Enoch and have them written down for no reason. The book of scripture I highly recommend is **The Book of Yahweh (from Yahweh.com).**

In the Book of Enoch, we see Enoch, son of Jared, speaks of the angels called '*the Watchers*' appointed to protect mankind. However, while watching over human beings, they lusted after the beautiful earthly women. The lure of what Yahuah has created for man i.e. women, proved too enticing to the Watchers, who decided to abandon heaven, and join women on Earth and live with them, i.e. they "fell from heaven to Earth" metaphorically speaking. From this union they had children and they taught their women and children magic, advanced knowledge of the workings of the solar system, the Zodiac, astrology, and other skills, previously unknown to humans. What they taught was very real and very true. It was because these angels taught humanity "knowledge" outside of the timing of Yahuah and without giving Yahuah the Glory that these angles "were judged" by Yahuah and fell from Grace. Humanity, seeking this knowledge from the angelic realm, likewise "fell" i.e. *ate of the proverbial apple* from the 'forbidden tree' which were the Angels. Man had been forbidden to seek knowledge from the Watchers and the Watchers forbidden to give man knowledge. From that point on humanity was led astray by these fallen angels into sun worship. Like I said, the knowledge given mankind by the Watchers was true including the Zodiac. It was "how it was given" that was in error.

The knowledge the Watchers gave humanity was not theirs to give, it was Yahuah's to give humanity. This knowledge was given outside of the plan of Yahuah. The Watchers used their advanced knowledge <u>to rule over humanity</u> and elevate themselves and their off-springs as rulers and Gods. The Zodiac was taught to man by the Watchers who instead of pointing man to a coming Messiah, they twisted the message as though it were speaking of them. The Zodiac was then used as the 'Divine Authority' by which the Watchers and their offspring ruled over humanity.

This is where the Sumerian culture and cuneiform tablets and wall relief comes into play! What is portrayed by the Sumerian cuneiform was exactly what Enoch declared… they ruled over the Sumerians and imparted sacred knowledge. It is from these fallen angels that the Zodiac and Astrology was disclosed to a human race that did not possess the technology to know this information otherwise.

As a result, the exact representation of the solar system is carved in stone and we even see evidence of space travel and much more on the walls of these ancient civilizations. Obviously the technology brought by these "Watchers" was equal to or beyond that which exists even today. Notice in the picture below, images of flight that look identical to the Apache helicopter of today, what appears to be submarines and planes! The middle image reveals these "gods" flying around in what would appear to be a spaceship! It is little wonder primitive man worshipped them. In the image on the far right we see depictions of our solar system with the exact number of planets orbiting the sun in their proper proportions and relative distances. This knowledge/information would be impossible for a civilization to know 5,000 years ago outside of an advanced race "giving" it to them.

Back to our storyline…These children of The Watchers were not exactly human as you can see in these quotes from the Book of Enoch. Enoch described these beings and what they did to

37

humanity, as Enoch was taken into the Spiritual Realm and literally introduced to the angels by name and given dominion over them.

The Book of Enoch – an eye witness to our origins

We see in the Book of Enoch (as he clearly described the horrible conditions on Earth under the rule of the Anakin or Nephilim) conditions that eventually required a flood to remedy. We see the "blood drinking" nature of these half breeds.

> **Chapter 7**
> 13 When they (the Nephilim or giants) turned themselves against men, in order to devour them; 14 And began to injure birds, beasts, reptiles, and fishes, to eat their flesh one after another, and to drink their blood.

We see below they were seeking "length of days" or eternal life like their fathers (angels), but were denied that lineage by Yahuah and their lifespan was limited to 500 years (about half that of their human counterparts at that time who lived nearly 1,000 years). Enoch tells us that the spiritual realm was populated by the spirits that came forth from the Nephilim whose physical bodies had died. We call them *demons* today.

> **Chapter 10**
> 10 (excerpted) for length of days shall they (the Nephilim) not have. And no request that they (i.e. their angelic fathers) make of thee shall be granted unto their fathers on their behalf; for they (the Nephilim) hope to live an eternal life (like their angelic fathers), and 11 that each one of them will live five hundred years.

> **Chapter 15**
> 3 for you: Wherefore have ye left the high, holy, and eternal heaven, and lain with women, and defiled yourselves with the daughters of men and taken to yourselves wives, and done like the children 4 of earth, and begotten giants (as your)

sons? And though ye were holy, spiritual, living the eternal life, you have defiled yourselves with the blood of women, and have begotten (children) with the blood of flesh, and, as the children of men, have lusted after flesh and blood as those also do who die 5 and perish... 11 And <u>the spirits of the giants</u> afflict, oppress, destroy, attack, do battle, and work destruction on the earth, and cause trouble: they take no food, but nevertheless 12 hunger and thirst (after blood), and cause offences. And these spirits (what we call demons) shall rise up against the children of men and against the women, because they have proceeded from them (the dead Nephilim).

Why the fallen angels hate YAHUAH?

Chapter 10
13 To Gabriel also Yahuah said, Go to the biters, to the reprobates, to the children of fornication; and destroy the children of fornication, the offspring of the Watchers, from among men; bring them forth, and excite them one against another. Let them perish by mutual slaughter; for length of days (eternal life) shall not be theirs.

We see the "reason" the fallen angels hate Yahuah so intently is because He made them watch the slaughter of these half breed children called Nephilim.

Chapter 12
4 "Enoch, scribe of righteousness. Go and inform the Watchers of Heaven, who have left the High Heaven and the Holy Eternal Place, and have corrupted themselves with women, and have done as the sons of men do and have taken wives for themselves, and have become completely corrupt on the earth. 5 They will have on Earth, neither peace, nor forgiveness of sin, for they will not rejoice in their sons. 6 The slaughter of their beloved ones they will see; and over the destruction of their sons they will lament and petition forever. But they will have neither mercy nor peace."

We see that Yahuah judged them for the information they taught humanity in "error" leading mankind to blaspheme and sin against Yahuah...

> **Chapter 13**
> 1 And Enoch went and said to Azazel: "You will not have peace. A severe sentence has come out against you that you should be bound. 2 And you will have neither rest nor mercy, nor the granting of any petitions, because of the wrong which you have taught, and because of all the works of blasphemy and wrong and sin which you have shown to the sons of men."
>
> **Chapter 14**
> 6 And before this, you shall have seen the destruction of your beloved sons, and you shall not be able to enjoy them, but they shall fall before you by the sword. 7 And your petition on their behalf shall not be granted, nor yet on your own: even though you weep and pray and speak all the words contained in the writing which I have written.

The Watchers taught humanity the heavenly secrets

What are the origins of the corrupt uses of astrology and magic? I'll explain what the difference between righteous uses and unrighteous uses later in this book. We see below that the workings of the solar system as viewed from Earth such (as the Zodiac) and the path of the Moon and astrology was given to man by these fallen angels. This is extremely important as I will bring out in this book. Astrology was the #1 focus of these lying Angles who sought to twist the message and corrupt the Heavenly Scroll (the Zodiac). We will learn why later in this book as well.

> **Chapter 8**
> 3 Amezarak taught all those who cast spells and cut roots, Armaros the release of spells, and Baraqiel astrologers, and Kokabiel portents, and Tamiel taught astrology, and Asradel taught the path of the Moon.

We see that Yahuah had orchestrated in His Creation *"eternal secrets preserved in heaven"* (written in the stars) and these secrets were perverted by the fallen angels when given to man.

Chapter 9
6 things, and nothing can hide itself from Thee. Thou seest what Azazel hath done, who hath taught all unrighteousness on earth *and revealed the eternal secrets which were (preserved) in heaven,* which 7 men were striving to learn:

Chapter 16
3 "You have been in heaven, but all the mysteries had not yet been revealed to you, and you knew worthless ones, and these in the hardness of your hearts you have made known to the women, and through these mysteries women and men work much evil on earth."

There we have it, in one of the most ancient writings known to humanity, the source of "sun worship" that eventually became the Mystery Religion of Babylon (that is the subject of book 2 in the *Original Revelation Series*). We see the origin of the myths of giants and vampires. We see the origin and twisting of the Heavenly Scroll into magic, sorcery, (improper use of) astrology, and evil. What we will discover in this book, is that the knowledge these Watchers gave to our early ancestors was in fact true. Things such as the Zodiac, Astrology, magic, divination, and so forth. We will see these exact things practiced by the prophets of Yahuah in a righteous manner. We will learn in this book the difference between righteous practices vs. the unrighteous practices.

Ancient Genetic Engineering

Today genetic engineering is not only possible, but in the "shadows" our scientific community (and military industrial complex) is actively engaged in engineering humans with animal traits to create "enhanced soldiers". While this may sound like the basis (and actually is the basis) of many Hollywood movies... it is also true. Just Google "military genetic engineering" and read all about it. If humanity has reached such lofty scientific heights, what is to say that these fallen angels did not employ the same techniques (after all their knowledge far exceeds our own)? We have many hybrid creatures in mythology and Astrology... are they truly just "myth" or is there evidence of ancient genetic engineering that resulted in these hybrids?

One such "myth" which appears very early in human history and is very prevalent in ancient hieroglyphics is The Sphinx! Why would there be images of such a genetically engineered half lion half man on walls, statues, and even megalithic structures such as the Egyptian Pyramids dedicated to such a "creature"? Maybe such a creature had been created! We also see many examples of "genetic engineering" in pictographs, hieroglyphics, and cuneiform tablets.

Creation Cries Out!

Below we see the Priest of Dagon the dragon wearing a dead fish draped over his head and shoulder (center of the first image looks like a walking turtle), to the right we see a half lion/half man:

We even see "non-human" beings in ancient Egyptian hieroglyphics...

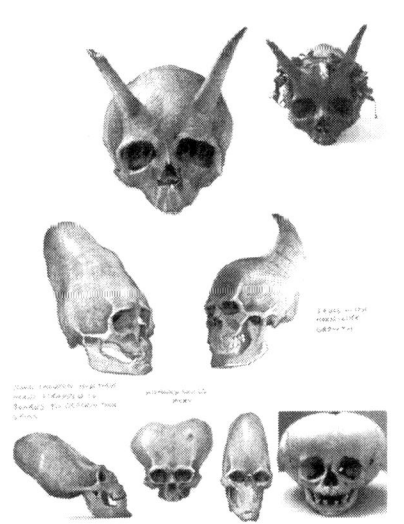

When looking at the fossil record it becomes quite obvious that "something" was being manipulated in our past... below are a few examples of skulls discovered. From the looks of these examples it is not hard to understand where such "myths" came from.

You can easily see from these examples of skulls found where the images of "demons" originated. Maybe it all isn't just "myth" after all?

43

Conclusion

The point I wanted to make is this: when searching for truth concerning our origins and our ancient past, mythology is the means our ancestors used to communicate their realities in the same way we explain our realities through science today.

As medicine looks more closely at ancient remedies and is finding some modern answers, as archaeology is looking at the Bible and finding references that explain what it is finding in archeological ruins, as history itself is taking a closer look at some ancient writings; <u>so we too (those who seek Yahuah) need to be very cautious about throwing out the old stories simply because they contain "mythological" elements</u>. We need to know if there are truths underneath the mythological wrappings. We need to pay more attention to what our ancestors have passed down to us if we hope to discover the truth behind the origin of man.

__We__ were not there, __they__ were!

With this in mind let us examine some of these "myths", especially as they relate to ***the Zodiac,*** and try and discern the truth in them and where mankind fell into idolatry. As we have just discovered in this chapter, Enoch was an eye-witness and told us the angelic realm <u>perverted the Zodiac</u>, which according to David (in Psalms 19) was created by Yahuah with a very important message to humanity!

That message contained in the Zodiac is... Original Revelation from the Creator to all mankind!

CHAPTER 2

YAHUAH CREATED AND NAMED THE STARS AND STRETCHES THEM OUT LIKE A HEAVENLY SCROLL...

Chapter 2 - Yahuah Created and Named the Stars!

> **Matthew 11:25**
> At that time Yahusha answered and said, I thank you, O Father, King of heaven (Strong's H8064 *'shamayim'* - the place where the stars are located, i.e. The Mazzaroth/Zodiac) and earth, because you have hid these things (secrets preserved in the stars/heaven *Enoch 9:6*) from the wise and prudent, and have revealed them unto babes.

I realize we have come to view the Zodiac in a negative light, as a tool used only in the hands of witches performing magic or stargazers attempting to predicting the future using the perverted means of Astrology. We associate the Zodiac with the '*hocus pocus*' in the daily newspaper horoscopes. However, the Bible declares that Yahuah named the stars and established them for signs and for seasons. The Zodiac is simply a tool that illustrates this fact as we will see. So we need to tread lightly when it comes to the Zodiac and not deny Glory Yahuah declares is His!

The ***wise men*** in Babylon knew this 2000 years ago, that is how the "*magi*" discerned the time and the place of the Messiah's birth… it was foretold in the heavens, a sign in the Zodiac! Abraham knew this as Yahuah "witnessed the Gospel in advance to Abraham" … by the stars in 'heaven' speaking directly of the Zodiac as we will find out. David knew this well, expressing in Psalms 19 of the glorious message found in the Zodiac. Enoch the "scribe of righteousness" taken to 'heaven' by Yahuah also knew this… and so too did the angels:

> **The Book of Enoch - Chapter 9**
> 6 things, and nothing can hide itself from Thee. Thou seest what Azazel hath done, who hath taught all unrighteousness on earth *and revealed the eternal secrets which were (preserved) in heaven*, which 7 men were striving to learn:

And finally, it was the angels who perverted this message leaving mankind swinging back and forth (as on a pendulum) from misusing the stars and Astrology for fortune-telling, magic, and sorcery… to the other end of the spectrum, denying the very existence of a Creator through science.

The message found in the heavens eludes us today in astronomy as we study the very creation that literally cries out His existence while denying there is a Creator. Enoch tells us there are actually *"eternal secrets preserved in heaven"* the men were striving to learn (just like we are today) and that angels fell from the Grace of Yahuah in order to pervert the message proclaimed by the Creator.

Let us go back and re-establish that message.

Once we re-establish that message then we can literally reconcile the information passed down across cultures over thousands of years as every culture in effect is saying the same thing! We just stopped listening.

Yahuah is the author of the Zodiac

We see clearly stated in the Bible that it was Yahuah who is the author of the Zodiac (*the path of the sun through the constellations*) not Satan or the fallen angels. Not the Sumerians with their sun gods, nor the Greeks with their Olympus, and not the Romans with their Pantheon. They simply perverted the message from Yahuah. We also know that there is a divine message found within the Zodiac that tells of the Glory of Yahuah and cries out the works of His hand. We see below that it was Yahuah who named every star!

Psalms 147:1-5
How good it is to sing praises to our Elohim, how pleasant and fitting to praise him! Yahuah builds up Jerusalem; he gathers the exiles of Israel. He heals the brokenhearted and binds up their wounds. *He determines the number of the stars and calls them each by name*. Great is our Elohim and mighty in power; his understanding has no limit.

Before I continue any further, allow me to define what the English word *'heaven'* actually means. The word Hellenized into English as 'heaven' is Strong's **H8064**, below is the definition.

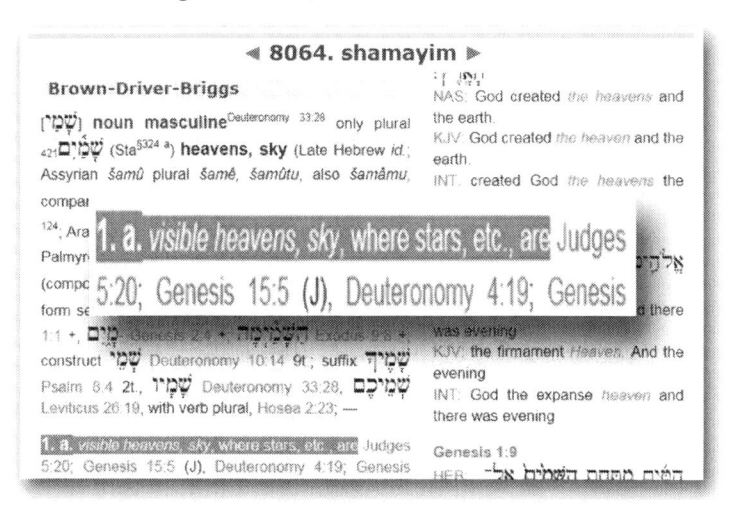

***Heaven**, is probably one of the most miss-understood mythical concepts in all of Christianity. That is why I wrote the book **The Kingdom**! Because **'Heaven'** and the **'Kingdom of Yahuah'** are two very different things.*

We see above that the primary definition of **H8064 *shamayim*** which is translated 'heaven' and 'sky' in English is '*the visible sky where the stars are located*'. It is specifically referring to the Zodiac.

> *Heaven is not some mythical place with angels flying around playing harps where "God", some old guy with a long white beard resides!*

No, we need to forget all these fairytales of established religion. They are more fabricated than mythology! At least mythology is based on real signs in the heavens! Heaven in Hebrew is speaking of *the Zodiac*, the place where the stars resides in the sky. Now that we understand that one word, the scriptures come alive before our very eyes and the Zodiac takes center stage. We see below, that it was Yahuah who created all the stars, and "starry hosts" (which are the constellations), and named both the stars and the constellations!

> **Isaiah 40:25-26**
> "To whom will you compare me? Or who is my equal?" says the Holy One. Lift your eyes and look to the *heavens* (H 8064 *shamayim*: means the Zodiac) Who created all these? He who brings out the starry host (constellations are the hosts of stars) one by one, and calls them each (constellation) by name. Because of his great power and mighty strength, not one of them is missing (there are 12 major constellations exactly among all cultures).

Isaiah 45
⁵ I am Yahuah, **and there is no other**; apart from me there is no God. ⁷ I form the light and create darkness, I bring prosperity and create disaster; I**, Yahuah, do all these things**. ¹² It is I **who made the earth and created mankind upon it**. My own hands stretched out the heavens (signs of the Zodiac along the ecliptic to reveal a hidden message *Psalms 19*); I marshaled their starry hosts (constellations).

Isaiah 44
²⁴ "This is what Yahuah says— your Redeemer, who formed you in the womb: I am Yahuah, *the Maker of all things*, who stretches out the heavens (signs of the Zodiac along the ecliptic to reveal a hidden message *Psalms 19*), who spreads out the earth *by myself*.
-
Isaiah 46
⁵ "**To whom will you compare me or count me equal**? To whom will you liken me that we may be compared? ⁸ "Remember this, fix it in mind, take it to heart, you rebels. ⁹ Remember the former things, those of long ago; I am God, **and there is no other**; I am God, and there is none like me. ¹⁰ I make known the end from the beginning (written in The Zodiac), from ancient times (creation), what is still to come. I say: My purpose (defined and written in the stars) will stand, and I will do all that I please (His will be done on Earth, as it is proclaimed in heaven i.e. written in the stars)

Isaiah 42
⁵ This is what Yahuah says— **He** who created the heavens (the stars and constellations... the Zodiac) and stretched them out (in order to proclaim a message), who spread out the earth and all that comes out of it, who gives breath to its people, and life to those who walk on it:

In Psalms below we see that as the sun and moon rises and sets daily and night after night... knowledge concerning The Plan of Yahuah is proclaimed without voice or speech from one end of the Earth to the other to all mankind.

Psalm 19

19 The heavens (H8064: shamayim - the stars and constellations of the Zodiac) are telling of the glory of Yahuah; And their expanse is declaring the work of His hands. 2 Day to day (the Zodiac) pours forth speech, And night to night (the Zodiac) reveals knowledge. 3 There is no speech, nor are there words; Their (stars and constellations of the Zodiac) voice is not heard. 4 Their line (ecliptic plane through which the sun appears to travel when viewed from Earth) has gone out through all the earth, And their utterances to the end of the world. In them (the constellations) He has placed a tent for the sun, 5 Which (the Sun) is as (a shadow or metaphor) a bridegroom (the Messiah) coming out of his chamber (to run the course of a wedding and marry the Bride); It rejoices as a strong man (Messiah) to run his course (Plan of Salvation). 6 Its rising is from one end of the heavens, And its circuit (that is what Zodiac means, "path or circuit") to the other end of them; And there is nothing hidden from its heat.

David is clearly describing the Zodiac, the chart of the sun moving across our skies and the "line of the sun" called the ecliptic that goes throughout all the earth, as it runs its course each year through the Signs of the Zodiac called constellations. David properly understood the message contained in the Zodiac as we will learn later in this book. The sun rises from one end of heaven and then its "circuit or Zodiac" is like a "bridegroom coming out of his chamber". This is fulfilled in Yahusha the Messiah. Yahusha proclaims himself the 'bridegroom' and says those who "hear his voice" speaking of the Zodiac (Psalms 19:2) rejoice; and it is Yahusha's joy to be the fulfillment of that message. Yes, the Zodiac is the original Gospel message proclaiming the Messiah as we will find out later in this book.

John 3:29

29 He who has the bride is the bridegroom; but the friend of the bridegroom, who stands and hears him, rejoices greatly because of the bridegroom's voice. Therefore this joy of mine is fulfilled.

Matthew 25
⁴The wise ones, however, took oil in jars along with their lamps. ⁵The bridegroom was a long time in coming, and they all became drowsy and fell asleep. ⁶ "At midnight the cry rang out: 'Here's the bridegroom! Come out to meet him!'

Revelation 19
⁹And the angel said to me, "Write this: Blessed are those who are invited to the marriage supper of the Lamb." And he said to me, "These are the true words of Yahuah."

The "marriage supper of the Lamb" was first proclaimed in the Zodiac, as we will find out. That is what John was referring to in Revelation 19. **The Zodiac contains "the true words of Yahuah"!**

In other words, David sees the Sun as a prototype for The Messiah. This physical metaphor of the sun as the bridegroom pointing to The Messiah is repeated throughout scripture. This is, in fact, true as the Sun was created as a witness of the coming of the Messiah and what the Messiah would do. This striking declaration in ***Psalms 19*** clearly tells us that Yahuah built into the Zodiac the story of redemption and through the stars He has been witnessing His Plan to all humanity in a unique view only from Earth. Later in this book we will learn that the message of the Zodiac is that of a bridegroom who redeems his bride!

Creation Cries Out!

God's Sun a metaphor for God's Son

Yes, 'Yahuah's Sun' in our solar system is a prophetic prototype of Yahuah's Son. The Sun of God is the "light of the world" as a physical metaphor of the Son of God as the "light of the world" Spiritually. The Sun of God saves humanity from the physical darkness bringing life giving light. This too is a physical metaphor of the Son of God who saves humanity from Spiritual darkness bringing the light of Spiritual Life. The center of the Enoch Zodiac is the 'throne of Yahusha' which is pictured on two wheels, because the Sun appears to 'move' throughout the sky.

The prophets Enoch, Ezekiel, Daniel, and John all described the center of the Zodiac in great detail with

- 2 sets of 4 living creatures
- 4 "wheels with a wheel"
- a rainbow throne
- 24 stars/elders falling at the feet of the One who sits on the throne

53

I will cover these prophesies in great detail later in this book. The Greeks then took the Zodiac given to Enoch and perverted the center of the Zodiac into mythology, re-envisioned the entire Zodiac into a Greek Appropriate Zodiac and the image in the center of the Zodiac as '***Helios riding his Sun chariot'***.
The Signs of the Zodiac were twisted into Greek Gods and idolized just like the Babylonians and Sumerians before them had done. The image on the left is the Enoch Zodiac, the one on the right is the Greek Zodiac. The image on the left is a pictograph of the Plan of Salvation, the one on the right... idolatry.

Later Constantine would do the same thing, and turn the 12 disciples into "gods" to whom his new religion would pray to and simply associated the 12 disciples with the pagan gods of the Zodiac and Pantheon. They were later assigned to "Saints" in an act of idolatry by Christianity. Greek coins were inscribed to this 'sun god' murals dedicated to him and so forth. The Romans then re-envisioned 'Helios' into 'Apollo' then Constantine merged all pagan god-men into Jesus.

Today when we think of "the Zodiac", images of pagan god worship given to us by the Greeks come to mind. We do not understand the origin, or message of the true Zodiac given to Enoch by Yahuah! You will understand completely by the time you finish this book!

Those who are not guided by the Spirit of Yahuah, and view the Zodiac literally have, elevated the Sun as God, instead of seeing it as a metaphor... the source of Sun worship.

The "throne of Yahuah" in The Heavenly Scroll was changed to the chariot of Helios the Sungod by the Greeks.

The Plan of Salvation laid out in The Heavenly Scroll

If we are ever going to fully comprehend the Scriptures, the prophets, and The Nazarene (Branch); we must understand what The Plan of Salvation is. That Plan was first written into the stars at creation called *The Heavenly Scroll*. Yahuah used The Heavenly Scroll to witness the Plan of Salvation to His prophets, and it was further defined in The Feast Cycle which is an annual celebration of *The Heavenly Wedding*.

The Feast Cycle is "*The Narrow Gate*" that we must walk as a bride making ready for her Groom. We are being misled and not taught the true meaning of these things, and being brought back into the immaturity of the letter following Rabbinical Judaism (which does not keep the Feasts properly out of ignorance of The Heavenly Scroll). In fact, by following Rabbinical Judaism, we are literally keeping PAGAN rituals and breaking The Law! For more information on The Feast Cycle and The Narrow Gate, please read my book *The Narrow Gate* free on my website and available on Amazon.

In all our attempts to be obedient to the letter of the Law, we again fail our Father in Spiritual Intent. We remain addicted to milk, lacking teeth to digest the meatier matters of what The Feast Cycle was designed to teach us (and what Yahusha's role is in that Plan as The Nazarene or Branch)... The Plan of Salvation was foretold in The Heavenly Scroll, fulfilled in The Yahushaic Covenant.

> **Hebrews 5**
> In fact, though by this time you ought to be teachers (of the intent of the Law), you need someone to teach you the elementary truths of Yahuah's word all over again. You need milk (the letter), not solid food (Spiritual Intent. The Law is Spiritually appraised *1 Corinthians 2:14*)!

As I will demonstrate, the "elementary Truths of Yahuah's Word" is The Plan of Salvation written in The Heavenly Scroll. Sha'ul openly declares that is the foundation of our faith! However, we are following "teachers" who bring us under condemnation to the "letter of the Law" outside of its intent (*which is what The Yahushaic Covenant is all about*). These teachers tell us everything has to be done "***just like this... or just like that***" and point us to the way Rabbinical Judaism does things, yet never tell us "why" these things are done; which is the more important MEAT... these teachers are a 'dime a dozen'!

These are infant teachers teaching infants, all feeding on milk!

Nothing has changed in 2,000 years! We still do not have mature teachers teaching the Spiritual Law or The Plan of Salvation (written in The Heavenly Scroll). Instead, we have immature teachers trying to "look knowledgeable" with all their impressive carnal/literal knowledge of the letter. We mistake these men as "teachers", when they are in as much need of instruction as the rest of us in Spiritual Things.

> **1 Corinthians 3**
> 1 Brothers, I could not address you as spiritually mature, but as worldly (immature with a literal/carnal approach to the Spiritual Law)—as infants in The Yahushaic Covenant. 2 I

> gave you milk, not solid food, for you were not yet ready for solid food. In fact, you are still not ready, 3 for you are still worldly (approaching the Spiritual Law from a literal mindset, putting the letter above intent, and totally missing the point).

In this chapter, my goal is to illustrate very simply where the Feast Cycle originated and what The Feast Cycle is pointing to, and rehearsing, so we can properly rehearse our role in these moedim as The Bride of the Messiah. The Spring Feasts rehearse the engagement and the Fall Feast are a rehearsal of the wedding all of which is based on the Plan of Salvation written in the stars!

We should approach our celebration of these moedim from that standpoint. If we do, not only will we please Yahuah, but we will mature from the milk of the Word to the meat of it. In the process, we will fulfill "the letter" and properly prepare ourselves as the Bride; and have our candles lit when Yahusha returns to receive us unto himself. If we do not approach The Heavenly Wedding properly and rehears as his Bride, we will remain infants feeding on the milk of the word, never maturing in the intent of things. Year after year, we go through the motions, "to the letter", just like ancient Israel had always done... causing them to MISS the Messiah when he came to fulfill The Heavenly Scroll.

The Blind Following the Blind

As we come out of total paganism (*Christianity*) and realize that we are to keep The Holy Days of Yahuah, we naturally look to Judaism for the answers. What we do not realize is, Judaism is a Hellenized pagan religion as much as Christianity!

> **Hellenization**
> *"The twentieth century witnessed a lively debate over the extent of Hellenization in the Levant and particularly among the ancient Palestinian Jews that has continued until today. The Judaism of the diaspora was thought to have succumbed thoroughly to its influences. Bultmann thus argued that Christianity arose almost completely within those Hellenistic confines and should be read against that background as*

opposed to a more traditional (Palestinian) Jewish background"

We see that Judaism abandoned The Heavenly Scroll, never understood the meaning of His Holy Days and failed to celebrate these important moedim properly! If they did, they would never have killed Yahusha on Passover because that is exactly what the Messiah came to do (as foretold in The Heavenly Scroll). Killing Yahusha on Passover only proved he is the one prophesied in The Heavenly Scroll and prophets!

Yahuah's Feasts are a "mystery", that is veiled in the "letter", and only revealed to the Chosen Few who mature in the meaning of these feasts:

> **1 Corinthians 2**
> 7 but we speak Yahuah's wisdom in a mystery, the hidden wisdom which Yahuah predestined before the ages to our glory (in The Heavenly Scroll); 8 the wisdom which none of the rulers of this age has understood; for if they had understood it they would not have crucified the King of glory (on Passover); 9 but just as it is written, "THINGS WHICH EYE HAS NOT SEEN AND EAR HAS NOT HEARD, AND which HAVE NOT ENTERED THE HEART OF MAN, ALL THAT GOD HAS PREPARED FOR THOSE WHO LOVE HIM."...

We see above that Sha'ul mentions the Mystery Language, and then speaks in this mystery language a parable and prophecy from the book of Isaiah. We are going to dig deeper into the mystery of the ages that Isaiah spoke about in

> **Isaiah 64:4**
> ""THINGS WHICH EYE HAS NOT SEEN AND EAR HAS NOT HEARD, AND WHICH HAVE NOT ENTERED THE HEART OF MAN, ALL THAT YAHUAH HAS PREPARED FOR THOSE WHO LOVE HIM."

… the Plan of Salvation, spoken of by Isaiah and referenced by Sha'ul (as a "mystery" or "hidden wisdom"), is found in the Spring and Fall Feasts of Yahuah which are based on Plan of Salvation written in The Heavenly Scroll as I will prove in this book!

> *These feasts are literally the Plan of Salvation written in the Stars played out on Earth each year.*

As we read in 1 Corinthians 2, those who "ruled" at that time (*the Pharisees who ruled the synagogues and Sadducees who ruled in the Temple*) did not understand the meaning of Yahuah's Holy Days. Why then, are we keeping these Holy Days in the way and example of Rabbinical Judaism? They do not now, nor did they then, understand the meaning of these Appointed Times and had abandoned The Heavenly Scroll. Nothing has changed in Rabbinical Judaism over the last 2000 years.

> *They have been doing it "**their way**"... and now <u>we</u> are doing it "**their way**" and they are no closer to seeing their Messiah.*

The same human traditions are carried forward today in Judaism, as they continue in bondage to the Letter "***ever seeing but cannot see; ever hearing but cannot hear, ever seeking but never understanding***" as they continue in the literal ritualistic adherence to the Letter outside of what these moedim mean Spiritually in context of the Plan of Salvation. **And we are the blind following the blind (Hebrew Roots "teachers") ... right off the cliff!**

Creation is crying out the Plan of Salvation

We read in 1 Corinthians 2:7 that Sha'ul mention "*predestined before the ages to our glory*"! If we are going to unlock the "mystery" of these moedim, we must begin there; **_before the ages_** as Sha'ul indicated. We must journey back to the very beginning and search for our answers as to "what" the Feast Cycle is telling us.

> *We are going to go back to the very beginning, before the Feasts of Yahuah were given orally to Adam – Moses, before they were written down in detailed instructions in the Mosaic Covenant... back to Creation!*

Why must we go back to day 4 of Creation? Because now, in The Yahushaic Covenant, they have found their ultimate meaning Spiritually; which was **_ordained before the foundation of the world and predestined before the ages_**, as Sha'ul stated.

We are going to unlock the "secrets preserved in the heavens" that Enoch spoke of and reveal The Plan of Salvation as Yahusha was "portrayed as crucified" in The Heavenly Scroll and given glory with Yahuah as "the coming King". Yahuah literally gave Yahusha "glory" before the world was, by witnessing of His coming King in the fabric of His Creation. Yahuah revealed His Plan on day 1 when He said "let there be light", then authored that plan into the stars on Day 4, then fulfilled that Plan on the 4th prophetic day. I will prove this in detail, and illustrate this fact, and show "how" Yahusha was "ordained before the foundation of the world" and "how" Yahusha was "as a lamb that has been slain".

The stars literally cry out the coming King! They foretell of his role in the Plan of Salvation, and lay out the annual wedding feast which would later become The Holy Days of Yahuah!

Plan of Salvation
The Feast Cycle foretold in The Heavenly Scroll

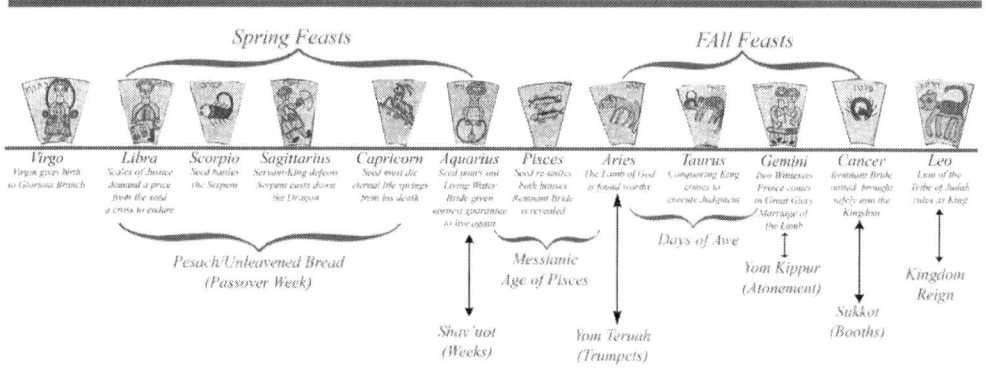

Spring Feasts — FAll Feasts

| Virgo | Libra | Scorpio | Sagittarius | Capricorn | Aquarius | Pisces | Aries | Taurus | Gemini | Cancer | Leo |

Pesach/Unleavened Bread (Passover Week)

Shav'uot (Weeks)

Messianic Age of Pisces

Yom Teruah (Trumpets)

Days of Awe

Yom Kippur (Atonement)

Sukkot (Booths)

Kingdom Reign

Image property of The Sabbath Covenant Ministry www.sabbathcovenant.com by Rav Sha'ul

Sha'ul, speaking of Yahuah's Feast Cycle, declared in *1 Corinthians 2* that the meaning of the Feasts of Yahuah were a mystery and hidden wisdom. He clearly understood what many even today do not comprehend. He stated that no one of this age (*this is still the same age, ages are 2000 years in duration*) understood the true meaning of these moedim. Sha'ul pointed us back to creation for the answer declaring: "**Yahuah predestined before the ages to our glory**". What is Sha'ul referring to? What is it in "creation" that is crying out to us, and what is it saying? Is there a message embedded in the fabric of creation, designed by The Creator, that will give us insight into His Appointed Times and Feasts?

> **Romans 1**
> "19 because that which is known about Yahuah is evident within them; for Yahuah made it evident to them (writing His Plan into the stars *Psalms 19*). 20 For <u>since the creation of the world</u> (he points out that creation is the Original Revelation that cries out) His invisible attributes, His eternal power and divine nature, have been clearly seen (in the stars), being understood through what has been made (The Heavenly Scroll)."

That message written in the stars was corrupted and very few understand what that message is telling us.

That message is the foundation of The Torah, the Feasts, the Prophets… and the reason Abraham attempted to sacrifice Isaac. It is the foundation of all pagan King's claim to rule mankind, and the foundation of every prophet's proclamations concerning The Messiah. It is a Divine Clock that dictates The Sabbath, foretells the exact timing of The Messiah's two comings, and much more.

The "key" to the Feast Cycle is found in The Heavenly Scroll as Yahuah's Word is preserved eternally in the heavens (*or rather, The Heavenly Scroll*). "Heaven" is a Hellenized word that robs us of the true meaning, that is pointing directly to The Heavenly Scroll.

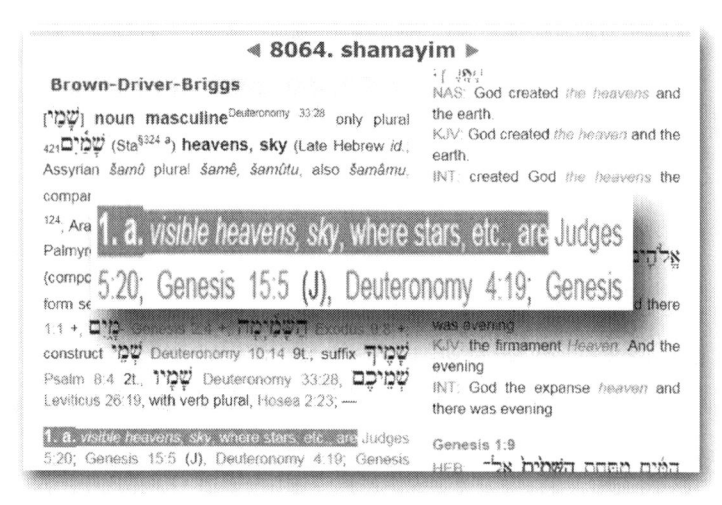

"Heaven" should have been translated "Heavenly Scroll" in many places.

The Hebrew word is 'shamayim' which is a direct reference to the stars, where The Heavenly Scroll stands eternally as Yahuah's witness of Yahusha as The Messiah.

> **Psalm 119:89**
> Your word, Yahuah, is eternal; it stands firm (written) in the heaven(ly Scroll)

It is in The Heavenly Scroll that Yahusha had "Glory" with Yahuah written into creation "before the world was". This witness in the stars called The Heavenly Scroll foretells of The Messiah defeating death through resurrection, and reigning as King eternally as we will learn in this book. Next, I am going to demonstrate how "key" The Heavenly Scroll is to our faith as every forefather, every prophet, the Messiah, and the messengers of The Yahushaic Covenant ALL preached The Heavenly Scroll.

Creation Cries Out!

The Heavenly Scroll is the FOUNDATION of the Earthly Scroll

Scripture is ripe with references to The Heavenly Scroll as it is the vehicle by which Yahuah revealed to mankind the coming Branch and Plan of Salvation through a mediating High Priest.

Amos

Amos 5:8
Yahuah who made the Pleiades (7 stars/Orion's Belt) and Orion (Orion represents the Son of Man and "coming of The Branch")

Amos 9:6
Yahuah builds His lofty palace in the heavens (Mazzaroth/Heavenly Scroll) and sets its foundation on the earth (the heavens and Earth are intimately connected, what is portrayed in the heavens, plays out on Earth).

King David

Psalm 19
2 The heavens (the place in the sky where the stars are located i.e. Zodiac) are telling of the glory of Yahuah (the Glory of Yahuah is Yahusha! *2 Corinthians 4:6*); And their expanse is declaring the work of His hands. 2 Day to day (The Heavenly Scroll) pours forth speech, And night to night reveals knowledge. 3 There is no speech, nor are there words; Their (signs of the Zodiac/Constellations) voice is not heard. 4 Their line (Zodiac means line or path of the sun) has gone out through (and seen by) all the earth, And their (signs of the Zodiac) utterances to the end of the world. In them (the constellations) He has placed a tent for the sun (the Zodiac), 5 Which is as a bridegroom (Yahusha) coming out of his chamber; It rejoices as a strong man (human Messiah) to run his course (of a wedding). 6 Its rising is from one end of the heavens (Zodiac), And its circuit (Zodiac means circuit or path or The Way) to the other end of them; And there is nothing hidden from its heat.

Psalm 119:89
Your word, Yahuah, is eternal; it stands firm (written) in the heaven(ly Scroll).

Moses

Deuteronomy 3:19
When you look up to the sky (sky is Hebrew *8064* shamayim/Zodiac) and see the sun, moon, and stars (speaking of the Zodiac) — the whole heavenly creation (Mazzaroth/Zodiac) — you must not be seduced to worship and serve them (signs of the Zodiac), for Yahuah your Elohim has assigned them (the signs of the Zodiac) to all the people of the world (they were created by Yahuah to proclaim the coming Messiah Yahusha, see Psalm 19, they are not gods).

Genesis 15:5
And he brought him forth abroad, and said, Look now toward heaven (the Zodiac), and (see if you can) tell (what) the stars (proclaim), if thou be able to number them (read them in order, there are 12): and he said unto him, So shall thy seed (Yahusha) be (they tell the story of his life and role he plays in The Plan of Salvation)

Job

Job 38:32
Yahuah said to His upright servant "Can you bring forth Mazzaroth (the 12 signs of the Zodiac) in their season.

Job 9:9
Yahuah is the Maker of the Bear (Ursa Major) and Orion, the (7 stars of) Pleiades and the constellations of the south.

Enoch

Enoch is the one who was "taken to Heaven" or rather, shown the meaning of The Heavenly Scroll and drew the diagram that has been passed down to us today. Enoch was shown how the Watchers perverted the meaning of The Heavenly Scroll into sun worship and magic and horoscopes. Enoch drew The Heavenly Scroll (side image) and that was passed down to future generations before lost when it was outlawed by the Pope and Rabbinical Judaism

Enoch Chapter 9

6 things, and nothing can hide itself from Thee. Thou seest what Azazel hath done, who hath taught all unrighteousness on earth and revealed the eternal secrets which were (preserved) in (the) heaven(ly scroll), which 7 men were striving to learn.

Enoch 35:3

I blessed Yahuah of glory, who had made those great and splendid signs (of the Zodiac), that they might display the magnificence of his works (The Plan of Salvation *Psalms 19*) to angels and to the souls of men; and that these (splendid signs in The Heavenly Scroll) might glorify all his works and operations; might see the effect of his power; might glorify the great labor of his hands; and bless him forever. (wow!)

Ezekiel

Ezekiel 2:9-10
Then I looked (into the heavens), and behold, a hand was extended to me; and lo, a scroll was in it (The Heavenly Scroll).

I will talk more about Ezekiel's vision later. The "4 Wheels within a Wheel" that Ezekiel described and "saw" when he looked into the heavens, was The Enoch Zodiac!

I have produced an in-depth video on what Ezekiel witnessed proving Yahuah was showing Ezekiel The Heavenly Scroll. It can be found on my YouTube Channel. Search "The Sabbath Covenant Channel" or go here:
https://www.youtube.com/channel/UCVLZgChmeSa78Mo7b228sjQ

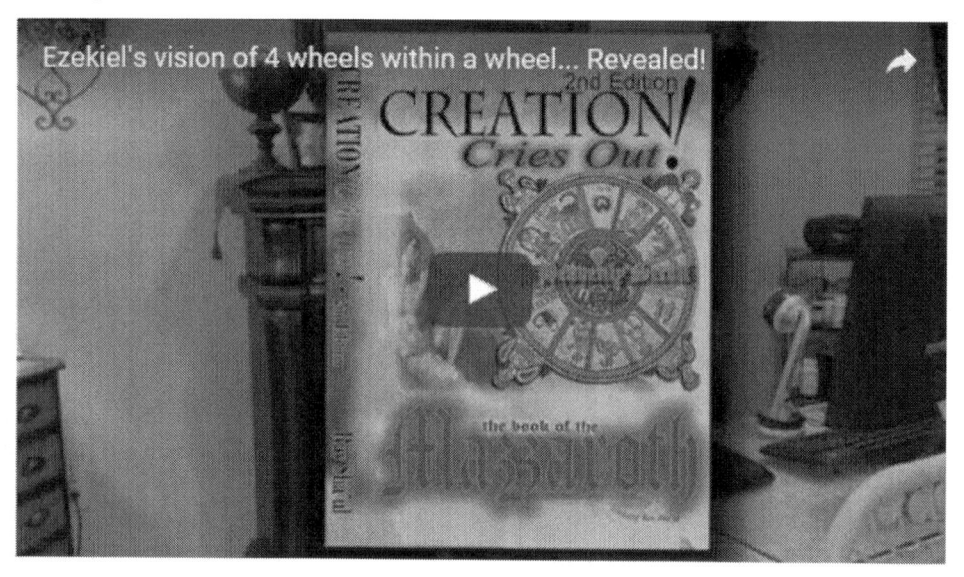

Zechariah

Zechariah 5:2-3
And he said to me, "What do you see (as you look into the heavens)?" And I answered, "I see a flying scroll (the Living Creature holding the Scroll has 2-sets of wings)!"

Isaiah

Isaiah 34:4
And all the host of heaven (Zodiac Signs/Constellations "host stars") shall be dissolved, and the heavens shall be rolled together as a scroll (i.e. The Heavenly Scroll).

Isaiah 9:6-7
"For to us a child is born (VIRGO), to us a son (of man) is given (ORION), and the government shall be on his shoulders (TAURUS) and he will be called Wonderful Counselor (AQUARIUS), (the perfect image of) Mighty God (CAPRICORNUS), (fore) Father of Everlasting (life) (CAPRICORNUS), and Prince of Peace (CANCER)." There will be no end to the increase of His government or of peace, on the Throne of David and over His Kingdom, to establish it (SAGITTARIUS) and to uphold it with justice and righteousness from then on and forevermore (LEO).

Isaiah went on to perfectly describe the Enoch Zodiac:

Isaiah 6:1-13
In the year that (good) king Uzziah died I saw (in the heavens) the Almighty sitting on a throne (the center of The

Enoch Zodiac), high and lifted up; and His train filled the temple. 2 Above Him stood the seraphim (living creatures with 2 sets of wings sitting on the 4 corners of the Enoch Zodiac): each one had six wings; with two it covered its face, and with two it covered its feet, and with two he it did fly (flying scroll of Zechariah). 3 One cried to another, and said, Holy, holy, holy is Yahuah of Hosts: the whole earth is full of his glory (a futuristic vision of the Sabbath Millennium). 4 The foundations of the thresholds shook at the voice (sounds and thunders) of Him who cried out, and the house was filled with smoke.

Isaiah 42
5 This is what Yahuah says— He who created the heavens (the stars and constellations... the Zodiac) and stretched them out (in order to proclaim a message), who spread out the earth and all that comes out of it, who gives breath to its people, and life to those who walk on it:

Isaiah 46
5 "To whom will you compare me or count me equal? To whom will you liken me that we may be compared? 8 "Remember this, fix it in mind, take it to heart, you rebels. 9 Remember the former things, those of long ago (at creation); I am ELOHIM, and there is no other; I am ELOHIM, and there is none like me. 10 I make known the end from the beginning (written in The Heavenly Scroll on Day 4 of Creation), from ancient times (creation), what is still to come. I say: My purpose (defined and written in the stars ***Psalms 119:89***) will stand, and I will do all that I please (His will be done on Earth, as it is proclaimed in heaven i.e. written in the stars ***Matthew 6:10***)

Isaiah 44
24 "This is what Yahuah says— your Redeemer, who formed you in the womb: I am Yahuah, the Maker of all things, who stretches out the heavens (signs of the Zodiac along the ecliptic to reveal a hidden message ***Psalms 19***), who spreads out the earth **by myself** (Yahusha did not exist, and was NOT co-creator).

Isaiah 45

5 I am Yahuah, and there is no other; apart from me there is no Elohim. 7 I form the light and create darkness, I bring prosperity and create disaster; I, Yahuah, do all these things. 12 <u>It is **I** who made the earth and created mankind upon it</u>. **My own hands** stretched out the heavens (signs of the Zodiac along the ecliptic to reveal a hidden message **Psalms 19**); I marshaled their starry hosts (constellations/signs which "host stars"... Yahusha did not exist, and was NOT co-creator)

Isaiah 48

11 For My own sake, for My own sake I will do it; for how could dishonor come to My Name (Yahuah)? I will not give My glory (as Creator) to another (not even Yahusha)! 12 Listen to Me, O Yaaqob and Yisrayl, My called; I am He; I am the Aleph, I also am the Tav (means 'Unity and Perfection' ... Yahuah not Yahusha). 13 **<u>My hand has laid the foundation of the earth</u>** (He alone is Creator and did it all by Himself *Isaiah 44:24*), and My right hand has spanned (authored) the heaven(ly Scroll *Psalm 19*); when I summon them together (i.e. the stars and constellations conspire together to hold a secret a message), they will minister together (to proclaim the Messiah/Plan of Salvation *Psalm 19*). 14 All of you, gather yourselves together and hear (what the stars proclaim day after day, night after night *Psalm 19*)! Who among them has foretold these things? Yahuah has loved him (spoken of in The Heavenly Scroll; Yahusha); He will do His pleasure on Babylon, and His arm will be on the Chaldeans. 15 I, even I, have spoken; yes, I have called him (Yahusha *Luke 4:18*). I have brought him (forth as The Branch as My Eternal High Priest see Zechariah Chapter 3), and his way (example of Mikveh, Circumcision, and Offering) will succeed (in producing perfection and resurrection, called The Way).

John the Revelator

Revelation 6:14

The heavens (Mazzaroth/Zodiac) receded like a scroll being rolled up.

Revelation 5 - *The Opening of the Scroll of the Mazzaroth*

5 Then I saw in the right hand of the one who was seated on

the throne a scroll written on the front and back (3-D scroll of heavenly pictographs) and sealed with seven seals (the 7 visible wandering stars were seen as seals over The Heavenly Scroll, also the 7 lampstand Heavenly Menorah).

Revelation Chapter 4

1 The Throne in Heaven After this I looked, and behold, a door was opened in heaven; and the first voice which I heard was (Yahuah, the Aleph/Tav), as it were, of a loud shofar blast talking with me, which said: Come up here, and I will show you things which must be after this. 2 And immediately I was in the Spirit (seeing a vision of The Heavenly Scroll); and behold (in the stars), a throne was set in (the middle of) The Heavenly Scroll, and One sat on the throne. 3 And He Who sat there had the appearance of a jasper and a sardius stone, and there was a rainbow surrounding the throne, like the appearance of an emerald. 4 And surrounding the throne were twenty-four seats, and sitting on the seats I saw twenty-four elders (represented by stars in the center of the Zodiac), clothed in white robes; and they had crowns of gold on their heads. 5

And out of the throne proceeded lightnings, and thunderings, and voices; and there were seven lamps of fire (Heavenly Menorah) burning before the throne, which signify and represent the complete plan of Yahuah (7-spirits/7 stars of Pleiades). 6 And before the throne there was a sea of glass, like crystal (blackness of space). And in the midst of the throne, and surrounding the throne, were four living creatures full of eyes before and behind (the "signs/constellation" wheel of Ezekiel's vision, image to the left).

7 And the first creature was like a **lion**, and the second creature like a **calf**, and the third creature had a face as a **man**, and the fourth creature was like a **flying eagle** (the 4 cardinal points of the Enoch Zodiac to the left). 8 And each of the four living creatures had six wings, they were full of eyes around and within; and they did not cease day and night, saying: Holy, holy, holy, Father Yahuah Almighty, Who was, and is, and is to come.

9 And when those creatures give glory, and honor, and thanks, to Him who sat on the throne, to Him Who lives forever and ever,

10 The twenty-four elders (stars) fall down before Him Who sat on the throne (in the Enoch Zodiac, there are exactly 24 stars and they are "falling" under the rainbow throne, the four beasts are seen singing "holy, holy, holy" pictured on previous page), and worship Him Who lives forever and ever, and bow with their kippot before the throne, saying: 11 You are worthy, O Yahuah, to receive glory, and honor, and power; for You created all things, and by Your will they exist and were created!

I have produced an in-depth video on what John witnessed proving Yahuah was showing John The Heavenly Scroll. It can be found on my YouTube Channel. Search "The Sabbath Covenant Channel" or go here: https://www.youtube.com/channel/UCVLZgChmeSa78Mo7b228sjQ

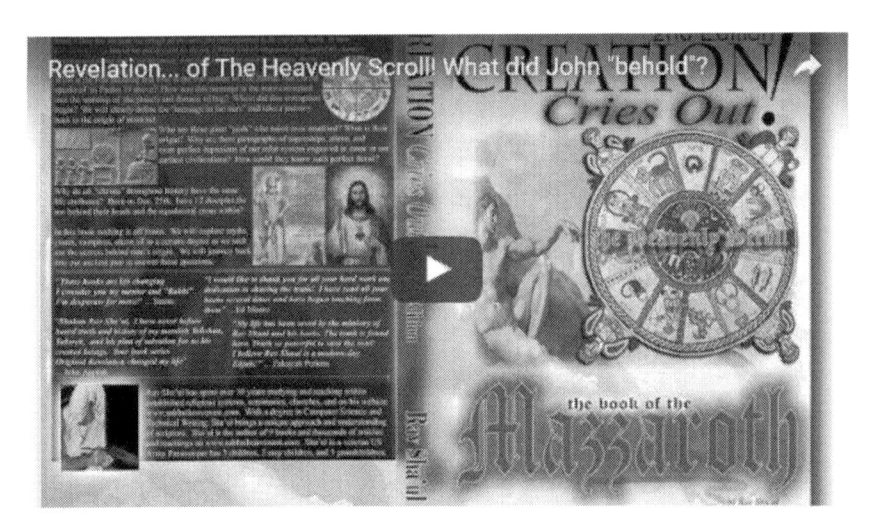

Daniel

Daniel 7
1 In the first year of Baalshazzar king of Babylon, Daniyl had a dream, and visions in his mind (as he studied the Heavenly Scroll of Enoch) as he lay on his bed (looking up at the stars and constellations). Then he wrote down his dream (H2493. A revelation from Yahuah, he was not asleep, he was wide awake writing down his visions), beginning the account of these matters: 2 Daniyl spoke, and said; I saw (The Heavenly Scroll) in my vision by night (by night - because he was observing the stars, not sleeping), and behold (The Heavenly Scroll), ... 9 I beheld (the Enoch Zodiac) until the 4 thrones were set in place (the 4 living creatures on the outer rim of the Enoch Zodiac that move it about until they had moved The Heavenly Scroll in position), and the Ancient of days (Yahuah) did sit (on the judgement seat), Whose vesture was white as snow, and the hair of His head like the pure wool; His throne was like the fiery flame, and His wheels (The Throne is pictured on "wheels" because it is represented by the Sun which "moves" through the constellations) as burning

fire.

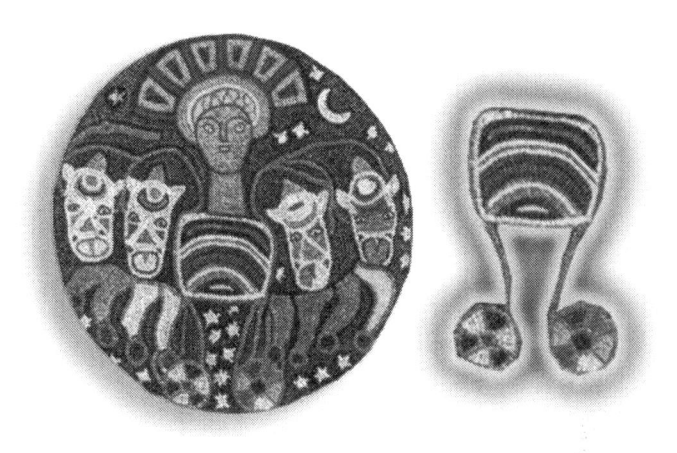

10 A fiery stream issued (from His mouth) and came forth from before Him (His words are like an all-consuming fire *Jeremiah 23:29* and *Hebrews 12:29*); thousands upon thousands (of stars in the heavens) ministered to Him, and ten thousand times ten thousand (of stars) stood before Him (Daniel was looking at The Heavenly Scroll, and all the stars in the heavens); the judgment was set (or rather the Judge Yahuah, had taken His seat, the battle is about to begin between the Son of Man and the Son of Perdition), and the books (of The Heavenly Scroll, there are 3 books as I revealed in my book **Creation Cries Out!** *The Mazzaroth*) were opened.

11 I beheld (The Heavenly Scroll), then, because of the voice of the great words which 'the horn' (**Strong's H7162** - should be 'Shofar', Yahuah's voice sounds like a loud Shofar blast *Hebrews 12:19*, do not confuse this with the other 'horns' in Daniel, this one is a musical instrument, the Shofar) spoke; I beheld (what is written in The Heavenly Scroll) until the beast was slain and his body destroyed, and given to the burning flame (message behind the pictographs of **Sagittarius**). 12 As concerning the rest of the beasts, they had their governments taken away; yet their lives were prolonged for a season and time (message behind the pictograph of **Taurus**). 13 I saw in the night (sky) visions (of The Heavenly Scroll, like I said he was laying down at night

looking at the stars), and behold (the constellation *Orion*), One like the Son of man (*Orion*) came with the clouds of heaven (the Milky Way), and (Yahusha and the Beast) came to the Ancient of days (Yahuah, who had taken His seat to judge between them), and they (both) were brought together before Yahuah (to declare who was the fulfillment of The Heavenly Scroll, the books had been opened). 14 And there was given Him (the Son of Man) ruling authority, and glory, and a kingdom, that all peoples, nations, and languages should obey Him; His government is an everlasting government, which will not pass away; and His kingdom is one which will not be destroyed (message behind the pictograph of Leo). 15 I, Daniyl, was grieved in my spirit within my body, and the visions (of The Heavenly Scroll) that passed through my mind (as he studied the Enoch Zodiac) troubled me (as he lay on his bed at night, looking up at the stars, he was not dreaming, he was writing these down as Yahuah gave him understanding as he said in verse 1). 16 I came near to one of those who stood by, and asked him the truth of all this (what do these constellations mean?). So he told me, and revealed the interpretation of these things to me (revealed the meaning behind the Heavenly pictographs).

Yahusha

Matthew 28:20
"and teaching them to obey everything I have commanded you. And surely I am with you always, to the very end of the age (of Pisces when he returns in the Age of Aquarius)."

Hebrews 10:7
Then I said, 'Here I am--it is written about me in the heavenly scroll-- I have come to do your will, my God! (*Matthew 6:10)*

Matthew 6:10
Your kingdom come, Your will be done, on earth as it is (written) in (the) heaven(ly scroll).

John 3:29
29 He who has the Bride is the Bridegroom (speaking of The Heavenly Scroll see ***Psalm 19***); but the friend of the Bridegroom, who stands and hears Him, rejoices greatly because of the Bridegroom's voice (the stars cry out with a loud voice day after day, night after night as "*a bridegroom coming out of his chambers*" in The Heavenly Scroll ***Psalms 19***). Therefore, this joy of mine is fulfilled (Yahusha fulfilled the message contained in The Heavenly Scroll, ***John Chapter 1*** he is the fulfillment of the Debar/Predestined Plan in the flesh).

John 17
5 And now, Father, glorify me in your presence (through resurrection as promised in The Heavenly Scroll) with the glory I had with you (written in The Heavenly Scroll) before the world began (the Light of ***Gen. 1:1***: written into the stars on Day 4, then fulfilled in Yahusha on the 4th prophetic day as the Debar/Plan was fulfilled in the flesh ***John 1***).

Matthew 11:25
At that time Yahusha answered and said, I thank you, O Father, King of The Heavenly Scroll (***Strong's H8064*** 'shamayim' - the place where the stars are located, i.e. The Mazzaroth/Zodiac) and earth, because you have hid these things (secrets preserved in the stars/heaven ***Enoch 9:6***) from the wise and prudent, and have revealed them unto babes.

Matthew 13:11
He replied, "Because the knowledge of the secrets of the kingdom of heaven (the Zodiac or Heavenly Scroll, the *"secrets preserved in the heavens" Enoch 9:6*) has been given to you, but not to them.

Peter

1 Peter 1:20
He was **chosen** (not created) before the creation of the world (as foretold in The Heavenly Scroll), but was revealed (manifested, born, created) in these last times (the 'Debar' or Predestined Plan fulfilled in the flesh *John 1*) for your sake (to fulfill The Plan of Salvation).

Sha'ul

2 Corinthians 4:6
6 Seeing it is Yahuah, that said, Light shall shine out of darkness (referring to day 1 of Creation when the "light" or Plan of Salvation was revealed), who shined in our hearts, to give the light of the knowledge (proclaimed by the stars *Psalms 19*) of the glory of Yahuah in the face of Yahusha the Messiah.

1 Corinthians 2 - *Sha'ul speaking to former pagans who knew and abused the Zodiac*
1 And so it was with me, brothers and sisters. When I came to you, I did not come with eloquence or human wisdom as I proclaimed to you the testimony of Yahuah (about Yahusha written in the stars). 2 For I resolved to know nothing while I was with you except Yahusha the Messiah and him crucified (before the foundation of the world written in the stars before our very eyes *Galatians 3*). 3 I came to you in weakness with great fear and trembling. 4 My message and my preaching were not with wise and persuasive words (of human literal wisdom), but with a demonstration of the Spirit's power, 5 so that your faith might not rest on (literal) human wisdom, but on Yahuah's power (in a Mystery Language). 6 We do, however, speak a message of (spiritual) wisdom among the (spiritually) mature, but not the wisdom of this age or of the rulers of this age (who viewed the Zodiac literally and

worshiped the signs and the Sun), who are coming to nothing. 7 No, we declare Yahuah's wisdom, a mystery that has been hidden (in the Heavenly Scroll *Enoch 9:6*) and that Yahuah destined for our glory before time began (writing it in the stars on day 4 of creation). 8 None of the rulers of this age understood it (because it was corrupted by the watchers *Enoch 9:6*)

Galatians 3
6 You foolish Galatians! Who has bewitched you (twisting the Zodiac into witchcraft)? Before your very eyes (in The Heavenly Scroll) Yahusha the Messiah was clearly portrayed as crucified ...7 Understand then (what is foretold in the stars), that those who have faith (in the message contained in the stars) are children of Abraham. 8 Scripture (the word written in the heavens *Psalm 119:89*) foresaw that Yahuah would justify the Gentiles by faith, and Yahuah announced the gospel in advance to Abraham (via The Heavenly Scroll *Genesis 15:5*; saying): "All nations will be blessed through you."

Romans 10:17
Consequently, faith comes from hearing the message, and the message is heard through the word about the Messiah (what "word" about Yahusha?). 18 But I ask: Did they not hear (what the stars proclaim night after night, day after day *Psalms 19*)? Of course they did: "Their voice (constellations) has gone out into all the earth, their words (concerning Yahusha) to the ends of the world." (Sha'ul quotes *Psalms 19*)

As we move ahead in this book, I will demonstrate exactly what is written in The Heavenly Scroll, how to read it, and its vital importance to our faith. The proof that Yahusha is the Messiah is that he fulfilled The Heavenly Scroll!

CHAPTER 3
YAHUAH CREATED AND NAMED THE STARS AND STRETCHES THEM OUT LIKE A HEAVENLY SCROLL

Chapter 3 - Sha'ul declared Faith comes from the message proclaimed by The Heavenly Scroll!

Isaiah 40:26
Lift up your eyes and look to the heavens: Who created all these? He who brings out the starry host (constellations) one by one (there are exactly 12 major constellations in every culture) and calls forth (in order) each of them by name (to proclaim a message Psalm 19). Because of his great power and mighty strength, not one of them is missing.

The true children of Yahuah have ALWAYS been "Nazarenes!". Nazarene means "those who follow the Branch" and that term "Branch" came from The Heavenly Scroll.

Virgo
A virgin will give birth to a beautiful glorious and righteous branch.

This is what Isaiah was prophesying when he said "Yahuah will give you a SIGN (*human women are not for 'signs', the STARS ARE **Genesis 1:14***) Behold (*in the stars*) a young maiden shall give birth to king/son" which was also The Sign of the Son of Man in the sky, when Jupiter the King Planet is in Virgo with the Sun. We do not understand this and it is taught that Isaiah was speaking of Miriam and we force her to be a "virgin" when that is not what Isaiah said (*he said young maiden*) and Isaiah was not talking about Miriam. He was proclaiming the Plan of Salvation written by the hand of The Creator into the fabric of creation on Day 4.

This is also what Isaiah was prophesying in Isaiah 9

> **Isaiah 9:6-7**
> "For to us a child is born (VIRGO), to us a son (of man) is given (ORION), and the government shall be on his shoulders (TAURUS) and he will be called Wonderful Counselor (AQUARIUS), (the perfect image of) Mighty God (CAPRICORNUS), (fore) Father of Everlasting (life) (CAPRICORNUS), and Prince of Peace (CANCER)." There will be no end to the increase of His government or of peace, on the Throne of David and over His Kingdom, to establish it (SAGITTARIUS) and to uphold it with justice and righteousness from then on and forevermore (LEO).

Then all throughout The Heavenly Scroll, he is called a "seed" as in the seed that produces the Branch. The prophets read the Scroll and that is where they got the term "the Branch". This "seed" or "Branch" is, as Sha'ul declared to the Galatians, portrayed as crucified in the stars since the creation of the world. Below is the message that cries out daily (***Psalm 19***) to all the world that Sha'ul declared "humanity is without excuse" for not accepting Yahusha as the Messiah... and chastised the Romans for twisting it into Sun Worship!

> **VIRGO**: A virgin will give birth to a beautiful glorious and righteous branch. The seed of the woman will be a man of humiliation to rise to be the desire of nations and will become exalted first as shepherd then as harvester. **LIBRA**: The scales demand a price to be paid of this seed, a cross to endure; the victim will be slain and purchase a crown. **SCORPIO**: There is a conflict between the seed and the serpent leading to a struggle with the enemy, the enemy is vanquished. **SAGITTARIUS**: The double-natured seed (servant/king) triumphs as a warrior and pleases the heavens, builds fires of punishment, casts down the dragon. **CAPRICORNUS**: Eternal life comes from his death, he's the Arrow of God, he is pierced, yet springs up again in abundant life. **AQUARIUS**: He pours out "living water" from on high, humanity drinks of the heavenly river and the faithful live again, he is the deliverer of the good news (Gospel), Carrying

the Cross over the earth. **PISCES**: The Redeemer's people multiplied, supported and led by the Lamb, The Bride is exposed on earth, the Bridegroom is exalted. **ARIES**: The Lamb is found worthy, the Bride is made ready, Satan is bound, the strong man triumphs. **TAURUS**: The conquering Ruler comes, the sublime vanquisher, to execute the great judgment, he is the ruling Shepherd King. **GEMINI**: The Marriage of the Lamb, the enemy is trodden down, the Prince comes in great Glory. **CANCER**: The great Bride, the two Houses of Judah and Israel are united, they are brought safely into the kingdom. **LEO**: The Lion King is aroused for rending, the Serpent flees, the Bowl of Wrath is upon him, his Carcass is devoured. The Lion of the tribe of Judah rules as King.

We see in this message... The Spring and Fall Feasts foretold, the Suffering Servant revealed who must die to pay the dowry for his Bride, the Bride revealed, the wedding take place, the "strongman/messiah" defeat the dragon and reign as Conquering King. The Heavenly Scroll is literally the foundation of the Torah/Prophets/Holy Days/Messiah. This is why Sha'ul declares The Heavenly Scroll is the "source of our faith" pointing to Abraham witnessing the stars and quoting David in *Psalm 19* declaring the meaning of the Zodiac in great detail.

We are going to show next, that Sha'ul said that Abraham was called "the father of faith" because he was the first not to fall for the corrupted version of Sun Worship, and even had so much faith in The Heavenly Scroll (*and knew it was speaking of his own seed*), that, thinking it was speaking of Isaac, marched Isaac atop Mt. Mariah to "fulfill the Scroll" which says his seed must die, and eternal life springs from his death:

CAPRICORNUS
Eternal life comes from his death, he's the Arrow of God, he is pierced, yet springs up again in abundant life.

So Abraham tried to sacrifice Isaac trying to fulfill The Heavenly Scroll himself! Much like Abraham tried to fulfill the promise of Yahuah that Sarah would bear him a son (*with Hagar*). Abraham was quite "motivated" and maybe a little impatient.... Yahuah stopped that sacrifice because the "seed" was not Isaac. That event was reckoned to Abraham as tremendous faith that he would offer his own "promised one" to Yahuah believing that Yahuah could and would raise Isaac as stated in the Scroll! So those who "have the faith of Abraham" i.e. believe in The Heavenly Scroll are his descendants!

Sha'ul explains that faith in The Heavenly Scroll is "the faith of Abraham" that is why ALL true Nazarenes (*which means followers of the Branch, foretold in The Heavenly Scroll*) have the foundation of The Heavenly Scroll. Abraham was the first "Nazarene"...

> **Romans 10**
> 17 Consequently, faith comes from hearing the message, and the message is heard through the word about the Messiah (what "word" about Yahusha is heard throughout the world?). 18 But I ask: Did they not hear? Of course they did: "Their (constellations) voice has gone out into all the earth, their words (concerning Yahusha) to the ends of the world." (Sha'ul quotes ***Psalms 19***)

Sha'ul explains that Yahuah witnessed the coming Messiah using The Heavenly Scroll to Abraham and it was in that way that "Abraham saw Yahusha's day and rejoiced". This is what Yahusha was talking about, when the Jews twisted his words to imply that Yahusha saw Abraham. That is NOT what Yahusha said, he said Abraham saw his day ***Gen 15:5***. Yahusha said "before Abraham was created, I am prophesied to come in The Heavenly Scroll"! The Jews had abandoned The Heavenly Scroll and had no clue what Yahusha was saying... (*just like humanity today*).

> **John 8**
> 56 Your father Abraham rejoiced at the thought of seeing my day (***Genesis 15:5***); he saw it (written in the stars) and was glad." 57 "You are not yet fifty years old," the Jews said to him, "and you have seen Abraham! (that is NOT what he said!)" 58 "I tell you the truth," Yahusha answered, "before Abraham was born, I am (prophesied to come in the stars as

he explained *Genesis 15:5*)!" 59 At this, they picked up stones to stone him, but Yahusha hid himself, slipping away from the temple grounds.

Genesis 15
5 And Yahuah brought Abraham forth abroad (outside), and said, Look now toward (the) heaven(ly Scroll), and (see if you can) tell (what) the stars (proclaim day after day, night after night **Psalm 19**), if thou be able to (discern the) number (and order of) them (the Starry Hosts i.e. constellations; there are 12 in every culture in human history): and he said unto him, So shall thy seed be.

This is the same point Sha'ul was making...

Galatians 3:8
8 Scripture (the eternal word written in The Heavenly Scroll **Psalms 119:89**) foresaw that Yahuah would justify the Gentiles by faith, and (THE STARS) announced the gospel in advance to Abraham (**Gen. 15:5**): "All nations will be blessed through you."

You see, Yahuah authored The Heavenly Scroll, named all the stars and gave them their meaning, gathered them together into "starry hosts" (*constellations host stars*) gave the constellations "meaning" and He SUMMONS THEM TOGETHER to proclaim The Plan of Salvation!

Isaiah 48
13 My right hand has spanned (authored) the heaven(ly Scroll *Psalm 19*); when I summon them together (i.e. the stars and constellations conspire together to hold a secret a message *Enoch 9:6*), they will minister together (to proclaim the Messiah/Plan of Salvation *Psalm 19*). 14 All of you, gather yourselves together and hear (what the stars proclaim day after day, night after night *Psalm 19*)! Who among them has foretold these things (understood The Heavenly Scroll)? Yahuah has loved him (spoken of in The Heavenly Scroll; Yahusha); He will do His pleasure on Babylon, and His arm will be on the Chaldeans. 15 I, even I, have spoken; yes, I have called him (Yahusha *Luke 4:18*). I have brought him (forth as The Branch as My Eternal High Priest see Zechariah

Chapter 3), and his way (example of Mikveh, Circumcision, and Offering) will succeed (in producing perfection and resurrection, called The Way).

Humanity has been "had" by tradition and religion. Lied to generation to generation, the Lying Pen of the Scribes have altered the meaning of the text, The Scriptures interpreted by unspiritual minds, outside of the context of The Plan of Salvation written in The Heavenly Scroll. I am going to show everyone what "tradition and religion" does not want you to "see" and "understand". I am going to show us how to have "eyes to see The Heavenly Scroll" and "ears to hear what the stars proclaim".

The Heavens Pour Forth Speech Day after Day

Sha'ul the Apostle asks of humanity below "did they not hear? Of course, they did, he exclaims!" and then Sha'ul quotes David in **Psalms 19** that declares the heavens are pouring forth speech, day after day, to all mankind as David describes the Zodiac in great detail.

'Hearing' and 'voice' are used anthropomorphically as physical to spiritual parallels by Sha'ul as he clearly teaches that the source of "faith" comes from the message proclaimed in the stars at creation. The very means by which Yahuah witnessed the Gospel to Adam, Enoch, Noah, Abraham, and all the prophets. He used the Heavenly Scroll.

> **Romans 10**
> 17 Consequently, faith comes from hearing the message, and the message is heard through the word about the Messiah (what "word" about Yahusha is heard throughout the world?). 18 But I ask: Did they not hear? Of course they did: "Their (constellations) voice has gone out into all the earth, their words (concerning Yahusha) to the ends of the world." (Sha'ul quotes **Psalms 19**)

The "*message that is heard through the word about the Messiah*", Sha'ul says is... the Zodiac, the 'Heavenly Scroll'; the Original Revelation to all mankind, the first and most complete Gospel of Yahusha the Messiah! After asking the question "*did they not hear*" the message of The Gospel, Paul literally quotes from **Psalm 19**, the most eloquent description of the Zodiac and its message I have ever read...it is a detailed account of the Zodiac proclaiming The Gospel Message to all mankind.

Yahuah witnessed the Gospel of Yahusha in advance (*of Yahusha being created to fulfill it*) to Abraham, and Abraham "saw Yahusha's Day" written in the stars!

> **John 8**
> 56 Your father Abraham was overjoyed to see My day. He saw it (written in the stars *Genesis 1:15)* and was glad." 57 Then the Jews said to Him, "You are not yet fifty years old, and You have seen Abraham?"

Notice that Yahusha did **NOT** say that he saw Abraham, he said Abraham saw his life story revealed in The Heavenly Scroll. Even today false teachers abound who preach incarnation saying that Yahusha "saw Abraham" and that is **NOT** what is said in this Scripture! Yahusha is "before Abraham" in preeminence, as Yahuah had given Yahusha "Glory" with Him at creation by writing his life in The Heavenly Scroll foretelling that He would glorify Yahusha through resurrection and crowning him King.

> **Genesis 15**
> 5 And he brought him forth abroad, and said, Look now toward heaven (the Zodiac), and (see if you can) tell (what) the stars (proclaim), if thou be able to number them (read them in order, there are 12): and he said unto him, So shall thy seed (Yahusha) be (they tell the story of his life).

Sha'ul understood this and this was the foundation of what Sha'ul told the Galatians! In Galatians Chapter 3, Sha'ul refers to *Gen. 15:5* and explains that is how Abraham was considered the "father of our faith". Abraham understood the message of The Heavenly

Scroll, then tried to fulfill it by killing Isaac (*because the "strong man" is foretold to die and eternal life springs from his death in The Heavenly scroll*) thinking Isaac was "the seed" that The Heavenly Scroll was speaking of! The Heavenly Scroll declares this "seed" must die and be resurrected to earn the right to rule as "The Lion of the Tribe of Judah".

Rav Sha'ul the Apostle made a significant statement in Galatians 3:8:

Galatians 3:8
8 Scripture foresaw that Yahuah would justify the Gentiles by faith, and announced the gospel in advance (of Yahusha being created) to Abraham: "All nations will be blessed through you."

Galatians 3:16
The promises were spoken to Abraham and to his seed (Genesis 1:15). Scripture does not say "and to seeds," meaning many people, but "and to your seed," meaning one person, who is Yahusha the Messiah (the stars were speaking of Yahusha!).

Again in Galatians 3, Sha'ul declares that "***before their very eyes Yahusha the Messiah was portrayed as crucified***". What does that mean?

The members of the church in Galatia (*who once were pagans*) were not present at the crucifixion some 50 years earlier. So, in what way was the messiah "***portrayed as crucified before their very eyes?***" It was written in the stars! The same way it was preached to Abraham. We see Sha'ul make the point that "the seed" proclaimed in "the heavens" to Abraham was in fact Yahusha the Messiah not Isaac (*so Abraham had misunderstood it that is why the Angel of Yahuah stopped that sacrifice*). The same Messiah was "***portrayed as crucified/A Lamb that was slaughtered before the world was***" right before the very eyes of the Galatians as well… in The Zodiac as I will prove:

Galatians 3
3 You foolish Galatians! Who has bewitched you? Before your very eyes (in the stars) Yahusha the Messiah was clearly portrayed as crucified (A lamb that was slaughtered before the foundation of the world).

Sha'ul then goes on to point the Galatians back to Abraham making the point that "the seed" or The Messiah was prophesied by the stars of heaven...

Galatians 3
5 So again I ask, does Yahuah give you his Spirit and work miracles among you by the works of the law (alone *James 2:14-26*), or by your believing what you heard (the stars proclaim day after day *Palms 19*)? 6 So also Abraham "believed Yahuah (when he read The Heavenly Scroll *Genesis 15:5*), and it was credited to him as righteousness (when he tried to fulfill the message in the stars by sacrificing Isaac)." 7 Understand, then, that those who have faith (in the Plan of Salvation proclaimed in the stars) are children of Abraham. 8 Scripture (The Heavenly Scroll, the 'word' eternally preserved in the stars *Psalms 199:89*) foresaw that Yahuah would justify the Gentiles by faith, and announced the gospel in advance to Abraham (through the stars *Genesis 15:5*): "All nations will be blessed through you." 9 So those who rely on faith (in The Heavenly Scroll) are blessed along with Abraham, the man of faith (in the message he witnessed in The Heavenly Scroll)...16 The promises (of eternal life and a mediator) were spoken to Abraham (via The Heavenly Scroll *Genesis 15:5*) and to his seed. Scripture does not say "and to seeds," meaning many people, but "and to your seed," meaning one person, who is the Messiah (is what the Stars proclaimed to Abraham, all the prophets, the Galatians, the Romans, and you and I today... *Psalms 19*!).

"How Yahuah preached the Gospel to Abraham"

by Barry Setterfield

<u>Star names and languages</u> *by Barry Sutterfield*

"One important fact emerges here. Many star and constellation names in a variety of languages around the world have a similar meaning. For example, one constellation was known as Virgo to the Romans, Bethulah to the Hebrews, Parthenos to the Greeks, and Kanya to the Indians, but all mean "VIRGIN". Linguistically, this strongly implies there was a common origin for the names. It is accepted theory that the three main linguistic branches from which most languages diverged had a common origin in Anatolia (see Gamkrelidze and Ivanov in *Scientific American* March 1990, or Colin Renfrew in *Scientific American* October 1989). Scripturally, this division of languages occurred at Babel, which was near Anatolia. This would imply an origin of star and constellation names prior to the Babel event which suggests that they may have been known as far back as Noah and the Flood. Linguistically, that is as far back as we can go. However, the Isaiah 40:26 statement takes us right back to the Creation and Adam.

> <u>Isaiah 40:26</u>
> Lift up your eyes and look to the heavens: Who created all these? He who brings out the starry host one by one and calls forth each of them by name. Because of his great power and mighty strength, not one of them is missing.

In the mid to late 19th century, star names became fixed by astronomical convention. The name chosen for a given star was sometimes the Latin, or Hebrew, or Chaldean, or Arabic version of the original name. As a result of this process, some names have been lost. However, those who studied this topic in detail, namely Frances Rolleston, Joseph A. Seiss, and E. W. Bullinger wrote at a time when the star names in other languages were still extant.

Some important information on these matters can also be found in Jamieson's Celestial Atlas of 1822 which appeared well before astronomical convention fixed the names.

Rolleston's work of 1862 comprised 221 pages of small typeface in four parts. The author died just prior to the completion of Part 4. In Part 2 there is an extensive study of star names in a variety of languages, and their primitive roots. Most give a concordant testimony. However, as noted by a number of recent commentators on the topic, modern Arabic interpretations are often discordant with the overall picture that emerges. However, Rolleston did point out the source of this problem on page 5 of Part 1. The difficulty arises because modern Arabic use of the basic roots of words gives meanings that are divergent from ancient Arabic. By reference to the ancient Arabic use of roots, corroboration of the story given by the other star names is usually obtained."

Seasons and constellations *by Barry Sutterfield*

"The time or season of the year used to be known by the constellations passing overhead or the one that the Sun was in. In Job 38:32 Yahuah said to His upright servant "Can you bring forth Mazzaroth (the 12 signs) in their season?" These 12 signs form the path that the Sun appears to take in the heavens, namely the Zodiac. The word ZODIAC comes from the Greek word ZOAD meaning "a way, a step, a circuit, a circle". In Chaldean the word has similar associated meanings. Psalm 19:6 actually uses the Hebrew equivalent of this word where it states that "(the Sun) goes from one end of heaven, and his CIRCUIT (or path i.e. Zodiac) is unto the other end of it:"

There is evidence that the constellation patterns making up the Zodiac, and indeed the rest of the night sky, were formed and named by Yahuah. In Job 26:13 we find the statement "By His Spirit He has garnished and decorated the heavens; His hand has formed the FLEEING SERPENT." Note that in Hebrew poetic style the heavens and the fleeing serpent are connected. So we ask

"Is there a fleeing serpent in the heavens?" The answer is YES! The constellation of HYDRA. It is a particularly apt constellation to remark upon as it is the longest constellation in the sky. It takes 7 hours to pass overhead. This comment in Job implies that the Spirit of Yahuah Himself formed and decorated the heavens with the constellation patterns, and, as shown above, He gave them their names as well. Obviously, Abraham was familiar with the constellation patterns and star names because Yahuah used the message therein to instruct him. What is this message?"

The stars carry a gospel message *by Barry Sutterfield*

"In Romans 10, Rabbi Sha'ul gives us some key verses to help with this. Verse 15 states "and how shall they preach except they be sent? As it is written 'How beautiful are the feet of them that preach the GOSPEL OF PEACE, and bring GLAD TIDINGS of good things'." So the bringing of the GOOD NEWS, the GOSPEL OF PEACE is what Sha'ul is talking about here in this context. In verse 18, Sha'ul then goes on to say: "But have they (the heathen) not heard? YES! Truly they have heard! For 'their sound went into all the earth and their words unto the ends of the world'." What a fascinating statement! Sha'ul says here that the heathen have heard the Gospel of Peace, because "THEIR sound went into all the earth and THEIR words unto the ends of the world." The question is who are the "THEY" that are doing the preaching? Well, if you have a marginal reference, you find that Sha'ul is quoting directly from Psalm 19:4 where the stars are being spoken of. Indeed, Psalm 19:3 gives the additional information that "there is no speech or language where (the stars) voice is not heard." Therefore, the "THEY" in Psalm 19 and Romans 10:18 are the stars in the heavens. As a consequence, it can only be concluded that it is the stars that are preaching the Gospel - in a particular way by their names and the arrangement of the constellation patterns."

The importance of the Sun *by Barry Sutterfield*

"The next point to note comes from Psalm 19:4-6. Dr. D. E. Spencer paraphrases verse 4 as "In amongst these starry witnesses, Yahuah has established a dwelling place for the Sun." The next verse goes on to describe the SUN as the Heavenly Bridegroom, who comes forth to run his race and returns to his place of origin. But in the Bible, John the baptizer speaks of the Messiah as coming down from heaven, and calls Him the "Bridegroom" (John 3:25-31). The beloved disciple John also refers to the relationship of the Messiah to His Called Out Ones (saints) as that of a heavenly bridegroom with an earthly bride, while Rabbi Sha'ul echoes the idea in Ephesians 5.

It is therefore apparent from Psalm 19 and the other passages that the Sun represents Yahusha, the heavenly Bridegroom.

This idea is accentuated by the prophet Malachi. He calls Israel's Messiah the SUN of Righteousness who will blaze forth for the sake of His people in the Last Day (Malachi 4:2). So the Sun represents the Messiah, the light of the world (John 8:12), who came from heaven, ran His race on earth, and returned to Heaven. The race that the Sun runs is given by the Zodiac constellations or star patterns, so all the strong-man figures along the Zodiac represent the Messiah, the SUN of Righteousness, and the work He was to do. Note further that Psalm 19 is in two parts: In Part 1 we have the message of the stars - In Part 2 we have the message of Yahuah's word, the Bible being discussed. One is set against the other in such a way that David, who wrote this Psalm about 1000 BC, is implying that **the message in the stars and the message in the Scriptures are one and the same.**"

The strong man constellation figures *by Barry Sutterfield*

"The story told by the strong man figures of the sky has been corrupted by Greek and Roman mythology. This was recognized by Jamieson in his Celestial Atlas published in 1822. On page 40 he states that "The Lion does not seem to have been placed among the zodiacal symbols because Hercules was fabled to have slain the Nemean Lion. It would seem, to the contrary, that Hercules, who represented the Sun, was said to have slain the Nemean Lion, because Leo was ALREADY a zodiacal sign." Notice here that this nineteenth century astronomer actually states that the Sun (the light of the world) is symbolized by the strong man Hercules. This is in agreement with the Biblical interpretation which identifies the strong man who runs his race along the path of the Sun as Messiah Yahusha the victor.

Another point is also pertinent. The Greeks thought of each of these "strong man" figures as being a different deity. In the Biblical interpretation they represent different works of the same person, namely Messiah Yahusha. Even though it will pre-empt the discussion later, an example may be appropriate. To the Greeks, the Zodiac sign of Gemini the Twins represented Apollo and Hercules, the twin sons of Zeus, the chief deity. The Roman equivalent was Castor and Pollux which star names are retained today. It is shown later that these two pictures are of the same anointed one... the Messiah Yahusha in His twin role as the Son of Yahuah and also the Son of Man."

The origin of mythology and tradition *by Barry Sutterfield*

"Interestingly enough, the skeptic Volney is recorded by Rolleston as saying that "Everywhere in antiquity is the existence of the tradition of the expected conqueror of the serpent, a divine person, born of a woman, who was to come." Rolleston noted that Volney "sees this tradition reflected in the constellations, but why it should be there he does not say."(Part 1 page 19). A very similar statement is made by Depuis in L'Origine des Cultes who admits that this tradition was prevalent in all nations. Greek, Roman and other pagan mythologies have been built around this message from the stars and as a result must be considered as a perversion of the original. Nevertheless as Dr. D. E. Spencer concluded "Pagan mythology still retains sufficient of the truth for you to recognize it." (Word Key "Mazzaroth," broadcast over radio HCJB 1972).

Rolleston (Part 1 p.23) elaborates on this: "Should the tradition of the Divine yet woman-born Conqueror of the serpent, crushing His foe, but suffering from its venom, be met with among all nations, it is only what might have been anticipated among the descendants of one common father. From the Grecian Hercules, half human and half divine, subduing the hydra and dying from its poison; from the Indian incarnation of the Divinity, the virgin-born Krishna, slaying a serpent and wounded by it in the heel; to the serpent-worship of Mexico, and that of the woman-born and unfathered deity Mexitli; this image is everywhere present, pointing to one origin of the tradition and the race."

Dr. Spencer gave a further example of interest. In mythology "Zeus, the supreme deity of the Greeks reigned on Mount Olympus 'in the midst' of the twelve lesser gods of the Greeks." He then points to the pre-existent truth that has been corrupted by this mythology and makes an important observation. "Is it not more than chance that just as the blazing fire of the Sun dwells in the midst of the twelve constellations of Mazzaroth, so the blazing pillar of fire was the dwelling place of Yahuah in the midst of the twelve tribes of Israel? Furthermore, can it be mere chance that Messiah Yahusha, 'the Light of the world', is the One who dwelt in a tabernacle of flesh in the midst of the twelve disciples?" (***The Gospel in the Stars, pp. 20, 53***)."

God's promise to Abraham *by Barry Sutterfield*

"As noted at the beginning, Galatians 3:8 says that Yahuah preached the Gospel unto Abraham. It is important that we know when He did this as the stars were mentioned by Yahuah to Abraham on two distinct occasions, once in Genesis 15, then again in Genesis 22. We must not confuse these two separate incidents. Galatians 3:6 gives us the answer to this question. Rabbi Sha'ul states that it was on the occasion when "Abraham believed Yahuah and it was counted to him for righteousness." Importantly as we search both Genesis passages, it becomes apparent that this quote comes directly from Genesis 15:6. The context was given by Genesis 15:5. Abraham was childless and had no heir. Then Yahuah "brought him forth abroad, and said, 'Look now towards heaven, and TELL the stars if you be able to list them'; and He said unto him, 'So shall your seed be'."

Several important points emerge from this interview that Abraham had with the Almighty. In the first place, the word "TELL" is the same census-taking word as used in Psalm 147:4 so the star names are in view here. The second point is vital. The Almighty made a key comment when Abraham had finished listing off the star names. He said: "So shall your seed be." Does this mean that Abraham was to have many children? We have Rabbi Sha'ul's exegesis of the original Hebrew on this. In Galatians 3:16, Sha'ul says: "Now to Abraham and his seed were the promises made. He said not, And to seeds (plural) as of many; but as of one, 'And to your seed (singular) WHICH IS THE MESSIAH!"

Here is an amazing statement! Abraham lists the star names in sequence from constellation to constellation telling the story of the stars from their names, and Yahuah says to him "So will your seed, the Messiah, be." Here was the promise to Abraham that the Messiah would come from his lineage. Furthermore, the Gospel was obviously associated with these star names as Galatians 3:8 states that Yahuah preached the Gospel to Abraham on that occasion - a Gospel associated with the coming of the Messiah, Yahusha.

It is important not to confuse this incident in Abraham's life with a later one. On the second occasion in Genesis 22:17, Abraham was promised seed like "the stars of heaven and the sand of the sea shore for multitude." This is a different interview with Yahuah when the Patriarch received a different promise. According to Sha'ul in Galatians 3, it was specifically on the first occasion in Genesis 15 that Messiah was promised from Abraham's lineage and Abraham believed Yahuah. Finally note that Yahuah preached the Gospel of Christ to Abraham by this method, and by faith Abraham accepted the message. The stars must therefore be preaching the same message in every language around the world, because Psalm 19 states that there is no speech or language where their voice is not heard."

The significance of the Sphinx *by Barry Sutterfield*

"Well, if there is a message in the stars, where does the story begin since the Zodiac is a circle. An important clue is obtained from the Sphinx in Egypt. The word SPHINX comes from the Greek word SPHIGGO which means to "bind closely together". The significance of this meaning becomes apparent when ancient Egyptian Zodiacs are inspected. In those zodiacs such as one in the tombs of the kings at Karnak, the sphinx curiously linked the 12 signs together. Its woman-like face gazed upon the sign of Virgo, while its lion-like body and tail pointed to Leo. Dr Spencer notes that several other places in the Near East have similar inscriptions. Dr Spencer writes: "The sphinx is the key symbol which shows where the story in the stars begins and ends. It begins with Virgo the Virgin and the first coming of Yahusha as Messiah; and closes with Leo the Lion, marking the Return of Messiah as the King of Glory. It begins with the story of His coming in humility and seeming defeat, and climaxes with the story of His coming again in power and overwhelming victory."

CHAPTER 4
A LAMB THAT HAS BEEN SLAUGHTERED

Chapter 4 - A lamb that has been slain from the foundation of the world

> **Enoch 35:3**
> I blessed Yahuah of glory, who had made those great and splendid signs (of the Zodiac), that they might display the magnificence of his works (The Plan of Salvation *Psalms 19*) to angels and to the souls of men; and that these (splendid signs in The Heavenly Scroll) might glorify all his works and operations; might see the effect of his power; might glorify the great labor of his hands

Mankind has denied Yahuah's witness of Yahusha, written into creation called ***The Heavenly Scroll***. As a result, we have been led astray by The Spirit of the False Messiah (*doctrine of incarnation*) by teachers who teach that Yahusha pre-existed with Yahuah as "*a lamb that has been slaughtered at creation*". These false teachers are not anointed to teach by Yahuah and by denying the most critical witness and original gospel (*The Heavenly Scroll*) they are not capable of understanding the Scriptures.

Yahuah promised that anyone who elevated the image of a man who died as God would be given over to a depraved mind and fall for the greatest lie of all… Incarnation.

> **Romans 1**
> "18 The wrath of Yahuah is being revealed from (the) heaven(ly scroll) against all the godlessness and wickedness of people, who suppress the truth (of the Zodiac's message and that there is one and only God, Yahuah *John 17:3*) by their wickedness (twisting The Heavenly Scroll into sun worship and denying Yahuah's immortality claiming He came to Earth and died!), 19 since what may be known about Yahuah (that He is invisible *Col. 1:15* and *John 1:18* and *1 John 4:12* and *Hebrews 11:27* and *1 Timothy 6:16* and *Ex. 33:20* and *Job 9:11* and *1 Timothy 1:17* and *Romans 1:20* and not

a man *Numbers 23:19* and *Hosea 11:9*) is plain to them, because Yahuah has made it plain to them (through Creation and His Word). 20 For since the creation of the world Yahuah's **invisible** qualities—his **eternal** power and **divine** nature (immortality)—have been clearly seen, being understood from what has been made (***Enoch 35:3***), so that people are without excuse (for denying a Lamb that has been slaughtered IN THE STARS). 21 For although they knew Yahuah, they neither glorified him as the **invisible**, **immortal** God nor gave thanks to him, but their thinking became futile (believing in incarnation) and their foolish hearts were darkened (to worship the stars/constellations). 22 Although they claimed to be wise (Hebrew Roots Teachers, Christian Pastors, etc.), they became <u>fools</u> 23 and exchanged the glory of the ***immortal*** God for images made to look like a mortal human being!" (they were full of The Spirit of the False Messiah and idolized the Messiah who died, and blasphemed the Creator) ... 28 Furthermore, just as they did not think it worthwhile to retain the knowledge of God (that He is IMMORTAL and INVISIBLE and SPIRIT found written in the stars ***Enoch 35:3***), so Yahuah gave them over to a depraved mind (they do not understand the Scriptures OR The Heavenly Scroll), so that they do what ought not to be done (blaspheme the Holy Spirit which declares Yahuah is immortal invisible Spirit NOT a mortal man who died and worship the Sun)."

The Heavenly Scroll is used by Yahuah to witness the coming Messiah to all the prophets and forefathers. We see written in Scripture in many places that Yahusha was predestined before the world was, as a lamb that would be slaughtered... in The Heavenly Scroll!

John 17
4 I have glorified You on earth by accomplishing the work You gave Me to do (laid out in The Heavenly Scroll ***Hebrews 10:7***). 5 And now, Father, glorify Me in Your presence with the glory I had with You (written in The Heavenly Scroll as the coming King) before the world existed (written into creation on Day 4).

Hebrews 10
7 Then I said, 'Here I am, it is written about Me in The Heavenly Scroll: I have come to do Your will, O God (*Matthew 6:10*).'"

Matthew 6:10
your kingdom come, your will be done, on earth as it is (written) in (the) heaven(ly scroll).

Ephesians 1
3 Blessed be the God and Father of our Master Yahusha the Messiah (he is NOT Yahuah, Yahuah is his God and Father just like Yahuah is ours), who has blessed us in The Yahushaic Covenant with every spiritual blessing in the heavenly realms (i.e. The Heavenly Scroll). 4 For Yahuah chose us in Yahusha before the foundation of the world (we were predestined in The Plan of Salvation just like Yahusha, written in The Heavenly Scroll as the Bride) to be holy and blameless in His presence. In love 5 Yahuah predestined us for adoption as His sons through The Yahushaic Covenant, according to the good pleasure of His will (to beget a family through resurrection, Yahusha the firstborn from the dead in that family)

1 Peter 1
19 but with the precious blood of Yahusha, a lamb without blemish or spot (foretold to come in The Heavenly Scroll). 20 He was known (in The Heavenly Scroll) before the foundation of the world (written in the stars on day 4 of creation *Psalm 19*), but was revealed (the Plan of Salvation was fulfilled 'in the flesh" when Yahusha was born *John Chapter 1*) in the last times for your sake (in the 4th prophetic day as foretold in The Heavenly Scroll). 21 Through (covenant with) Yahusha you believe in Yahuah, who raised Yahusha from the dead (this is when Yahusha became Divine, NOT at creation) and glorified Him (with the Glory Yahuah has spoken of him written in The Heavenly Scroll POST resurrection not before creation); and so your faith and hope are in Yahuah (who authored The Heavenly Scroll *Isaiah 46*)....

Sha'ul confirms that Yahusha did not pre-exist, but was PORTRAYED as a lamb that would be slaughtered before all humanity, written in the stars.

2 Corinthians 4:6
6 Seeing it is Yahuah, that said, Light shall shine out of darkness (day 1 when the light or Plan of Salvation was revealed), (now Sha'ul is teaching the metaphor of the Sun/Son in The Heavenly Scroll *Psalm 19*) who shined in our hearts, to give the light of the knowledge (proclaimed by the stars as the Sun is a metaphor of the Son. The Sun gives physical light unto the world, the Son gives Spiritual light *Psalms 19*) of the glory of Yahuah in the face of Yahusha the Messiah.

1 Corinthians 2 - *Sha'ul speaking to former pagans who knew and abused the Zodiac*
1 And so it was with me, brothers and sisters. When I came to you, I did not come with eloquence or human wisdom as I proclaimed to you the testimony of Yahuah (about Yahusha written in the stars). 2 For I resolved to know nothing while I was with you except Yahusha the Messiah and him crucified (before the foundation of the world written in the stars before our very eyes *Galatians 3*). 3 I came to you in weakness with great fear and trembling. 4 My message and my preaching were not with wise and persuasive words (of human literal wisdom), but with a demonstration of the Spirit's power, 5 so that your faith might not rest on (literal) human wisdom, but on Yahuah's power (in a Mystery Language). 6 We do, however, speak a message of (spiritual) wisdom among the (spiritually) mature, but not the wisdom of this age or of the rulers of this age (who viewed the Zodiac literally and worshiped the signs and the Sun), who are coming to nothing. 7 No, we declare Yahuah's wisdom, a mystery that has been hidden (in the Heavenly Scroll *Enoch 9:6*) and that Yahuah destined for our glory before time began (writing it in the stars on day 4 of creation). 8 None of the rulers of this age understood it (because it was corrupted by the watchers *Enoch 9:6*)

Galatians 3
You foolish Galatians! Who has bewitched you (and twisted The Heavenly Scroll into witchcraft)? Before your very eyes (in The Heavenly Scroll) Yahusha the Messiah was clearly portrayed as crucified (as a witness to all mankind *Psalms 19*)...7 Understand then (what is foretold in the stars), that

those who have faith (in The Heavenly Scroll) are children of Abraham. 8 Scripture (the word written in the heavens *Psalm 119:89*) foresaw that Yahuah would justify the Gentiles by faith, and Yahuah announced the gospel in advance to Abraham (via The Heavenly Scroll *Genesis 15:5*; saying): "All nations will be blessed through you."

Romans 10:17
Consequently, faith comes from hearing the message, and the message is heard through the word about the Messiah (portrayed as crucified.. what "word" about Yahusha?). 18 But I ask: Did they not hear? Of course they did: "Their voice (constellations) has gone out into all the earth, their words (concerning Yahusha) to the ends of the world." (Sha'ul quotes *Psalms 19*)

John confirms that Yahusha is portrayed as a lamb that was slain in The Heavenly Scroll in Revelation. We see John literally witness, in a vision, The Heavenly Scroll and given revelation as to what it says.

Revelation Chapter 5
And I saw in the right hand of Him Who sat on the throne, a (heavenly) scroll written inside and on the back (scroll made up of 3D Heavenly "signs"/pictographs), sealed with seven seals (7 classical planets). 2 And I saw a mighty malak proclaiming with a loud voice: Who is worthy to open the (heavenly) scroll, and to release its seals? 3 And no one in

heaven, nor in earth, neither under the earth was able to open the (heavenly) scroll, neither to look at it. 4 And I wept bitterly, because no one was found worthy to open and to read the (heavenly) scroll, neither to look upon it. 5 But one of the elders said to me: Do not weep! Behold (in the Heavenly Scroll, the pictograph of Leo, the last sign in the Plan of Salvation written in the stars), the Lion of the tribe of Yahdah (*Leo* the Lion, associated with the tribe of Yahdah/Judah), the Root of David, has overcome (the Dragon, *Draco*... the meaning behind the constellation *Leo*) to open the (heavenly) scroll and to release its seven seals (7 stars of *Pleiades*). 6 And I looked (into the stars), and behold (in The Heavenly Scroll), in the midst of the throne and the four living creatures, and in the midst of the elders, **stood a Lamb as though it had been slain**, having complete power and complete knowledge and understanding, which signify and represent the complete plan of Yahuah (the 7 Spirits/7 stars of *Pleiades*) sent forth into all the earth (*Psalm 19*). 7 And He came and took the (Heavenly) scroll out of the right hand of Him Who sat upon the throne. 8 And when He had taken the (heavenly) scroll, the four living creatures and twenty-four elders fell down before the Lamb, each one of them having a harp (constellation *Lyra*), and golden bowls full of incense (constellation *Crater*), which are the prayers of the saints. 9 And they sang a new song, saying: You are worthy to take the (heavenly) scroll, and to open its seals (Meaning of the pictograph *Aries*); for You were slain (meaning of the pictograph *Libra*), and have redeemed us to Yahuah by Your blood out of every tribe, and language, and people, and nation (meaning of the pictograph of *Pisces*); 10 And have made us kings and priests to our Father (meaning of the pictograph of *Cancer*); and we will reign upon the earth (meaning of the pictograph of *Leo*);. 11 And I looked, and I heard the voice of many malakim (he was

Creation Cries Out!

looking at the stars) surrounding the throne, and the (4 living) creatures, and the (24) elders; and the number of them (the stars in the sky which represent malakim/angels) was ten thousand times ten thousand, and thousands of thousands, 12 Saying with a loud voice: **Worthy is the Lamb Who was (portayed as) slain** (in The Heavenly Scroll *Galatians 3:1*)) to receive power, and riches, and wisdom, and strength, and honor, and glory, and blessing! 13 And every creature which is in heaven, and on the earth, and under the earth, and such as are in the sea, and all that are in them, I heard saying: Blessing, and honor, and glory, and power belongs to Him Who sits on the throne (of Creation, Yahuah), and to the Lamb (who sites on Yahuah's right hand), forever and ever! 14 And the four living creatures (the 4 seraphim in the center throne room of The Enoch Zodiac) said: HalleluYahweh! And the twenty-four elders (represented by stars in the inner circle of The Enoch Zodiac) fell down and worshiped Him Who lives forever and ever.

We are taught by false teachers that this is proof that he pre-existed as these teachers have been given over to a depraved mind and cannot understand what they read (**Romans 1:28**). We do not realize the context of each one of these verses (*that refer to Yahusha as 'a lamb that would be slaughtered'*) is speaking of The Heavenly Scroll where Yahuah gave Glory to the coming King in The Heavenly Scroll at creation!

Isaiah 46
9 "Remember the former things long past (written in the stars at creation), For I am God, and there is no other; I am God, and there is no one like Me, 10 Declaring the end from the beginning (written in the stars at creation), And from ancient times (before the world was *John 17:5* and *Ephesians 1:4* and *1 Peter 1:20*) things which have not been done, Saying, My purpose (to send a human mediating High Priest and King) will be established (as foretold in The Heavenly Scroll), And I will accomplish all My good pleasure (the Plan of Salvation written in the stars)'; 11 Calling a bird of prey from the east, The man (not demi-god) of My purpose (the one spoken of in The Heavenly Scroll) from a far country (out of

Egypt *Matthew 2:15* and *Hosea 1:1*). Truly I have spoken; truly I will bring it to pass. I have planned it (The Plan of Salvation from creation), surely I will do it (and that 'Debar' or predestined plan written in the stars became "flesh" and fulfilled when Yahusha was born *John Chapter 1*)

Psalm 19
2 The heavens (the place in the sky where the stars are located i.e. Zodiac) are telling of the glory of Yahuah (the Glory of Yahuah is Yahusha! *2 Corinthians 4:6*); And their expanse is declaring the work of His hands. 2 Day to day (The Heavenly Scroll) pours forth speech, And night to night reveals knowledge. 3 There is no speech, nor are there words; Their (signs of the Zodiac/Constellations) voice is not heard. 4 Their line (Zodiac means line or path of the sun) has gone out through (and seen by) all the earth, And their (signs of the Zodiac) utterances to the end of the world. In them (the constellations) He has placed a tent for the sun (the Zodiac), 5 Which is as a bridegroom (Yahusha) coming out of his chamber; It rejoices as a strong man (Glorious Righteous Branch/human Messiah) to run his course (of a wedding, the Feast Cycle). 6 Its rising is from one end of the heavens (Zodiac), And its circuit (Zodiac means circuit or path or The Way) to the other end of them; And there is nothing hidden from its heat.

Again, below is the message The Heavenly Scroll proclaims:

VIRGO: A virgin will give birth to a beautiful glorious and righteous branch. The seed of the woman will be a man of humiliation to rise to be the desire of nations and will become exalted first as shepherd then as harvester.
LIBRA: The scales demand a price to be paid of this seed, a stake/cross to endure; the victim will be slain and purchase a crown. **SCORPIO:** There is a conflict between the seed and the serpent leading to a struggle with the enemy, the enemy is vanquished. **SAGITTARIUS:** The double-natured seed (servant/king) triumphs as a warrior and pleases the heavens, builds fires of punishment, casts down the dragon. **CAPRICORNUS:** Eternal life comes from his death, he's the Arrow of God, he is pierced, yet

springs up again in abundant life. **AQUARIUS:** He pours out "living water" from on high, humanity drinks of the heavenly river and the faithful live again, he is the deliverer of the good news (Gospel), Carrying The Way by example over the earth. **PISCES:** The Redeemer's people multiplied, supported and led by the Lamb, The Bride is exposed on earth, the Bridegroom is exalted. **ARIES:** The Lamb is found worthy, the Bride is made ready, Satan is bound, the strong man triumphs. **TAURUS:** The conquering Ruler comes, the sublime vanquisher, to execute the great judgment, he is the ruling Shepherd King. **GEMINI:** The Marriage of the Lamb, the enemy is trodden down, the Prince comes in great Glory. **CANCER:** The great Bride, the two Houses of Judah and Israel are united, they are brought safely into the kingdom. **LEO:** The Lion King is aroused for rending, the Serpent flees, the Bowl of Wrath is upon him, his Carcass is devoured. The Lion of the tribe of Judah rules as King.

Yahusha is the fulfillment of the Plan of Salvation (*Debar*) written in The Heavenly Scroll "in the flesh" when he was born. That is the proper translation of John Chapter 1. Yahusha was given Glory by Yahuah as the Passover Lamb and King of Kings in the stars.

Matthew 28:20
"and teaching them to obey everything I have commanded you. And surely I am with you always, to the very end of the age (of Pisces when he returns in the Age of Aquarius)."

Hebrews 10:7
Then I said, 'Here I am--it is written about me in the heavenly scroll-- I have come to do your will, my God! (*Matthew 6:10*)

Matthew 6:10
Your kingdom come, Your will be done, on earth as it is (written) in (the) heaven(ly scroll).

John 3:29
29 He who has the Bride is the Bridegroom (speaking of The Heavenly Scroll see *Psalm 19*); but the friend of the Bridegroom, who stands and hears Him, rejoices greatly because of the Bridegroom's voice (the stars cry out with a loud voice day after day, night after night as "*a bridegroom coming out of his chambers*" in The Heavenly Scroll *Psalms 19*). Therefore, this joy of mine is fulfilled (Yahusha fulfilled the message contained in The Heavenly Scroll, John Chapter 1 he is the fulfillment of the Debar/Predestined Plan in the flesh).

John 17
5 And now, Father, glorify me in your presence (through resurrection as promised in The Heavenly Scroll) with the glory I had with you (written in The Heavenly Scroll) before the world began (the Light of *Gen. 1:1*: written into the stars on Day 4, then fulfilled in Yahusha on the 4th prophetic day as the Debar/Plan was fulfilled in the flesh *John 1*).

Matthew 11:25
At that time Yahusha answered and said, I thank you, O Father, King of The Heavenly Scroll (Strong's H8064 'shamayim' - the place where the stars are located, i.e. The Mazzaroth/Zodiac) and earth, because you have hid these things (secrets preserved in the stars/heaven *Enoch 9:6*) from the wise and prudent, and have revealed them unto babes.

Matthew 13:11
He replied, "Because the knowledge of the secrets of the kingdom of heaven (the Zodiac or Heavenly Scroll, the "*secrets preserved in the heavens*" *Enoch 9:6*) has been given to you, but not to them.

Understanding The Heavenly Scroll and the Lamb that was Slaughtered

But how, exactly, is Yahusha portrayed in The Heavenly Scroll as a lamb that was slain? To understand how Yahusha is seen as a Lamb slain, we must understand how to read The Heavenly Scroll as the prophets of old. The Heavenly Scroll portrays the plan of salvation counter clockwise beginning with Virgo ending with Leo. The Plan for Mankind (*a 7,000-year plan*) is foretold going

Ages & Epochs of Mankind
The Heavenly Scroll of Enoch

Heavenly Scroll
The Heavenly Scroll is held by the living creature over the Age of Gemini/creation of man... and ends with the position of the next "living creature" over the Age of Aquarius/The Sabbath Kindgom!

clockwise beginning at the cusp of Gemini and Taurus. We see the Seraphim sitting just over that cusp, holding The Heavenly Scroll. The Plan for Mankind ends with the next Seraphim sitting over the Age of Aquarius.

Yahusha was foretold to come on the cusp of Aries and Pisces by drawing a direct line across from Virgo in the Plan of Salvation to the other side where the timeframe is laid out.

Birth of Messiah foretold in The Heavenly Scroll

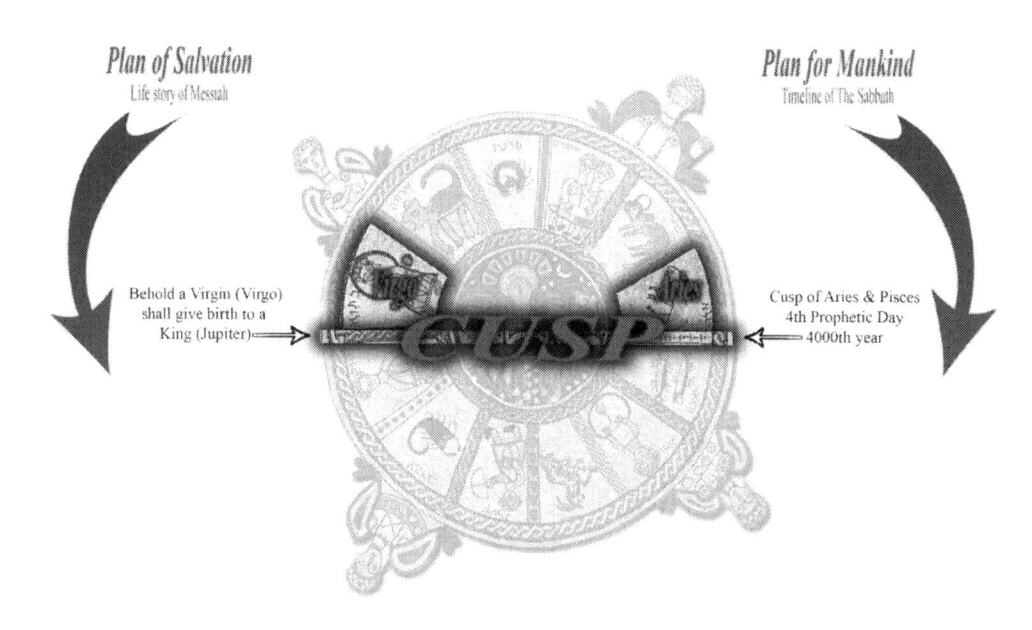

Plan of Salvation
Life story of Messiah

Behold a Virgin (Virgo) shall give birth to a King (Jupiter)

Plan for Mankind
Timeline of The Sabbath

Cusp of Aries & Pisces
4th Prophetic Day
4000th year

Each age is 2,000 years so Yahusha was seen in The Heavenly Scroll as coming in the 4,000th year when the Sign of the Son of Man is in the sky marking the transition of the ages.

Mankind has used these signs in the sky to mark the age in which they lived. The bull was worshiped in Egypt during the Age of Taurus (that is why the Israelites coming out of Egypt made a *Golden Calf*). The Ram (***Aries***) was the substitute for Isaac, then the Passover Lamb annual sacrifice marked the entire age of Aries. Yahusha's disciples used the fish as a symbol during Pisces, and so forth.

As each age ended, the 'mascot' was said to have died out, and there was a birth of a new age and new mascot. This is why the Golden Calf was such a mistake, not that Yahuah didn't know what they were doing attempting to Glorify Him by exalting the Age of Taurus, but because they demonstrated a total lack of knowledge of The Heavenly Scroll in doing so.

On the following page, I show "how" Yahusha was portrayed as a lamb that had been slaughtered since creation. It was foretold in The Heavenly Scroll that Yahusha would fulfill the Plan of Salvation in the 4,000th year (*4th prophetic day*). That is when the Age of Aries the Lamb metaphorically "dies" as the age comes to an end.

The Spring Feasts are written in the stars where the Messiah is foretold to "endure a cross and die" which was fulfilled as the "lamb dies" at the transition of the ages! The prophets knew this, understood The Plan of Salvation written in the stars and that is why Yahusha was known as "a lamb that was slaughtered"! Not because he pre-existed as some type of butchered animal at Creation as we are misled to believe by those filled with The Spirit of the False Messiah.

Lamb Slaughtered / Age of Aries Ends
before the world was... portrayed as crucified in The Heavenly Scroll

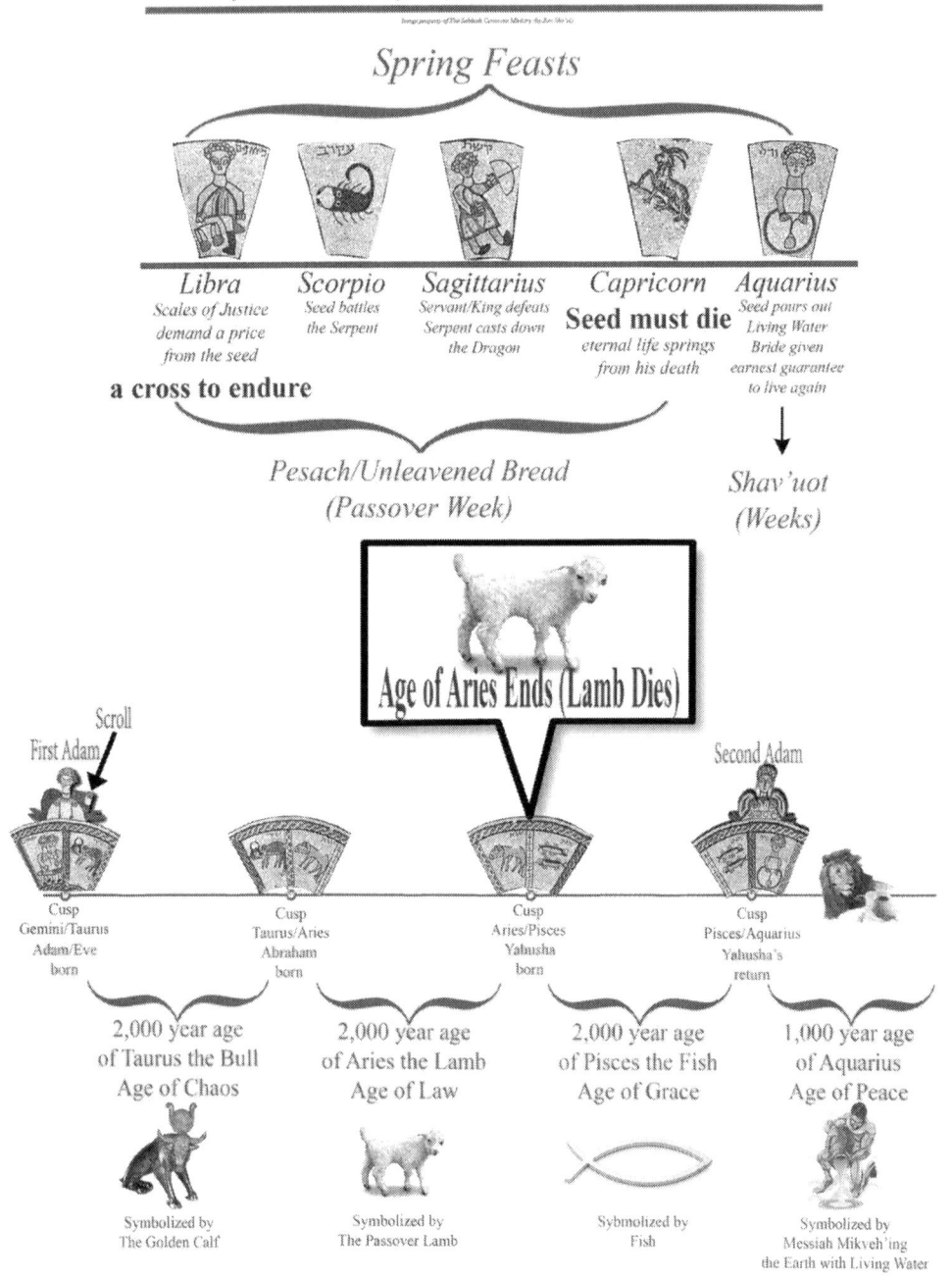

Spring Feasts

Libra	Scorpio	Sagittarius	Capricorn	Aquarius
Scales of Justice demand a price from the seed	Seed battles the Serpent	Servant/King defeats Serpent casts down the Dragon	**Seed must die** eternal life springs from his death	Seed pours out Living Water Bride given earnest guarantee to live again

a cross to endure

Pesach/Unleavened Bread (Passover Week) — *Shav'uot (Weeks)*

Age of Aries Ends (Lamb Dies)

Scroll — First Adam — Second Adam

Cusp Gemini/Taurus Adam/Eve born	Cusp Taurus/Aries Abraham born	Cusp Aries/Pisces Yahusha born	Cusp Pisces/Aquarius Yahusha's return
2,000 year age of Taurus the Bull Age of Chaos	2,000 year age of Aries the Lamb Age of Law	2,000 year age of Pisces the Fish Age of Grace	1,000 year age of Aquarius Age of Peace
Symbolized by The Golden Calf	Symbolized by The Passover Lamb	Symbolized by Fish	Symbolized by Messiah Mikveh'ing the Earth with Living Water

Revelation of The Heavenly Scroll Prophesied by Yahusha

Many today accuse Yahusha of being a False Prophet because, they claim, he prophesied that he would return in his own lifetime. He did not return so therefore he is a False Prophet and not the Messiah the accusation goes. The prophecy in question is:

Matthew 16:28
"Truly I tell you, some who are standing here will not taste death before they see the Son of Man coming in his kingdom."

How do we understand this? Is Yahusha a False Prophet or did this prophecy come true making Yahuah as True Prophet? Could it be that Yahuah has turned us over to a depraved mind for denying and twisting The Heavenly Scroll (***Romans 1***) so that we are now helplessly lost in our own ignorance and deception?

Romans 1
18 The wrath of Yahuah is being revealed from (the) heaven(ly scroll... Shamayim/Mazzaroth) against all the godlessness and wickedness of people, who suppress the truth (of its message) by their wickedness (turning The Heavenly Scroll into witchcraft ***Galatians 3:6-8*** and worship the signs of the Zodiac, Sun, Moon, and stars), 19 since what may be known about Yahuah (the Plan of Salvation) is plain to them (proclaimed in The Heavenly Scroll day after day, night after night Psalms 19), because Yahuah has made it plain to them (by authoring the life of Yahusha into the fabric of Creation on Day 4 this message goes out unto all the Earth ***Psalms 19***, given to all mankind ***Deuteronomy 3:19***). 20 For since the creation of the world (day 4 of Creation when Yahuah created the sun, moon, and stars) Yahuah's invisible qualities—his eternal power and divine nature—have been clearly seen (written in the stars at creation ***Enoch 35:3*** in The Zodiac), being understood from what has been made (in heaven), so that people are without excuse (for denying Yahusha). 21 For although they knew Yahuah (is The Creator), they neither

glorified Him as Elohim nor gave thanks to Him (for the Plan of Salvation written in the stars), but their thinking became futile (twisting the Zodiac and signs into 'gods' and witchcraft) and their foolish hearts were darkened (to worship the creation over The Creator). 22 Although they claimed to be wise (through religion, tradition, philosophy and mythology), they became fools 23 and exchanged the glory of the immortal Elohim (the Glory of Yahuah is Yahusha *2 Corinthians 4:6*! So they exchanged *Yahusha*) for images made to look like a mortal human being (incarnated demi-gods) and birds and animals and reptiles (the signs of The Zodiac).

...

28 Furthermore, just as they did not think it worthwhile to retain the knowledge of God (that He is IMMMORTAL and INVISIBLE and SPIRIT found written in the stars *Enoch 35:3*), so Yahuah gave them over to a depraved mind (they do not understand the Scriptures OR The Heavenly Scroll), so that they do what ought not to be done (blaspheme the Holy Spirit which declares Yahuah is immortal invisible Spirit NOT a mortal man who died and worship the Sun)."

This is where we are today. We have denied The Heavenly Scroll all together and come against its message saying it is witchcraft! With that knowledge, let us see what Yahusha prophesied exactly!

Matthew 16:28 in context

What was Yahusha actually prophesying; his return or the revelation of The Heavenly Scroll? We see Yahusha say "see the Son of Man coming in his Kingdom" and we immediately assume this is speaking of The Second Coming! This is because we have turned our backs on The Heavenly Scroll and do not recognize or understands these Scriptures.

"***See the Son of Man coming in his kingdom***" is an idiom for The Heavenly Scroll where Orion (*the Son of Man*) is coming on the clouds of heaven (*Milky Way*) in The Heavenly Scroll".

Here again, we are met with very poor translation outside of the context of The Heavenly Scroll.... and our blindness because we have denied The Original Revelation and do not understand The Mystery Language the Bible is written in.

Yahusha was making a reference to The Heavenly Scroll and telling his disciples that Yahuah would confirm to them that he was the 'Conquering King to come' by revealing to them The Heavenly Scroll. The constellation Orion means "the coming of the Branch" as a Conquering King. Yahusha was not saying they would live to see his literal return, in fact, Yahusha told them that would not happen until the end of The Age of Pisces on the cusp of Aquarius…

> **Matthew 28**
> ...19 Therefore go and make disciples of all nations, Mikveh'ing them into the covenant that bears my name (The Yahushaic Covenant), 20 and teaching them to obey all that I have commanded you. And surely I am with you always, to the very end of the age (ages are 2,000 years! He knew the Plan of Salvation as it is written in The Heavenly Scroll)."

Yahusha was telling his disciples that some of them would receive the revelation contained in The Heavenly Scroll where he is pictured by Orion coming as Conquering King on the "clouds of heaven".

Prophecy fulfilled in their lifetimes

We see this come true when Stephen was stoned, he was the first one to understand the witness of the Messiah as the "heavens opened up" and Steven saw Yahusha "coming in the clouds of heaven" in a vision (*read The Heavenly Scroll properly*)... so just like Yahusha said "before you die, you will know him as the coming Conquering King" as Stephen was given that witness as he was being stoned to death just before he died!

Steven sees "the Son of Man coming in his Kingdom"

> **Acts 7**
> 55 But Stephen was filled with the Holy Ruach (Yahuah breathed on Stephen). He looked toward (the) heaven(ly Scroll), where he saw our glorious Elohim and Yahusha standing at his right side (in The Heavenly Scroll). 56 Then Stephen said, "I see the heaven(ly scroll) open (like a Scroll ***Revelation 6:14*** and ***Hebrews 1:12***) and the Son of Man (Orion) standing at the right side of Yahuah (coming in the clouds of heaven the Milky Way)!"

Then later, all the rest of his disciples received the revelation of Yahusha in the stars, as Orion riding on the clouds of heaven as King... the clouds of heaven is the Milky Way... The Heavenly Scroll is the confirming witness of Yahuah that Yahusha is the coming King (Leo) the Lion of the Tribe of Judah...

Sha'ul sees "the Son of Man coming in his Kingdom"

Then Sha'ul had the same vision as he was "taken to the third heaven"! Sha'ul deflects the attention away from himself with the age old technique "I have a friend who" because he doesn't want to boast. He then goes on to say he was taken to the third heaven which is a metaphor for "shown advanced revelations of The Heavenly Scroll". The number 3 in The Mystery Language means:

> "Three, therefore, stands for that which is solid, real, substantial, complete, and entire."... ***Numbers in Scripture by E.W, Bullinger***

Sha'ul, below, is saying that Yahuah had given him visions of what is contained in The Heavenly Scroll that were "solid, real, substantial, complete, the ENTIRE revelation".

> **2 Corinthians 12**
> 1 I must go on boasting. Although there is nothing to be gained, I will go on to visions and revelations from Yahuah (he did not literally go to a place called the third level of heaven, he saw VISIONS and REVELATIONS). 2 I know a man in covenant with Yahusha (he is speaking of himself in third person) who fourteen years ago (when Sha'ul was nearly stoned to death, like Stephen he too saw the Heavenly Scroll open up) was caught up to the third heaven (was given 'solid, real, substantial, complete' understanding of The Heavenly Scroll). Whether it was in the body or out of the body I do not know— Yahuah knows (Sha'ul was unconscious from being stoned half to death). 3 And I know that this man—whether in the body or apart from the body I do not know, but God knows— 4 was caught up to paradise (shown The Heavenly Scroll like Daniel, Ezekiel, John, Enoch who were all 'taken to heaven' in the same way?) and heard inexpressible things, things that no one is permitted to tell (they are secrets preserved in The Heavenly Scroll ***Enoch 9:6***). 5 I will boast about a man like that, but I will not boast about myself, except about my weaknesses. 6 Even if I should choose to

boast, I would not be a fool, because I would be speaking the truth. But I refrain, so no one will think more of me than is warranted by what I do or say, 7 or because of these surpassingly great revelations (he was shown Yahusha coming as King of Heaven in The Heavenly Scroll).

John sees "the Son of Man coming in his Kingdom"

And so did John in the book of Revelation as he witnessed and literally described The Heavenly Scroll and its meaning, he described and identified Orion as the "coming of the Branch" riding on the clouds of Heaven...

Revelation 1
12 And I turned to see (in The Heavenly Scroll) the voice that spoke with me (Yahuah had spoken, identified Himself as Aleph/Tav, the Father). And having turned (he didn't see Yahuah), I saw (in The Heavenly Scroll) a golden seven lamp lampstand (7 classical planets also seen as the seals over The Heavenly Scroll); 13 And in the midst of the seven lamp lampstand (in The Heavenly Scroll / stars) One like the Son of Man (constellation Orion represents the Son of Man in the Heavenly Scroll), clothed with a garment (of the High Priest) down to the feet (tallit - *Psalms 110:3*) with a girdle of gold about His chest (chest plate of the High Priest Zachariah Chapter 3, Yahusha was consecrated High Priest by Yahuah and adorned the garments of the High Priest). 14 The hair of His head was white like wool (John begins describing the constellation Orion), as white as snow; and His eyes were as a flame of fire; 15 And His feet glowed like bronze which had been fired in a furnace; and His voice sounded like many (Living) waters (reference to the Water Bearer of *Aquarius*). 16 And in His (Orion's) right hand He had seven stars (constellation Pleiades); and out of His mouth went a sharp, two-edged sword (the sword of Orion, a metaphor of the Word of Yahuah); and His face was like the sun (the sun is a metaphor of the Messiah see *Psalms 19*)

shining in its strength. 17 And when I saw Him, I fell at His feet as though dead (literally "scared to death" so to speak).

Daniel sees "the Son of Man coming in his Kingdom"

Daniel 7
11 I beheld (The Heavenly Scroll), then, because of the voice of the great words which 'the horn' (***Strong's H7162*** - should be 'Shofar', Yahuah's voice sounds like a loud Shofar blast ***Hebrews 12:19***, do not confuse this with the other 'horns' in Daniel, this one is a musical instrument, the Shofar) spoke; I beheld (what is written in The Heavenly Scroll) until the beast was slain and his body destroyed, and given to the burning flame (message behind the pictographs of Sagittarius). 12 As concerning the rest of the beasts, they had their governments taken away; yet their lives were prolonged for a season and time (message behind the pictograph of Taurus). 13 I saw in the night (sky) visions (of The Heavenly Scroll, like I said he was laying down at night looking at the stars), and behold (the constellation Orion), One like the Son of man came with the clouds of heaven (the Milky Way).

Orion is the Son of Man in Heaven

The star names that tell the story of Orion, the light bearer are:

- Star name: Betelgeuse = The coming of the branch.
- Star name Rigol = the foot that crushes the serpent.
- Star name Al Nitak = the wounded one (wounded by the serpent).

Story behind the pictograph of Orion:

> "*as the coming prince, the light, the one who holds the double-edged sword in his hand, he is the coming of The Branch, the one wounded by the serpent, the foot that crushes the head of the serpent.*"

This is why Yahusha references the son of man, Orion, 87 times! He was telling us clearly, that he is the fulfillment of that original revelation and prophecy written in the stars. He is "the coming of the branch". This is why the prophets called him "the Branch", each and every prophet read The Heavenly Scroll and understood the meaning of the Heavenly Pictograph of Orion. This is why he is called Yahusha the Nazarene (*Branch*)!

Now to our original question: "Is Yahusha a False Prophets or did his prophecy come true?" I leave it to you to decide.

Chapter 5

What is the Zodiac?

Chapter 5 - What is the Zodiac?

Most Christians cringe at the mention of the Zodiac; being taught it is "evil". Knowing absolutely nothing about the Zodiac, most people simply do not realize the amazing witness of Yahuah found within it; *because its message was corrupted.* We, the sons of Yahuah, must reclaim the Zodiac for His Glory from those who would defile it in idolatry. Yahuah is <u>THE CREATOR</u> especially of... the Zodiac.

Let me quickly explain what the Zodiac is and what it represents as to dispel any myths associated with it being evil in nature. As I explained earlier: The Book of Enoch tells us fallen angels perverted the message in the heavens and taught a corrupted version of it in order to lead man into worship of the creature above The Creator. Corrupting Astrology (*fortune telling*) and so forth perverts the true meaning of the Zodiac. The Watchers instead taught man to worship false god-men (*solar messiahs*), the Sun/planets, and the Signs of the Zodiac. So let me explain what the Zodiac really is.

> *The Zodiac is simply a map of the Sun as it travels through the star constellations over the course of a year as visible from planet Earth. It marks the seasons, the equinoxes and solstices. It is a divine clock showing the lifespan of man (70 years), the Ages of mankind, and proclaiming the Sabbath Covenant. It is a pictograph of the Plan of Salvation. It is...*
> **The Heavenly Scroll!**

In the following image, you can see the Earth orbiting the Sun through the 4 seasons and the constellations in the sky during those seasons as they are visible from Earth (*if you believe the Earth if flat, you will have to do your own research as to how The Heavenly Scroll, star chart, etc. fit into that cosmology. In this book, I use the most accepted view of cosmology and this is not an endorsement of either one. Just the one most people understand as not to confuse this issue with undless dabates of which no one really can prove either side*):

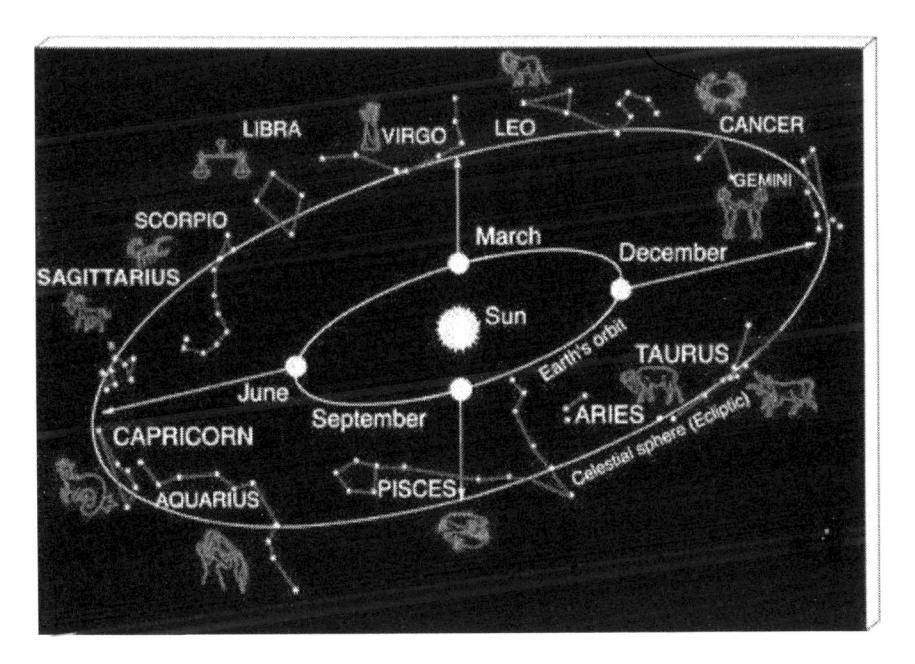

The image above shows our solar system which was organized into a star chart called the Zodiac Chart. It is an accurate representation of the stars as seen from Earth. Nothing to fear!

On the left is the Zodiac Chart divided into 4 quadrants to illustrate the 4 different seasons. The Sun is in the middle and we see the Earth orbiting the Sun. The two lines that intersect to form a cross are the "Equiluxes". It is at these two Equiluxes (*not Equinoxes*) that daylight is equal to the darkness of night.

An equinox occurs twice a year (*around 20 March and 22 September*), when the tilt of the Earth's axis is inclined neither away from nor towards the Sun, the center of the Sun being in the same plane as the Earth's equator. The term equinox can also be used in a broader sense, meaning the date when such a passage happens. The name "equinox" is derived from the Latin aequus (*equal*) and nox (*night*), because around the equinox, the night and day have approximately equal length. The Equinox, however, is not the day of equal light/darkness that is a human tradition. It is when the sun is over the equator.

The Equilux is The Great Sabbath Sign of equal light and darkness, the one day a year that mimics the first day of creation. For more on this, read my book ***The Narrow Gate***.

The Zodiac Chart is a true representation of our Solar System as seen from Earth. It contains the Sun, the Earth, and the constellations of stars visible from Earth. The same star constellations the Bible says that Yahuah named and "ordered" in the heavens as "signs" are illustrated in the Zodiac. It is simply a harmless chart that shows the sun, the 12 constellations it travels through, the four seasons, and the two lines of the Equiluxes. The fact that it has been so corrupted should tell us one simple fact...

> *The Zodiac embodies some very important information that is being diluted and corrupted from our knowledge by the enemy.*

So let us seek this hidden information that the Bible says contains the very witness of Yahuah of His chosen human Messiah. What was so important that the fallen angels wanted to hide it and corrupt it so as to redirect worship to themselves?

The reason we need to embrace the Zodiac, as sons of Yahuah, **and restore its message** is because the premier battleground between the sons of Yahuah and the fallen angels is the message foretold in the heavens. The battle between the Mystery Religion of Babylonian sun worship and the Truth told in the Bible. That battleground began with the Zodiac and continues even today. It was the perversion of this message (that led to the worship of the planets) that was handed down through many cultures and eventually evolved into what we call "Christianity" today through syncretism (the blending of pagan sun worship with the Bible). It is this very religion, Christianity, that abolished the Zodiac and has taught you not to look at it!

The False Messiah and The True Messiah are found within the context of this battle. The False Messiah is the result of the corrupted message; the true Messiah is foretold in the uncorrupted message. This is why in the ***Book of Revelation*** we are told to come out of the Mystery Religion of Babylonian Sun Worship that, in the end, will have misled the entire planet. We are at 'the end' of that Age (more on Ages later) and Christianity is the largest religion on Earth!

The 12 Signs of the Zodiac

The Zodiac contains 12 "signs" or constellations made up of star clusters as seen from Earth; as the Earth travels around the sun over the course of a year. Below are the anthropomorphic or "personified" images, symbols, and names of the constellations or signs of the Zodiac. These images are pictographs as we will see.

The above images are modern depiction of the pictographs (constellations). They are not "circle of animals"! These are also known as "signs" corresponding to a distinct time frame during the course of a year when the sun is seen moving through their respective constellations. Below are the true images or pictographs of the "starry hosts" or constellations that host stars as seen by Enoch (*they are not a "circle of animals" either!*)

What is interesting to note, is that the same number, shape, symbols, and names <u>have remained constant</u> among all cultures since creation. This is because Yahuah named the stars and organized them into their constellations (*heavenly hosts of stars*) and called those constellations out by name!

<u>Psalms 147</u>
4 He determines the number of the stars (*in each constellation*) and calls them (*the constellations*) each by name.

To demonstrate this amazing fact, what follows is a list of the twelve signs of the modern zodiac with their Latin, Greek,

127

Sanskrit, and Babylonian names (but note that the Sanskrit and the Babylonian name equivalents denote the constellations only, not the tropical zodiac signs). Also, the "English translation" is not usually used by English speakers. The Latin names are Standard English usage. The point is the consistency across time/cultures:

№	Symbol	Latin	English	Greek	Sanskrit	Original Babylonian Meaning
1	♈	Aries	Ram	*Krios*	Meṣha	The Agrarian Worker
2	♉	Taurus	Bull	*Tauros*	Vṛiṣabha	The Steer of Heaven
3	♊	Gemini	Twins	*Didumoi*	Mithuna	The Great Twins
4	♋	Cancer	Crab	*Karkinos*	Karkaṭa	The Crayfish
5	♌	Leo	Lion	*Leōn*	Siṃha	The Lion
6	♍	Virgo	Maiden	*Parthenos*	Kanyā	The Furrow
7	♎	Libra	Scales	*Zugos*	Tulā	The Scales
8	♏	Scorpio	Scorpion	*Skorpios*	Vṛścika	The Scorpion
9	♐	Sagittarius	Archer	*Toxotēs*	Dhanuṣa	soldier
10	♑	Capricorn	"Goat-horned"	*Aigokerōs*	Makara	The Goat-Fish
11	♒	Aquarius	The Water-Bearer	*Hudrokhoos*	Kumbha	pitcher
12	♓	Pisces	The Fish	*Ikhthues*	Mīna	fish-cord

Why is it that throughout human history and across cultures and languages the number of constellations and the name of the "signs" remain constant? The only real explanation is that there is a Creator behind the workings of the Universe who named them just as the Bible declares. The only thing that changed was the languages as Yahuah confused the languages at the Tower of Babel in Babylon because the people were attempting to "reach the stars" in an act of idolatry. The Tower of Babel was being built as a monolithic Temple to Ba'al the sun god.

What we must come to understand is that the Zodiac is a function of creation that is itself a manifestation of The Creator whose name is Yahuah. The Bible declares that it was Yahuah who gave the stars (*and their resulting constellations*) their names and ordered them into 12.

Isaiah 40
²⁶ Lift up your eyes and look to the heavens (the place in the sky where the stars are located, the Zodiac): Who created all these? He who brings out the starry host (constellations) one by one and calls forth each of them by name (signs of the Zodiac).

Job 38:32
Yahuah said to His upright servant "Can you bring forth Mazzaroth (the 12 signs) in their season?"

Far from being evil, the Zodiac is in fact a divine portrait designed to "witness to all mankind" of The Creator's Plan of Salvation. Understanding that one simple fact brings into sharp focus "why" the Zodiac was the focus of knowledge given to mankind by fallen angels whose goal was to "corrupt" humanity. The Watchers and The Nephilim had to first pervert Yahuah's message (*the Zodiac*) to humanity concerning His Messiah in order to lead man away from his Creator.

Just like Enoch said, it was the fallen angels who perverted the message of the Zodiac and taught magic, astrology, and idolatry of creation in order to conquer mankind.

Book of Enoch Chapter 8
3 Amezarak taught all those who cast spells and cut roots, Armaros the release of spells, and Baraqiel astrologers, and Kokabiel portents, and Tamiel taught astrology, and Asradel taught the path of the Moon.

Book of Enoch Chapter 9
6 things, and nothing can hide itself from Thee. Thou seest what Azazel hath done, who hath taught all unrighteousness on earth *and revealed the eternal secrets which were (preserved) in heaven*, which men were striving to learn

In the next chapter, I will clearly demonstrate that the Bible in fact declares the Zodiac as a message from Yahuah, the Creator of ALL things… given to all of mankind.

CHAPTER 5
WHAT IS THE HEAVENLY SCROLL?

Chapter 5 – What is The Heavenly Scroll?

Notice on the Enoch Zodiac, the "living being" that sits over the transition from the Age of Gemini (*illustrated with a pictograph of Adam/Eve*) to the Age of Taurus (*a pictogram of a bull*) is the only one of the 4 living creatures (*who guard the Zodiac*) to hold a "scroll".

This is because, as we will later see, the Heavenly Scroll is a message to all humanity of a coming Messiah. What is this scroll in 'heaven' that Yahusha alone is found worthy to open? You see, before the foundation of the world, Yahuah literally authored (*in the stars*) the Plan of Salvation through a human Messiah called the Heavenly Scroll or Mazzaroth or Zodiac!

> **Revelation 13:8**
> All inhabitants of the earth will worship the beast--all whose names have not been written in the Lamb's book of life, the Lamb who was slain from the creation of the world (in The Heavenly Scroll).

1 Peter 1:20
He was <u>chosen</u> before the creation of the world (in The Heavenly Scroll), but was revealed (created to fulfill The Heavenly Scroll) in these last times (4th prophetic day) for your sake (to show us The Way unto salvation).

The Bible calls this scroll in the stars the Mazzaroth. Remember, "Mazzaroth" is Hebrew for what we call the Zodiac:

[Wikipedia screenshot: "Mazzaroth" article. Mazzaroth (Mazarot מַזָּרוֹת, LXX μαζουρωθ) is a hapax legomenon (i.e., a word appearing only once in a text) of the Hebrew Bible, found in Job 38:31-32. The similar word mazalot (מַזָּלוֹת) in 2 Kings 23:3-5 may be related. The word's precise meaning is uncertain, but its context is that of astronomical constellations, and it is often interpreted as a term for the zodiac or the constellations thereof. In Yiddish, the term mazalot came to be used in the sense of "astrology" in general, surviving in the expression "mazel tov," meaning "good luck". 6th-century depiction of the zodiac, mosaic in Beit Alpha, Israel.]

==Many times, when you see the English words "heaven" or "sky", it is referring to the Book of the Mazzaroth (*the Zodiac*)! Yahuah stretched out the "heavens" or Zodiac signs like a scroll across the ecliptic plane (*the path of the Sun*):==

Revelation 6:14
The heavens receded like a scroll being rolled up (to be read)

Isaiah 34:4
All the stars in the sky will pine away (longing to be fulfilled) and the heavens rolled up like a scroll (to be read)

Isaiah 45
I, Yahuah, do all these things. 12 It is I who made the earth and created mankind upon it. My own hands stretched out the heavens (the place where the stars are located; shamayim, Zodiac); I marshaled their starry hosts (constellations host stars, the signs of the Zodiac).

Also keep in mind, the Hebrew word translated "sky" and "heaven" is shamayim, which means "the place in the sky where the stars are located" referring specifically to the Zodiac.

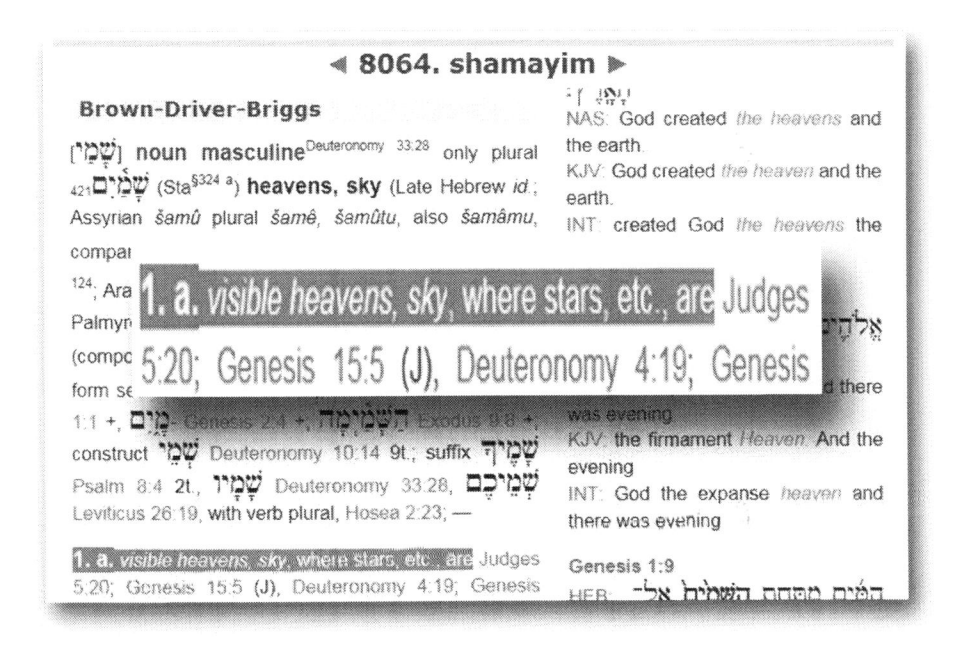

◀ 8064. shamayim ▶

Brown-Driver-Briggs

[שָׁמַי] noun masculine^{Deuteronomy 33:28} only plural שָׁמַיִם (Sta§324 a) **heavens, sky** (Late Hebrew id.; Assyrian šamû plural šamê, šamûtu, also šamâmu, ...

1. a. visible heavens, sky, where stars, etc., are Judges 5:20; Genesis 15:5 (J), Deuteronomy 4:19; Genesis ...

NAS: God created *the heavens* and the earth.
KJV: God created *the heaven* and the earth.
INT: created God *the heavens* the ...

KJV: the firmament *Heaven*. And the evening
INT: God the expanse *heaven* and there was evening

Genesis 1:9
HEB: ...

Isaiah 44: 24
"This is what Yahuah says— your Redeemer, who formed you in the womb: I am Yahuah, the Maker of all things, who stretches out the heavens (like a scroll i.e. Mazzaroth/Zodiac),

The Zodiac is stretched out in the heavens, the signs created by Yahuah (*Zodiac Signs*) are laid out across the ecliptic plane like a scroll and read like pictograph in order as the Sun goes through each sign each year. They proclaim the Plan of Salvation.

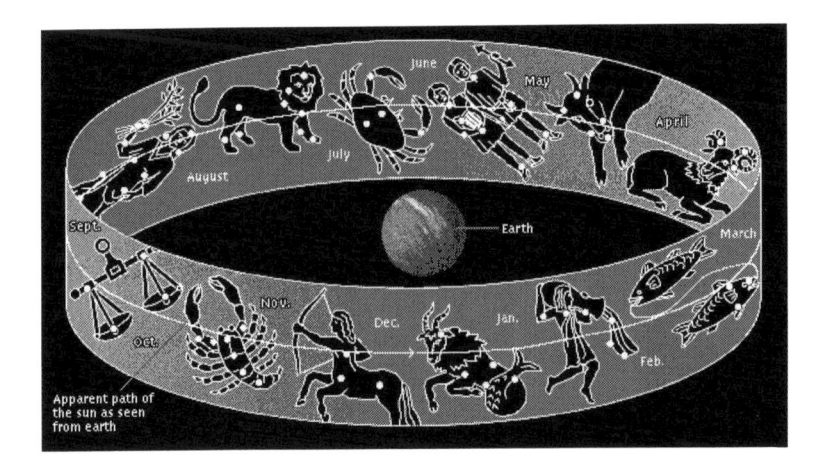

It is Yahuah who prophesied the end from the beginning, writing His Plan of Salvation in the stars in the Heavenly Scroll we call the Zodiac.

Isaiah 46
I am Elohim, and there is no other; I am Elohim, and there is none like me. 10 I make known the end from the beginning (written in The Zodiac), from ancient times (the foundation of the world), what is still to come. I say: My purpose (proclaimed in the Zodiac) will stand, and I will do all that I please.

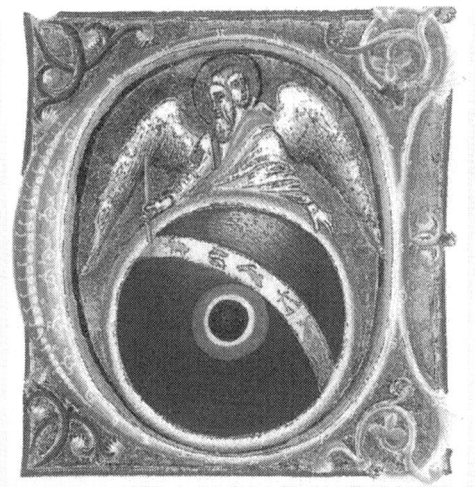

Our ancestors understood this truth, left is a painting depicting Yahuah authoring The Heavenly Scroll with "Yahusha on His mind"! His instructions for Earth, i.e. Plan of Salvation are securely written in the Heavenly Scroll, safe from human hands.

Psalms 119
O Yahuah, your instructions endure; they stand secure in heaven (originally written in the stars, untouched by human hands).

Yahusha prayed the will of Yahuah be done on Earth as it laid out in the Heavenly Scroll of the Mazzaroth/Zodiac.

> **Matthew 6:10**
> your kingdom (proclaimed in the heavenly scroll) come, your will be done, on earth as it is (written) in (the) heaven(nly Scroll... the place where the stars are i.e. the Zodiac).

We see that once the Heavenly Scroll is fulfilled, that the "heavens open up like a scroll" as the Book of the Mazzaroth is opened. The "starry hosts" or signs of the Zodiac "fall" at the feat of the one found worthy to open the Heavenly Scroll as they are fulfilled.

> **Revelation 6:14**
> The heavens (the Zodiac) receded like a scroll being rolled up

> **Isaiah 34:4**
> All the stars in the sky (Zodiac) will be dissolved and the heavens (Zodiac) rolled up like a scroll; all the starry host (signs of the Zodiac) will fall (before the one who fulfills them)

==It is only after Yahusha fulfills the final Zodiac Sign of Leo and conquers the dragon, that the Lion of the Tribe of Judah is revealed==. Having fulfilled the 'Heavenly Scroll', he is found to be the only one worthy to open it, and read it publicly to proclaim that he was chosen by Yahuah from the foundation of the World. The "heavenly scroll' is that witness to confirm that he alone is the Messiah.

> **Revelation 5**
> 5 Then I saw in the right hand of the one who was seated on the throne (of Creation ... Yahuah) a scroll written on the front and back (3-D scroll of the Zodiac signs along the ecliptic plane) and sealed with seven seals (the 7 visible planets from Earth, seen as seals over the scroll). 2 And I saw a powerful angel proclaiming in a loud voice: "Who is worthy to open the scroll and to break its seals?" 3 But no one in heaven or on earth or under the earth was able to open the scroll or look into it. 4 So I began weeping bitterly because no one was found who was worthy to open the scroll or to look into it. 5

Then one of the elders said to me, "Stop weeping! Look, the Lion of the tribe of Judah (Yahusha fulfills the sign of Leo; completing the Heavenly Scroll), the root of David, has conquered (the dragon, the meaning of the sign of LEO); thus (because only he has fulfilled the meaning of the scroll) he can open the scroll and its seven seals."

Then John continues describing the center of the Zodiac in great detail confirming the meaning of the "Heavenly Scroll"...

Rev. 5... continued
6 Then I saw standing in the middle of the throne and of the four living creatures, and in the middle of the elders, a Lamb that appeared to have been killed. He had seven horns and seven eyes, which are the seven spirits of God sent out into all the earth. 7 Then he came and took the scroll from the right hand of the one who was seated on the throne, 8 and when he had taken the scroll, the four living creatures and the twenty-four elders (stars) threw themselves to the ground before the Lamb... 14 And the four living creatures were saying "Amen," and the elders (stars) threw themselves to the ground and worshiped.

I will go further into these images and prophesies later in this book.

The contents of the Heavenly Scroll or book of the Mazzaroth is held secret, revealed through the Ruach (Spirit) to His chosen prophets. It is *"the secrets contained in the heavens"* perverted by the watchers twisting the meaning of the Zodiac. It is not read publicly until it is fulfilled completely, and only he who fulfills it is found worthy to break the seals, and read the scroll. Proclaiming to all that Yahuah's will has been done on Earth, as it is written in the Heavenly Scroll!

Matthew 13:11
He replied, "Because the knowledge of the secrets of the kingdom of heaven (the Zodiac or Heavenly Scroll) has been given to you, but not to them

Faith comes from 'hearing' the message in the stars!

As I explained in Chapter 3, Sha'ul asks of humanity below "did they not hear? Of course they did, he exclaims!" Then Sha'ul quotes David in Psalms that declares the heavens are pouring forth speech day after day to all mankind. *'Hearing'* and *'voice'* are used anthropomorphically as physical to spiritual parallels by Sha'ul as he clearly teaches the source of "faith" is the Zodiac!

> **Romans 10:17**
> Consequently, faith comes from hearing the message (proclaimed in the heavens), and the message is heard through the word (Heavenly Scroll) about the Messiah. 18 But I ask: Did they not hear? Of course they did: "Their (Signs of the Zodiac) voice has gone out into all the earth, their words (concerning Yahusha) to the ends of the world." (Sha'ul quotes ***Psalms 19:4***)

The "message that is heard through the word about the Messiah" Sha'ul says is... ***the Zodiac***, the 'Heavenly Scroll'; the Original Revelation to all mankind, the first and most complete Gospel of Yahusha the Messiah!

After asking the question "did they not hear" the message of the Gospel, Sha'ul literally quotes from Psalm 19, the most eloquent description of the Zodiac and it's message I have every read...it is a detailed account of the Zodiac proclaiming The Gospel Message to all mankind.

> **Psalm 19**
> 2 The heavens (the place in the sky where the stars are located i.e. Zodiac) are telling of the glory of Yahuah (the Glory of Yahuah is Yahusha!); And their expanse is declaring the work of His hands. 2 Day to day pours forth speech, And night to night reveals knowledge. 3 There is no speech, nor are there words; Their (signs of the Zodiac/Constellations) voice is not heard. 4 Their line (Zodiac means line or path of

the sun) has gone out through (and seen through) all the earth, And their (signs of the Zodiac) utterances to the end of the world. In them (the constellations) He has placed a tent for the sun (the Zodiac), 5 Which is as a bridegroom (Yahusha) coming out of his chamber; It rejoices as a strong man to run his course (through the ecliptic). 6 Its rising is from one end of the heavens (Zodiac), And its circuit (Zodiac means circuit or path) to the other end of them; And there is nothing hidden from its heat.

Yes, the Zodiac is the Original Revelation to all mankind. It is the foundation of all prophecy and "faith"; as it is Yahuah's witness of the Messiah Yahusha.

Of course, we did what we always do and perverted it, then abolished it (*like we did The Law, the Sabbath, His Holy Name*) ... that is why this is so shocking to us today. We allowed the enemy to twist Yahuah's revelation in the stars and abuse it, to the point we will not even "look at or consider it" because we have been misled to believe it is 'evil'.

We were told the Zodiac is Yahuah's gift to all mankind, and we were not supposed to worship it. But, we did just that.

Deuteronomy 3:19
When you look up to the sky ('sky' is Hebrew shamayim/Zodiac) and see the sun, moon, and stars (speaking of the Zodiac) — the whole heavenly (Hebrew shamayim/Zodiac) creation — you must not be seduced to worship and serve them (signs of the Zodiac), for Yahuah your Elohim has assigned them (the signs of the Zodiac) to all the people of the world (they were created by Yahuah to proclaim the coming Messiah Yahusha, see Psalm 19, they are not

gods).

The Heavenly Scroll or Zodiac has been used by Yahuah to witness the Gospel all the way back to Adam, Enoch, even Abraham...

> **Genesis 15:5**
> And Yahuah brought Abram forth abroad (out under the stars), and said, Look now toward heaven (shamayim/Zodiac), and (see if you can) tell (what) the stars (proclaim), if thou be able to number them (read them in order, there are 12): and he said unto him, So (what they proclaim) shall thy seed (Yahusha) be (they tell the story of his life)

And Abraham believed the message he saw written in the stars! Abraham then became the 'Father of our Faith' because the source of "faith"... is The Heavenly Scroll! Just like Sha'ul said to the Galatians, Yahuah witnessed the Gospel to Abraham through the stars.

> **Galatians 3:8**
> 8 Scripture foresaw that Yahuah would justify the Gentiles by faith, *and announced the gospel in advance to Abraham*: "All nations will be blessed through you."

The Bible declares that creation cries out His existence and the Glory of Yahuah, which is the Gospel of the coming Messiah Yahusha.

We must shed the blinders of the "Church" in this one area concerning looking to the stars for knowledge and "reading the stars" as a witness from Yahuah to all mankind (*not fortune telling and horoscopes*).

Once these blinders are removed, we then begin to see the Bible instructing us to do just that… "Look up into the heavens" at the message found in the Zodiac. It must become obvious as we go back to the very foundation of the Universe, as we look to understand the workings of our Solar System; that Yahuah had a Plan and disclosed that plan in "the heavens". Why wouldn't He? He is ***The Creator*** and it was His predestined plan all along to deliver this planet through a human Messiah. That plan (Hebrew 'debar' mistranslated into Greek as 'logos') was with Yahuah in the beginning. Everything that was done in creation was done according to that predestined plan. It was Yahuah's plan!

> **John 1**
> 1 In the beginning was the *plan of Yahuah*, and *the plan* was with Yahuah (and defined His purpose in creation), and *the plan* was Yahuah's. 2 The same *plan* was in the beginning with Yahuah. 3 All things were done according to the *plan of Yahuah*, and without the *plan of Yahuah* nothing was done, that was done. 4 In *this plan* was (predestined) life (through a human Messiah's sacrifice), and that life was the light (revelation) to mankind.

Yes, it was Yahuah's plan from the very beginning and Yahuah, ***THE CREATOR***, literally wrote that plan into the stars in an elaborate display for all mankind to see. He didn't just name these stars and constellations for identification purposes; but for signs to be used as prophetic markers for coming days, seasons, and years… but also as signs with meaning that tell the story of Yahusha the Messiah!

> **Genesis 1**
> And Yahuah said, "Let there be lights in the expanse of the sky to separate the day from the night, and let them serve as signs, and to mark seasons and days and years"

However, very early on (*as we see in The Book of Enoch*) mankind was led astray from The Creator. We were taught to worship His creation in idolatry by "The Watchers" (*also known as fallen angels*). As we have read in several passages that these fallen angels taught a "worthless message" and corrupted the message in the heavens, and taught the use of astrology:

> **The Book of Enoch Chapter 8**
> 3 Amezarak taught all those who cast spells and cut roots, Armaros the release of spells, and Baraqiel astrologers, and Kokabiel portents, and Tamiel taught astrology, and Asradel taught the path of the Moon.
>
> **The Book of Enoch Chapter 9**
> 6 things, and nothing can hide itself from Thee. Thou seest what Azazel hath done, who hath taught all unrighteousness on earth and revealed the eternal secrets which were (preserved) in heaven, which 7 men were striving to learn:
>
> **The Book of Enoch Chapter 16**
> 3 "You have been in heaven, but all the mysteries had not yet been revealed to you, and you knew worthless ones, and these in the hardness of your hearts you have made known to the women, and through these mysteries women and men work much evil on earth."

This corrupted version of The Gospel Message was to worship the Sun and planets and Zodiac signs ... Sun Worship as it evolved from Babylon to modern day Christianity. We read in The Book of Daniel that the magic arts, divination, and astrology were central to the Mystery Religion of Babylon. Moses presented a clear warning to Israel before taken into Babylonian captivity NOT <u>to fall for sun worship</u>.

> **Deuteronomy 4**
> 19 And when you look up to the sky (the Zodiac) and see the sun, the moon and the stars—all the heavenly array (of the Zodiac)—do not be enticed into bowing down to them (the signs of the Zodiac/constellations) and worshiping things (the Zodiac) Yahuah your Elohim has apportioned to all the nations under heaven (as a witness to the coming Messiah).

And Moses further warned Israel against using the Zodiac for astrology to tell fortunes and divination and forbids the use of any of the knowledge given by The Watchers (*fallen angels*):

Deuteronomy 18
9 When you enter the land Yahuah your God is giving you, do not learn to imitate the detestable ways of the nations there. 10 Let no one be found among you who sacrifices their son or daughter in the fire (to Ba'al), who practices divination or sorcery, interprets omens, engages in witchcraft, 11 or casts spells, or who is a medium or spiritist or who consults the dead. 12 Anyone who does these things is detestable to Yahuah; because of these same detestable practices Yahuah your Elohim will drive out those nations before you. 13 You must be blameless before Yahuah your Elohim.

Idolatry consists of revering the created thing rather than the Creator. Behind the worship of the sun, moon and stars are the demonic powers of the heavenly realm (1Cor. 10:20).

Angels, fallen and un-fallen, are Yahuah's instruments in the government of the physical world and nature (***Hebrews 2:5***). Seeking answers about the future in the stars-then or now-brings us under the control of demonic agencies (*to our own harm and destruction*).

That, however, does not preclude us from looking up into the heavens to "see" the message of The Gospel written for all humanity and that is exactly why the Zodiac was created. It is also why the Zodiac was the focus of corruption.

The Heavenly Scroll is opened

Leo, the Lion of the Tribe of Judah opens the book of the Mazzaroth, the Heavenly Scroll

Revelation 5 - *The Opening of the Scroll of the Mazzaroth*
5 Then I saw in the right hand of the one who was seated on the throne a scroll written on the front and back (3-D scroll of heavenly pictographs) and sealed with seven seals (the 7 visible wandering stars were seen as seals over The Heavenly Scroll, also the 7 lampstand Heavenly Menorah).

Revelation Chapter 4
1 The Throne in Heaven After this I looked, and behold, a door was opened in heaven; and the first voice which I heard was (Yahuah, the Aleph/Tav), as it were, of a trumpet talking with me, which said: Come up here, and I will show you things which must be after this. 2 And immediately I was in the Spirit; and behold, a throne was set in The Heavenly Scroll, and One sat on the throne. 3 And He Who sat there had the appearance of a jasper and a sardius stone, and there was a rainbow surrounding the throne, like the appearance of an emerald. 4 And surrounding the throne were twenty-four seats, and sitting on the seats I saw twenty-four elders,

clothed in white robes; and they had crowns of gold on their heads. 5 And out of the throne proceeded lightnings, and thunderings, and voices; and there were seven lamps of fire burning before the throne, which signify and represent the complete plan of Yahuah (7-spirits/7 stars of Pleiades). 6 And before the throne there was a sea of glass, like crystal (blackness of space). And in the midst of the throne, and surrounding the throne, were four living creatures full of eyes before and behind (the "signs/constellation" wheel of Ezekiel's vision, image to the left).

7 And the first creature was like a **lion**, and the second creature like a **calf**, and the third creature had a face as a **man**, and the fourth creature was like a **flying eagle** (the 4 cardinal points of the Enoch Zodiac to the right). 8 And each of the four living creatures had six wings, they were full of eyes around and within; and they did not cease day and night, saying: Holy, holy, holy, Father Yahuah Almighty, Who was, and is, and is to come.

9 And when those creatures give glory, and honor, and thanks, to Him who sat on the throne, to Him Who lives forever and ever, 10 The twenty-four elders (stars) fall down before Him Who sat on the throne (in the Enoch Zodiac, there are exactly 24 stars and they are "falling" under the rainbow throne, the four beasts are seen singing "holy, holy, holy" pictured below)

, and worship Him Who lives forever and ever, and bow with their kippot before the throne, saying: 11 You are worthy, O Yahuah, to receive glory, and honor, and power; for You created all things, and by Your will they exist and were created!

I have produced an in-depth video on what John witnessed proving Yahuah was showing John The Heavenly Scroll. It can be found on my YouTube Channel. Search "The Sabbath Covenant Channel" or go here:
https://www.youtube.com/channel/UCVLZgChmeSa78Mo7b228sjQ

CHAPTER 6
THE HEAVENLY WEDDING PORTRAIT

Chapter 6 - The Zodiac proclaims the Feast Cycle

With that introduction to the Heavenly Scroll (*the Zodiac*), we are now prepared to examine the 12 signs of the Zodiac to see what story is told to all mankind in the heavens (***H8064** – the visible place in the sky where the stars are located*). As we now know, this mystery was revealed to King David. In Psalms 19, we see that as the sun and moon rises and sets daily, and night after night… knowledge concerning The Plan of Yahuah is proclaimed without voice or speech from one end of the Earth to the other to all mankind.   Remember, Sha'ul told the Galatians that before their very eyes, the Messiah was "seen" as crucified in the stars. Sha'ul also proclaims in **Romans Chapter 1** that mankind is without excuse, because the Plan of Salvation is evident in creation! We see then David define the Zodiac in detail as that message.

> **Psalm 19**
> 1 The heavens (H8064, speaking of the Zodiac) are telling of the glory of Yahuah; And their expanse is declaring the work of His hands. 2 Day to day pours forth speech, And night to night reveals knowledge. 3 There is no speech, nor are there words; Their (the stars and constellations) voice is not heard. 4 Their line (ecliptic, the path of the sun through them) has gone out through all the earth, And their utterances to the end of the world. In them (the constellations) Yahuah has placed a tent for the sun, 5 Which (the Sun) is as a bridegroom coming out of his chamber (a metaphor of Yahusha who is the Bridegroom); It rejoices as a strong man to run his course (of a wedding). 6 Its (the Sun's) rising is from one end of the heavens, And its circuit (through the constellations, Zodiac means 'circuit') to the other end of them; And there is nothing hidden from its heat (a metaphor of the message shining down from heaven to all mankind).

The sun rises from one end of heaven and then its "circuit or Zodiac" is like a "bridegroom coming out of his chamber" to run the course of a wedding says King David. The Messiah Yahusha understood this too, knowing that he was the fulfillment of that Plan of Salvation. He was the Bridegroom and that role was defined in the *Original Revelation* in the stars called the Zodiac.

> **John 3:29**
> [29] He who has the bride is the bridegroom (***Psalm 19***); but the friend of the bridegroom, who stands and hears him, rejoices greatly because of the bridegroom's voice. Therefore, this joy of mine is fulfilled.

Yahusha's joy was fulfilled in knowing that he was the one spoken of in the message the Zodiac contains! Yahusha explains, in Matthew 25, that the "message of the Bridegroom" found written in the stars was a long time coming before he was born to fulfill it. Mankind "fell asleep" and the message of the Zodiac, which proclaims the bridegroom and the wedding, was forgotten:

> **Matthew 25**
> [4] The wise ones, however, took oil in jars along with their lamps. [5] The bridegroom was a long time in coming, and they all became drowsy and fell asleep. [6] "At midnight the cry rang out: 'Here's the bridegroom! Come out to meet him!'

This is the meaning of the parable of the 10 virgins. We read in this parable that most people (*5 virgins*) would disregard the Zodiac and the message it contained of the coming Bridegroom (*let the oil in their lamps run out*). Others would study and retain the knowledge written in the stars, and be prepared for the arrival of the Bridegroom. Because his return is a "sign in the sky" or a prophetic marker in the constellations of the Zodiac.

We see that only those who understand the meaning of this message, and the reality of how the Feast Cycle is a fulfillment of the Plan of Salvation, are invited to the "wedding" foretold in the heavens that we "forgot":

> **Revelation 19**
> ⁹ And the angel said to me, "Write this: Blessed are those who are invited to the marriage supper of the Lamb." And he said to me, "These are the true words of Yahuah."

"These are the true words of Yahuah" is, in context, speaking of the marriage supper of the Lamb which is found prophesied in the Zodiac since the creation of the Universe. As I pointed out earlier, in addition to this message being of the Bridegroom running the course of a wedding (**Psalms 19**), it also speaks of "a Lamb that was slain" at creation (**Revelation 13:8** and **Revelation 5:6**). In this way, the "true words of Yahuah" is the message contained in the Zodiac; the original gospel!

David sees the Sun as a prototype for The Messiah as a bridegroom and the path it takes through the constellation is the course of a wedding. This physical metaphor of the sun as the bridegroom (*pointing to The Messiah*) is repeated throughout scripture. This is, in fact, true as the Sun was created as a witness of the coming of the Messiah and what the Messiah would do. In other words, *the sun of Yahuah is a physical to spiritual parallel of the son of Yahuah.*

This striking declaration in Psalms 19 clearly tells us that Yahuah built into the Zodiac the story of redemption, and through the stars has been witnessing His plan to all humanity in a unique view only from Earth. The Original Revelation of Yahuah of Yahusha, *found written in the stars represented by the Zodiac*, is only told from the vantage point of Earth as we look up into the heavens at the eternal secrets they have preserved.

We read in 1 **Corinthians 2:7** that Sha'ul mentions that he came to proclaim the "testimony of Yahuah" which is a message of wisdom concerning the sacrifice of Yahusha which is "***predestined before the ages to our glory***". That message is that of a Lamb that was slaughtered before the foundation of the world (*as John proclaimed in **Revelation***). All these references of Yahusha being proclaimed speaking directly of the Gospel message contained in the Zodiac. We read below this message, *predestine before the ages*, is a "***mystery that has been hidden** that Yahuah destined for our glory **before time began**". In other words Yahuah wrote the Plan of Salvation into the stars!

> **Corinthians 2:7**
> And so it was with me, brothers and sisters. When I came to you, I did not come with eloquence or human wisdom as **I proclaimed to you the testimony of Yahuah** (about Yahusha which is The Heavenly Scroll). ² For I resolved to know nothing while I was with you except Yahusha the Messiah and him crucified (as portrayed in The Heavenly Scroll). ³ I came to you in weakness with great fear and trembling. ⁴ My message and my preaching were not with wise and persuasive words, but with a demonstration of the Spirit's power, ⁵ so that your faith might not rest on human wisdom, but on Yahuah's power (displayed in Creation *Enoch 35:3*). ⁶ We do, however, **speak a message of wisdom** among the mature, but not the wisdom of this age or of the rulers of this age (who twisted the Zodiac into withcraft), who are coming to nothing. ⁷ No, **we declare Yahuah's wisdom, a mystery that has been hidden and that Yahuah destined for our glory before time began (authoring The Plan of Salvation into the heavens on Day 4)**. ⁸ None of the rulers of this age understood it (because it was corrupted by the watchers), for if they had, they would not have crucified the King of glory (The Heavenly Scroll *Psalm 19* 'the heavens tell of the Glory of Yahuah').

If we are truly going to unlock the "mystery" of the moedim (*annual Feast Cycle*), we must begin there, before the ages (*as Sha'ul indicated*) with the message proclaimed in the stars. We must journey back to the very beginning and search for our answers as to "what" the Feast Cycle is telling us. The message in the stars is "the true original words of Yahuah" (***Revelation 19:9***).

We must look before the Feasts of Yahuah were given orally to Adam thru Moses, before they were written down in detailed instructions in the Mosaic Covenant. Why? Because now, in the Yahushaic Covenant, they have found their ultimate meaning;

meaning which was ordained before the foundation of this earth and predestined before the ages as Sha'ul stated. That meaning, as King David proclaimed, is that of a Bridegroom running the course of a wedding.

This fundamental message, written into the stars by The Creator as a witness to all mankind, is further revealed in covenants made between The Creator and mankind. Each and every covenant in the Bible is a "marriage covenant" and the Law is the "marriage vows". This Plan of Salvation through a wedding was further revealed to us in parables and idioms.

- Parable of the Wedding Banquet in Matthew 22
- Parable of the Faithful Servant in Matthew 24
- Parable of the 10 Virgins in Matthew 25
- Revelation 19

We find that Yahusha, who is the bridegroom, constantly taught the same message written in the stars, giving us more and more insight into the Plan of Salvation… the plan of the bridegroom redeeming his bride.

The Annual Wedding Portrait

The Appointed Times (*or the Feast of Yahuah*) each year are a literal rehearsal of this divine wedding proclaimed in the heavens (*the Zodiac*).

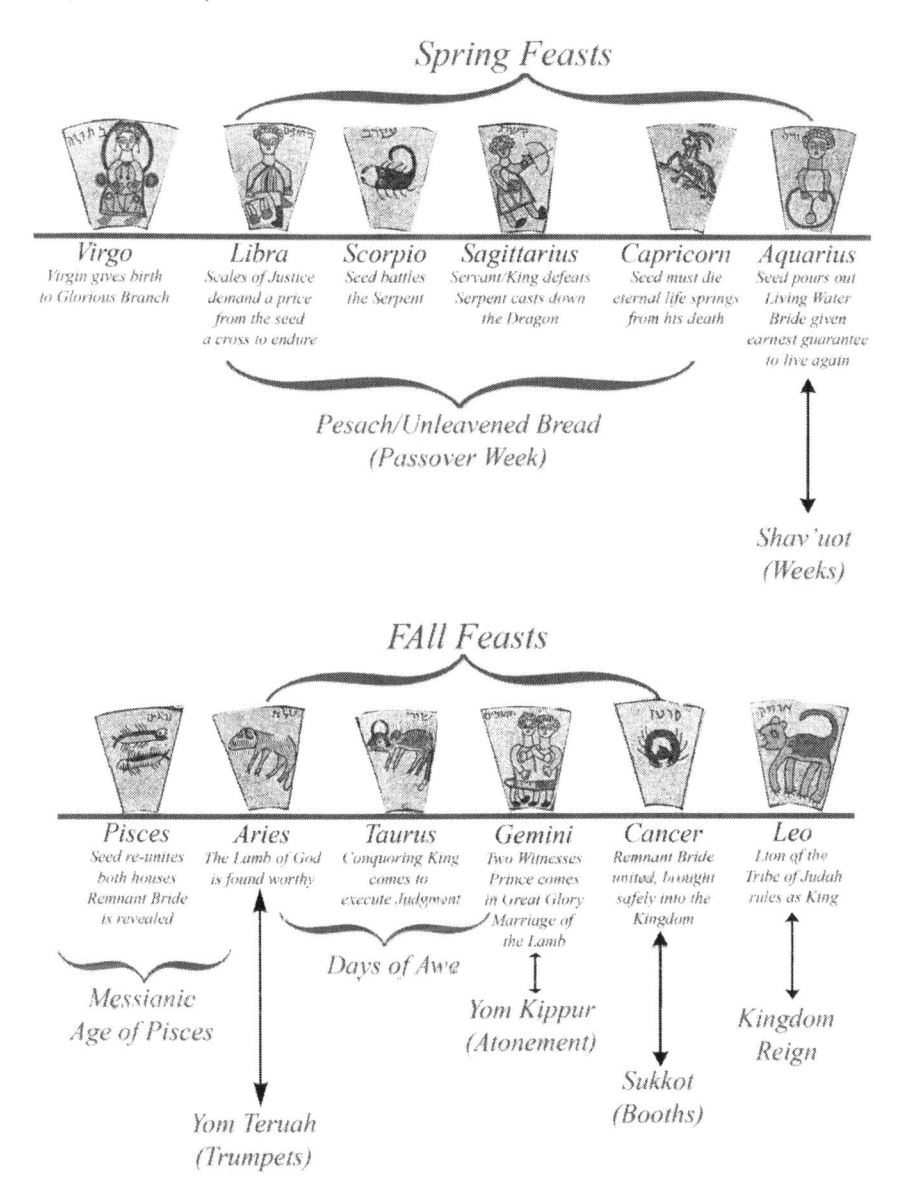

Spring Feasts

Virgo
Virgin gives birth to Glorious Branch

Libra
Scales of Justice demand a price from the seed a cross to endure

Scorpio
Seed battles the Serpent

Sagittarius
Servant/King defeats Serpent casts down the Dragon

Capricorn
Seed must die eternal life springs from his death

Aquarius
Seed pours out Living Water Bride given earnest guarantee to live again

Pesach/Unleavened Bread (Passover Week)

Shav'uot (Weeks)

FAll Feasts

Pisces
Seed re-unites both houses Remnant Bride is revealed

Aries
The Lamb of God is found worthy

Taurus
Conquoring King comes to execute Judgment

Gemini
Two Witnesses Prince comes in Great Glory Marriage of the Lamb

Cancer
Remnant Bride united, brought safely into the Kingdom

Leo
Lion of the Tribe of Judah rules as King

Messianic Age of Pisces

Yom Teruah (Trumpets)

Days of Awe

Yom Kippur (Atonement)

Sukkot (Booths)

Kingdom Reign

This message and meaning behind the annual feasts is hidden knowledge revealed only to those "invited to the wedding". Like Sha'ul said, it was not understood by the leaders of Israel in the second temple period, or by those who lead us in this age even now.

The Messiah ben David and Messiah ben Joseph

The Messiah is represented in The Heavenly Scroll to die first and suffer; to earn the right to reign as King. The prophets understood this and represent the Messiah in Scripture as a double natured servant/king. These prophecies are known as **The Messiah ben Joseph** (*The Suffering Servant*) and **The Messiah ben David** (*The Conquering King*). The Spring Feast give us the role of Messiah ben Joseph, as the Messiah must suffer and die for the forgiveness of sin. Then the Messiah is raised from the dead, granted eternal life, and returns as Conquering King (*Messiah ben David*) which is foretold in the Fall Feasts.

The Jews lost sight of The Heavenly Scroll which dictates the order the Messiah must fulfill the Plan of Salvation. He MUST come first as "shepherd" and die, then as "harvester" to gather into one the two houses and rule as King (***Leo***). Being weary after spending over 500 years in captivity, they simply did not want to submit to The Plan of Salvation therefore denying Yahusha as the Messiah because he did not come as their "King" first. He came to fulfill The Heavenly Scroll… not their selfish desires.

In The Heavenly Scroll, we see the dual nature/role of the Messiah foretold in the starry hosts (*constellations*) Virgo, Sagittarius, and Taurus! We see in these pictographs the Messiah will come "**first as shepherd then as harvester**", he will be a "**doubled natured seed**", and the "**ruling Shepherd/King**"! There is an order in The Plan of Salvation, the prophets, and the Feast Cycle all based on The Heavenly Scroll that the Messiah must fulfill. Until the Jews come out of there rebellion against The Plan of Salvation, deny themselves, and accept this divine order, they will remain outside of The Yahushaic Covenant!

> ***VIRGO:*** A virgin will give birth to a beautiful glorious and righteous branch. The seed of the woman will be a man of humiliation to rise to be the desire of nations and will become exalted **first as shepherd then as harvester**.
>
> ***SAGITTARIUS:*** The **double-natured seed** (*servant/king*) triumphs as a warrior and pleases the heavens, builds fires of punishment, casts down the dragon.
>
> ***TAURUS:*** The conquering Ruler comes, the sublime vanquisher, to execute the great judgment, he is **the ruling Shepherd King**.

We see *The Suffering Servant* portrayed in the heavenly hosts (*constellations*) *Libra* through *Capricorn* which became the foundation of The Spring Feasts:

LIBRA: The scales demand a price to be paid of this seed, a cross to endure; the victim will be slain and purchase a crown. ***SCORPIO:*** There is a conflict between the seed and the serpent leading to a struggle with the enemy, the enemy is vanquished. ***SAGITTARIUS:*** The double-natured seed (*servant/king*) triumphs as a warrior and pleases the heavens, builds fires of punishment, casts down the dragon. ***CAPRICORNUS:*** Eternal life comes from his death, he's the Arrow of God, he is pierced, yet springs up again in abundant life.

We see *The Conquering King* portrayed in the heavenly hosts (*constellations*) Aries through *Leo* which were later articulated in the Fall Feasts!

PISCES: The Redeemer's people multiplied, supported and led by the Lamb, The Bride is exposed on earth, the Bridegroom is exalted. ***ARIES:*** The Lamb is found worthy, the Bride is made ready, Satan is bound, the strong man triumphs. ***TAURUS:*** The conquering Ruler comes, the sublime vanquisher, to execute the great judgment, he is the ruling Shepherd King. ***GEMINI:*** The Marriage of the Lamb, the enemy is trodden down, the Prince comes in great Glory. ***CANCER:*** The great Bride, the two Houses of Judah and Israel are united, they are brought safely into the kingdom. ***LEO:*** The Lion King is aroused for rending, the Serpent flees, the Bowl of Wrath is upon him, his Carcass is devoured. The Lion of the tribe of Judah rules as King.

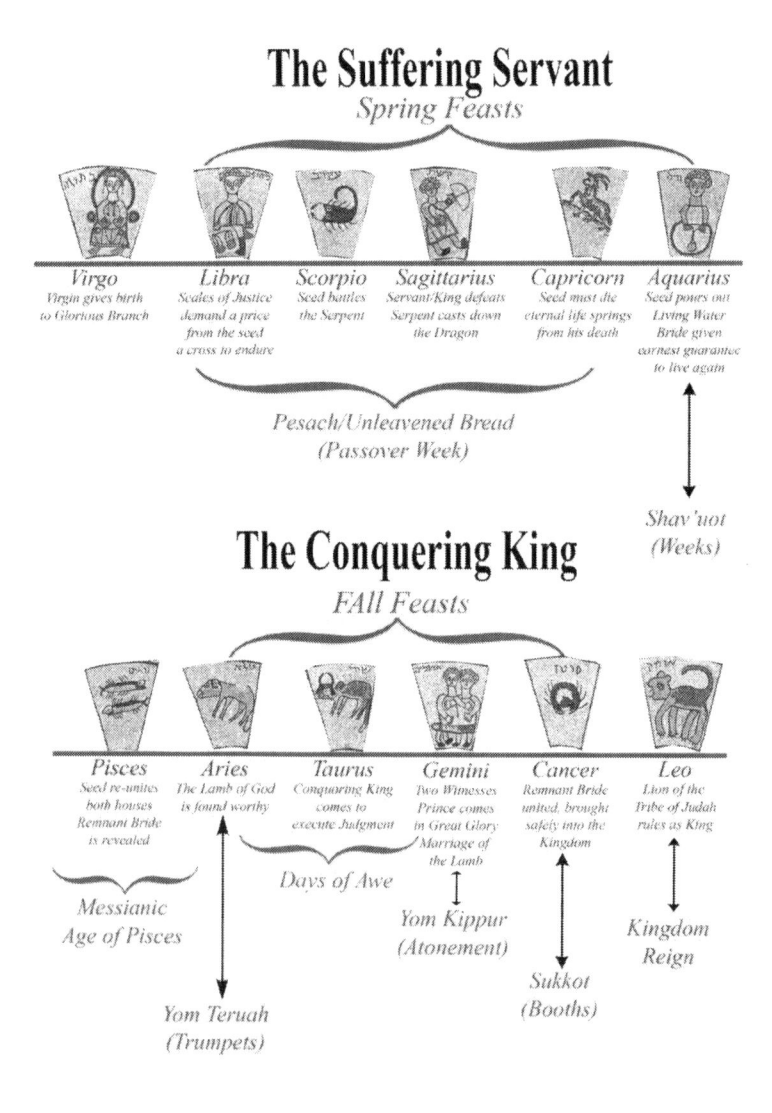

The Suffering Servant
Spring Feasts

Virgo — Virgin gives birth to Glorious Branch
Libra — Scales of Justice demand a price from the seed a cross to endure
Scorpio — Seed battles the Serpent
Sagittarius — Servant/King defeats Serpent casts down the Dragon
Capricorn — Seed must die eternal life springs from his death
Aquarius — Seed pours out Living Water Bride given earnest guarantee to live again

Pesach/Unleavened Bread (Passover Week)

Shav'uot (Weeks)

The Conquering King
FAll Feasts

Pisces — Seed re-unites both houses Remnant Bride is revealed
Aries — The Lamb of God is found worthy
Taurus — Conquering King comes to execute Judgment
Gemini — Two Witnesses Prince comes in Great Glory / Marriage of the Lamb
Cancer — Remnant Bride united, brought safely into the Kingdom
Leo — Lion of the Tribe of Judah rules as King

Messianic Age of Pisces

Yom Teruah (Trumpets)

Days of Awe

Yom Kippur (Atonement)

Sukkot (Booths)

Kingdom Reign

The Physical Shadow of Greater Truths

Hebrew/Jewish weddings were pre-arranged marriages. They consisted of

1. the father choosing a qualified groom
2. the groom paying the dowry or "ransom" for the bride
3. the groom introducing himself to her father
4. the bride presenting herself to the bridegroom
5. the bridegroom going away to prepare a place for her in his father's estate
6. the bridegroom returning for his bride
7. the wedding
8. the wedding banquet

Remember, in Psalms 19, David described the Zodiac in great detail. He said the Sun was a shadow picture of the Messiah as the Bridegroom ran the course of a wedding. With this in mind, let me show how perfectly the Feasts Cycle or Appointed Times of Yahuah reflect the physical marriage process of a Hebrew wedding. As foretold in the stars, the Bridegroom running his course.

Keeping in mind that a marriage between a man and a woman is a physical to spiritual parallel that should help us understand our roles as the Bride in the Spring and Fall Feasts:

- *The father choosing a qualified Groom* – this is reflected in Yahuah's choice of the Messiah Yahusha as proclaimed through the prophets.

- *The Rehearsal Dinner* – the Chagigah meal on the 14th of Abib is a "remembrance meal" where we are to discuss the upcoming wedding rehearsal, and what each day represents. This is called "The Last Supper" in our Hellenized English Bibles. I explain all this in my upcoming book *The Narrow Gate*. We see Yahusha teach the meaning of the upcoming

Passover and that it is to be celebrated each year "in remembrance/Chagigah) of him (1 Corinthians 11:24 and Luke 22:19).

- ***The Groom paying the dowry or "ransom" for the Bride*** – this is a shadow of Passover as Yahusha "paid the debt to the Father of the Bride" and redeemed us from our prior lives into a new life in covenant with Yahuah through Yahusha. He paid the dowry, or ransom, owed to our Father - **Matthew 20:28** *"just as the Son of Man did not come to be served, but to serve, and to give his life as a ransom for many."*

- ***The Groom introducing himself to the Father of the Bride*** – Feast of First fruits. **John 20:17** *"Yahusha said, "Do not hold on to me, for I have not yet ascended to the Father."*

- ***The Bride presenting herself to the Bridegroom and agreeing to the marriage vows*** – Shav'uot. On Shav'uot we are to follow the example set by Yahshua during Passover. We are to Mikveh ourselves, bring our own lives as an offering at the altar of Yahuah (a lamb without blemish), and then present ourselves properly to our Bridegroom on Shav'uot. We agree to the wedding vows (the Law) by saying "this we will do" or "I do" as they did at the foot of Mt. Sinai. It is a celebration of the giving of the Wedding Vows and our accepting them. Sha'ul expressed the way we are to present ourselves in following Yahusha's example of Mikveh, circumcision, and bringing an offering. Again we see the Plan of Salvation is a marriage covenant:

Ephesians 5 – *Sha'ul likens the example Yahusha set to marriage. Like I said, the feasts are a marriage celebration. We see below, Sha'ul teaches the example of Mikveh, circumcision, and offering*
25 Husbands, love your wives, just as the Messiah loved the assembly and gave himself up for her (as The Passover Lamb paying the dowry) 26 to set her apart, (ritually) cleansing her by the washing with water according to the commandments

(of Mikveh), 27 and to present her (consecrated) to himself (with a circumcised heart) as a radiant assembly, without spot or wrinkle or any other blemish (as we offer our lives as living sacrifices), but holy and blameless (as the spotless Bride of Yahusha).

- ***The bridegroom going away to prepare a place for the bride in his father's estate*** - **John 14** Yahusha says "<u>2</u> "*In My Father's house are many dwelling places; if it were not so, I would have told you; for I go to prepare a place for you. <u>3</u>"If I go and prepare a place for you, I will come again and receive you to Myself, that where I am, there you may be also. <u>4</u>"And you know the way where I am going.*" Here Yahusha is speaking in the ***Mystery Language*** a parable and idiom confirming the wedding. Yahusha goes and prepares a place for us in The Kingdom of Yahuah. He is not referring to a physical place (because we reign with him on Earth), he is referring to a place in the family of Yahuah. Yahusha is going to perform the duties of High Priest and offer the proper gifts and sacrifices before the throne of Yahuah.

- ***The Bridegroom returning for his Bride*** – Feast of Trumpets or Yom Teruah. This is a portrait of the second coming of the Bridegroom to receive his Bride. This occurs on the Feast of Trumpets (Yom Teruah) which is celebrated over a two-day period at the beginning of the 7th month, because it is the only feast based on the timing of the new moon. Yom Terauh became known therefore as the idiom "***the feast of which no man knows the day or hour***" because we don't know the exact timing of the new moon. Yahusha confirmed his return on the Feast of Trumpets when he used an idiom for this feast in **Matthew 24:36** ""*But about that day or hour no one knows, not even the angels in heaven, nor the Son, but only the Father.*" Here Yahusha was both confirming his return on the Feast of Trumpets and the arranged marriage using another idiom "*no one knows, not even the angels in heaven, nor the Son, but only the Father*". You see, the marriage was arranged by the father unknown to the son.

- ***The wedding*** – Yom Kippur or Day of Atonement. This is the actual wedding day celebration. The Groom atones for himself and for his new bride.

- ***The wedding banquet*** – Sukkot or The Feast of Tabernacles. This feast is known as the Wedding Banquet as portrayed in Revelation 19 and was the meaning behind the Parable of the Wedding Banquet in Matthew 22.

It is outside the scope of this first book to explain in detail the Feasts of Yahuah, how they fulfill the Plan of Salvation written in the stars, and our role in properly keeping them as His Bride. I cover this in great detail in this book series in my book '**The Narrow Gate –** *The Annual Celebration of the Wedding* '.

My point here in this book is that David understood the true meaning of the Zodiac! The message in the Zodiac is told from the standpoint of a "wedding" as the bridegroom comes out of his chambers and runs his course! The fundamental message to all humanity written in the stars at creation is that of a "groom" coming forth, paying the ultimate price for his bride with his life, and redeeming her from death, and ruling together as King and Queen!

Later in this book we will examine this message in great detail. This message was further defined by Yahuah and laid out in His Ordained Feast Cycle, as we celebrate The Plan of Salvation and rehearse our role each year. A message that goes out to all the Earth as the Sun travels its course through the Zodiac:

Feast of Passover – the groom pays the dowry.

Feast of First Fruits – the Groom presents himself to the Father of the Bride spotless and ready for his Bride.

Feast of Weeks – the groom goes to prepare a place for the Bride in his Father's estate.

Feast of Shav'uot – the Bride presents herself to the Groom spotless and ready and the wedding vows are agreed upon.

Feast of Trumpets – the Groom returns for his Bride, is announced and comes forth. The Bride is revealed.

Feast of the Day of Atonement – the Groom makes atonement for himself and his Bride as they become "one" through covenant in a wedding ceremony.

Feast of Tabernacles – the Wedding Banquet

Now let us look at the message contained in the Zodiac proclaimed in the heavens from the foundation of the world, predestined for our Glory. Does this message proclaim a Bridegroom running the course of a wedding? Is the message in the heavens the foundation of the annual Feast cycle?

CHAPTER 7
RIGHTEOUS ASTROLOGY?

Chapter 7 – Righteous Astrology?

The goal of this book is to determine the ***Original Revelation*** from Yahuah to man that creation cries out. We are doing so by looking further into what is the oldest revelation to mankind… the Zodiac. It was Yahuah, the Creator, who named the stars, ordered them into constellations, and brings those formations forth by name!

> **Psalms 147**
> 4 He determines the number of the stars (*in each constellation*) and calls them (*the constellations*) each by name.

Let's take a closer look at "the circuit of the Sun" that David proclaimed was a Bridegroom running the course of a wedding. What is the true message it reveals from heaven condemning all those who would pervert that message and worship His creation above the Creator as Sha'ul proclaimed in ***Romans 1***?

To understand the true meaning of the Zodiac, we must know where the "circuit" or "circle" of the sun moving through the constellations begins. We, the sons of Yahuah, know where the story begins through the prophet Isaiah.

> **Matthew 1:23**
> 22 Now all this took place to fulfill what was spoken by Yahuah through the prophet (*Isaiah 7:4*): 23 " Therefore Yahuah himself will give you a sign (stars are for signs): The virgin (***Virgo***) will conceive and give birth to a son,

All signs are given in the stars as Yahuah declared in ***Genesis 1:14***, Yahuah never instructed us to look for a human woman as a sign. Later in this book I am going to breakdown the restrictions in the Torah concerning the abuse of the Zodiac. I will explain that what we call "Astrology" today is much different than how it is used in the Bible.

Whether we want to admit the obvious concerning the Zodiac and even divination and astrology in the Bible, there is a righteous means by which the Zodiac is to be used and an unrighteous use.

The Babylonian Chaldean Astrologers trained by the prophet Daniel (*who was the chief astrologer in multiple dynasties and Kings*) were looking for the celestial sign; they were not running around knocking on every door from Babylon to Bethlehem looking for a pregnant virgin!

Using the Zodiac to seek 'divine counsel" from Yahuah through Astrology (*in the sense of understanding the Heavenly Scroll*) is the way Yahuah intended the Zodiac to be used. If we deny that reality because we have been brainwashed by the Catholic Church (*who abolished the Zodiac along with everything else holy to Yahuah*), that just makes us "ignorant" of the truth and "stiff necked" people.

Daniel the Chief Astrologer

Daniel is a very good example that using the Zodiac, interpreting dreams, and deciphering omens with the proper 'spirit' and seeking those answers from the Creator is acceptable. The Prophet Daniel was the "*Chief Astrologer*" in the Babylonian Court (*actually under several empires/kings*)... so good was Daniel at his craft of *divination* (*means seeking Divine Revelation*), he was made King of the Chaldeans who were renowned Astrologers dating back to Babylon!

The Bible calls those who use divination techniques to seek counsel from Yahuah... Prophets. Those who use divination and seek counsel from other gods... false prophets, soothsayers, etc.

Daniel was a Eunuch; he had no children/heirs. Daniel amassed a fortune serving at the highest levels of multiple empires and Kings as their 'advisor' i.e. chief astrologer... Daniel became the right hand of the Kings who deemed Daniel their King "by proxy". Daniel was one of the most powerful and wealthy men across several dynasties and Kings. Daniel trained the Chaldean Astrologers how to properly understand The Zodiac and how it foretold of the coming King/Messiah. He left specific instruction to those in his 'school of astrology' called Chaldean Astrologer how to find the newborn King using astrology and the signs in the sky/Zodiac (the one defined in Revelation 12, a sign in the constellation Virgo that announced the birth of the king).

Astrologers the only ones to find the King

Daniel's fortune, a King's ransom literally, was passed down through the centuries by the Chaldean Astrologers trained by Daniel to give this King's ransom to the newborn Messiah (*because Daniel had no heirs*). At the time of Yahusha's birth, the messianic expectations of all of Israel was at a very high state, they all knew it was time according to Daniel's prophecies the Messiah would be born. The Priests in the Temple, the Zealots, all the people in Israel, and THE ENTIRE ARMY of Herod (who sought to kill the child) were all looking for the birth of the Messiah. I cover this in great detail in my book; **Melchizedek and the Passover Lamb**.

> *You could say it was one of the largest man-hunts in human history....*

The only, I repeat... **THE ONLY** ones to find the Messiah were astrologers! The Bible calls these astrologers "wise men'... trained by the master astrologer himself ... Daniel. And they delivered to the newborn King, the wealth of several Empires! No one else, NO ONE ELSE found him! Not the High Priests, not the Zealots, not the Army of Herod, no one in Israel at all... only those who knew how to read The Zodiac signs!

Yahusha the Astrologer?

Keep in mind, when I use the term 'astrologer' here I am using in the proper sense of the word divination (*divine revelation*) which is seeking divine counsel **from Yahuah** not in the sense we think of it today as fortune telling. Yahusha shows that he too was an "astrologer" who understood the meaning of the Zodiac properly. He commanded us to seek out the **Sign of the Son of Man** (*defined in **Rev. 12***) among the stars; the same sign that heralded his birth... heralds his return.

> **Matthew 24:30**
> "Then will appear the sign of the Son of Man in (the) heaven(ly scroll H8064 – the visible place in the sky where the stars are located). And then all the peoples of the earth will mourn when they (are given Spiritual eyes to) see the Son of Man coming on the clouds (the Milky Way) of (the) heaven(ly scroll), with power and great glory.

Yahusha is specifically instructing us to understand and watch for a specific "sign" in the stars. When that day arrives, Yahusha prophesied that we will be given "eyes to see" The Heavenly Scroll! I will discuss this in detail later in this book. Just like the only ones who found the newborn King 2000 years ago were astrologers... so too the only ones who will know of the timing of his return will be "astrologers". All of us you are looking for the *Sign of the Son of Man* which is a sign in the constellation of the Zodiac known as Virgo are what we would call 'astrologers'.

This sign is of a "woman giving birth to a son/king" among the stars. It is what Yahusha the Messiah called "*the sign of the son of man*" in the sky/H8064 which is "the place in the sky where the stars are located". It is when the King Planet Jupiter moves into the womb of the constellation Virgo. Once Jupiter is inside the "*womb*" of Virgo, it goes into retrograde motion and literally bounces around inside the womb of Virgo for exactly 9 months (*the exact time of human gestation*). Then Jupiter exits out of the birthing canal (between the legs of Virgo). This is the "woman giving birth" and "birth pains" spoken of in Revelation Chapter 12 which describes this "sign in the Zodiac" in great detail. Below is the upcoming event on Yom Teruah 2017:

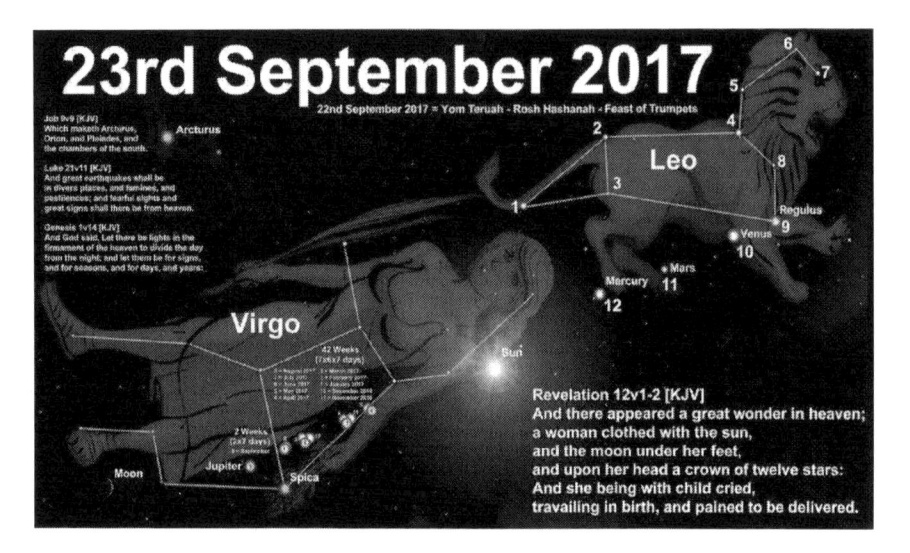

Revelation 12

12 And then a great wonder appeared in heaven (H8064 – the Zodiac): There was a woman (Virgo) who was clothed with the sun, and the moon was under her feet. She had a crown of twelve stars on her head. ² She was pregnant and cried out with pain because she was about to give birth... ⁵ The woman gave birth to a son, who would rule all the nations with an iron rod. And her child was taken up to Yahuah and to his throne.

What constellation do you suppose the sun is moving through in late September each year when the Messiah was born during the Sukkoth? ***Virgo***! That is why Isaiah said "***Behold!*** *(*the Zodiac*), a*

virgin shall give birth to a son." This is how the Chaldean astronomers knew when to begin looking for the birth of the Messiah, he would be born in late September when the sun is moving through Virgo and she would be "*clothed with the sun*" as we see in **Revelation Chapter 12**.

They knew the exact year he would be born because of the unique event where the King planet Jupiter moves into the womb of Virgo and spends 9 months bouncing around in retrograde motion. They knew the general timing because he was to be born during the transition from the Age of Aries to the Age of Pisces. This was the same "sign" spoken of by Isaiah ... Virgo is that woman. Daniel taught the Chaldean Astrologers the meaning of Ages and when the next Age should occur; so they began looking for the "*sign of the son of man*" probably around 100 years or so before Yahusha's birth knowing that was the timing of the Age of Aries transitioning to the Age of Pisces.

Once they saw that sign approaching, they knew he would be born in the Fall around September *the year Jupiter entered the womb of Virgo* with the Sun at her back and the moon at her feet. They knew to find him in Bethlehem because it was so prophesied:

> **Micah 5:2**
> "But you, Bethlehem Ephrathah, though you are small among the clans of Judah, out of you will come for me one who will be ruler over Israel, whose origins are (foretold) from of old, from ancient times (in the Zodiac)."

The Sign of the Son of Man

This "sign of the son of man" in the Zodiac occurs roughly every 2,000 years marking what the Bible callas "*Ages*". Ages progress backward through the signs of the Zodiac. I will discuss '*Ages*' later in this book. This sign heralded the birth of Abraham around the year 2000BC (*the transition from the Age of Taurus to the Age of Aries*). This same sign in the Zodiac then heralded the birth of the Messiah 2,000 years later (*the transition from the Age of Aries to the Age of Pisces*). This same sign in the Zodiac returns in the heavens to herald the return of the King and Age transition from Pisces to Aquarius on Yom Teruah 2017! I am not saying Yahusha returns on the specific day. I am saying that it marks the progression of the Ages. Yahusha said he will be with us until the 'end of this Age of Pisces', and then told us what Sign in the Zodiac to look for. So we see Yahusha understood 'astrology' from a righteous standpoint and referred to it quite often as we will learn in this book.

> **Matthew 28:20**
> teaching them to observe all that I have commanded you. And behold, I am with you always, to the end of the Age (*of Pisces the Fish*)."

We read in the Book of Jasher the events surrounding the birth of Abraham were identical to that of Yahusha.

> **Jasher 8:1-4**
> And it was in the night that Abram was born, that all the servants of Terah, and all the wise men of Nimrod, and his conjurors came and ate and drank in the house of Terah, and they rejoiced with him on that night. 2) And when all the wise men (astrologers) and conjurors went out from the house of Terah, they lifted up their eyes toward heaven (the Zodiac) that night to look at the stars (constellations of the Zodiac), and they saw (the sign of the son of man), and behold one very large star came from the east and ran in the heavens, and he swallowed up the four stars from the four sides of the heavens. 3) And all the wise men of the king and his conjurors

were astonished at the sight and the sages understood this matter, and they knew its import (to mark the progression of the Age of Taurus to the Age of Aries). 4) And they said to each other, this only betokens the child that has been born to Terah this night, who will grow up, and be fruitful, and multiply, and possess all the earth, he and his children forever, and he and his seed will slay great kings, and inherit their lands.

As Bob Wadsworth wrote in ***The Open Scroll***

> *The planets were seen rising from the east. The planets and the stars as well as the sun, rise in the east and set in the west.*
>
> *In their forward movement through the zodiac and against the background stars, the planets move in the opposite direction, from the west to the east. But Venus would have been seen here in the moment as coming from the east, since it is from the east that it was seen rising into the heavens. This is very similar to the description given of the star from the east seen at or around the time of Yahusha's birth.*

So (*we who know Yahuah*) know where the story begins in the Zodiac. It begins with the constellation Virgo as that is the sign of the birth of the King. But, as we know the watchers gave humanity this message contained in the stars as well; although they corrupted its message. Is there confirmation among the pagan religions, showing us they understood there was a message written in the Zodiac? Is there confirmation among those earliest pagan sun worshipping religions that the story begins in Virgo? Did the watchers tell them where the message begins and ends in the constellations... YES! It is called *the Sphinx*!

There is a reason why these ancient peoples build massive monuments to the Sphinx. The Sphinx represents the beginning and ending point of the Plan of Salvation foretold in the heavens.

171

While we have Yahuah telling us where the story begins with the "sign of the son of man" or Virgo giving birth to Jupiter as a "sign", the ancients had the Sphinx.

The meaning of the Sphinx

The Zodiac is a circle. In order to accurately decipher the message of the Zodiac, we must know from which sign or constellation the story begins and ends. The sphinx provides the clue where the Zodiac story begins and ends. It is a story told by the Sun... of Yahuah's Son throughout the course of a year as the sun travels through the sky. Like David proclaimed in ***Psalms 19***, the Sun runs its course like a "strong man" or Savior and like a bridegroom receiving his bride.

The ancients left us the "key" to this puzzle in the Sphinx. The Sphinx is this mysterious mythical figure that is half woman and half lion. Obviously the importance of the Sphinx to the beginning cultures of humanity cannot be understated. They made monuments that to this day survive them as a message to all mankind.

Notice the picture on the right of man "listening" as the Sphinx whispers a secret message! The sphinx is a combination of the two signs where the story begins and ends. It begins with Virgo the "virgin" woman and ends with Leo the Lion.

CHAPTER 8
HOW TO READ THE HEAVENLY SCROLL

The message in The Zodiac begins with Virgo and ends with Leo

Head of Virgo — Body of Leo

Chapter 8 - How to read the scroll in Heaven

Revelation 6:14
13 and the stars of the sky fell to the earth, as a fig tree casts its unripe figs when shaken by a great wind. 14 The heavens were split apart like a scroll when it is rolled up!

Isaiah 34:4
All the stars in the heavens will be dissolved and the heavens rolled up like a scroll; all the starry host will fall like withered leaves from the vine, like shriveled figs from the fig tree.

Where did the images come from?

Have you ever noticed how the pictures associated with each constellation have nothing to do with how the stars that supposedly make up that constellation appear when connected together? How did our ancient ancestor, across all cultures and over thousands of years, come up with the same images to represent the same 12 constellations and 36 Decans (*smaller constellations*)?

The images associated with each constellation do not represent the physical "connect the dots" representation of the stars that make up each constellation. The images represent the "meaning" or story told by the constellation. The story told by each constellation is derived from the meaning of the names of the stars the constellation contain! The meaning of the major 12 constellations also factor in the meaning of the associated Decans around each constellation. The Signs are pictographs, pictures that tell a story.

We know from scripture that it was Yahuah who named each star, grouped them into constellations, and brought each constellation forth by name. We see below that it was Yahuah who named every star!

Psalms 147:1-5
How good it is to sing praises to our Elohim, how pleasant and fitting to praise him! Yahuah builds up Jerusalem; he gathers the exiles of Israel. He heals the brokenhearted and binds up their wounds. *He determines the number of the stars and calls them each by name.* Great is our Elohim and mighty in power; his understanding has no limit.

We see below, that it was Yahuah who created and named the "starry hosts" which are the constellations (groups that "host" stars):

Isaiah 40:25-26
"To whom will you compare me? Or who is my equal?" says the Holy One. Lift your eyes and look to the heavens: Who created all these? He who brings out the starry host (constellations) one by one, and calls them each (constellation) by name. Because of his great power and mighty strength, not one of them is missing (there are 12 major constellations exactly among all cultures).

Because Yahuah named each star and the constellation that hosts the stars, every culture has exactly 12 major constellations along the path of the sun (*ecliptic*). Every culture has the same names (*in their own language*) for the constellations and the stars in them. In every culture the names of the stars/constellation mean the same thing. To determine the image of a constellation, every culture simply looked at the meaning behind the names of the stars in that constellation. The stars are "read" in the order of their brightness in the sky.

Then based on the "story" told when looking into the meaning of the stars, they would understand the story of the constellation itself. Then they would create an "image" for the constellation base on the story it told, not by "connecting the dots" i.e. by the shape of the stars in the constellation. So the "images" are pictographs. Pictographs on a 'scroll' that visually tell the story of salvation.

That is why the images of each Zodiac Sign (*constellation*) looks (*in some cases*) nothing like you would get if you drew a line connecting all the stars! Some actually do resemble the image, but others are a real stretch because the image is not really based on the shape but the story.

Constructing the images of the Signs of The Zodiac

This is what the grouping of stars in each constellation looks like to the naked eye:

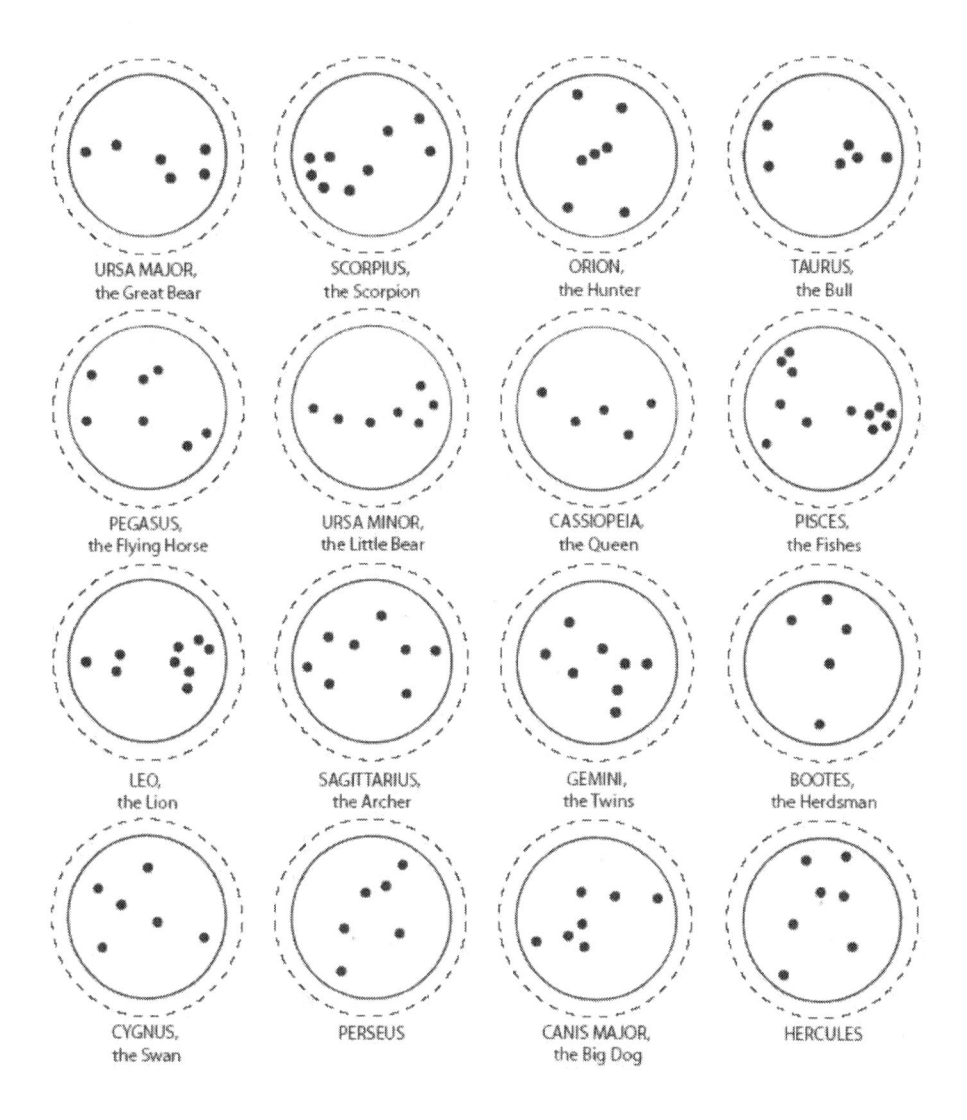

URSA MAJOR, the Great Bear	SCORPIUS, the Scorpion	ORION, the Hunter	TAURUS, the Bull
PEGASUS, the Flying Horse	URSA MINOR, the Little Bear	CASSIOPEIA, the Queen	PISCES, the Fishes
LEO, the Lion	SAGITTARIUS, the Archer	GEMINI, the Twins	BOOTES, the Herdsman
CYGNUS, the Swan	PERSEUS	CANIS MAJOR, the Big Dog	HERCULES

This is what you get "connecting the dots":

If you look really hard you can almost "see" the resulting characters associated with them. But it is a stretch and definitely doesn't account for why every culture has the exact same images and stories.

This is a sample of the images/characters drawn to represent the story told:

Decans

Within each "sign" or constellation, there are 3 nearby constellations called Decans; for a total of 36 minor constellations. These minor constellations, like the major ones, derive their image the same way; from the names of the stars within them.

Creation Cries Out!

Each major constellation's story also includes the story told by the associated 3 Decans nearby them. The Decans are not on the ecliptic (the Sun does not go through them) that is the difference between the 12 major signs and the minor signs. Below is a chart showing the 12 major signs color coded and the associated Decans (minor constellations) that factor into the overall story told by each major constellation.

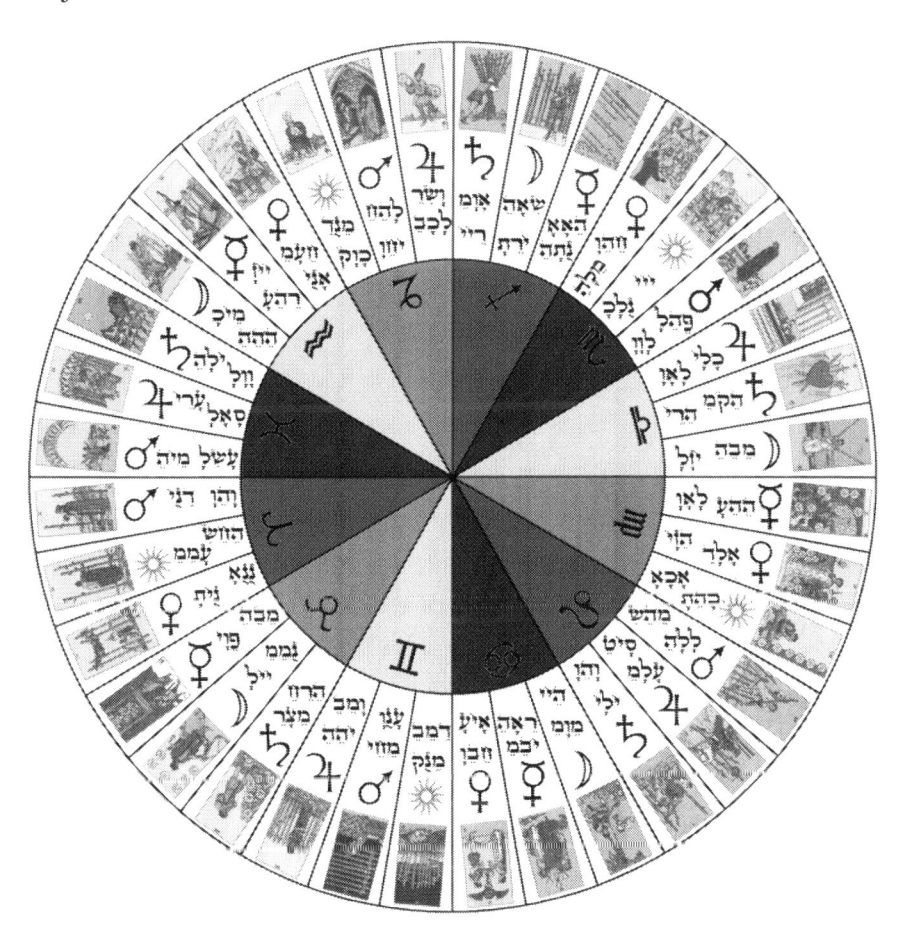

On the following pages, I will breakdown each major sign in the Zodiac. I will explain each major star and the associated Decans to show why every culture dating back to the origin of man has come up with the same images and stories.

181

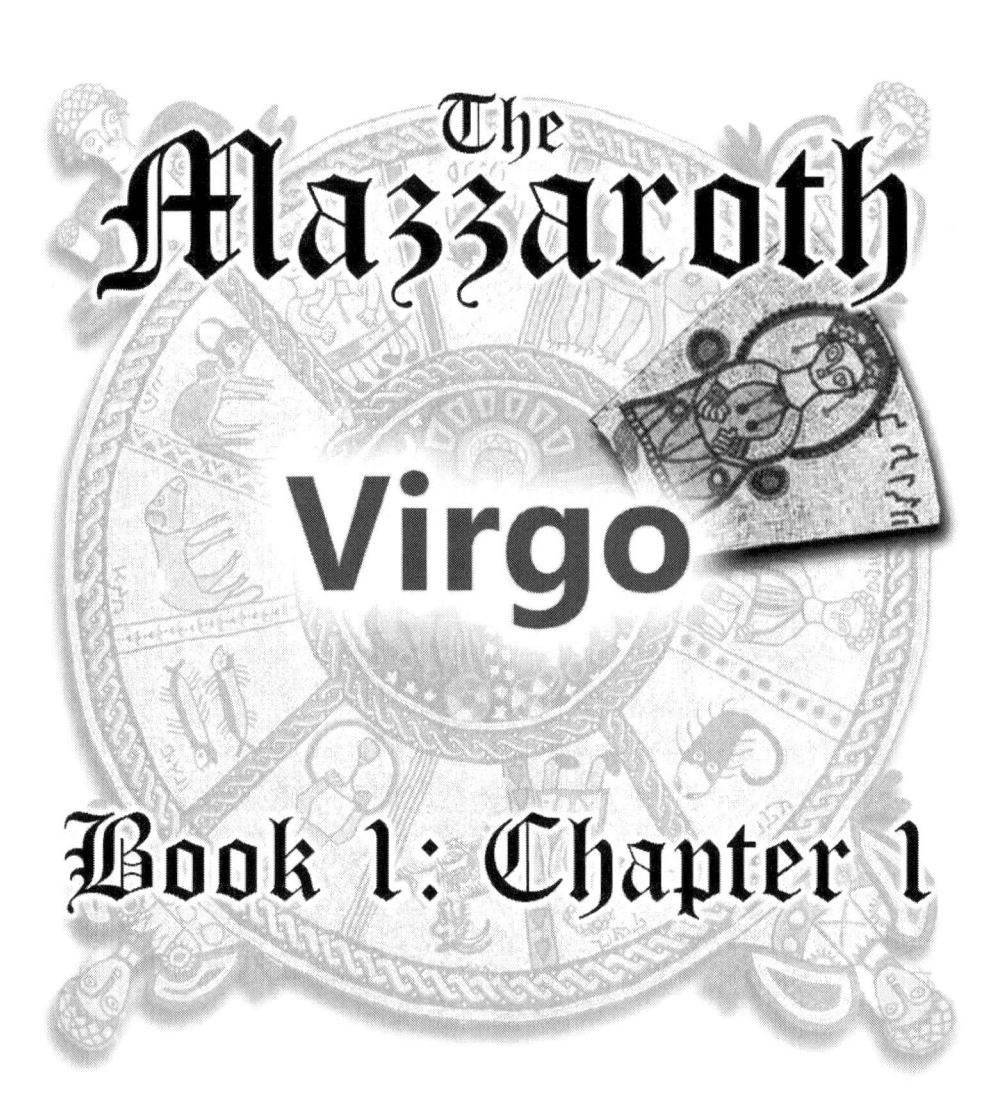

Virgo

The Mazzaroth

Virgo

Book 1: Chapter 1

Short Story: The Virgin / Young Maiden

Virgin gives birth to a King, great shepherd and harvester

Tribe of Israel: *Naphtali*

Primary star

Spica – means "ear of wheat/corn/grain". Hebrew word for this star is *Tsemech* which means "the branch". Jer 23:5-6, Zech 3:8, 6:12, Isaiah 4:2. There are 20 different Hebrew words that mean "branch", yet only *Tsemech* is used of the Messiah; the same word for the name of the brightest star of Virgo. Virgo has a branch/ear of barely in one hand (John 12:21-24) and a "seed" in her other (Gen 3:15)

Secondary star

Zavijaveh, meaning "gloriously beautiful." - Isaiah 4:2

Decans (secondary constellations)

Decan constellation Coma

Idol worship from Babylon to Egypt to Rome based on Coma

Coma decan – meaning "the infant is the desired one" (Haggai 2:7). The image of this constellation is a woman holding an infant child. As the Egyptians were led astray into worshipping the "creation over the creator" they idolized the image of Coma and myths were created around this Decan of the Madonna and Child. This is where the worship of

Semaramis and Tammuz (Babylon), Isis/Horus (Egypt), and many other pagan myths are derived.

Centaurus decan – meaning "the dart piercing a victim"
Bootes decan – meaning "the great shepherd and harvester"

Overall story told by VIRGO

Seed of the Woman, Desire of nations, Man of humiliation, becomes exalted Shepherd and Harvester. A virgin holding a branch and an ear of corn. Corn = **seed** (Latin Spica, the modern name of this bright star. Old name was Arabic Al Zimach meaning seed). Star Zavijaveh means "gloriously beautiful". So according to all cultures since the beginning of mankind, the constellation Virgo means "a virgin holding a branch and a seed that will be gloriously beautiful".

Let's look at what the prophets of Yahuah spoke concerning the Messiah Yahusha and see if the meaning of Virgo is truly a prophetic sign of the coming messiah Yahusha:

<u>Isaiah 7</u>
14 Therefore Yahuah himself will give you a sign: *The virgin will conceive and give birth to a son*

Jeremiah 23
⁵ "The days are coming," declares Yahuah, "when I will raise up for David ***a righteous Branch***, ... This is the name by which he will be called: Yahuah Our Righteous Savior.

Note: Jeremiah named the name of the Messiah specifically here. *"Yahusha" in Hebrew is how you say: "Yahuah Our Righteous Savior". It is said Yahuah Yasha but Hebrew tradition was to shorten an expression into a personal name with meaning. The short poetic form of Yahuah "Yah" and the short poetic form of the salvation "sha". The Hebrew name of the Messiah fulfills this prophecy perfectly; his name was **Yahusha** not "Jesus". Yahusha is short for Yahuah Yasha which means "Yahuah Our Righteous Savior" or Yahuah is our savior. I will cover the name of The Messiah in detail in this book series.*

Isaiah 4
² In that day *the **Branch** (**who is Yahusha**)* of Yahuah ***will be beautiful and glorious***

So, the prophets of Yahuah proclaimed a virgin will give birth to a beautiful glorious and righteous branch, the seed of Abraham. Perfect match.

Libra

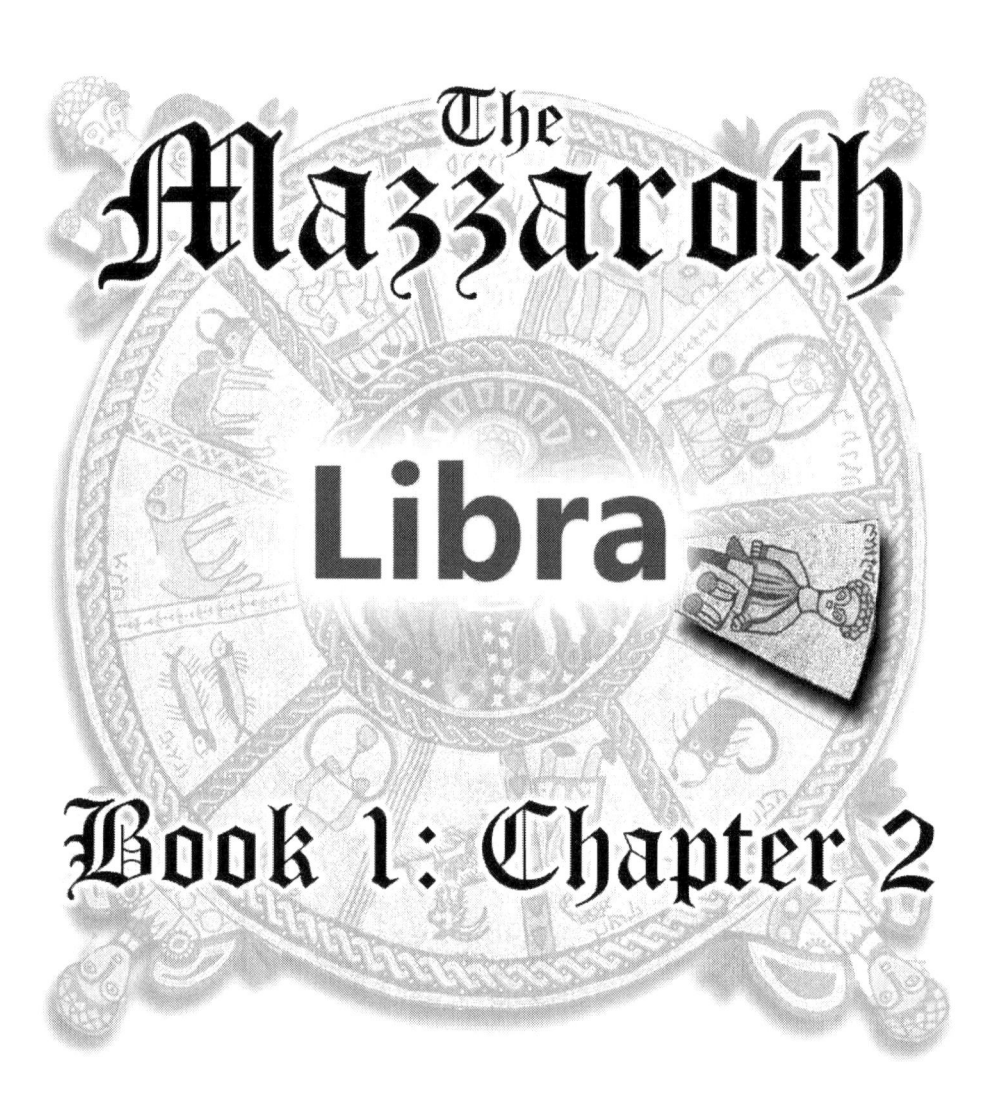

The Mazzaroth

Libra

Book 1: Chapter 2

Short Story: The Scales

The scales demand a price to be paid, Cross to endure, the Victim slain, a Crown purchased.

Tribe of Israel: *Asher*

Primary star

> *Alpha: Zuben al Genubi* – means price deficient (Ps 49:7, 62:9

Secondary star

> *Beta: Zuben al Chemali* – means price that covers (Rev 5:6). So "we fall short, another covers the gap)

Third star

> *Gamma: Zuben al Akrab* – price of the conflict as it points toward Centaurus and victim slain

Decans (secondary constellations)

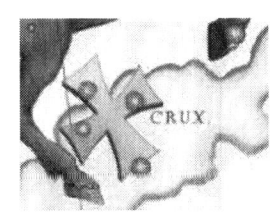

The Cross - Hebrew is Adom means "cut off"

Lupus – the victim, pierced to death, Hebrew Asedah "to be slain". Egyptian name is Sura which means "lamb" (Isa 53:7)

Corona – the crown (Heb 2:9). Hebrew word Atarah means "royal crown" (Rev 5:9, Mt 27:29, Jas 1:12, Zech 9:16).

To the south of Libra, we find the cosmic struggle of Serpens and Ophiuchus a man wrestling with serpent while treading on the head of a scorpion and the other foot is on the scorpions head.

Overall story told by Libra

The Balance, or Scales, symbolizes measurement and balance in general as well as justice and commerce. Speaking of the Messiah:

> **Job 31**
> ⁶ let Yahuah weigh me in honest scales and he will know that I am blameless
>
> **Revelation 6**
> ⁵ When the Lamb opened the third seal, I heard the third living creature say, "Come!" I looked, and there before me was a black horse! Its rider was holding a pair of scales in his hand.

An accurate balance with accurate weights was a symbol of justice. Yahuah has perfect Justice based upon His absolute Righteousness. The scales of divine Justice are accurately calibrated. Divine Judgment is without partiality (Deut 10:17; Acts 10:34; Rom 2:11; Gal 2:6; Eph 6:9). Yahuah (His proxy King Yahusha) is the final Judge (2 Tim 4:1; Heb 4:12; 10:30; 12:23; Jas 4:12).

Scorpio

The Mazzaroth

Scorpio

Book 1: Chapter 3

Short Story

A Conflict, Serpent's coils, Struggle with the Enemy, the Evil Vanquisher. The "strong man" wrestles with the serpent who is reaching for the crown. The scorpion is stinging the heel of the strong man, who is treading on the scorpion.

Tribe of Israel: *Dan*

Primary star

> *Antares* - wounding, cutting, tearing

Secondary star

> ***Beta: Zuben al Chemali*** – means price that covers (Rev 5:6). So "we fall short, another covers the gap)

Third star

> ***Gamma: Zuben al Akrab*** – price of the conflict as it points toward Centaurus and victim slain

Decans (secondary constellations)

Serpens and Ophiuchus decans – the serpent and the **Serpent Bearer**, or **Healer**. A man wrestling with the serpent. He has one foot on the scorpions head and the other on the scorpion's tail.

<u>**Genesis 3:15**</u> - I will put enmity between you (the serpent) and the woman, And between your seed

and her seed; He shall crush your head, And you shall crush his heel.

Hercules decan – the mighty man. This Decan is the foundation of myths and idols of the Greeks.

Overall story told by Scorpio

Scorpius, the Scorpion, symbolizes Satan, the enemy of Yahuah and His chosen family. Satan was the enemy of the Messiah in Hypostatic Union, who inspired the execution on the stake (Jn 13:2, 27), but was defeated at the stake through resurrection (Jn 3:14-15, 12:31-32, 16:11). The scorpion (Dt 8:15; Ezek 2:6; Lk 10:19; 11:12) is a desert creature, as is the snake, which also symbolizes Satan.

Snakes and scorpions, the symbols of Satan, were the enemies of Israel. "Fiery serpents" is the Hebrew nachash, serpent, and saraph, meaning burning, fiery, or serpent. The two words together mean literally burning snakes, which were so called for their inflammatory bite, filled with heat and poison.

The constellation, Scorpius, is near other snake symbols. It is near the constellation Serpens, the Serpent, and Ophiuchus, the Snake Holder. Since both snakes and scorpions are symbols of Satan, the sign of Scorpius applies to both. Therefore, scripture for snakes as well as scorpions apply in the study of Scorpius.

The scorpion is also a symbol of the Centaur demon assault army of Abaddon (Rev 9:3, 5, 10), which, of course, is from Satan. Scorpius symbolizes the enemy attack of Satan, but it also symbolizes the victory at the stake (Yahusha was nailed to a stake or tree not a cross). The Greek word for serpent is o[fi" (ophis), which is also used in the Septuagint for the serpent in the Garden (Gen 3:1), the fiery serpents (Deut. 8:15), and the brass serpent in the desert (Num 21:6-9).

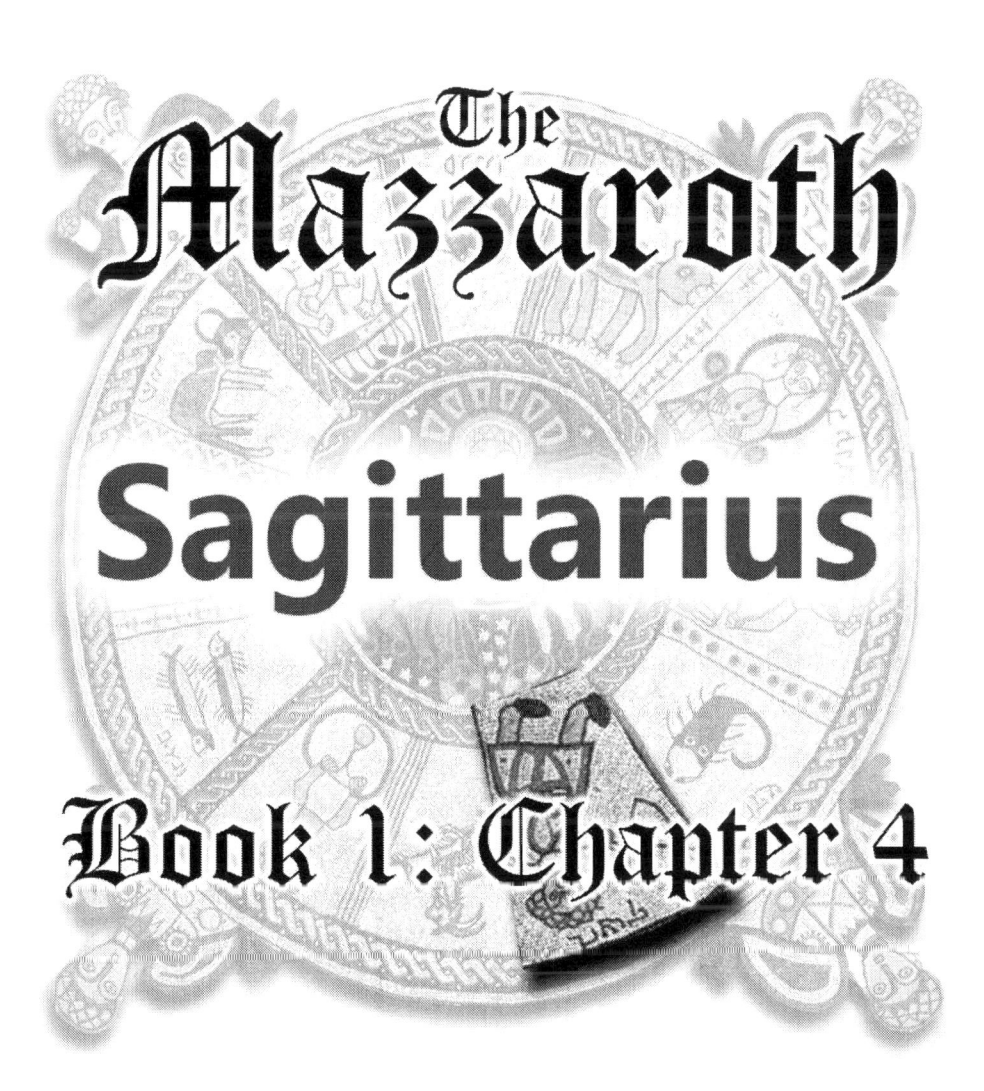

Sagittarius

The Mazzaroth

Sagittarius

Book 1: Chapter 4

Rav Sha'ul

Short Story: The Archer

The double-natured One triumphs as a Warrior, Pleases the Heavens, Builds fires of punishment, Casts down the Dragon. Same meaning in several languages (Rev. 6:2). Star Naim = The gracious one.

Tribe of Israel: *Benjamin*

Primary star

El Asieh – "the one to whom we bow" (Isaiah 45:23)

Secondary star

Beta: Zuben al Chemali – means price that covers (Rev 5:6). So "we fall short, another covers the gap)

Third star

Gamma: Zuben al Akrab – price of the conflict as it points toward Centaurus and victim slain

Decans (secondary constellations)

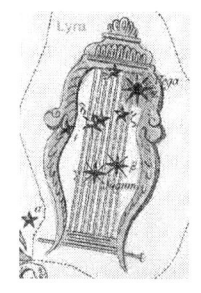

Lyra - The harp. The name indicates the praise of Yahuah. Brightest star is **Vega** = He shall be exalted. (Ps. 2 1:13)

Ara - the Altar. The burning fire prepared for His enemies.

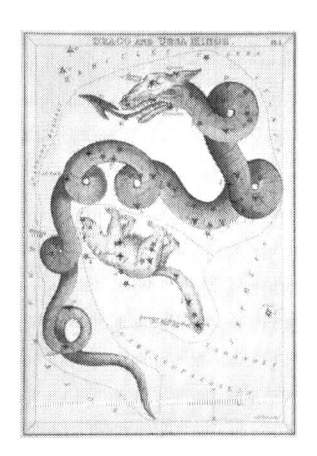

Draco - The Dragon. The name comes from the Greek = Trodden on (Ps. 91:13). Brightest star Thuban = The subtle. Names of other stars all refer to similar aspects of the dragon.

Overall story told by Sagittarius

The heavenly sign shows the archer with his bow bent and an arrow fitted to the string. It is aimed directly at Antares, the star in the heart of Scorpio. In Sagittarius the emphasis shifts from the wounding by the adversary, to one of victory. The arrows of God are shot at the heart of the enemy. In the Zodiac of Dendera under the image of this constellation is the word Knem, meaning "He conquers." We find the same word under the last sign of the Dendera Zodiac, that of Leo the Lion who is standing upon a serpent. This affirms that the Lion of Leo, and the Centaur of Sagittarius, refer to the same person. Numerous Scriptures come to mind in relation to this sign.

Psalms 45:3-5
Gird Your sword upon Your thigh, O Mighty One, with Your glory and Your majesty. And in Your majesty ride prosperously because of truth, humility, and righteousness; And Your right hand shall teach You awesome things. Your arrows are sharp in the heart of the King's enemies; The peoples fall under You.

Psalms 64:7
God shall shoot at them with an arrow; Suddenly they shall be wounded.

Revelation 6:2
And I looked, and behold, a white horse, and he who sat on it had a bow; and a crown was given to him; and he went out conquering, and to conquer.

Capricorn

The Mazzaroth

Capricorn

Book 2: Chapter 1

Short Story: Goat / Scapegoat

Life comes from death; He's the Arrow of God, Pierced, springs up again in abundant life.

Ancient pictures are half goat, half fish; i.e. the sacrifice and those who it is sacrificed for.

Tribe of Israel: *Zebulun*

Primary star

Gedi - Hebrew for "cut off"

Secondary star

Daneb Al Gedi - meaning "The Sacrifice Comes." (Isaiah 53:7-8)

Decans (secondary constellations)

Sagitta Decan – the Arrow

Aquila Decan – the Eagle

Delphinus Decan – the Dolphin

Overall story told by Capricorn

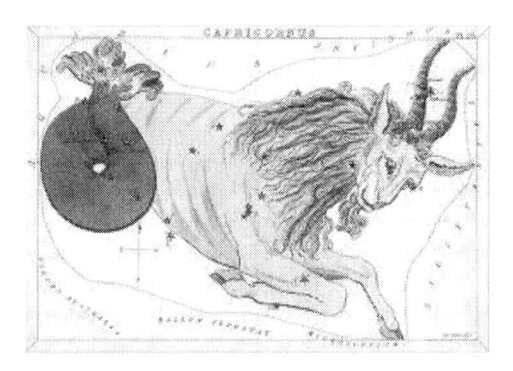

Capricorn is the top half of a goat, and the bottom half is the tail of a fish. It is called the **Sea Goat** (Capricornus). It is wounded and on one knee, and some of the ancient star names indicated that it is a sacrifice. The goat was one of the sacrificial animals in the Law of Yahuah given to Moses. It was the animal used as the scapegoat that took upon itself the sins of Israel on the Day of Atonement (Lev. 16:10). After John the Immerser Mikveh'd Yahusha and laid his hands on our Messiah's head, Yahusha "fled into the wilderness" in fulfillment of the shadow picture of the scapegoat.

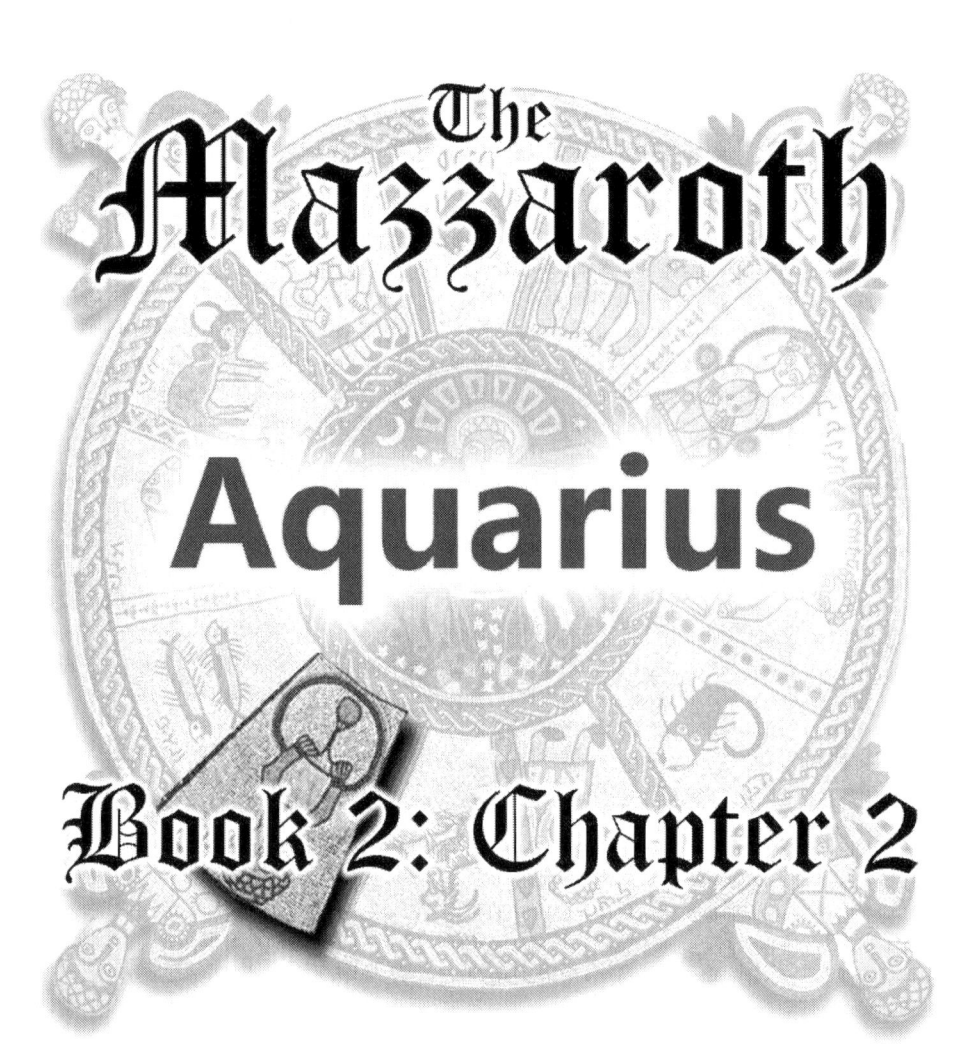

Aquarius

The Mazzaroth

Aquarius

Book 2: Chapter 2

Short Story: The Water Bearer

Life-waters from on High, Drinking the heavenly river, delivering the Good News, Carrying the wood of the sacrifice over all the earth.

Tribe of Israel: *Reuben*

Primary star

Sa'ad Al Melik - means "record of the outpouring"

Secondary star

Al Sund – means "the pourer out."

Decans (secondary constellations)

Picus Australis – the southern fish. Star Fom al Haut = the mouth of the fish.

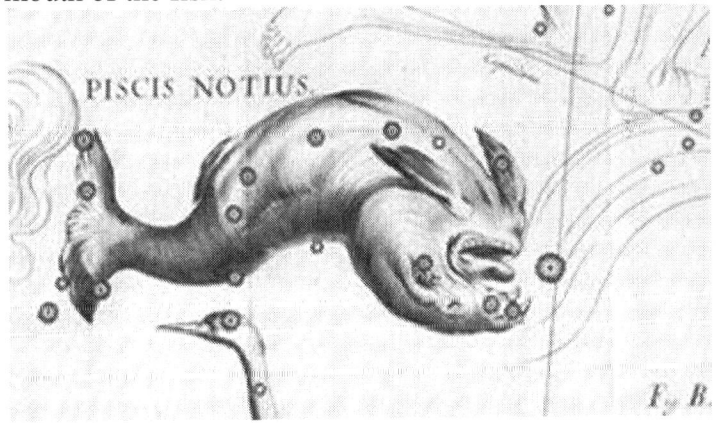

Pegasus – the winged horse

Cygnus – The Swan. Brightest star Deneb = The Judge or Adige = flying swiftly.

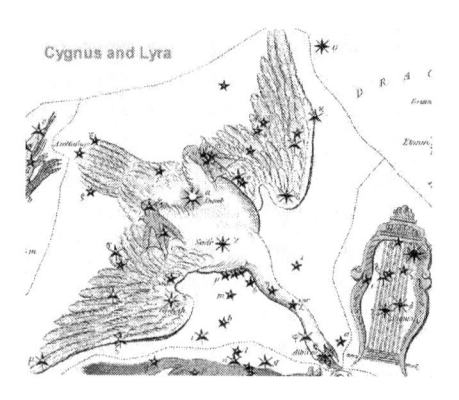

Overall story told by Aquarius

A man pouring out water on the Earth, living water (John 4:10, John 7:37-38, Isaiah 44:3-4). Aquarius is a Latin name meaning "the pourer forth of water." The brightest star is located in the right shoulder and is called Sa'ad Al Melik, meaning "record of the outpouring." The next star in brightness is Al Sund, "the pourer out." A star in the urn bears the Egyptian name Mon, or Meon, being interpreted "the urn." It is not difficult to find in the Scriptures references to Yahusha and the pouring forth of water.

When Yahusha encountered the woman of Samaria at the well, He said, "If you knew the gift of God, and who it is who says to you, 'Give Me a drink,' you would have asked Him, and He would have given you living water" (John 4:10). In John 7:37-38 Yahusha cried out at the water ceremony of Sukkot "'If any man is thirsty, let him come to Me and drink. He who believes in Me, as the Scripture said, 'From his innermost being shall flow rivers of living water.'"

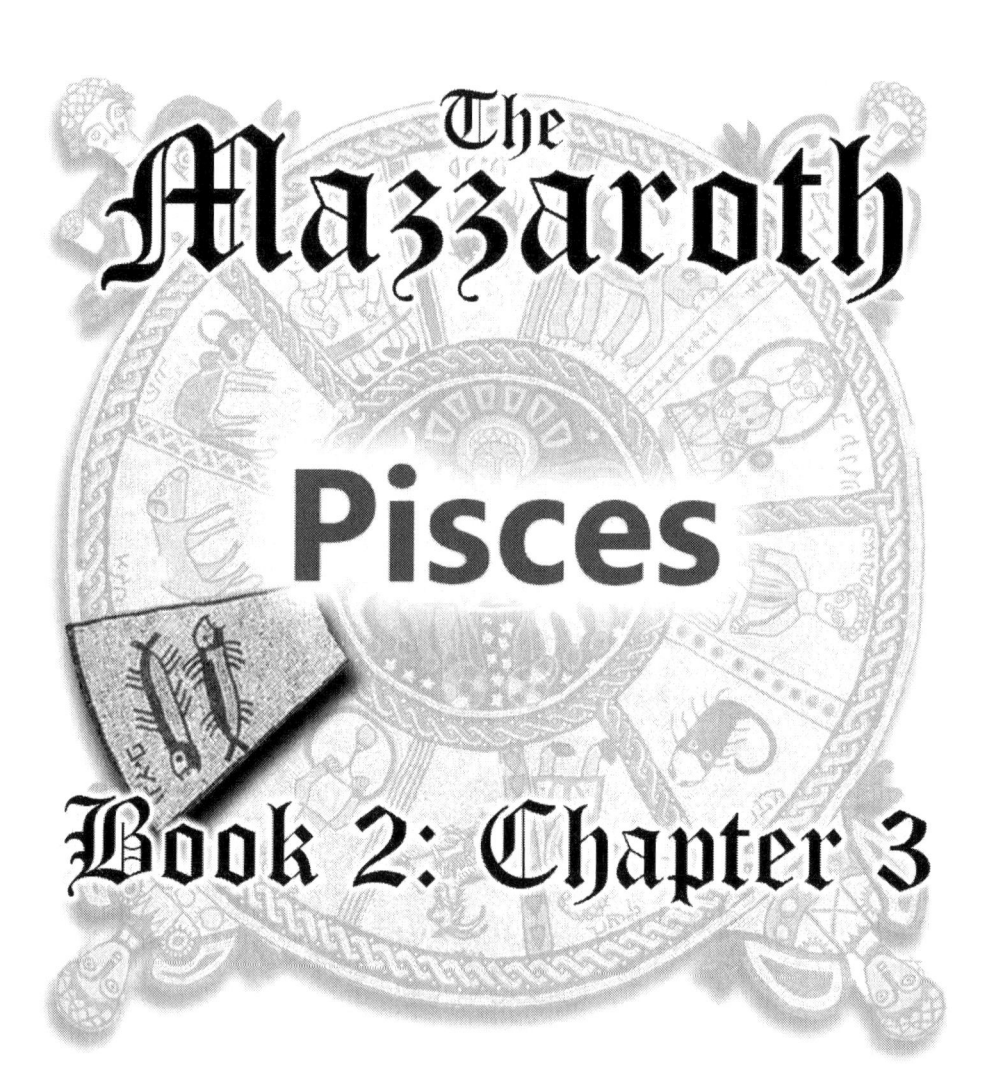

Pisces

The Mazzaroth

Pisces

Book 2: Chapter 3

Short Story: The Two Fish / Two Houses of Israel

The Redeemer's People multiplied, Supported and led by the Lamb, The Bride is exposed on earth, the Bridegroom is exalted. Star names indicate "the fish (multitudes) of those who will follow"- i.e. The chosen of Yahuah (Ps. 115:14).

Tribe of Israel: *Simeon*

Primary star

Al Deramin - means the Quickly-Returning.

Secondary star

Al Phirk - means the Redeemer **Decans (secondary constellations)**

The Band - (that unites the two fish) (Hos. 11:4, Ephesians 2:15)

Andromeda - The Chained Woman (who will be delivered).

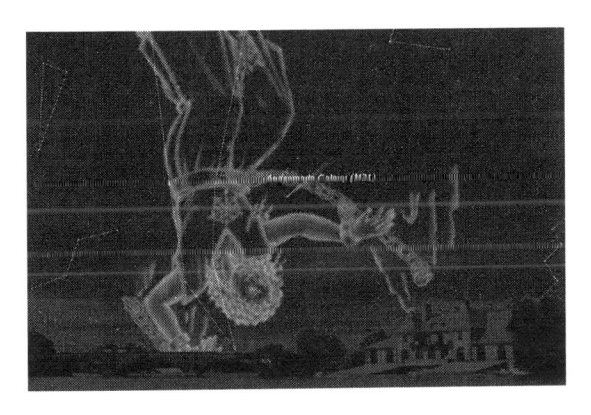

Cepheus - The Crowned King.

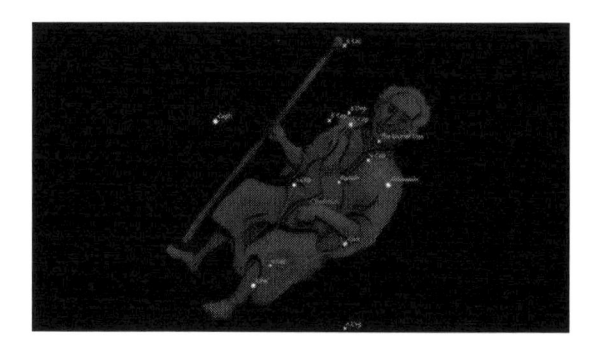

Overall story told by Pisces

The unusual feature of this constellation is that the two fish are drawn as being held together by a band. This band is a shadow picture of the Messiah who makes out of the two houses of Israel (the two fish) one new "man" or Remnant Israel.

> **Ephesians 2**
> [14] For Yahusha is our peace, who hath made both (Jews and Gentiles) one, and hath broken down (the death decrees in The Law which were) the middle wall of partition between us; [15] Having abolished (nailed the death decrees to the cross) in his flesh which were the *cause of the enmity* (our fear of the death) *toward* the law, commandments and ordinances; for to make in himself of two, one new man, so making peace.

Pisces, of course, is symbolic of the redeemed of Yahuah, His called out sons. Yahusha told His disciples, "I will make you fishers of men."

The shackles (on the Bride/Andromeda) of sin weigh down all mankind and have need of being broken. Isaiah, spoken by Yahusha as He began His ministry, were cited. "He has sent Me to proclaim release to the captives, and recovery of sight to the blind, to set free those who are downtrodden, to proclaim the favorable year of Yahuah." In Pisces, we see the conflict of man, a conflict that Yahusha triumphantly overcame.

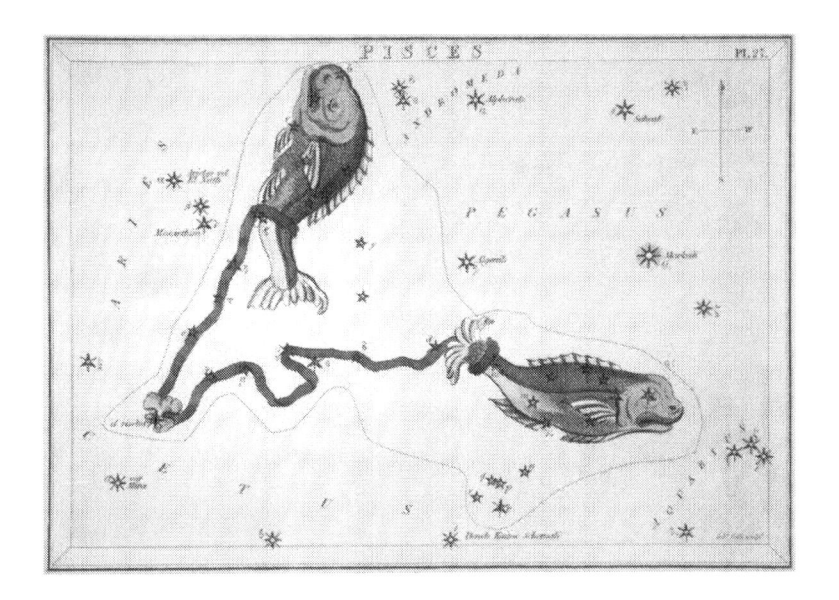

Aries

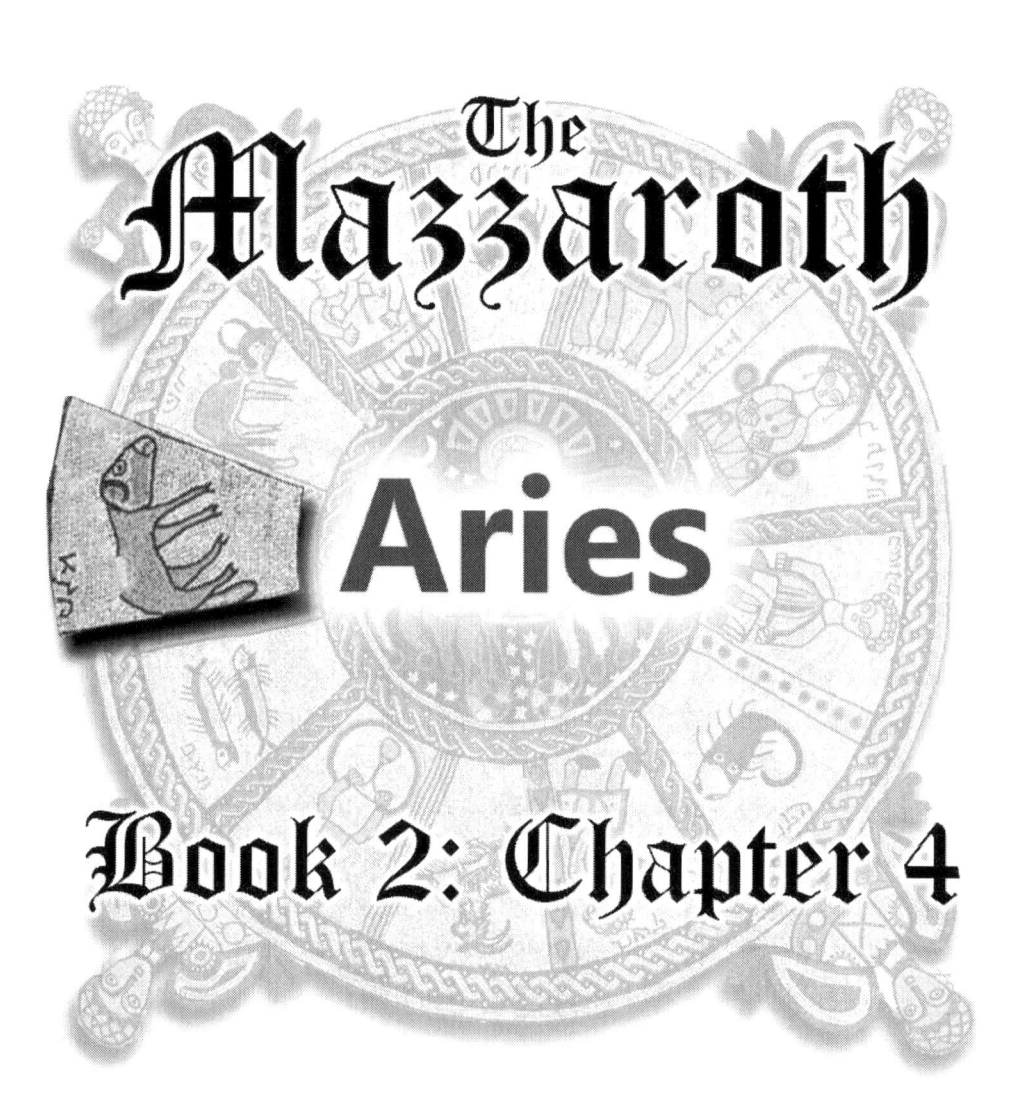

The Mazzaroth

Aries

Book 2: Chapter 4

Short Story: The Ram / Lamb

The Lamb is found worthy, the Bride (after being released from chains of sin) is made ready, Satan is bound, the Breaker (of chains) triumphs. Brightest star El Nath = wounded, slain; (others similar).

Tribe of Israel: *Gad*

Primary star

El Nath - wounded, slain; (others similar).

Secondary star

Schedir - (Hebrew) = freed.

Third star

Caph - The Branch (of victory). (Is. 54:1-8, 62:3-5).

Decans (secondary constellations)

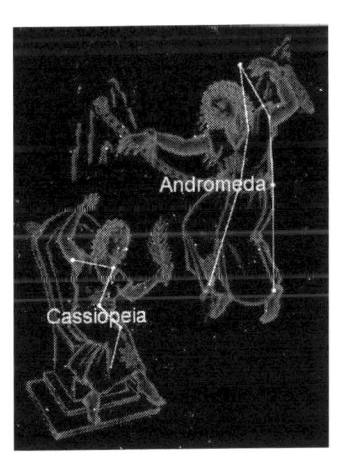

Cassiopcia - The Beautiful Enthroned Woman. The captive woman (Andromeda) now delivered.

Cetus - the sea monster (Revelation 13). The enemy bound.

Perseus - The Breaker. Hebrew = Peretz. Greek = Perses (Micah 2:13). Winged feet = coming swiftly. Head he carries wrongly called Medusa by Greeks; Hebrew Rosh Satan = Head of the Adversary.

Overall story told by Pisces

Let me quote from Kenneth Fleming, in God's Voice in the Stars:

> *"Aries is the last of the signs in the second group, which includes Capricorn, Aquarius, Pisces, and Aries. This quartet of signs pictures the blessings of salvation. Capricorn signifies the blessings of salvation. Capricorn signifies the blessing of life from death. Aquarius pictures the blessing of*

salvation's fullness. Pisces signifies the delay of the promised blessing. Now in Aries we see the blessing fully realized...

Aries has a most interesting and instructive message for the student of the biblical prophecy and the history of salvation. Aries usually carries the symbol of the ram, but many of the oldest zodiacs portray a lamb (with no horns), and in some ancient zodiacs the lamb has a circular crown on its head... The Hebrew name for Aries was Taleh, which means Lamb, while the Arabic name, Hamal, means Sheep, Gentle, Merciful... In Syriac the name for Aries is Amroo, meaning Lamb. The New Testament in that language uses the same word for the Lord Jesus; John the Baptist cried, "Behold the Lamb of God!" (John 1:29)"

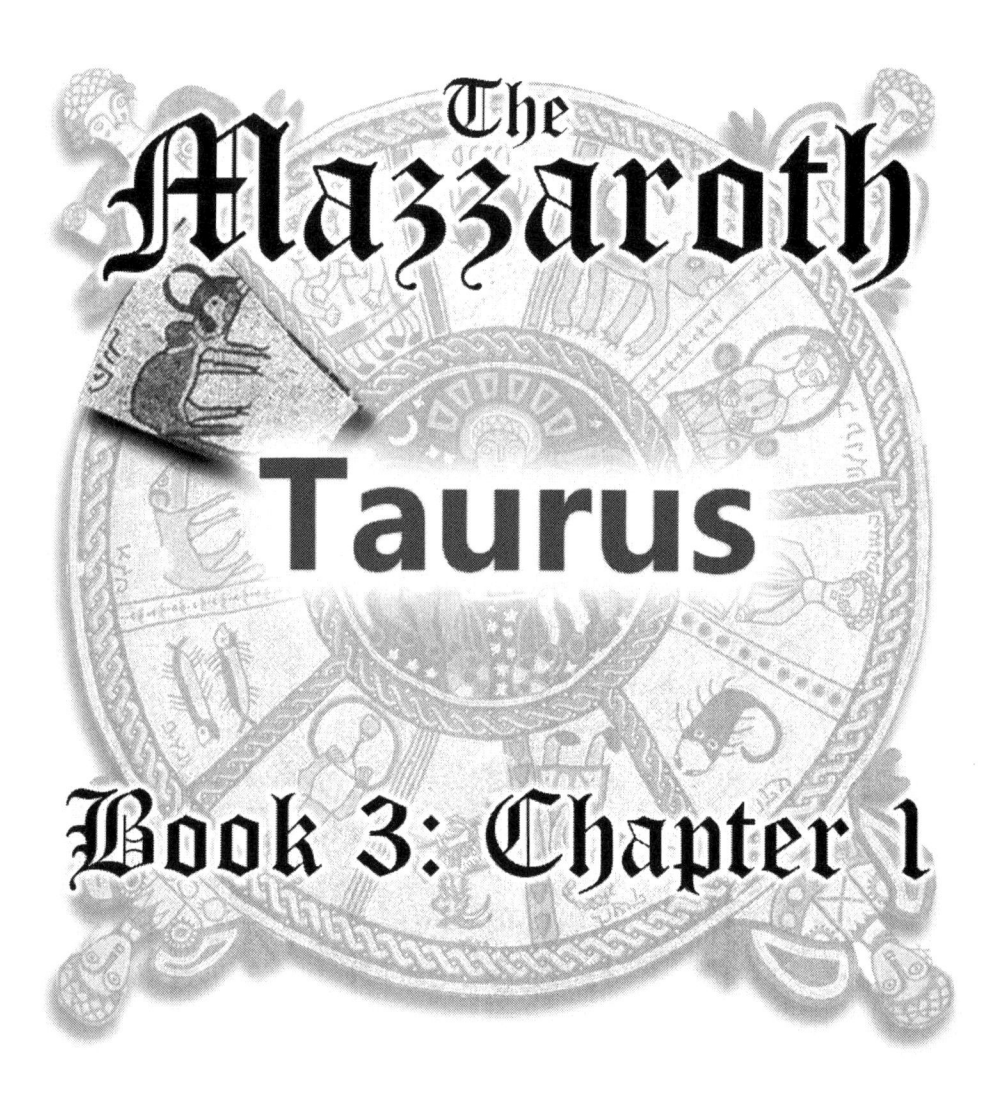

Taurus

The Mazzaroth

Taurus

Book 3: Chapter 1

Short Story: The Bull

The conquering Ruler comes, the sublime Vanquisher, the great Judgment, the ruling Shepherd. The Pleiades = The congregation of the judge.

Tribe of Israel: *Ephraim*

Primary star

Al Nitak - the wounded one.

Secondary star

Capella - she goat

Third star

The Pleiades - The congregation of the judge.

Decans (secondary constellations)

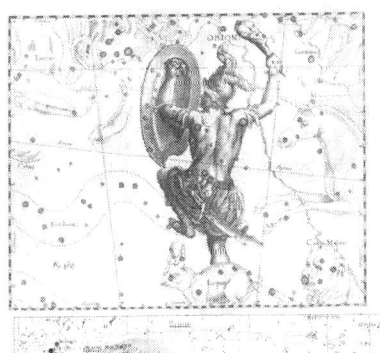

Orion - The coming Prince. Hebrew Oarion = light. He holds a club and the head of "the roaring lion" (1 Pet. 5:8). Betelgeuz = The coming of the branch. Rigol = the foot that crushes. Al Nitak = the wounded one.

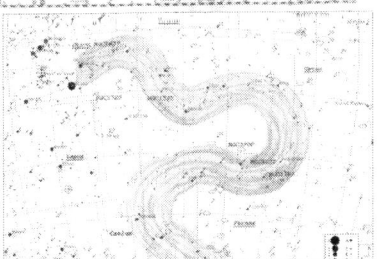

Eridanus - The River of the Judge. Star names refer to "flowing" etc. (Dan. 7:10; Nahum 1:8).

Auriga - The Shepherd (Isaiah 40:10-11). Hebrew root = shepherd. Star Capella (Latin) = she goat.

Overall story told by Taurus

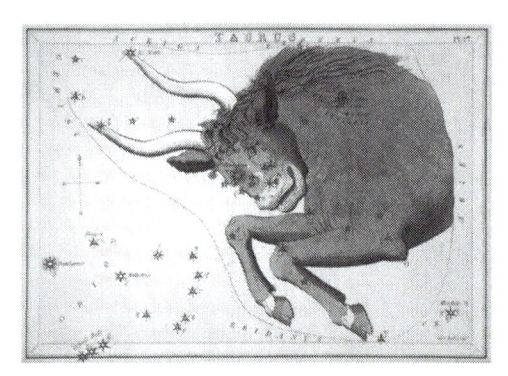

He is a great white bull of the variety of wild ox which has two long forward-pointing golden horns. His forelegs suggest that he is charging forward. On the other hand, he has seven doves on his back (the Seven Sisters), and some have suggested that the bent legs indicate that he is peacefully reclining. Here it is not the Greek myths, but the Book of Enoch (section 4, Chapter 85) which makes it clear what the white bull represents. It is the millennial Kingdom of Yahuah which will soon govern the earth for a thousand years, after the destruction of the wicked.

Gemini

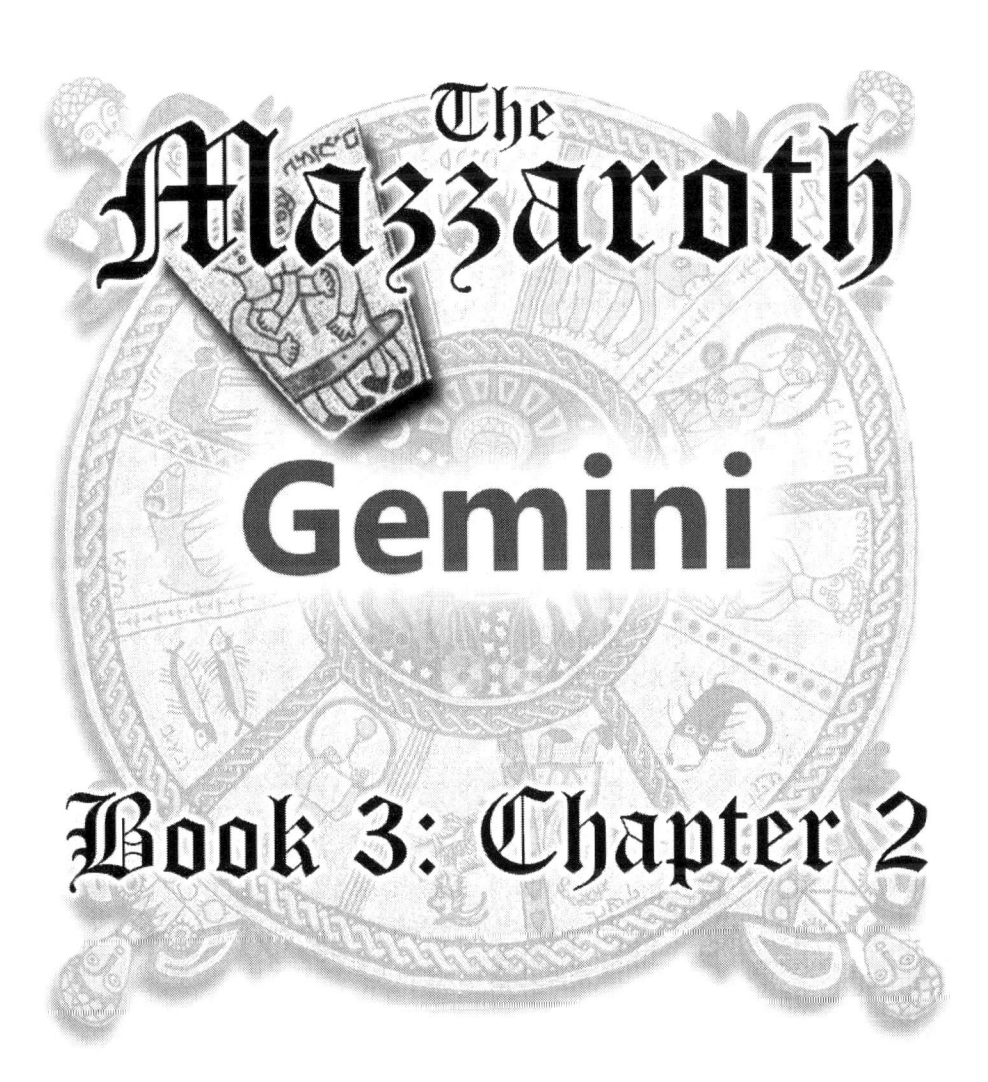

The Mazzaroth

Gemini

Book 3: Chapter 2

Short Story: The Twins

The Marriage of the Lamb, the Enemy is trodden down, the Prince comes in great Glory. There is some confusion of the pictures for this constellation in the different languages, but they generally refer to two people probably referring to the House of Israel and the House of Judah.

Tribe of Israel: *Manasseh*

Primary star

Sirius - is the brightest of all stars. (Is. 9:6).

Secondary star

Star Procyon - Redeemer.

Decans (secondary constellations)

Lepus - The Hare (the enemy); trodden under Orion's foot. Star names refer to "the deceiver" etc.

Creation Cries Out!

Canis Major (The Dog) or Sirius (The Prince). Sirius is the brightest of all stars. (Is. 9:6). And **Canis Minor** - The Second Dog. Star Procyon Redeemer.

Overall story told by Gemini

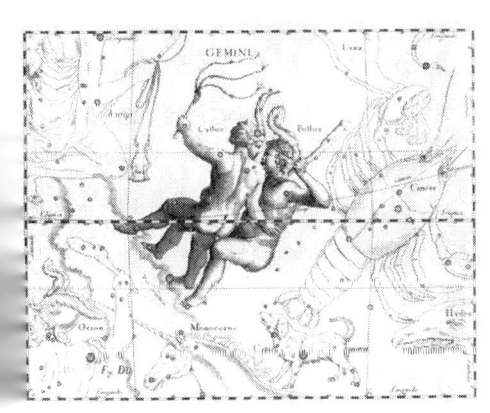

The tenth zodiac constellation is the **Twins** (Gemini), who are two brothers, with one usually being considered immortal and the other mortal. This constellations has many "meanings" depending on the culture looking at it. If we consider the Plan of Salvation this constellation could be in reference to the dual nature of the Messiah. First coming as a man, the suffering servant; then returning divine as the conquering king.

When looking at this constellation in terms of "2000 year ages" it would be symbolic of Adam and Eve.

217

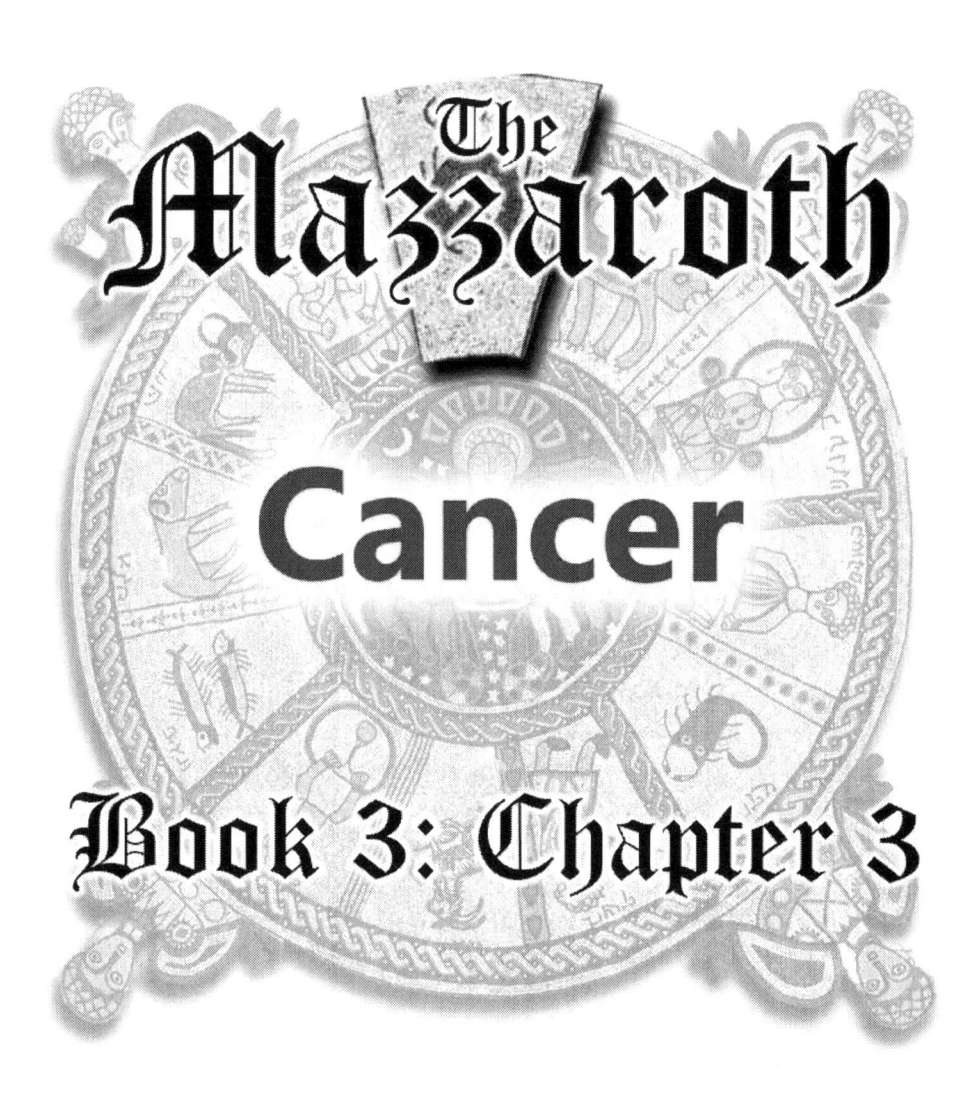

Cancer

The Mazzaroth

Cancer

Book 3: Chapter 3

Short Story: The Crab

The great Bride, the two Houses of Israel and Judah, are brought safely into a united kingdom. There are a variety of pictures for this constellation.

Tribe of Israel: *Issachar*

Primary star

Castor - "the mortal Twin",

Secondary star

Pollux - "the immortal Twin"

Decans (secondary constellations)

Ursa Minor - The Little Bear. No bears found in any ancient Zodiacs. Confusion may be from Hebrew Dohver Sheepfold, Dovh Bear.

Ursa Major - The Great Bear. Possibly "Sheepfold" as Ursa Minor as Al Naish "assembled together"; Dubhe = "Herd of animals or a flock" etc. Many stars similarly named.

Argo - Meaning is the "Return of the travelers".

219

Overall story told by Cancer

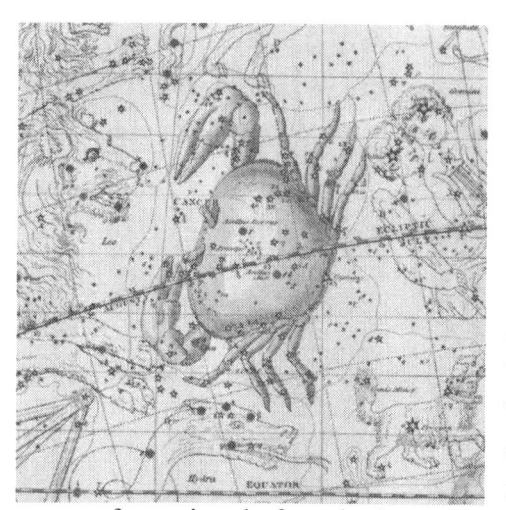

The crab can pick up things in its powerful right hand and deliver them to the desired destination. The Great Deliverer descended into hell and the gates of hell could not prevent him from delivering his people to freedom from the bondage of death and hell. This deliverance has not only happened in the past, it will yet happen in the future just before the beginning of the millennial reign of Yahusha. At that time, the righteous will again be delivered from the grasp of the seven-headed dragon kingdom (which has enslaved much of the entire world). This is where we are currently in the Heavenly Scroll.

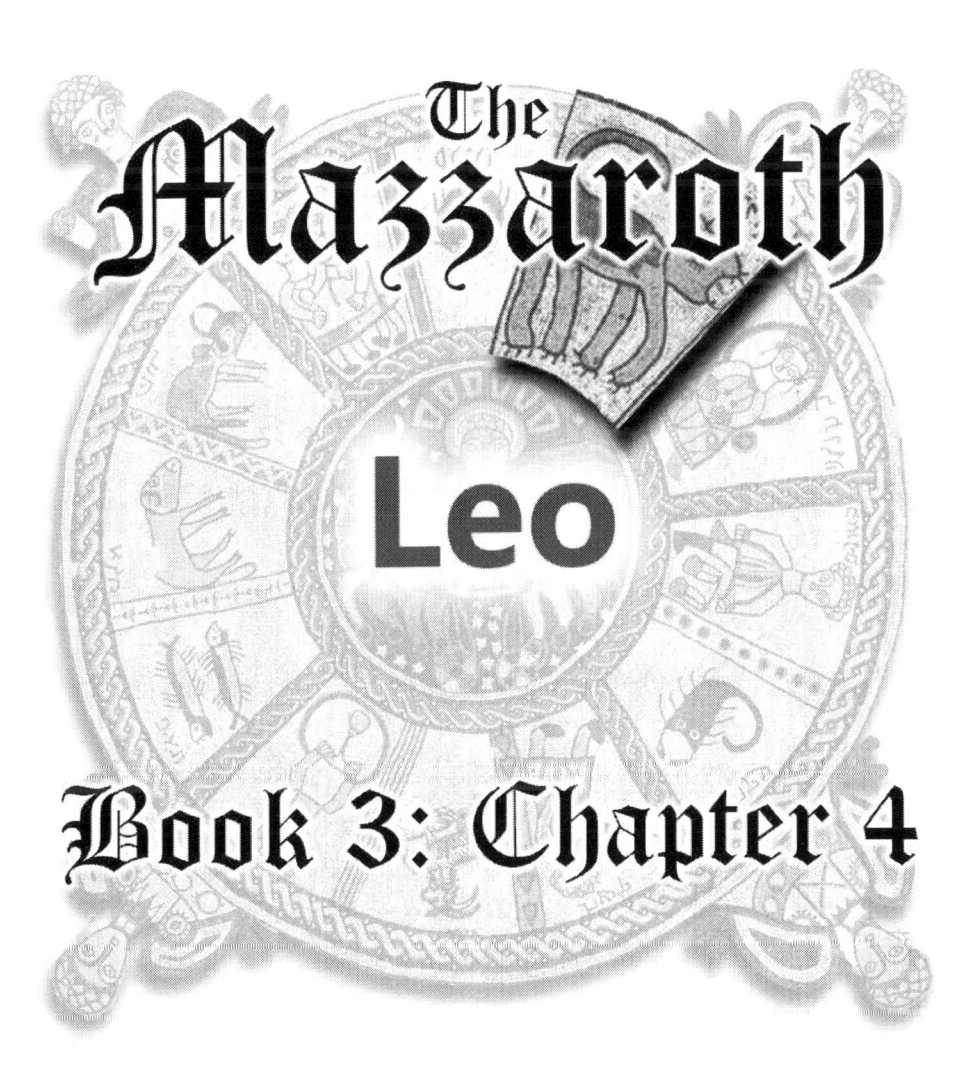

Leo

The Mazzaroth

Leo

Book 3: Chapter 4

Short Story: The Lion of the Tribe of Juda

The Lion King is aroused for rending, the Serpent flees, the Bowl of Wrath is upon him, and his Carcass is devoured. The Lion of the tribe of Judah (Rev. 5:5). Hebrew name means "Lion hunting down its prey". Name in other languages similar. Denebola Judge who cometh.

Tribe of Israel: *Judah*

Primary star

Alpha Regulus - treading under foot

Secondary star

Denebola - the judge comes (Num 24:8-9, Rev 5:5)

Decans (secondary constellations)

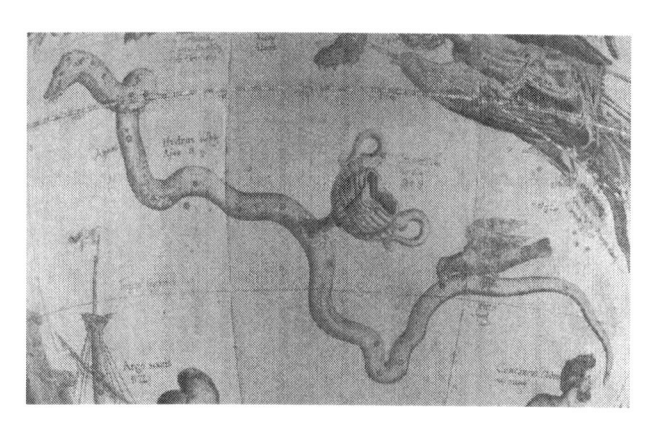

Hydra - The Serpent. Hydra means "He is abhorred". Star names similar.

Crater - The Cup. The pouring out of wrath on the wicked. (Ps 75:8, 11:6, Rev 14:10)

Corvus - The Raven. Birds of prey devouring the Serpent. (Prov 30:17, Rev 19:1)

Overall story told by Leo

The twelfth and last zodiac constellation is the **Lion** (Leo). He is a magnificent Lion which is pouncing on the head of the fleeing giant Water Serpent. In the Egypian planisphere, he is shown actually standing on the serpent. So once again, a hero is attacking a serpent; and apparently focusing on crushing its head.

The religious symbolism of the lion is similar. Yahusha is referred to as the "Lion of the tribe of Judah" (Rev. 5:5), and the lion seems to refer to Yahusha the Messiah in his role as *King*. This constellation most likely refers to the Messiah as King of Kings, reigning all during the coming Millennium, after he has destroyed the beast.

So Isaiah (and the Sphinx) tells us to begin with Virgo and end with Leo, to reveal the "message in the heavens". Let us see what that message contains that has witnessed to all mankind since creation.

The Gospel message contained in the Heavenly Scroll is:

VIRGO: A virgin will give birth to a beautiful glorious and righteous branch. The seed of the woman will be a man of humiliation, to rise to be the desire of nations; and will become exalted first as shepherd then as harvester. *LIBRA:* The scales demand a price to be paid of this seed, a cross to endure; the victim will be slain and purchase a crown. *SCORPIO:* There is a conflict between the seed and the serpent, leading to a struggle with the enemy, the enemy is vanquished. *SAGITTARIUS:* The double-natured seed (servant/king) triumphs as a warrior and pleases the heavens, builds fires of punishment, casts down the dragon. *CAPRICORNUS:* Eternal life comes from his death, he's the Arrow of Yahuah, and he is pierced, yet springs up again in abundant life. *AQUARIUS:* He pours out "living water" from on high, humanity drinks of the heavenly river, and the faithful live again. He is the deliverer of the good news (Gospel), Carrying the wood of the sacrifice over the earth. *PISCES:* The Redeemer's people multiplied, supported and led by the Lamb, The Bride is exposed on earth, and the Bridegroom is exalted. *ARIES:* The Lamb is found worthy, the Bride is made ready, Satan is bound, the strong man triumphs. *TAURUS:* The conquering Ruler comes, the sublime vanquisher, to execute the great judgment, he is the ruling Shepherd King. *GEMINI:* The Marriage of the Lamb, the enemy is trodden down; the Prince comes in great Glory. *CANCER:* The great Bride, the two Houses of Judah and Israel are united; they are brought safely into the kingdom. *LEO:* The Lion King is aroused for rending, the Serpent flees, the Bowl of Wrath is upon him, and his Carcass is devoured. The Lion of the tribe of Judah rules as King.

Truly, "their sound went into all the earth, and their words unto the ends of the world'." Mankind is left with no excuses. Now that we know the REAL meaning of the Zodiac, it becomes obvious why the enemy has made it the focus of perversion!

The Solar Messiah

To the ancients, the signs of the Zodiac correspond to what they called "The Grand Man" that we know as the Messiah. This image of a man is still pictured in modern almanacs with each sign corresponding to a part of his body;

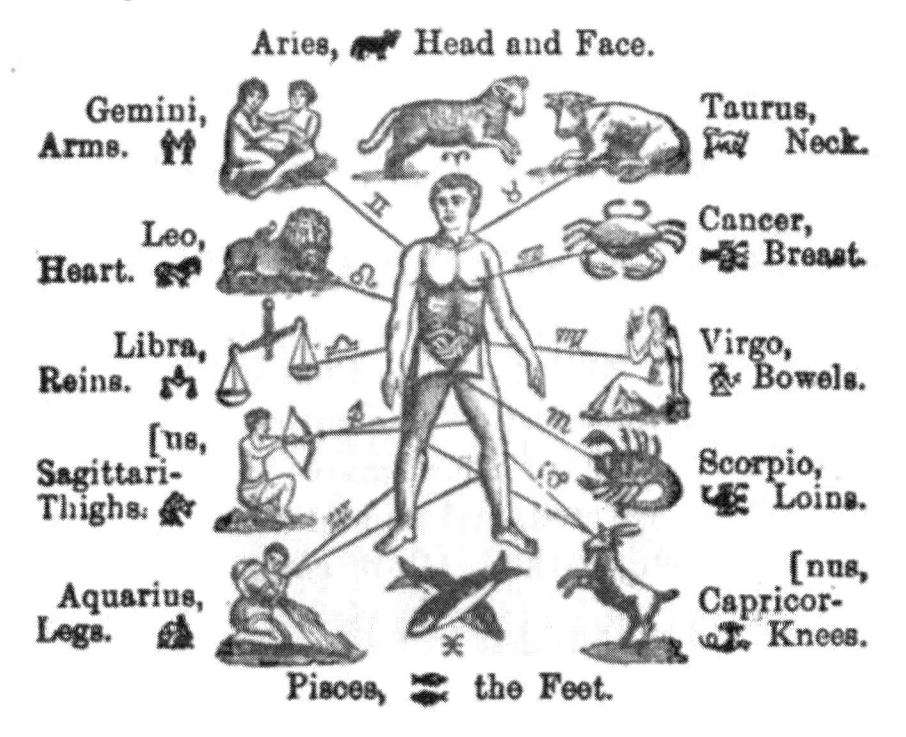

Aries, Head and Face.
Gemini, Arms.
Taurus, Neck.
Leo, Heart.
Cancer, Breast.
Libra, Reins.
Virgo, Bowels.
Sagittarius, Thighs.
Scorpio, Loins.
Aquarius, Legs.
Capricornus, Knees.
Pisces, the Feet.

The Zodiac was the for runner of modern science, astronomy, and medicine. Before modern technology, doctors would study the Natal Chart of their patience to help diagnose illness.

Medical Astrology is the branch of astrology that deals with the workings of the human body. A competent medical astrologer can analyze a person's birth chart and determine bodily strengths and weaknesses, proneness to various disease states, and nutritional deficiencies. In the event of illness or disease, a medical astrologer

225

will use predictive methods to try to determine the severity and duration of the disease. Sometimes a medical astrologer can help determine the course of a disease by the use of a chart called a decumbiture chart.

We see this Messiah figure at the center of the Zodiac Chart. The Sun is a metaphor for him; it is the basis for Leonardo Da Vinci's medicine man and our universal medical symbol.

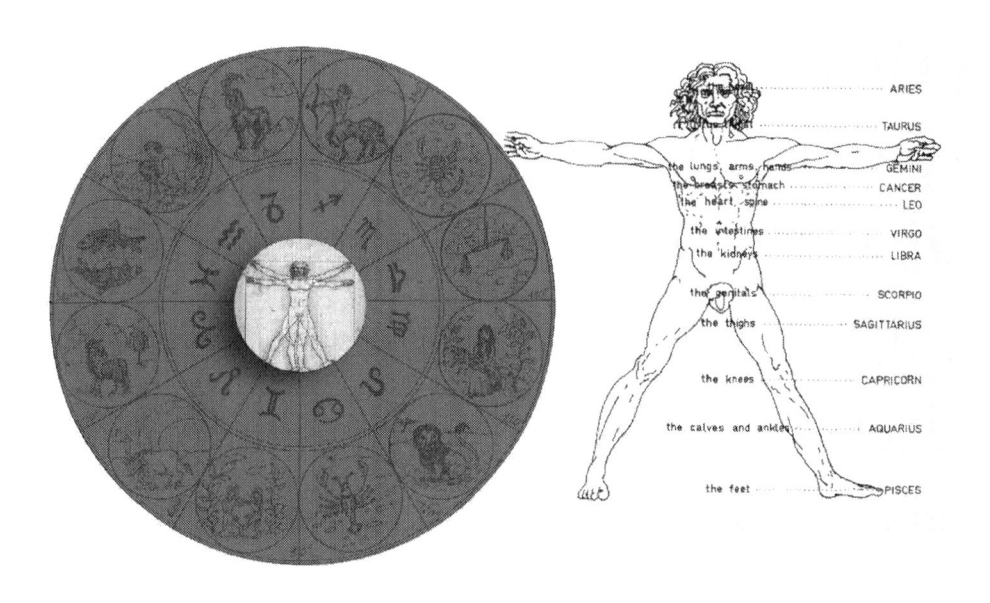

It is this Messiah or Grand Man pictured within the Zodiac that is pointed to by the 12 signs of the Zodiac. As we have demonstrated, this "solar messiah" or Grand Man is Yahusha, the Messiah of Israel, the son of Yahuah.

The "symbol" of the Grand Man or Solar Messiah came to be the center of the Zodiac because the Sun is a metaphor for him. A cutout of the center of the Zodiac became the universal symbol of all the mythical figures and false messiahs humanity created across cultures. Below is an illustration of the origin of the cross, it is taken from the center of the Zodiac.

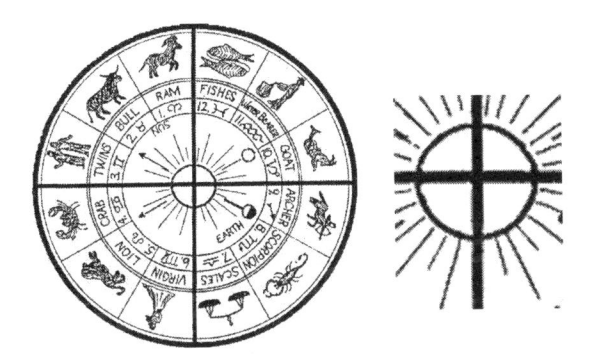

The ancients didn't understand its message and the Cross became the symbol of all the myths made up around this message. All "Christs" are shown with the Sun and the Zodiac "Cross" behind their head. This symbol is what identifies them as "Solar Messiahs".

It remains today the symbol of Jesus H. Christ adorning the tops of churches world-wide.

I will cover this symbol in greater detail throughout this book series. Let us look now at "why" Sun worship became so prevalent in ancient cultures.

The Sun foretells the crucifixion and resurrection

Many of the world's mythical sacrificed god men have their traditional birthday on December 25 which is where we get Christmas. This represents the ancient recognition that (from a perspective in the northern hemisphere) the sun makes a yearly descent southward until December 21 or 22, the winter solstice, when it stops moving southerly for three days and it "hangs" on the North Cross in the sky. After 3 days of appearing to stand still very low on the horizon, the sun then starts to move northward again or is "resurrected". During this time, people back then believed that "God's sun" had "died" for three days and was "born again" on December 25. After December 25, the Sun moves 1 degree, this time north, foreshadowing longer days. And thus it was said, the Sun died on the cross, was dead for 3 days, only to be resurrected or born again.

The Sun is a physical metaphor of the Son

In the Gospel of Luke below, The Messiah's very advent is depicted as a visitation from the "dayspring on high": "Through the tender mercy of our Elohim; whereby the dayspring from on high hath visited us..." The word for "dayspring" or "day" in the original Greek is ἀνατολή or *anatole*, which means "**sunrise, east**." We see a clear picture that the sun in the sky was created by Yahuah as a metaphor of The Messiah. The sun of Yahuah is metaphorically in the heavens a picture of The Son of Yahuah.

> **Luke 1**
> 67 His father Zechariah was filled with the Spirit of Yahuah and prophesied: 68 "Praise be to Yahuah, the Elohim of Israel, because he has come to his people and redeemed them. 69 He has raised up a horn of salvation for us in the house of his servant David 76 And you, my child, will be called a prophet of the Most High; for you will go on before Yahuah to prepare the way for Him, 77 to give his people the knowledge of salvation through the forgiveness of their sins, 78 because of the tender mercy of our God, *by which the rising sun will come to us from (the) heaven(ly scroll)* 79 to shine on those living in darkness and in the shadow of death, to guide our feet into the path of peace."

We see this metaphor used many times tying the role of the sun in the sky to the role of the Messiah on Earth:

> **Matthew 17** - *The Transfiguration*
> 17 After six days Yahusha took with him Peter, James and John the brother of James, and led them up a high mountain by themselves. 2 There he was transfigured before them. His face shone like the sun and his clothes became as white as the light.

> **Revelation 1**
> 16 In his right hand he held seven stars, and coming out of his mouth was a sharp, double-edged sword. His face was like the sun shining in all its brilliance.

Malachi 4
2...the sun of righteousness will rise with healing in its wings.

In these verses Yahusha is symbolized as sunlight:

- A red sunset, signifying Yahusha's bleeding. "This is my blood of the covenant, which is poured out for many." - **Mark 14:24**
- "I have come into the world as a light, so that no one who believes in me should stay in darkness." - **John 12:46**
- "In him was life, and that life was the light of all mankind. The light shines in the darkness, and the darkness has not overcome it. There was a man sent from Yahuah whose name was John. He came as a witness to testify concerning that light, so that through him all might believe. He himself was not the light; he came only as a witness to the light." - **John 1:4-8**
- "The true light that enlightens every man was coming into the world." - **John 1:9**
- "...the Messiah will shine on you." - **Ephesians 5:14**

- "I am the light of the world that every eye will see." - **Revelations 1:7**

If every eye can see this "light of the world," it is understandable that many people in ancient times believed the Messiah to be the sun itself, as they had with numerous gods preceding Yahusha's first coming. It is not only natural but logical that thousands of people in the earliest days of Christianity would have believed Yahusha to be the same as the gods they were already worshipping, the bulk of which possessed attributes of the solar messiah and were often considered to be sun gods to a significant extent.

At lower angles the sun has more atmosphere to punch through, so red sunrises and sunsets appear with increasing frequency. Ancients saw these natural events as their sun god weakening as it was falling and bleeding. We see the sun's metaphor clearly below:

- The sun is the "Light of the World." - **John 8:12**
- The sun is "anointed" when its rays dip into the sea.
- The sun rising in the morning is the "Savior of mankind," as well as the "healer" or "savior" during the day.
- The sun wears a corona, "crown of thorns" or halo.
- The sun "walks on water," describing its reflection. - **John 6:19**
- The sun's "followers," "helpers" or "disciples" are the 12 months and the 12 signs of the zodiac or constellations, through which the sun travels about annually.
- The sun at 12 noon is "Most High" in the sky; thus, "he" begins "his Father's work" at "age" 12.
- The sun enters into each sign of the zodiac at 30°; hence, the "Sun of God" begins his ministry at "age" 30.
- The sun's warmth turns water into wine through ripening grapes.

The Messiah as 'The Son of Man'

The Son of Man in the Gospels can be linked to the constellation Orion. Revelation's description of the Son of Man fits the pattern of stars in the constellation Orion. The star on his right shoulder is bright red (upper left star). The three stars at his waist were later seen as to shadow three wise men who announced the birth of the Messiah.

The Son of Man has a cluster of stars in the background that look like the clouds upon which the Son of Man rides. Astronomical maps show the Milky Way behind the constellation Orion. From earth, they look like clouds.

> **Revelation 1:12-20**
> "Then I turned to see the voice that was speaking to me, and on turning I saw seven golden lamp stands, and in the midst of the lamp stands one like a son of man, clothed with a long robe and with a golden girdle round his breast; his head and his hair were white as white wool, white as snow; his eyes were like a flame of fire, his feet were like burnished bronze, refined as in a furnace, and his voice was like the sound of many waters; in his right hand he held seven stars, from his mouth issued a sharp two-edged sword, and his face was like the sun shining in full strength."
>
> **Revelation 14:14-20**
> "And I looked, and behold a white cloud, and upon the cloud one sat like unto the Son of Man, having on his head a golden crown, and in his hand a sharp sickle."

Orion, as seen in human form, has his right hand holding a sickle or a club or a sword. His left hand could be holding an animal skin, a shield or a bow. The Milky Way is behind him. The arc above him represents the Sun's path. The line going through his waist is the celestial equator which runs parallel to earth's equator.

> **Matthew 17:22-23**
> "As they were gathering in Galilee, Yahusha said to them, 'The Son of Man is to be delivered into the hands of men, and they will kill him, and he will be raised on the third day.' And they were greatly distressed."

When the sun goes below the equator into the dark days, it is said to be delivered to the enemy. While the earth rotates, the stars appear to be moving westerly until they dip below the horizon. Three days later they reappear in the eastern horizon.

Matthew 26:63-64
..."'tell us if you are the Messiah, the Son of Yahuah.' Yahusha said to him, 'You have said so. But I tell you; hereafter you will see the Son of man seated at the right hand of Power, and coming on the clouds of heaven.'"

When facing North, Orion's rising in the East can be seen as rising from the right. Orion appears at the right hand of the Sun.

The constellation Orion is clearly declared to be a creation of Yahuah in scripture, further supporting the truth that the Zodiac and all the signs are His creation.

Amos 5:8
[Seek him] that maketh the seven stars and Orion, and turneth the shadow of death into the morning, and maketh the day dark with night: that calleth for the waters of the sea, and poureth them out upon the face of the earth: Yahuah [is] his name:

Job 38:3
Canst thou bind the sweet influences of Pleiades, or loose the bands of Orion?

Job 9:9
Which maketh Arcturus, Orion, and Pleiades, and the chambers of the south.

Job 38:31-32
Canst thou bind the sweet influences of Pleiades, or loose the bands of Orion?

Psalms 127:4
As arrows [are] in the hand of a mighty man; so [are] children of the youth.

The Messiah as the Bread of Heaven

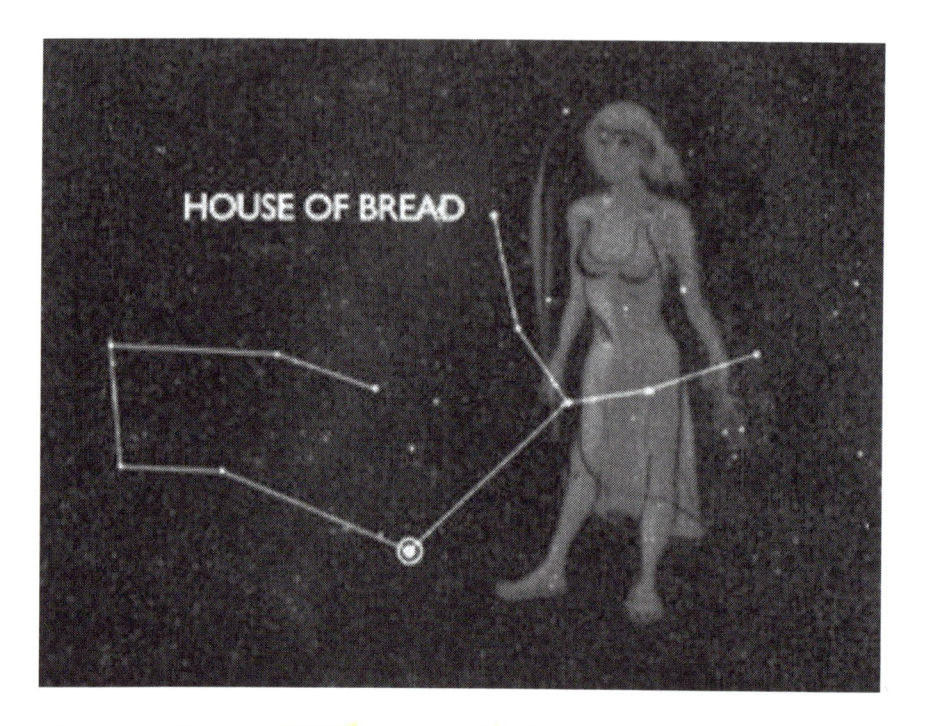

The constellation Virgo is associated with the heavenly bread. We see Yahusha the Messiah declare he is the living bread that came down from heaven, the one whom Yahuah has given his "seal of approval". Could that "seal of approval" be the *Original Revelation* found in the Gospel message of the Zodiac by the constellation Virgo? Yahusha encourages the Jews below to "believe in the one whom Yahuah has sent" that as I have demonstrated in this book was revealed by the Zodiac in the heavens.

Below in this one passage of scripture Yahusha references the living bread (Virgo/Manna) in heaven and the Son of Man (Orion):

John 6
25 When they found him on the other side of the lake, they asked him, "Rabbi, when did you get here?" 26 Yahusha answered, "Very truly I tell you, you are looking for me, not because you saw the signs I performed but because you ate the loaves and had your fill. 27 Do not work for food that spoils, but for food that endures to eternal life, *which the Son of Man* will give you. For on him Yahuah the Father has placed his seal of approval." 28 Then they asked him, "What must we do to do the works Yahuah requires?" 29 Yahusha answered, *"The work of Yahuah is this: to believe in the one he has sent."* ... 32 Yahusha said to them, "Very truly I tell you, it is not Moses who has given you *the bread from heaven (manna)*, but it is my Father who gives you the *true bread from heaven. 33 For the bread of Yahuah is the bread that comes down from heaven and gives life to the world."*

The Four Horesman

Revelations 4:7 The first living creature was like a lion, the second was like an bull, the third had a face like a man, the fourth was like a flying eagle.

Ezekiel 1:10 Their faces looked like this: Each of the four had the face of a man, and on the right side each had the face of a lion, and on the left the face of an bull; each also had the face of an eagle.

C = cardinal
F = fixed

Cardinal signs burst forward as horses.
Fixed signs sit as horsemen.

Beast 1 bull = Rider Taurus
Horse = Aries Spring

Beast 2 lion = Rider Leo
Horse = Cancer Summer

Beast 3 Eagle = Rider Scorpio
Horse = Libra Fall

Beast 4 Man = Rider Aquarius
Horse = Capricorn Winter

The 4 horses are the four cardinal points Spring, Summer, Fall, Winter

The 4 faces of the beasts (horsemen) are the 4 fixed signs Taurus (bull,) Leo (lion,) Scorpio (eagle), Aquarius (man)

CHAPTER 9
ENOCH'S ZODIAC EXPLAINED

Chapter 9 – Enoch's Zodiac Explained

Before we begin, let me make it very clear that this is not "Astrology" in the sense of divination, fortune telling, card reading, horoscopes, palm reading, magic, or any other abominable practice that has corrupted the Mazzaroth (Zodiac). What I am bringing to light in this book is <u>*HISTORY*</u> and the meaning of the stars and constellations. We are looking to Yahuah's creation to find the "secrets contained" therein. These secrets, which Yahuah had written into the stars at creation, were revealed to Enoch.

> **<u>E. W. Bullinger, (Witness of the Stars, Bullinger, p.9).</u>**
>
> *"If we turn to history and tradition, we are at once met with the fact that the Twelve Signs are the same, both as to the meaning of their names and as to their order in all the ancient nations of the world. The Chinese, Chaldean and Egyptian records go back to more than 2,000 years B.C. Indeed, the Zodiacs in the temples of Denderah and Esneh, in Egypt, are doubtless copies of Zodiacs still more ancient, which, from internal evidence, must be placed nearly 4,000 years B.C., when the summer solstice was in Leo."*
>
> *"Josephus hands down to us what he gives as the traditions of his own nation, corroborated by his reference to eight ancient Gentile authorities, whose works are lost. He says that they all assert that 'God gave the antediluvians (pre-flood ancestors) such long life that they might perfect those things which they had invented in astronomy.'"*

Bullinger goes on:

> *"Ancient Persian and Arabian traditions ascribe its [the Zodiac/Mazzaroth] invention to Adam, Seth, and Enoch.*

> *Josephus asserts that it originated in the family of Seth; and he says that the children of Seth, and especially Adam, Seth, and Enoch, that their revelation might not be lost as to the coming judgments of Water and Fire, made two pillars (one of brick, the other of stone), describing the whole of the predictions of the stars upon them, and in case the brick pillar should be destroyed by the flood, the stone would preserve the revelation" (p.10).*

The reality is that the Zodiac is not some evil pagan invention, or a function of mythology. Mythology was invented by man (to try and understand the Zodiac and turn it into god worship). Not the other way around. The Zodiac has been corrupted, and it is used for all types of nonsense and idolatry. However, it was created by Yahuah, then given to Enoch, and passed down through the ages; because there really are *"secrets preserved in the The Heavenly Scroll"*. The word for "heaven" means "the place where the stars are" in Hebrew referring to The Mazzaroth/Zodiac.

We see in Enoch Chapter 9, that these secrets were then given to all mankind in by the Watchers:

> **ENOCH CHAPTER 9**
> 4. And they said to the Lord of the ages: 'Lord of lords, God of gods, King of kings, ⟨and God of the ages⟩ , the throne of Thy glory (standeth) unto all the generations of the ages, and Thy name holy and glorious and blessed unto all the ages! 5. Thou hast made all things, and power over all things hast Thou: and all things are naked and open in Thy sight, and Thou seest all things, and nothing can hide itself from Thee. 6. Thou seest what Azâzêl hath done, who hath taught all unrighteousness on earth and revealed the eternal secrets which were (preserved) in The Heaven Scroll, which men were striving to learn.

In Genesis, Yahuah created the stars as "signs" as they are arranged into constellations and they are to give "light" on the Earth.

Light is the physical metaphor for Spiritual Truth.

> **Genesis 1:14**
> 14Then Yahuah said, "Let there be lights in the expanse of the heavens to separate the day from the night, and let them be for signs (constellations) and [also] for seasons and [also] for days and [also] years (The Heavenly Scroll is a Diving Clock); 15 and let them [also] be for lights in the expanse of the The Heavenly Scroll to give light (spiritual truth) on the earth"

So not only do they (*the constellations*) give off physical light, they pour forth speech and reveal spiritual truth:

> **Psalm 19**
> The Heavenly Scroll (Mazzaroth/Zodiac) declare the glory of Yahuah; the sky (Shamayim/Zodiac) displays his handiwork. 2 Day after day it (Mazzaroth/Zodiac) speaks out; night after night it (The Heavenly Scroll) reveals His greatness. 3 There is no actual speech or word, nor is its voice literally heard. 4 Yet its (Mazzaroth/Zodiac) voice echoes throughout the earth; its words carry to the distant horizon.

Mazzaroth in Hebrew means constellations of the Zodiac. From ***Franz Delitzsch, Biblical Commentary on the Book of Job, Volume 2, T. & T. Clark, 1866, p. 324.***

> ***Mazzaroth*** *(Mazarot מַזָּרוֹת, LXX μαζουρωθ) is a hapax legomenon (i.e., a word appearing only once in a text) of the Hebrew Bible, found in Job 38:31-32. The similar word mazalot (מַזָּלוֹת) in 2 Kings 23:3-5 may be related. The word's precise meaning is uncertain, but <u>its context is that of astronomical constellations, and it is often interpreted as a term for the zodiac or the constellations thereof.</u>*

We see this word 'Mazzaroth' or the Zodiac in the book of Job as he declares that Yahuah is the author and specifically names a few of the signs found in the Zodiac.

Job 38:31-32
31 "Can you bind the (7 star) cluster of the Pleiades, Or loose the belt of Orion? 32 Can you bring out Mazzaroth (the Zodiac) in its season? Or can you guide the (Zodiac sign of the) Great Bear with its cubs (Zodiac sign of the Little Bear)?

We see King David confirm this fact, that Yahuah is the author of the Zodiac, and that they declare The Creator's Glory:

Psalms 19:1
The Heavenly Scroll (the Mazzaroth/Zodiac) declare the glory of Yahuah

We see David declare the Zodiac proclaims the glory of Yahuah and His handiwork. Sha'ul understood this, and further defined "the glory of Yahuah" is Yahusha...

2 Corinthians 4:6
For it is Yahuah who once said, "Let light shine out of darkness," who has made his light shine in our hearts, the light of the knowledge of Yahuah's glory shining in the face of the Messiah Yahusha.

Put these two verses together; replace "*glory of Yahuah*" in Psalms 19:1 with "Yahusha" as Sha'ul explained and we get:

Psalms 19:1
The Heavenly Scroll (the Mazzaroth/Zodiac) declares Yahusha!

Exactly! There is only one "future" foretold in the Zodiac written in the stars, and that is Yahusha's... Obviously the watchers showed this to "women" in the earliest days of humanity and fooled them into thinking everyone's future is foretold in the stars resulting in such things as horoscopes! So the watchers showed secrets that were true, then used that truth to twist the Zodiac into idolatry.

The Mazzaroth/Zodiac is the Original Gospel of Yahusha the Messiah! All the Gospels (*Mazzaroth, 4 Gospels in the NT, and the Gospel of Revelation*) tell the exact same story and Plan of Salvation! However, the Heavenly Scroll (*Zodiac*) is the most complete covering both the first and second coming of Yahusha.

We often wonder "where did mankind learn about the Zodiac, the names of the stars, and names of the constellations?" We are misled today by the Christian Church to believe the Zodiac is "evil" and given to us by the Greeks. While the Greeks did create and center their mythology on the Zodiac and pervert it even further, they were not the authors. The Greeks, in fact, borrowed the Zodiac from the Hebrews as it was originally given to Enoch

> **Enoch 35:3**
> I blessed Yahuah of glory, who had made those great and splendid signs (Mazzaroth), that they (the signs of the Zodiac) might display the magnificence of his works to angels and to the souls of men; and that these might glorify all his works and operations; might see the effect of his power; might glorify the great labor of his hands; and bless him forever."

Every prophet foretold The Plan of Salvation by reading The Heavenly Scroll.

Isaiah 9:6-7

"For to us a child is born (*VIRGO*), to us a son (of man) is given (*ORION*), and the government shall be on his shoulders (*TAURUS*) and he will be called Wonderful Counselor (*AQUARIUS*), (the perfect image of) Mighty God (*CAPRICORNUS*), (fore) Father of Everlasting (life) (*CAPRICORNUS*), and Prince of Peace (*CANCER*)." There will be no end to the increase of His government or of peace, on the Throne of David and over His Kingdom, to establish it (*SAGITTARIUS*) and to uphold it with justice and righteousness from then on and forevermore (*LEO*).

We see then, the word Zodiac would be of Hebrew origin not Greek. In Hebrew the word Zodiac is derived from the primitive

Hebrew root 'zodi' and 'sodi' meaning "the way" or "step". According to scripture, the Mazzaroth (Zodiac) proclaims "the way" of salvation from the foundation of the world! It foretells the life story of the Messiah Yahusha. Yahusha also referred to "the way" to describe his example in the same way.

Another Hebrew root in the etymology chain is 'sode' meaning "secret counsel", a circle of friends, a council of familiar conversation with The Creator. The Divine Counsel.

http://studybible.info/strongs/H5475

Brown-Driver-Briggs' Hebrew Definitions of 'sode'

סוד

1. council, counsel, assembly
a. council (of familiar conversation)
1. divan, circle (of familiar friends)
2. assembly, company
b. counsel
1. counsel (itself)
2. secret counsel
3. familiar converse, intimacy (with God)

From the word יסד 'yâsad' meaning 'to establish, appoint, ordain a foundation.

Notice in Thayer's Greek Lexicon, Yahusha brought this knowledge of The Divine Counsel (Zodiac) with him!

Thayer's Greek Lexicon

STRONGS NT 305: ἀναβαίνω

that those persons are figuratively said ἀναβεβηκέναι εἰς τόν οὐρανόν, who have penetrated the heavenly mysteries: John 3.13, cf. Deuteronomy 30:12; Proverbs 24:27 (); Baruch 3.29. But in these latter passages also the expression is to be understood literally. And as respects John 3.13, it must be remembered that Christ brought his knowledge of the divine counsels with him

The Heavenly Scroll is the foundation of the Earthly Scroll and all prophesies. So the signs of the Zodiac (from Zodi) would be a ***The Divine Counsel***, circle of "friends" in secret counsel, and intimacy with Yahuah. Exactly what Enoch said, they are "secrets of Yahuah preserved in the heavens".

We see the word '*yasad*' used by Job referring to the "secret of Yahuah" established before the creation of man:

> **Job 15**
> 7 Art thou the first man that was born? or wast thou made before the hills? 8 Hast thou heard *the secret of Yahuah*?

So to get the full sense of the meaning for Zodiac, looking at the various languages and their meanings and roots I offer the following definition:

> **Definition: Zodiac** – The Divine Counsel. The arrangement of constellations or signs as given to Enoch by the messenger of Yahuah. A circuit or circle the sun appears to travel through the 12 signs along the ecliptic over the course of a year. A company of "signs" in close deliberation, consulting together to hold a "secret". "The secret preserved in the heavens/Heavenly Scroll", a familiar conversation with Elohim. The Original Revelation, and the ordained foundation of the Plan of Salvation appointed and establish by Yahuah, <u>written into the stars.</u>

The book of Job declares Yahuah the author of the Zodiac or Mazzaroth:

> **Job 9:9-10**
> 9 who made the Bear and Orion, the Pleiades and the chambers of the south; 10 who does great things beyond searching out, and marvelous things beyond number

John the revelator was told "see" the Lion of the Tribe of Judah has triumphed. What was John looking at that he could "see" the triumph of the Lion?

> **Revelation 5:5**
> 5and one of the elders said to me, "Stop weeping; behold (the Heavenly Scroll), the Lion that is from the tribe of Judah

(Sign of Leo), the Root of David, has overcome (the serpent) so as to open the book and its seven seals." 6 And I saw between the throne (with the four living creatures) and the elders a Lamb standing, as if slain, having seven horns and seven eyes, which are the seven Spirits of God, sent out into all the earth....

Was John given the understanding of the Mazzaroth, the secrets of the Zodiac? Could it be the "book/scroll" in Heaven is the Zodiac?

Revelation 6:14
13 and the stars of The Heavenly Scroll (sky/shamayim) fell to the earth, as a fig tree casts its unripe figs when shaken by a great wind. 14 The sky (Hebrew 8064: *shamayim* i.e. Zodiac) was split apart like a scroll when it is rolled up! ... The Heavenly Scroll

Isaiah 34:4
All the stars in the Heavenly Scroll (sky/Shamayim) will be dissolved and the heavens (Hebrew 8064: *shamayim* i.e. Zodiac) rolled up like a scroll; all the starry host (constellations that host stars) will fall like withered leaves from the vine, like shriveled figs from the fig tree.

We have already shown that yes, the Zodiac is, in fact, the Heavenly Scroll and each constellation falls as Yahusha reads the scroll and it is shown they are each fulfilled in him.

Enoch's Zodiac in detail

We know from the book of Enoch that Yahuah revealed the Mazzaroth (Zodiac) to him personally "face to face" and revealed the secrets contained within. Enoch then preserved this knowledge in what is known as The Enoch Zodiac or Ancient Hebrew Zodiac called the Heavenly Scroll.

In Enoch's Zodiac, *the Ancient Hebrew Zodiac*, we see the 12 signs/constellations displayed in reverse order. The Enoch Zodiac was literally a "clock" or timepiece showing the progression of 2,000 year 'ages'.

We see in this Ancient Hebrew Zodiac, 4 creatures before the throne and "he who sits on the throne" in the middle. There are 24 stars surrounding the throne along with the moon. These 4 creatures were signs in the Zodiac. Each of the 12 signs was associated with one of the 12 tribes of Israel.

This original revelation of Enoch revealed in the Enoch Zodiac, became the architectural structure reflected in the camp of Israel in the desert.

Below is an illustration of the Israelite's camp, and we see it is an identical reflection of the center of Enoch's Zodiac:

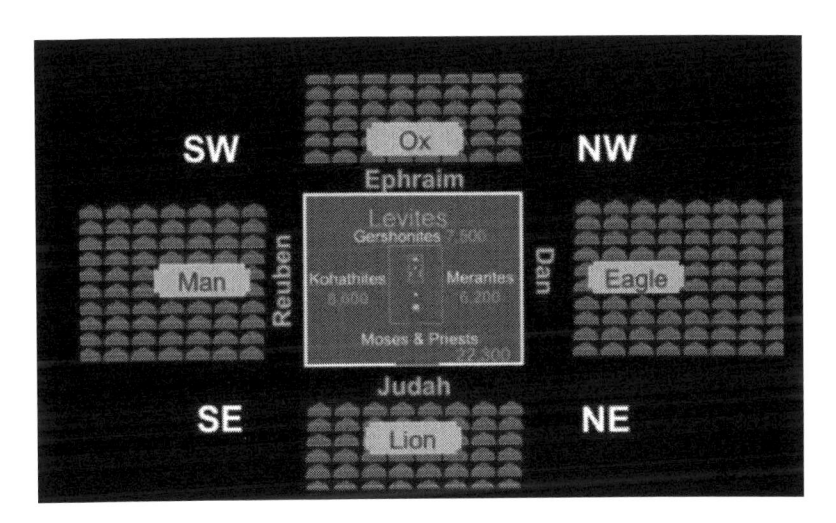

In camp, the Tabernacle rested in the middle. The Camp of Judah, composed of 3 Tribes, rested on the East, with its Standard bearing the figure of a **LION (Leo)**. The Camp of Ephraim, composed of 3 Tribes, rested on the West, with its Standard bearing the figure of an **OX (Taurus)**. The Camp of Reuben, composed of 3 Tribes, rested on the South, with its Standard bearing the figure of a **MAN (Aquarius)**. The Camp of Dan, composed of 3 Tribes, rested on the North, with its Standard bearing the figure of an **EAGLE (Scorpio, who becomes and Eagle after being shot with a bow)**.

Therefore, the Tabernacle in the center of the Camp, the place of Yahuah's Presence, was surrounded and protected by Standards that bore the figures of Ezekiel's and John's "Living Creatures." Like the Camp, the **Heavenly Scroll** also contains 4 books with 3 chapters each as I demonstrated earlier.

John reveals the meaning of Enoch's Zodiac

John the Revelator was told "see", that the Lion of the Tribe of Judah has triumphed. As we now understand, that was the message proclaimed in the Mazzaroth/Zodiac. The story told by the heavenly signs ends with the triumph of Leo and the defeat of the serpent. What was John looking at that he could "see" the triumph of the Lion? John was confirming the shadow picture of Enoch's Zodiac in great detail.

Notice below in the center of Enoch's Zodiac is the Lamb (with a crown on his head) standing before his throne with what appears to be a book perched on a pedestal, surrounded by 4 beasts, and exactly 24 stars (elders). The four beasts have their mouth open as if to sing "Holy Holy Holy" before the throne. The stars have fallen before the throne. This is what John was told to look at and "behold"…

> Revelation 5:5
> 5 and one of the elders said to me, "Stop weeping; *behold (Enoch's Zodiac)*, *(Leo)* the Lion that is from the tribe of Judah, the Root of David, has overcome so as to open the book (Zodiac/Heavenly Scroll) and its seven seals." 6And I saw *(now John describes the center of the Enoch Zodiac)* between the throne *(with the four living creatures)* and the elders a Lamb standing, as if slain, having seven horns and seven eyes, which are the seven Spirits of Yahuah, sent out into all the earth….

We see in Revelation Chapter 4, that there are 4 creatures (Lion – Leo, Ox – Taurus, Man – Aquarius, Eagle – Scorpio) that confirm the exact physical shadow picture of the Tabernacles in the wilderness. In the camping and marching order of Israel in the

Wilderness, there was a fixed relation of the Twelve signs of the Zodiac and the 12 Tribes of Israel. Below, John reveals the secrets of the Enoch Zodiac as he was shown the secrets preserved in the heavens, the following description is identical to the Enoch Zodiac.

Revelation 4:6-11

6 and before the throne there was as it were a sea of glass, like crystal. And around the throne, on each side of the throne, are four living creatures, full of eyes in front and behind: 7 the first living creature like a lion (***Leo***), the second living creature like an ox (***Taurus***), the third living creature with the face of a man (***Aquarius***), and the fourth living creature like an eagle in flight (Scorpio which turns into an Eagle and flies away). 8 And the four living creatures (representing the tribes of Ephraim, Dan, Judah, and Reuben), each of them with six wings, are full of eyes all around and within, and day and night they never cease to say (to Yahuah),

"Holy, holy, holy, is the Yahuah Elohim Almighty, who was and is and is to come!"

9 And [then] whenever the living creatures give glory and honor and thanks to him (Yahusha) who is seated on the throne, who lives forever and ever (they don't worship Yahusha, they give him praise), 10 the twenty-four elders fall down (notice the 24 stars have fallen before the King in the center of the Enoch Zodiac) before him who is seated on the throne and worship (bow down in respect for authority) him who lives forever and ever.

Ezekiel's vision of the Enoch Zodiac

We see in Ezekiel Chapter 1, another exact representation of the Enoch Zodiac.

Ezekiel Chapter 1

[4] As I watched, I noticed a windstorm coming from the north—an enormous cloud, with lightning flashing, such that bright light rimmed it and came from it like glowing amber from the middle of a fire. [5] In the fire were what looked like four living beings. In their appearance they had human form... [15] Then I looked, and I saw one wheel on the ground beside each of the four beings. [16] The appearance of the wheels and their construction was like gleaming jasper, and all four wheels looked alike. Their structure was like a wheel within a wheel. [17] When they moved they would go in any of the four directions they faced without turning as they moved. [18] Their rims were high and awesome, and the rims of all four wheels were full of eyes all around.

[19] When the living beings moved, the wheels beside them moved; when the living beings rose up from the ground, the wheels rose up too. [20] Wherever the spirit would go, they would go, and the wheels would rise up beside them because the spirit of the living being was in the wheel. [21] When the living beings moved, the wheels moved, and when they stopped moving, the wheels stopped. When they rose up from the ground, the wheels rose up from the ground; the wheels rose up beside them because the spirit of the living being was in the wheel.

[22] Over the heads of the living beings was something like a platform, glittering awesomely like ice, stretched out over their heads. [23] Under the platform their wings were stretched out, each toward the other. Each of the beings also had two wings covering its body. [24] When they moved, I heard the sound of their wings—it was like the sound of rushing waters, or the voice of the Almighty, or the tumult of an army. When they stood still, they lowered their wings.

[25] Then there was a voice from above the platform over their heads when they stood still. [26] Above the platform over their heads was something like a sapphire shaped like a throne.

High above on the throne was a form that appeared to be a man. ²⁷ I saw an amber glow like a fire enclosed all around from his waist up. From his waist down I saw something that looked like fire. There was a brilliant light around it, ²⁸ like the appearance of a rainbow in the clouds after the rain. This was the appearance of the surrounding brilliant light; it looked like the glory of Yahuah. When I saw it, I threw myself face down, and I heard a voice speaking.

Ezekiel describes two sets of 4 living creatures, one set on the inner circle of the 'wheel' and the other set on the outer 4 corners of the '4 wheels within a wheel'. The inner 4 beasts are the Ox (*Taurus*), the Man (*Aquarius*), the Eagle (*Scorpio*), and the Lion (*Leo*) exactly as John described them in Revelation.

Among the 4 living creatures in the center of the "wheel" is the Messiah and his throne, and 24 stars that have fallen. Ezekiel describes the appearance of the Messiah as fire moving about among the 4 living creatures with lightening emanating from him.

We see that within this "wheel within a wheel" is a rainbow throne, and a man who sat upon it. This is the exact representation found in the Enoch Zodiac above. It is 4 wheels within a wheel with spokes, two sets of 4 living creatures, one set surrounding a man on a throne that looks like a rainbow. The man is wearing a crown emanating out what could be described as rays of light or lightening. Surrounding this wheel within a wheel on the outer 4 corners are 4 more living creatures with two wings! The four living creatures surround the Zodiac "carry it about" and are positions over the signs of the inner 4 beasts (Leo, Taurus, Aquarius, and Scorpio).

We see in Ezekiel Chapter 1, the vision of a "wheel within a wheel". It is comprised of 4 wheels within each other.

The 4 "wheels within a wheel"

When looking at the Enoch Zodiac, we see:

1. The outer most 'wheel' or layer where the 4 winged beasts sit on the four corners who "move the wheel"
2. The 'wheel' or layer with the signs of the Zodiac,
3. Another 'wheel' or layer of intertwined rope, connected to the outer layer of rope by spokes.
4. The center of the Zodiac with the other set of 4 living creatures singing "holy, holy, holy" before the man on the throne with 24 stars/elders most already fallen at his feet..

"Full of eyes all around" vs. 18

¹⁸ Their rims were high and awesome, and the rims of all four wheels were full of eyes all around.

The wheel is "full of eyes all around" vs. 18. We see in Enoch's Zodiac, the inside is full of living creatures with eyes (12 signs of the Zodiac). They are position "around" the inner wheel. Two eyes for each of the 12 signs of the Zodiac round about the wheel. Not to mention the eyes on the angelic creatures at the 4 corners, and the eyes on the 4 beasts and man in the middle... Eyes everywhere round about.

The throne like a rainbow

Ezekiel also described the "rainbow" we see on the throne in the middle of Enoch's Zodiac. The throne is on wheels as to "move about the 4 living creatures" exactly as Ezekiel described.

Ezekiel 1:26-28

"I saw the likeness of a throne, as the appearance of a sapphire stone, and upon (it) was the likeness as the appearance of a man... I saw as it were the appearance of fire, and it had brightness round about... as the appearance of the bow that is in the cloud in the day of rain."

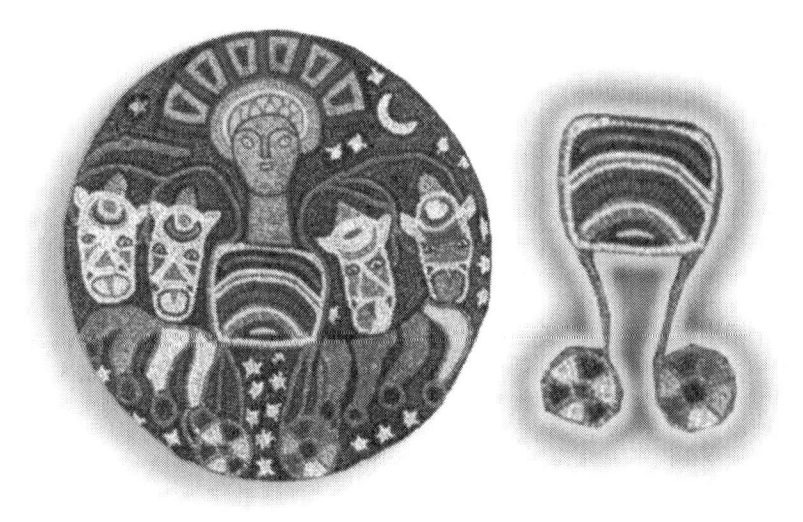

It should be quite obvious to anyone at this point that whatever Enoch was shown that he illustrated into what we now call the Zodiac was the exact same thing Ezekiel witnesses in his vision!

Ezekiel's 4 "wheels within a wheel"
Ezekiel Chapter 1
verse 16 - "all four wheels looked alike. Their structure was like a wheel within a wheel"

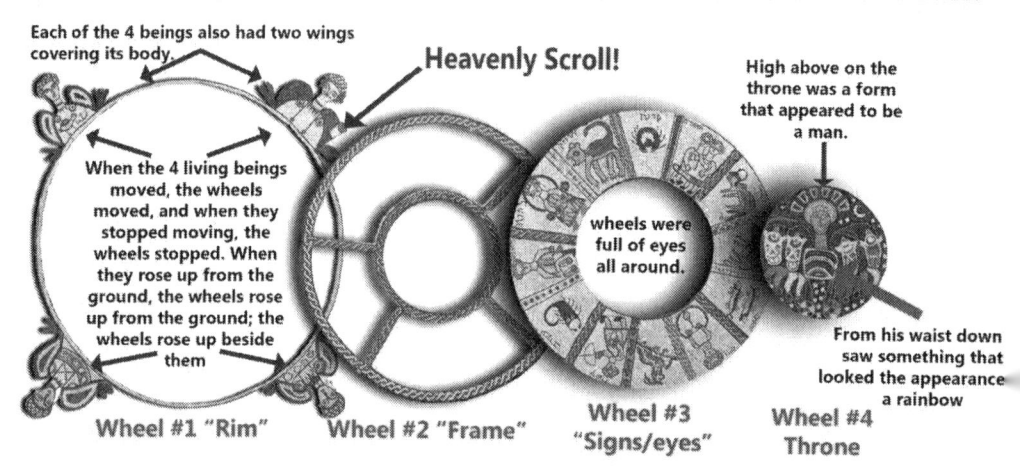

Each of the 4 beings also had two wings covering its body.

Heavenly Scroll!

High above on the throne was a form that appeared to be a man.

When the 4 living beings moved, the wheels moved, and when they stopped moving, the wheels stopped. When they rose up from the ground, the wheels rose up from the ground; the wheels rose up beside them

wheels were full of eyes all around.

From his waist down saw something that looked the appearance a rainbow

Wheel #1 "Rim"   Wheel #2 "Frame"   Wheel #3 "Signs/eyes"   Wheel #4 Throne

John's vision of the 'heavenly' throne
'heavenly' in Hebrew is Shamayim - "the visible stars i.e. the Zodiac"

At once I was in the Spirit, and there before me was a throne in heaven/shamayim (stars) with someone sitting on it.

Rev 4 - A rainbow that shone like an emerald encircled the throne. In the center, around the throne, were four living creatures singing holy, holy, holy. The twenty-four elders (stars) fall down before him who sits on the throne

Rainbow Throne

Exactly 24 stars falling before the throne

4 beasts, mouths open singing holy, holy, holy

Rev 5:6 Then I saw a Lamb, looking as if it had been slain, standing at the center of the throne, encircled by the four living creatures and the 24 (stars) elders... 14 The four living creatures said, "Amen," and the (stars)elders fell down and worshiped

Heaven – is the Mazzaroth?

By Hellenizing the scriptures, the reality of the Mazzaroth '*the Heavenly Scroll*' is hidden from our view. "Heaven" in Hebrew means "*visible sky where the stars are located*" and is speaking of the Mazzaroth where Yahuah authored the Plan of Salvation. Understanding this simple truth brings new meaning to the scriptures and when we remove the effects of Hellenism the reality of these scriptures come to life!

For instance, when Yahusha prays to Yahuah:

Matthew 6:10
"your kingdom come, your will be done, on earth as it is in heaven."

Below is the Hebrew word for Heaven which is *shamayim*:

Brown-Driver-Briggs entry H8064

1. a. *visible heavens, sky*, where stars, etc., are located

We see that the primary definition 1.A is "*visible sky where the stars are located*" i.e. the Mazzaroth! What Yahusha REALLY said and meant is this:

Matthew 6:10
"your kingdom come, your will be done, on earth as it is (proclaimed) where the stars are visible in the sky (Mazzaroth)"

You see, Yahusha understood that the entire Plan of Salvation, His Kingdom, and His Will were originally written in the stars! He was proclaiming his desire to see that ***Original Revelation*** come true on Earth exactly as it is written in the Mazzaroth. Let us look at other occurrences of the word '*shamayim*' in scripture and let us reveal the real meaning of those passages.

Exodus 20 – You shall have no other gods in my face!

Let's begin with Exodus where Yahuah condemns the practice of idol worship. To understand "why" this command was given is paramount. Yahusha teaches us to seek out the "intent behind the letter" so that we can mature as sons of Yahuah.

First a little background, the Israelites had just come out of 500 years of bondage in Egypt. In Egypt, they worshipped the signs of the Zodiac/Mazzaroth and depending on the "Age" they were currently in, they would erect Idols of that "Age".

During the Age of Taurus, they made images of Bulls and created 'gods' for themselves around the symbol of that Age. In Egypt they created the 'god' Apis the black bull. Below is a photo of this 'god' as the idol was made in the image of a calf:

Sacred bull Apis. Limestone (originally painted), days of Nectenabo I (?), 30th Dynasty. Found at the Serapeum of Saqqarah, in a chapel next to the processional way leading to the catacombs of the sacred bulls.

This was the real story behind the Israelites creating the "Gold Calf". This "Golden Calf" was an abomination to Yahuah because they had begun worshipping the signs of the Zodiac, like the

Egyptians. Yahuah had to formally forbid this practice from that point forward in His Law. Now with that background, let us look at the commandment to have no other 'gods' in the face of Yahuah. Note, "before me" is a lousy translation, it actually should read "in my face".

> **Exodus 20**
> Yahuah spoke all these words: 2 "I, Yahuah, am your Elohim, who brought you from the land of Egypt, from the house of slavery. 3 "You shall have no other gods before me (in My face). "You shall not make for yourself a carved image or any likeness of anything that is in heaven (shamayim i.e. the Mazzaroth) above or that is on the earth beneath or that is in the water below.

We now better understand why Yahuah had to make this clear to the Israelites. The word "heaven" is *'shamayim'* which means *"visible sky where the stars are located"* and specifically is speaking of the Mazzaroth/Zodiac. The image of the Golden Calf was just that, an image of Taurus the bull! They picked up that practice in Egypt and had mistaken Yahuah for Taurus.

Deuteronomy 3 – *gods in heaven*

In Deuteronomy Chapter 3 we see another reference to the 'gods" of the Mazzaroth. We see Moses proclaim that Yahuah was greater than any other "god in Heaven"! We know there are no other 'gods' at all, much less where Yahuah resides! No, Moses was simply referring to all the 'gods' the pagans had created around the sign of the Mazzaroth/Zodiac as to worship them. When we remove that Hellenized word "heaven" from scriptures, and properly replace it with *'shamayim'* (which is specifically speaking of the Mazzaroth/Zodiac), then Moses declaration makes perfect sense!

> **Deuteronomy 3**
> 23 Moreover, at that time I pleaded with Yahuah, 24 "O, Yahuah Elohim, you have begun to show me your greatness and strength. What god in heaven (the Mazzaroth/Zodiac) or earth can rival your works?

Deuteronomy 3 – The whole heavenly creation given to all humanity

Again in Deuteronomy Chapter 3, we see that Yahuah authored the Zodiac and assigned each sign in the stars as a witness to all humanity.

> **Deuteronomy 3**
> 19 When you look up to the sky (sky is Hebrew shamayim/Zodiac) and see the sun, moon, and stars *(speaking of the Zodiac)* —the whole heavenly creation (Mazzaroth/Zodiac) —you must not be seduced to worship and serve them (signs of the Zodiac), for Yahuah your Elohim has assigned them (the signs of the Zodiac) to all the people of the world (they were created by Yahuah to proclaim the coming Messiah Yahusha, see ***Psalm 19***, they are not gods).

Sha'ul declares this same truth to the Galatians, proclaiming that the Lamb had been slaughtered since the foundation of the world i.e. written in the Zodiac.

Sha'ul tells them that the Lamb was slaughtered right there before their very eyes. Then Sha'ul goes on to explain that, through the Zodiac, Yahuah witnessed the gospel in advance to Abraham.

> **Galatians 3**
> 3 You foolish Galatians! Who has bewitched you? Before your very eyes (in the Zodiac) Yahusha the Messiah was clearly portrayed as crucified (in the Heavenly Scroll) ... 8 ***Scripture foresaw that Yahuah would justify the Gentiles by faith, and announced the gospel in advance to Abraham***: "All nations will be blessed through you."

Sha'ul was referring to:

> **Genesis 15**
> 5 And he brought him forth abroad, and said, *Look now toward heaven, and tell (what the) the stars (proclaim),* if thou be able to discern the order of them (the Zodiac): and he said unto him, So shall thy seed be (the Messiah proclaimed by the Zodiac)

Psalms 119 - Yahuah's instructions/plan preserved in heaven

Again we see David in **Psalms 119** declare that Yahuah's "instructions" endure, they stand secure in heaven i.e. *shamarym*/Zodiac.

The Mazzaroth/Zodiac is Yahuah's **Original Revelation** to all mankind, laying out His Plan for Man (the timeframe through 2000 year reverse Ages) and His Plan of Salvation through Yahusha the Messiah (*as told by the 12 signs from Virgo-Leo*).

Let's shed the light of "context" on this passage with Psalm 19

> **Psalms 119**
> O Yahuah, your instructions endure; they stand secure in heaven (shamayim - written in the stars, untouched by human hands).
>
> **Psalm 19**
> 1 The heavens (shamayim - stars and constellations) declare the glory of Yahuah; the skies proclaim the work of his hands. 2 Day after day they pour forth speech; night after night they reveal knowledge. 3 They have no speech, they use no words; no sound is heard from them. 4 Yet their voice goes out into all the earth, their words to the ends of the Age. In the heavens (shamayim - among the Stars and Constellations) Yahuah has pitched a tent for the sun (the Zodiac). 5 It is like a bridegroom (Yahusha) coming out of his chamber (to wed the Bride, Remnant Israel), like a champion (Conquering King) rejoicing to run his course (through the ecliptic). 6 It rises at one end of the heavens (Zodiac) and makes its circuit (Zodiac means circuit of circle or path) to the other; nothing is deprived of its warmth.

We see Isaiah declare the exact same reality below. Remember "heavens" is actually specifically referring to the place in the sky where the stars are... i.e. The Zodiac. "Starry hosts" are those which hosts the stars i.e. constellations...

> **Isaiah 40:26**
> Lift up your eyes and look to the heavens (the Zodiac): Who

created all these? He who brings out the starry host (constellations) one by one and calls forth each (of the constellations) of them by name. Because of his great power and mighty strength, not one of them is missing (there are exactly 12 constellations in every culture dating back to the origin of man!).

Psalms 11 – The Throne of Yahuah in heaven

We see in Psalms 11, King David proclaim that Yahuah's throne is in "heaven". What is David referring to? We already know in Psalms 19, David proclaimed the meaning of the Zodiac in great detail.

Psalms 11
4 Yahuah is in his holy temple; Yahuah's throne is in heaven (shamayim/Zodiac). His eyes watch; his eyes examine all people.

We also see Isaiah proclaim:

Isaiah 66:1
This is what Yahuah says: "Heaven (shamayim/Zodiac) is my throne, and the earth is my footstool. Where is the house you will build for me? Where will my resting place be?

Yahuah had revealed to David, like He did Abraham, Ezekiel, Daniel, Sha'ul, Yahusha, John and all the prophets, the true meaning behind the Mazzaroth/Zodiac called ***the Heavenly Scroll***.

Yahuah gave that Zodiac to Enoch, and in the middle of Enoch's Zodiac is the "throne of God" that was detailed in great detail by Ezekiel, and Daniel, and John the revelator...

Ezekiel, Daniel, and John described Enoch's Zodiac in great detail. The 4 wheels within a wheel, eyes of the Zodiac Signs all around, 4 beasts crying out "Holy, Holy, Holy" before the King standing at a podium about to open the sealed book. The 24 stars/elders fallen at his feet. The other 4 beasts with 2 wings stationed at the 4 corners of the "wheel"... a perfect match!

I will stop there as I am sure we all get the message. I encourage everyone to go back into the Bible, and seek out every instance where the word "heaven" is used, and reconsider the meaning in context of "the place in the sky where the stars are" or *shamayim* which is speaking specifically of the Mazzaroth/Zodiac in many cases.

Origin of the Book of the Mazzaroth

Tehillim (Psalms) 147:1-5 – *Yahuah is the one who named every star, not the Greeks!*

> *Praise Yahuah. How good it is to sing praises to our Elohom, how pleasant and fitting to praise Him! Yahuah builds up Jerusalem; He gathers the exiles of Israel. He heals the brokenhearted and binds up their wounds.* **He determines the number of the stars and calls them each by name.** *Great is our Elohim and mighty in power; His understanding has no limit.*

Revelation 8:10-11 – *We see references to star names and the constellation Eridanus the River*

> *The third angel sounded his trumpet, and a great star, blazing like a torch, fell from the sky on a third of the rivers and on the springs of water-- The name of the star is Wormwood. A third of the waters turned bitter, and many people died from the waters that had become bitter.*

Yeshayah (Isaiah) 40:25-26 – *Yahuah named each constellation, each sign of the Zodiac*

> *"Lift your eyes and look to the heavens: Who created all these? He who brings out the starry host (constellations) one by one, and calls them each by name. Because of his great power and mighty strength, not one of them is missing.*

Iyov (Job) 9:7-10 - *We see specific signs of the Zodiac named by name in scripture, and Yahuah the maker of them*

> *He speaks to the sun and it does not shine; he seals off the light of the stars. He alone stretches out the heavens and treads on the waves of the sea. He is the Maker of **the Bear** and **Orion**, the Pleiades and the constellations of the south.*

Iyov (Job) 38:28-33 - *We see the only two constellations bound by "gravity" identified, and proof that Yahuah named and created the Zodiac and established laws of Heaven that have dominion over the Earth! That maybe the goal of the 3rd Edition of Creation Cries Out!*

> *Does the rain have a father? Who fathers the drops of dew? From whose womb comes the ice? Who gives birth to the frost from the heavens? When the waters become hard as stone, when the surface of the deep is frozen? "Can you bind the beautiful Pleiades? Can you loose the cords of Orion? Can you bring forth the constellations in their seasons or lead out the Bear with its cubs? Do you know the laws of the heavens? Can you set up [Yahuah's] dominion over the earth?*

Amos 5:6-10 – *Another reference of specific signs of the Zodiac by name.*

> *Seek Yahuah and live, or he will sweep through the house of Joseph like a fire; it will devour, and Bethel will have no one to quench it. You who turn justice into bitterness and cast righteousness to the ground. **He who made the Pleiades and Orion**,*

Shoftim (Judges) 5:19-20 – *Another references to the "courses of the stars" and specific names of constellations*

> Kings came, they fought; the kings of Canaan fought at Taanach by the waters of Megiddo, but they carried off no silver, no plunder. From the heavens the stars fought, from their courses they fought against Sisera.

Yeshayah (Isaiah) 13:6-10 – *Another reference to the constellations of the Zodiac*

> Wail, for the day of Yahuah is near; it will come like destruction from the Almighty. Because of this, all hands will go limp, every man's heart will melt. Terror will seize them, pain and anguish will grip them; they will writhe like a woman in labor. They will look aghast at each other, their faces aflame. See, the day of Yahuah is coming--a cruel day, with wrath and fierce anger--to make the land desolate and destroy the sinners within it. The stars of heaven and their constellations will not show their light. The rising sun will be darkened and the moon will not give its light.

At this point, it should be quite obvious neither the Greeks nor the Egyptians authored the Zodiac. No, not even the Sumerians and not the watchers before them...

Yahuah is the creator of all things...
HalleluYahuah!!!

CHAPTER 10
AGES AND EPOCHS

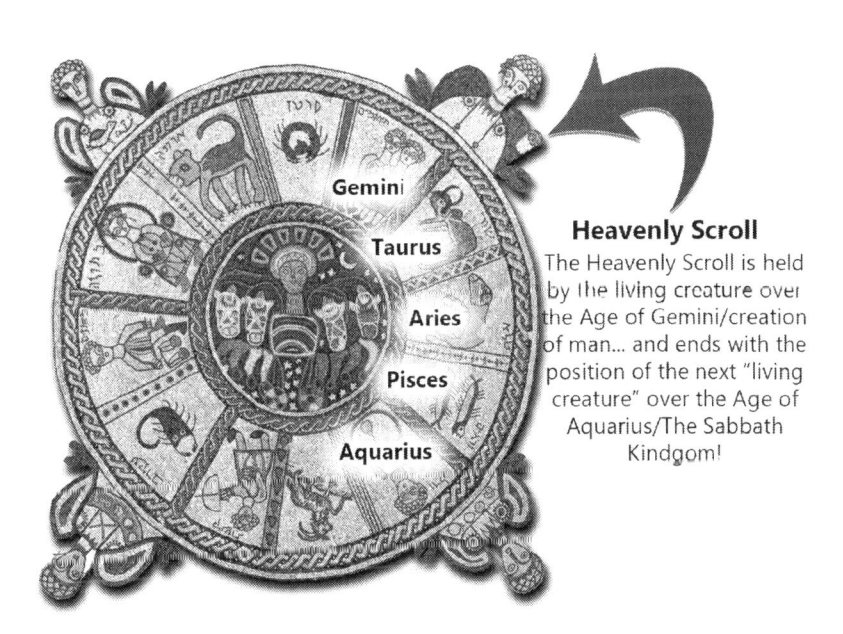

Ages & Epochs of Mankind
The Heavenly Scroll of Enoch

Heavenly Scroll
The Heavenly Scroll is held by the living creature over the Age of Gemini/creation of man... and ends with the position of the next "living creature" over the Age of Aquarius/The Sabbath Kindgom!

Chapter 10 – Ages & Epochs of Mankind

We all have heard the song that goes something like: "this is the dawning of the Age of Aquarius". We have all become familiar with the term *The New Age*. We also know to stay away from that "New Age" stuff. Like all the truths of Yahuah, there are those who deny Him in a humanistic attempt to tie in "evolution" and that is exactly what the modern New Age Movement is all about. With it's promise of the next evolutionary step of mankind led by the Ascended Masters... the watchers are still at, misleading mankind trying to take credit for what they know is coming.

In reality it simply refers to the transition from The Age of Pisces the fish to The Age of Aquarius the water bearer. What are these "ages"? The Bible calls them "epochs"; and yes, the Bible talks about the dawning of The Age of Aquarius along with the transition from The Age of Taurus to The Age of Aries to The Age of Aquarius. The Messiah also specifically referenced the transition from Pisces to Aquarius. Before we get into what the Bible says about these "ages" of the Zodiac, let's first establish what an "age" or "epoch" really is. Then we will get to the bottom of what this means in scripture and how these ages are prophesied and fulfilled.

An "age" or "epoch" is the time it takes the Earth to "wobble" on its axis called a Great Year divided by 12 (the number of constellations in the Zodiac). This wobble or great cycle of time is called the *Progression of the Equinoxes* and lasts approximately 26,000 years. An "age" then is approximately 2,200 years in duration (26,000 / 12) give or take a few hundred years. Each astrological age is based on the passage of the vernal equinox measured against the actual zodiacal constellations. Each of those twelve sections of what is called the ***Great Year*** can be called either an Astrological Age, Processional Age or a ***Great Month***. "Great Month" is the most common term for each of the 12 ages

(2000 year periods) in a ***Great Year*** (26000 year cycle of the Earth's wobble).

We currently are on the cusp of The Age of Pisces turning to The Age of Aquarius and the beginning of a new "Great Year" cycle of approximately 26,000 years. Very exciting times we are living in no doubt. That is what the Mayan Calendar is all about and all the "fuss" about December 2012. It would seem that great changes occur on Earth at the transition of each Great Year.

The Bible, however, was silent about 2012. This is because the transitions of "Great Months" or Ages is not measured by a pagan calendar! These Age transitions are marked by Yahuah with "signs in the sky" as He so instructed in Genesis.

> **Genesis 1:14**
> And Yahuah said, "Let there be lights in the expanse of the heavens to separate the day from the night. And let them be for signs and for seasons, and for days and years.

The "sign in the sky" that marks every Age transition is described in Revelation Chapter 12, known as 'the sign of the son of man'. I discuss this in more detail as we go forward.

"The Great Year"

In astronomy, axial precession is a gravity-induced, slow and continuous change in the orientation of an astronomical body's rotational axis.

In particular, it refers to the gradual shift in the orientation of Earth's axis of rotation, which, like a wobbling top, traces out a pair of cones joined at their apices in a cycle of approximately 26,000 years (called a Great or Platonic Year in astrology).

Below is a graphic of the Earth's "wobble". As the Earth spins clockwise around the equator, it wobbles counterclockwise on its axis.

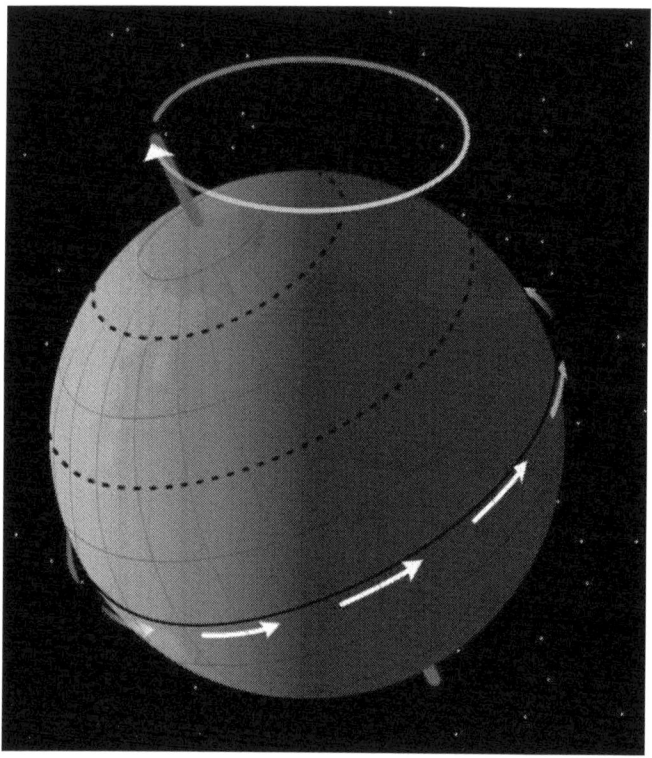

Normally, during the course of the astrological year, the Sun moves through the zodiacal signs commencing with Virgo and ending with Leo. However, the astrological ages proceed in the reverse direction through the signs of the Zodiac just as the "wobble" of the Earth on its axis is a counterclockwise motion. Therefore, after the Age of Pisces, the next age is the Age of Aquarius, followed by the Age of Capricorn, and so on.

There is a third aspect of the astrological ages that has very wide consensus amongst astrologers. Though astrologers cannot agree upon the year, century or millennium for the start of any age, they generally agree upon the core historical events associated with the recent Ages since the start of the Holocene Epoch.

For example, the *Age of Gemini* is associated with the Age of Innocents represented by Adam and Eve before the fall.

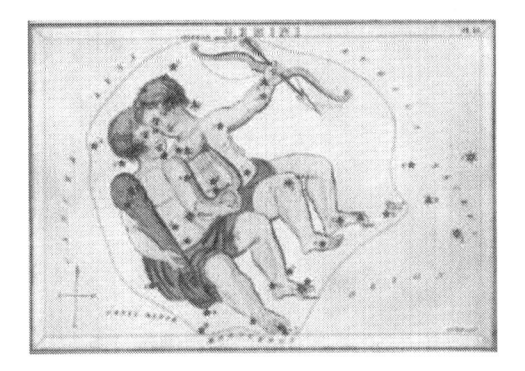

The *Age of Taurus* with Ancient Egypt and its massive pyramids and Bull worship

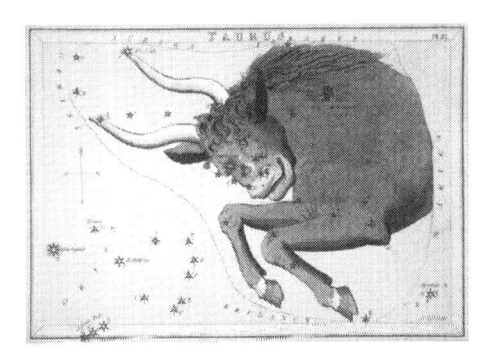

The *Age of Aries* with the Iron Age and the substitutionary Ram sacrifices. Followed by the annual Passover Lamb rehearsal.

The *Age of Pisces* with the Messianic age to reclaim the Lost Sheep of the House of Israel and unit it with the House of Judah… the two fish bound by the Messiah.

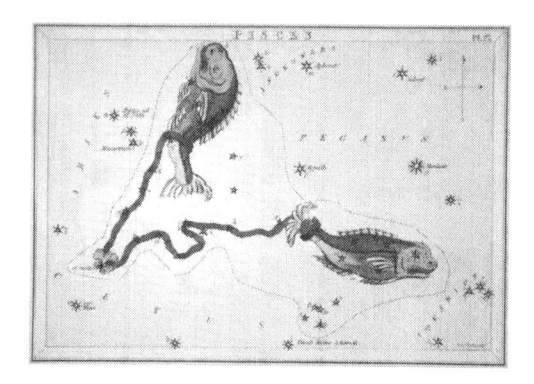

The *Age of Aquarius* the Water Bearer associated with the Kingdom reign of Leo the Lion of the Tribe of Judah. The Messiah being the living water poured out over Earth to Mikveh and cleans it in preparation for the kingdom reign.

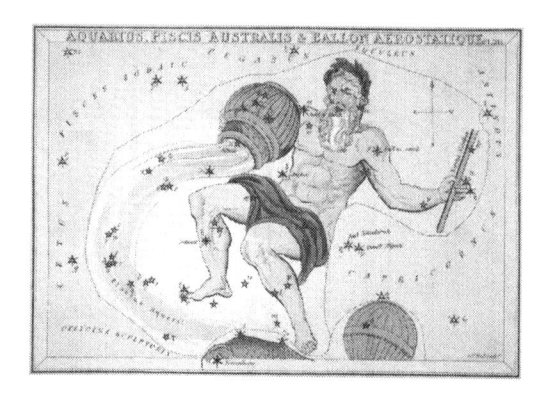

Ages are approximately 2,000 years each

Many astrologers find ages too erratic based on either the vernal point moving through the randomly sized zodiacal constellations or sidereal zodiac and, instead, round all astrological ages to exactly 2000 years each. This is because modern Astrology has denied Yahuah as the creator and failed to acknowledge the "sign of the son of man" as the transitional sign. We who know Yahuah can easily go back in time (with modern computer software) and find the sign of the son of man in the sky in human history and know the exact timing of the age transitions and length of each age.

/ Yahuah's Celestial Clock

The Zodiac is Yahuah's divine celestial 'clock'. The second hand moves about at clicks of 72 years, the minute hand every month along the 12 signs, and the hour hand moving backward every 2,000 years among the 12 signs. So one full rotation of the hour hand around this divine clock is a **Great Year** and every "tick" on the hour hand is a **Great Month**.

The Human Lifespan

There is a one-degree shift (the second hand on the clock) approximately every 72 years (the lifespan of man), so a 30-degree movement requires 2160 years to complete (a Great Month or Age, which has been rounded to 2000 years for simplicity).

> Psalm 90:10
> *The years of our life are seventy,* or even by reason of strength eighty; yet their span is but toil and trouble; they are soon gone, and we fly away.

The Plan of Salvation

With that introduction of the divine clock known as the Zodiac, let us now look at the Enoch Zodiac which is unique among the Zodiacs. Most Zodiac charts show the signs of the Zodiac from the standpoint of the Plan of Salvation as the "minute hand" of the clock rotates around the clock clockwise. You see below beginning with Virgo it moves around clockwise back around to Leo.

Notice that the constellation Virgo is just after the 3 O'clock position in the image above, this is when the Messiah was born. Keep that in mind for later

The Sabbath Covenant

The Enoch Zodiac is unique in that it is in "reverse order" i.e. the Zodiac Signs and the Plan of Salvation rotate counterclockwise.

The Enoch Calendar is designed to illustrate the progression of the ages. The first "tick" mark on the clock accurately represents the first age of modern man with the creation of Adam; the Age of Gemini and then progresses through the ages of mankind!

Age of Gemini (Innocence)

Age of Taurus (Chaos)

Age of Aries (Law)

Age of Pisces (Messianic)

Age of Aquarius (Kingdom)

The "hand on the clock" currently resting on the age transition from Pisces to Aquarius. This is 6,000 years since the fall of Adam when Gemini transitioned to Taurus. So we have since mankind fell and the Earth fell under the curse of Adam:

- *Age of Taurus – 2000 years* ... ended with the birth of Abraham announced by the "sign of the son of man" in the sky. *More on that later...*
- *Age of Aries – 2000 years* ... ended with the birth of Yahusha announced by the "sign of the son of man" in the sky. *More on that later...*

- *Age of Pisces – 2000 years* ... ends with the "sign of the son of man" in the sky in 2017. *More on that later…*

6,000 years complete, we enter the Sabbath Rest in the Age of Aquarius the Water Bearer. I will explain these ages and how they foretell of the Messiah as we go.

The Enoch Calendar is a divine witness to The Sabbath Covenant! 6,000 years we labor under the curse of Adam; then we enter the Sabbath Rest (very soon) in the Age of Aquarius!

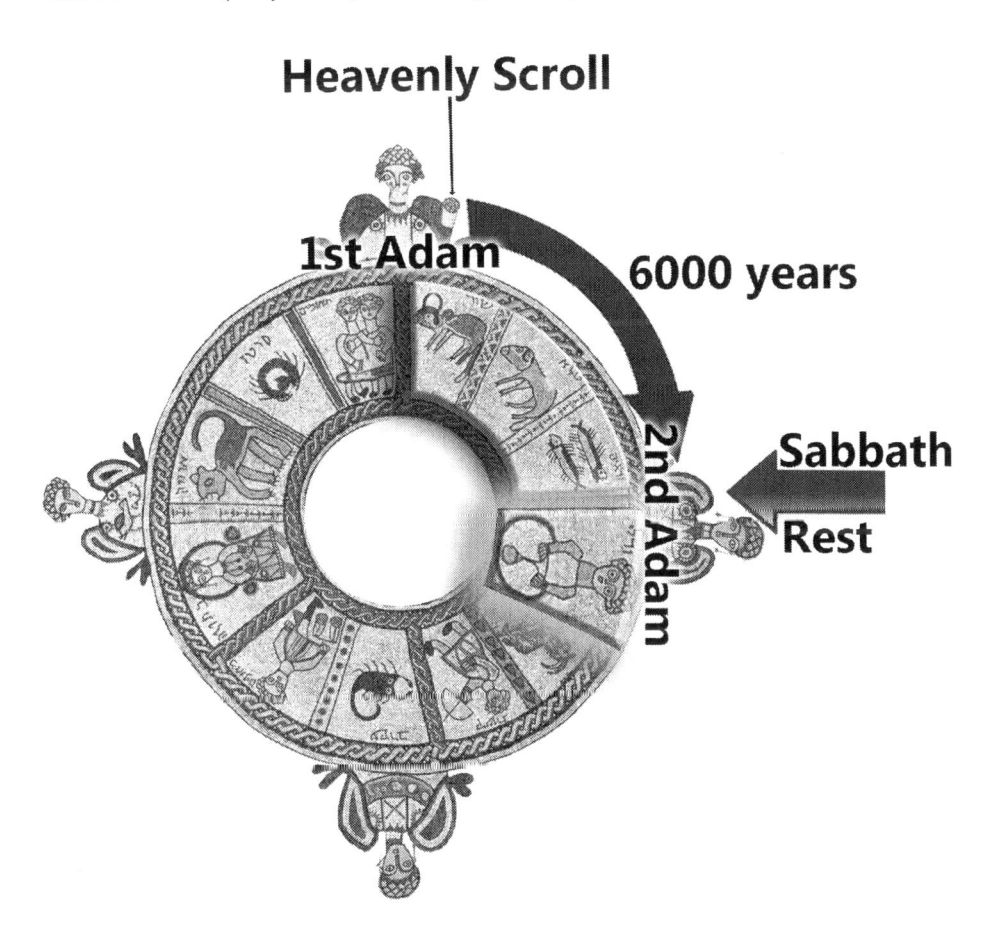

The Messiah's birth synchronized

Notice on both calendars regardless if it is a Zodiac that features the Plan of Salvation clockwise or the Enoch Calendar which features the Sabbath Covenant clockwise… the Messiah's birth is synchronized. Notice: Virgo *the sign of his birth* (as prophesied by Isaiah - the Sun moves through Virgo during the Feast of Sukkot), and Pisces *the Messianic Age announced by his birth* align perfectly!

Enoch's Timepiece – the Zodiac Ages

As I explained: an age is roughly 2,000 years. Each age has a heavenly sign known as "the sign of the son of man" that marks its transition.

Ages & Epochs of Mankind
The Heavenly Scroll of Enoch

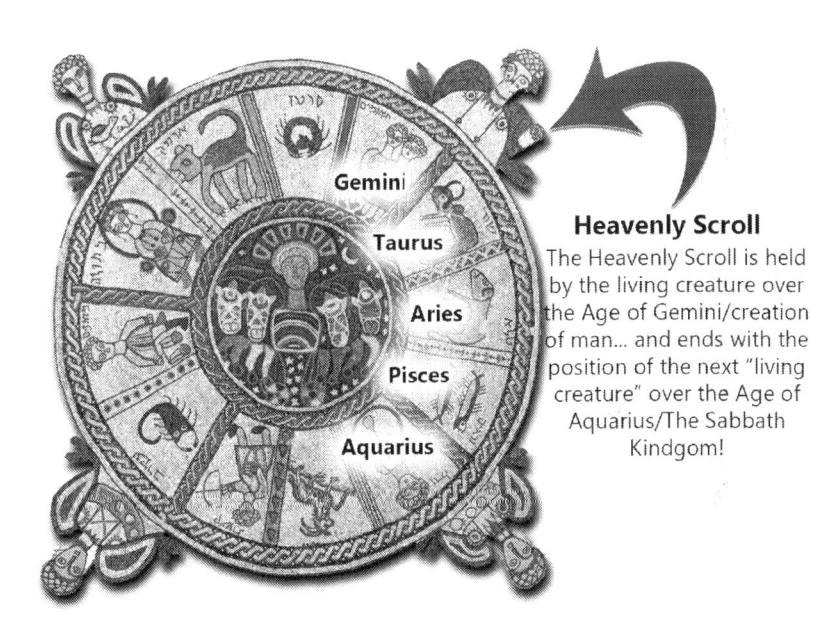

- Gemini
- Taurus
- Aries
- Pisces
- Aquarius

Heavenly Scroll
The Heavenly Scroll is held by the living creature over the Age of Gemini/creation of man... and ends with the position of the next "living creature" over the Age of Aquarius/The Sabbath Kindgom!

The reality of Ages and how they relate to human history has given rise to the Doctrine of Dispensations. There are many aspects of the Doctrine of Dispensations from which come Replacement Theology; some aspects of *"dispensations"* are true and others false. It is outside the scope of this book to go into this topic at length. This author teaches progressive revelation through covenants called **Covenantal Theology** and outright rejects **Replacement Theology**. There are not "two covenants; 1 new and 1 old" but rather 7 covenants whereby Yahuah revealed Himself to mankind. There is no distinction between "Law and Grace" both work hand in hand. There is no distinction between Israel and the Church. There is only <u>Remnant Israel</u>. Every covenant with man established by Yahuah is still very much active and relevant. But covenants have nothing to do with the various ages. They are separate and unrelated. I cover these topics in great detail in my book ***The Kingdom***. The basic covenant of Yahuah that illustrates the progression of "Ages" is the ***Sabbath Covenant***. As the Sabbath Covenant is not a covenant made "with man" but rather "for man". Each day in a 7-day weekly cycle is a shadow picture of a 1,000 years. The effects of sin span a 6,000 year period from the Age of Taurus, through the Age of Aries, to the end of the age of Pisces. Then the Millennial Reign begins with the second coming of the Messiah at the transition to the Age of Aquarius. This is when the curse of Adam is lifted and creation liberated.

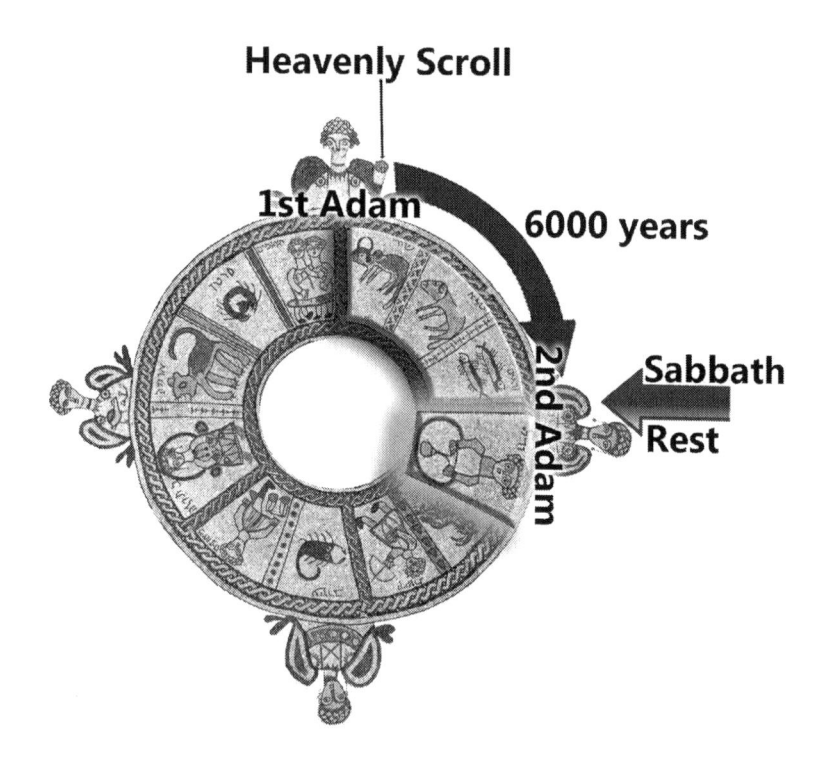

Due to the nature of this topic, and the proliferation of "New Age" dogma (which perverts the simple truth); I am simply going to illustrate what scripture reveals concerning ages and how these ages relate to progression of the signs in the Enoch Zodiac.

My goal here is to simply introduce the Biblical concept of Ages and demonstrate that each age is, in fact, represented by signs in the Enoch Zodiac and confirmed in scripture.

What does the Bible say about 'ages'?

The word 'age' in Greek is 'aion' or "eon" in English. Let's take a journey through scripture and see how 'ages" are handled and defined. Just like we did with the Zodiac, we must restore the concept of '*Ages or Epochs'* back to The Creator, Yahuah, who established them. We see Sha'ul below declare Yahuah is the author of *Ages*:

> ### Hebrews 1:1-2
> 1 Yahuah, who at various times and in various ways spoke in time (Ages/Epochs) past to the fathers by the prophets (during the Ages of Taurus and Aries), 2 has in these last days (since the beginning of the Age of Pisces) spoken to us by His Son, whom He has appointed heir of all things, **for whom also Yahuah made the ages** (ages - aion).

Sha'ul also speaks to the fact that there are present Ages and Ages to come. Here Sha'ul is making reference to the Age of Pisces (the Messianic Age), until the Age of Aquarius (The Kingdom Age):

> ### Ephesians 1:20-21
> 20 Which Yahuah worked in Yahusha when Yahuah raised Yahusha from the dead and seated Yahusha at His right hand in the heavenly places, 21 far above all principality and power and might and dominion, and every name that is named, not only in this Age (of Pisces) but also in that [Age of Aquarius] which is to come.

Sha'ul proclaims that the Plan of Salvation through a human Messiah was hidden throughout the previous Ages, and revealed when Yahusha came to usher in the Kingdom of Yahuah.

> **Ephesians 3:8-9**
> 9 and to make all see what is the fellowship of the mystery, which from the beginning of the Ages has been hidden in Yahuah, who created all things for Yahusha the Messiah (as an inheritance).

> **Colossians 1:26**
> 26 the mystery which has been hidden from Ages and from generations, but now has been revealed to His saints.

The disciples too understood that the comings of the Messiah marked the transition between ages:

> **Matthew 24:3**
> Now as He sat on the Mount of Olives, the disciples came to Him privately, saying, "Tell us, when these things will be? And what will be the sign of Your coming, and of the end of the age (aion)?"

We see Yahusha understood the progression of 2,000 year ages and confirmed the Sabbath Covenant. Yahusha's first coming was prophesied and fulfilled in the 4,000th year since the fall of Adam. Yahusha's return is in the 6,000th year since the fall of Adam. We see below, Yahusha confirms his return would not be for another 2,000 years (after the Age of Pisces) at the transition to the Age of Aquarius.

This 2,000 year period is the Messianic Age when Yahuah reclaims the lost from among the nation.

> **Matthew 28:20**
> Teaching them to observe all that I have commanded you. And behold, I am with you always, to the end of the age."

So with all the Christian false doctrines of "any minute now, in the twinkling of an eye" and so forth, we should never have expected the return of the King any sooner than, well... now! Yahusha knew the Sabbath Covenant, his role as Messiah ben Joseph and then 2,000 years to reclaim the lost sheep and return as Messiah ben David. All of this is proclaimed in the Zodiac! The image of Pisces is not one fish (as Christianity believes), but TWO fish; the House of Israel and the House of Judah! The two fish are bound together with a chord... the Messiah. So while they appear to be fighting to get away from one another... they are held fast by the Messiah.

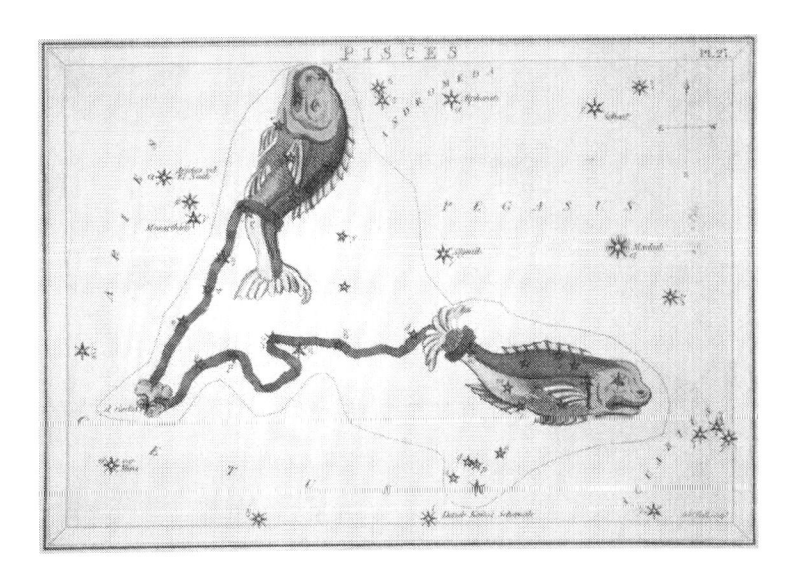

Age Transitions

The Book of the Mazzaroth, which is laid out in the Enoch Zodiac shows the progression of the ages as the signs of the Zodiac are reflected in reverse order. It is as though the Zodiac is a clock with one hand and 2,000 year tick marks!

Age of Gemini (Innocence)

Age of Taurus (Chaos)

Age of Aries (Law)

Age of Pisces (Messianic)

Age of Aquarius (Kingdom)

Currently, the "hand" is on the next tick mark as we are transitioning from Pisces to Aquarius. By all accounts no matter who is doing the reckoning, we are at the 6,000 year mark since Adam and 2,000 year mark since Yahusha's first coming.

Yahusha explained when ask about the sign of his return that we should be looking once again for the ***Sign of the Son of Man*** to appear in the sky.

> **Matthew 24**
> 29"But immediately after the tribulation of those days THE SUN WILL BE DARKENED, AND THE MOON WILL NOT GIVE ITS LIGHT, AND THE STARS WILL FALL from the sky, and the powers of the heavens will be shaken. 30"**And then the sign of the Son of Man will appear in the sky**, and then all the tribes of the earth will mourn, and they will see the SON OF MAN COMING ON THE CLOUDS OF THE SKY with power and great glory. 31"And He will send forth His angels with A GREAT TRUMPET and THEY WILL

Creation Cries Out!

GATHER TOGETHER His elect from the four winds, from one end of the sky to the other.

That sign is defined in great detail in the book of Revelation.

Revelation 12
12 And then a great wonder appeared in *heaven* (H8064: shamayim/Zodiac): There was a woman (Virgo) who was clothed with the sun, and the moon was under her feet. She had a crown of twelve stars on her head. ² She was pregnant and cried out with pain because she was about to give birth... ⁵ The woman gave birth to a son, who would rule all the nations with an iron rod. And her child was taken up to Yahuah and to his throne.

This exact sign is so unique; it is proven to have only appeared in the sky 2 times prior in human history. 2,000 years ago at the time

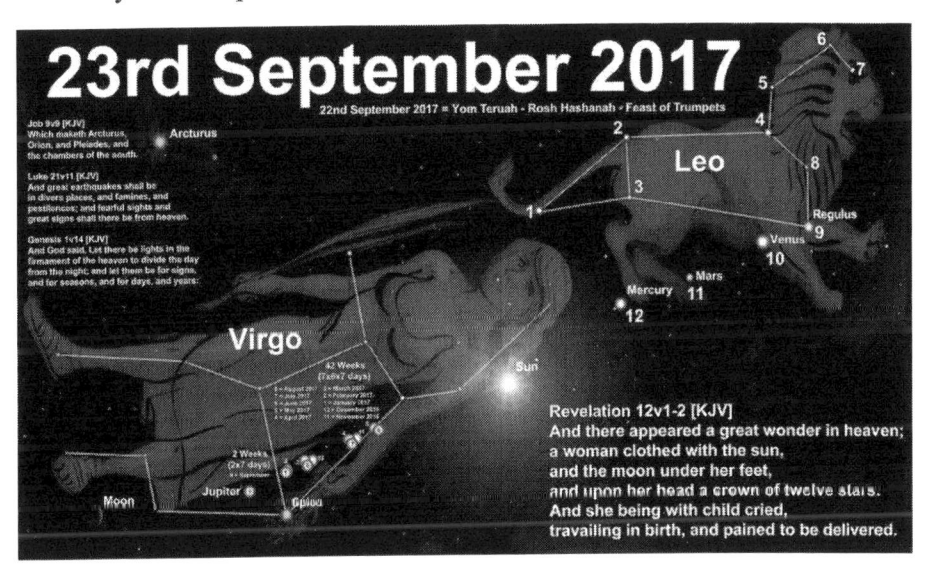

23rd September 2017

22nd September 2017 = Yom Teruah - Rosh Hashanah - Feast of Trumpets

Job 9v9 [KJV]
Which maketh Arcturus, Orion, and Pleiades, and the chambers of the south.

Luke 21v11 [KJV]
And great earthquakes shall be in divers places, and famines, and pestilences; and fearful sights and great signs shall there be from heaven.

Genesis 1v14 [KJV]
And God said, Let there be lights in the firmament of the heaven to divide the day from the night; and let them be for signs, and for seasons, and for days, and years:

Revelation 12v1-2 [KJV]
And there appeared a great wonder in heaven; a woman clothed with the sun, and the moon under her feet, and upon her head a crown of twelve stars. And she being with child cried, travailing in birth, and pained to be delivered.

of the Messiah's birth and 4,000 years ago at the time of Abraham's birth as the scriptures record. With modern astronomy software, we can look into the future for this exact celestial alignment which is slightly different than the two previous... it never appears again for the next 10,000 years! However, it does appear again on the Feast of Trumpets in 2017. Right on time to transition from the Age of Pisces to the Age of Aquarius just like, well... clockwork.

The Ages

Below are the ages in scripture, as they progress backward through the signs of the Zodiac:

1. *The pre-Adamic Age* – Alluded to, but undefined, in scripture. Deemed not relevant to our understanding the Plan of Salvation for mankind.

2. *The Age of Innocence / The Age of Gemini* – The twin figures in the symbol representing Adam and Eve.

3. *The Age of Chaos / The Age of Taurus the Bull* – this age began with the fall of mankind. The worship of the Bull in Egypt

4. *The Age of Law / The Age of Aries the Ram* – this age began with the birth of Abraham and the promise of the substitutionary Ram for Isaac's life. Then further laid out in the sacrifice of the Passover Lambs.

5. *The Messianic Age / The Age of Pisces the Fish* – symbolized by the fish symbol, to re-unite the two houses.

6. *The Kingdom Age / The Age of Aquarius the Water* Bearer – symbolized by living water poured out over the Earth.

7. *The Eternal Age of Kingdom Rule over the Universe* - Alluded to, but undefined, in scripture. Deemed not relevant to our understanding the Plan of Salvation.

The Age of Gemini
(The Twins - Innocence)

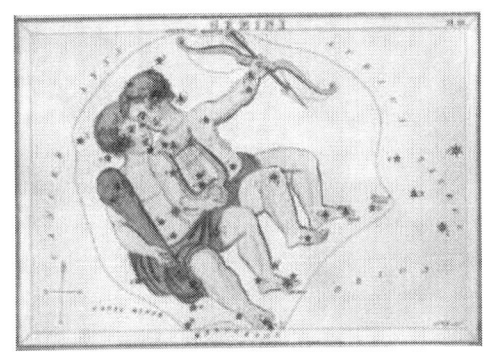

Adam and Eve were created at the end of the Zodiac Age of Gemini, the Twins, on the cusp of the Age of Taurus. Each Zodiac Age lasts over 2000 years (2160). On the ancient maps of the heavens, Gemini was always seen as Adam and Eve. Gemini was the age of duality among many other things. This is one of the reasons the Book of Genesis in the beginning chapters introduces us to the law of opposites; Heaven/Earth, light/darkness, land/sea, male/female, good/evil.

The Age of Taurus
(The Bull - Chaos)

Taurus also is a symbol of divine judgment or correction. One of the sub-constellations of Taurus is Eridanus, the river of Judgment. This is the period from the fall of man until the birth of Abraham. It was during this time period (initiated by Cain killing Abel) that mankind reached the breaking point of Yahuah's mercy. During this timeframe, the Watcher's (fallen Angels) had illicit sexual relations with human women. This is the Age in which Enoch lived and documented the apostasy of the Angels and humanity. Yahuah judged the fallen Angels and their offspring the Nephilim, and then destroyed all living creatures above on the surface of the Earth save Noah and his family. This Age is known as the Age of Chaos:

> **Songs of the Sage** *(4Q510-511)[43] fragment 1*:
> And I, the Instructor, proclaim His glorious splendor so as to frighten and to te[rrify] all the spirits of the destroying angels, spirits of the bastards, demons, <u>Lilith</u>, howlers, and [desert dwellers...] and those which fall upon men without warning to lead them astray from a spirit of understanding and to make their heart and their [mind] desolate during the present dominion of wickedness and predetermined time of humiliations for the sons of lig[ht], by the guilt of the ages of [those] smitten by iniquity – not for eternal destruction, [bu]t for an era of humiliation for transgression.

The Book of Enoch was written during this period of time. In the book of Enoch we see the prophetic shadow picture of the Bulls beginning in Enoch Chapter 85:

> **Enoch Chapter 85**
> 1,2 And after this I saw another dream, and I will show the whole dream to thee, my son. And Enoch lifted up (his voice) and spake to his son Methuselah: ' To thee, my son, will I speak: hear my words-incline thine ear to the dream-vision of thy father. Before I took thy mother Edna, I saw in a vision on my bed, and behold *a bull came forth from the earth, and that bull was white; and after it came forth a heifer, and along with this (latter) came forth two bulls, one of them black and* 4 *the other red. And that black bull gored the red one and pursued him over the earth, and thereupon* 5 *I could no longer see that red bull. But that black bull grew and that heifer went with him, and* 6 *I saw that many oxen proceeded from him which resembled and followed him. And that cow, that first one, went from the presence of that first bull in order to seek that red one, but found him* 7 *not, and lamented with a great lamentation over him and sought him. And I looked till that first* 8 *bull came to her and quieted her, and from that time onward she cried no more. And after that she bore another white bull, and after him she bore many bulls and black cows.* 9 *And I saw in my sleep that white bull likewise grow and become a great white bull, and from Him proceeded many* white bulls, and they resembled him. And they began to beget

many white bulls, which resembled them, one following the other, (even) many.

Over 6000 years ago, the Sun moved from Gemini to Taurus, a new age. Taurus' symbol is the Bull. On some charts he is seen as a red bull, symbolizing the red earth (and Red Heifer). During the pagan religions of the Age of Taurus, the Bull and Cow were deified and worshiped as gods of fertility, and abundance of the earth. This is the age that the cult of Mithra thrived. In Egypt, Apis the black bull was worshiped as the Bull of Memphis. The Greeks thought that Zeus had disguised himself as the Bull of heaven and worshiped it. The Hindus of India for 5000 years have counted the Bull or Cow as sacred even until this very day. The ancient people were aware of the movements of the heavens and their practice of worship evolved as the Sun moved through the Zodiac.

During this Age of Taurus the Bull, we find that every ancient culture and every religion worshipped the Bull. The Bull represented strength and power and the ancients would seek out their bull deities for divine blessings over their crops, their harvest, and in battle. In ancient Egypt, the god Hapi of the Nile River was the object of worship.

Even though the Israelites were taken into Egyptian captivity in the Age of Aries after the birth of Abraham, the bull was still worshipped in Egypt. The story of the Israelites making a "Golden Calf" at the foot of Mt. Sinai (***Exodus 32:19-24***) is evident of this practice coming out of Egypt. Over the long 500 year period of captivity, the Israelites lost the reckoning of time laid out by Enoch and the ages. In the Biblical story, the Israelites truly believed that the Golden Calf would be pleasing to Yahuah.

Prior to the written Law and lost in Egyptian captivity, the Israelites lost the knowledge of Yahuah and His Law as it was given to Abraham. Not only were they forbidden from making any graven images to worship, but by making an image of the Golden Calf (bull), they proved that they had lost sight of His message in the Zodiac. They made an image of a bull, when they were in the

Age of Aries the Ram! So not only did they make an image to worship, they made the wrong image too!

From ***Secrets of the Red Heifer***:

> *"4000 years ago the Sun equinox in the Zodiac sign of Aries, thus bringing in the Age of Aries, the Ram. This age would last just over 2000 years. Each time there is a new age, there must be a prophet on earth to declare it. Abraham declared on earth what the heavens declared. In Genesis 15, he offered a Ram. In Genesis 22, the Ram was in the bush and sacrificed instead of Isaac. The lamb/Ram became the choice animal for sacrifice and the blowing of the Ram's Horn announcing the Age of Aries and the end of the Age of Taurus the Bull. Near the end of the age of Taurus, Mithra slayed the Bull further announcing the end of the Bovine worship-worship of materialism. "*
>
> *3500 years ago, during the Age of Aries, there were others in Egypt and around the world yet worshiping the Bull or Cow. Israel while in Egypt was familiar with Apis, the Bull god and its worship. While waiting for Moses to return from the cloudship hovering over Mt Sinai, they got impatient. They wanted a god that they could see and worship, Aaron, Moses' brother built the Golden Bull Calf.*
>
> *When Moses arrived they were dancing and proclaiming the Age of Taurus, they had reverted back to the "old time religion". Moses destroyed the golden bull calf, ground it to power and threw it into the water and made them drink the gold water. Since they were so willing to worship gold, he made them drink it.*

The Law was then restored to them via Moses and the Passover Lamb was re-instituted. The Passover Lamb, in addition to being a reminder of coming out of Egypt, was an annual reminder of the debt owed on Mt. Mariah; where a Ram (Aries) was substituted for Isaac (the Bull). We see in the Book of Enoch that people were shadow pictured by bulls. So among the many types and shadows involved in Abraham sacrificing Isaac, we see the Age transition.

So the Ram replaced the Bull in the times of Abraham and the transition of the Ages from Taurus to Aries.

Calf Worship in the ISBE Bible Encyclopedia

Ancient Calf Worship. The origin of animal worship is hidden in obscurity, but reverence for the bull and cow is found widespread among the most ancient historic cults. Even in the prehistoric age the influence of the bull symbol was so powerful that it gave its name to one of the most important signs of the Zodiac, and from early historic times the horns of the bull were the familiar emblem of the rays of the sun, and solar gods were very commonly represented as bull-gods.

Timeframe: From the fall of man (Adam) through the birth of Abraham

Symbol: Bull/Golden Calf/Ox http://www.bible-history.com/biblestudy/bullworship.html

Transition: The transition from Taurus to Aries was marked by a very significant event in the Zodiac. This event, known today as the Sign of the Son of Man, heralded the birth of Abraham. The description of Abraham's birth is identical to that of Yahusha's birth because both were Age transitions and marked by the same sign that Yahuah had orchestrated in the Zodiac signs. We read of this event in the Book of Jasher.

The Book of Jasher is not a canonical book of the Bible, but is referred to in Joshua 10:13 and II Samuel 1:18.

Jasher 8:1-4

And it was in the night that Abram was born, that all the servants of Terah, and all the wise men of Nimrod, and his conjurors came and ate and drank in the house of Terah, and they rejoiced with him on that night. 2) And when all the wise men and conjurors went out from the house of Terah, they lifted up their eyes toward heaven that night to look at the stars, and they saw, and behold one very large star came from the east and ran in the heavens (the Zodiac), and he swallowed up the four stars from the four sides of the heavens. 3) And all the wise men of the king and his conjurors were astonished at the sight and the sages understood this matter, and they knew its importance. 4) And they said to each other, this only betokens the child that has been born to Terah this night, who will grow up, and be fruitful, and multiply, and possess all the earth, he and

The Age of Aries
(Ram/Lamb and the Law)

Yahuah witnessed The Plan of Salvation to Abraham through the Zodiac as we know. Abraham understood the "Life of the Messiah" was laid out annually as the sun progressed through the constellations and that Plan involved the sacrifice of a Lamb. However, Abraham also understood the TIMING of Yahuah's Plan was laid out through 2000 year Ages that progress backward through the signs! The Age of Aries began with the Sign of the Son of Man in the sky which heralded Abraham's birth. Abraham understood Isaac to be the one spoken of in the stars (by mistake) and went to fulfill the prophecy by sacrificing his own son. Yahuah prevented it and delivered a RAM as a substitute. Abraham recognized the RAM as a substitute because he understood the Ages and that we had just entered the Age of Aries... the Ram. Then the children of Israel were taken into captivity in Egypt. They lost the knowledge contained in the stars and only retained what the Egyptians knew. In the desert at Sinai if you read the story, they really thought they were honoring Yahuah by building an image of the Bull (Taurus), but by doing so they only illustrated their ignorance of the Plan of Salvation... as they were not in the Age of Taurus any longer, but in the Age of Aries. So this was an abomination to Yahuah on multiple levels, both building an "image" and at that... building the wrong one as I said earlier.

So Yahuah laid out His instructions in detail and the Passover Lamb properly represented the "Age of Aries" until the Age transitioned again... with the Sign of the Son of Man which heralded the birth of the Messiah and the transition from Aries to Pisces...

The Age of Pisces
(the Fish - Messianic Age to re-unite Israel)

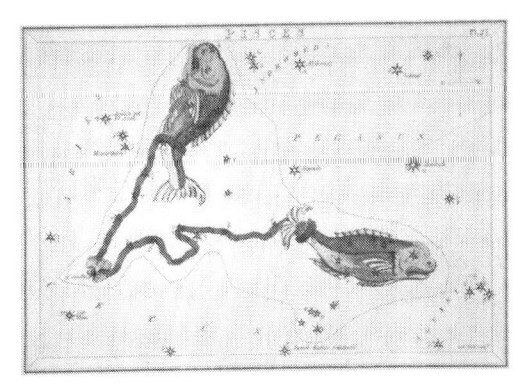

The early Nazarenes, taught by Yahusha, understood this transition and the sign of a fish was a "sacred symbol" by which they identified themselves. The two fish represent the two Houses of Israel bound by the Messiah.

The fish symbol was used to mark meeting place, and tombs.

The Messianic Age was an age of the "fisher of men" whereby the Messiah would as a "fisher of men" cast his net among the nations and "catch" the chosen among them. Yahusha came specifically to reclaim lost sheep of the House if Israel (who had been scattered among the nations.

Matthew 15:24
He answered, "I was sent only to the lost sheep of Israel."

The Age of Aquarius
(the Water Bearer - Kingdom Age)

The Age of Aquarius (which begins in 2017) is marked by the *Sign of the Son of Man* in the sky (on Yom Teruah). NOTE: I am not stating the Messiah returns on this date, I am just saying the Age of Aquarius begins on this date because of this sign. Per the book of Revelation, there is still 3.5 years from the date we see the Sign of the Son of Man in the sky.

What about... the Age of Aquarius the Water Bearer? What does this Age mean in the Zodiac, and how does Yahusha fulfill it? Is the Age of Aquarius in scripture? Shouldn't the prophets speak of this Age? Shouldn't there be an annual rehearsal for it since it is the fulfillment of the Fall Feasts?

Yes... Yes... and YES!

There certainly is, but we are not properly taught the meaning of scripture, and do not have "eyes to see" the Mystery Language in which it is written.

As I have demonstrated so far, the means by which Yahuah revealed the Plan of Salvation to Enoch, then Abraham, and then to all the prophets was via the Mazzaroth...

I showed how Ezekiel and John's visions were describing Enoch's Zodiac in great detail. I explained how the Heavenly Scroll is a divine clock proclaiming the Sabbath, the first and second comings, and every Age or Epoch of mankind.

The 4 wheels within a wheel, eyes of the Zodiac Signs all around, 4 beasts crying out "Holy, Holy, Holy" before the King standing at a podium that looks like rainbow about to open the sealed book. The 24 stars/elders fallen at his feet. The other 4 beasts with 2 wings stationed at the 4 corners of the "wheel"... a perfect match! So the prophets understood the "secret" message contained in the Stars; and they wrote about the Plan of Salvation describing it as they were told to "behold!" Enoch's Zodiac the Heavenly Scroll!

But what about ***The Age of Aquarius the Water Bearer***? Where is that in scripture? Where is the annual rehearsal for that?
Good questions. We see in Isaiah Chapter 44, that Isaiah understood the meaning of the *Age of Aquarius*:

> <u>Isaiah 44:3</u>
> For I will pour out water on the thirsty land And streams on the dry ground; I will pour out My Spirit on your offspring And My blessing on your descendants; 4 And they will spring up among the grass Like poplars by streams of water.'

Now look below at the symbol of the Age of Aquarius! It is the Messiah pouring out water to Mikveh the Earth and vegetation springs up fed by living water from Heaven. Read again what Isaiah just said in 44:3 above and compare to this image below!

Isaiah speaks of this again in Isaiah Chapter 12

Isaiah 12:2
"Behold, Yahuah is my salvation; I will trust, and will not be afraid; for Yahuah Elohim is my strength and my song, and He has become my salvation (by fulfilling His promise to send a Messiah)." 3 With joy you will draw water from the wells of salvation."

Again Isaiah is speaking of the Age of Aquarius. You see, Yahuah "preached the Gospel" to all the prophets using The Book of the Mazzaroth and they described the Plan of Salvation as foretold in the heavens in great detail. The Heavenly Scroll (Mazzaroth/Zodiac) was literally the foundation of revelation to the prophets. If the Age of Aquarius is speaking of the Kingdom Age, shouldn't we have some type of rehearsal during the Fall Feasts of Yahuah as a shadow picture of what Isaiah is referring to in his prophetic utterances?

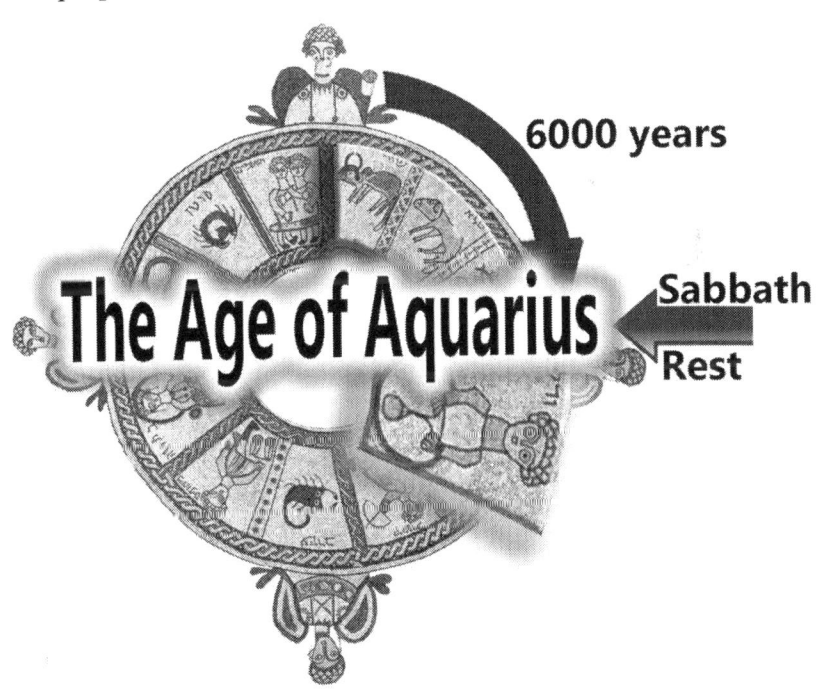

The Festival of Water Libation

The Festival of Water Libation on the last Great Day of Sukkot is the rehearsal for the Age of Aquarius! Read about the Festival of Water Libation from The Temple Mount Institutes website:

http://www.templeinstitute.org/water_libation_festival.htm

Also called "the water drawing ceremony"...

http://www.chabad.org/holidays/JewishNewYear/template_cdo/aid/1971019/jewish/The-Joyous-Water-Drawing-Ceremony.htm

Each year on Sukkot, which is the celebration of the beginning of the Millennial Kingdom (The Age of Aquarius), there was a water ceremony on the Temple Mount where the priests drew "living water" from the well. Then the priests would pour that water over the Altar to Mikveh the Altar. This was a rehearsal of what the prophet Isaiah spoke of in Isaiah 44:3 and Isaiah 12.

This was the meaning behind the Water Ceremony on the last day of Sukkot... it was a celebration of the coming day when we would see 'Yahuah's Salvation', and He would pour out His spirit, and we would "draw living water from the wells of salvation (Yahusha)".

Yahusha attended that Water Ceremony on the last Great Day of the Feast of Sukkot. Just as the priests were drawing living water from that well, as all stood by in eager expectation, watching the elaborate spectacle of priests dancing around and such... Yahusha stood up and literally screamed out load so that everyone would hear him... well, let's just read it:

> **John 7:38, 37**
> Now on the last day, the great day of the feast of Sukkot, Yahusha stood [up] and cried out in a loud voice, saying, "If anyone is thirsty, let him come to Me and drink. 38 "He who believes in Me, as the Scripture said, 'From his innermost being will flow rivers of living water.'"

Apparently, Yahusha said that Isaiah was speaking of him specifically and naming him by name! That is exactly what Isaiah did. Let's take a closer look at that scripture.

> **Isaiah 12:2**
> "Behold, Yahuah is my salvation; I will trust, and will not be afraid; for Yahuah Elohim is my strength and my song, and he has become my salvation (by fulfilling His word to send a Messiah)." 3 With joy you will draw water from the wells of [Yahuah's] salvation.

At the end of verse 3 above, 'Yahuah' is implied; there is no salvation outside of Him. So the end of that verse, we could add the word that is implied, and it would legally read "Yahuah's salvation". The translators left "Yahuah" out because it is implied. We know that Yahu'sha is a contracted sentence name (many names were back then, they gave Yahuah Glory as it was a common practice among the Hebrews to take a word and attach it to Yahuah then contracting it down to a name with meaning).

We know that Yahu'sha is a contraction of Yahuah and Yasha (salvation). So Yahseph and Miriam contracted the phrase "Yahuah is my salvation" into Yahu'sha, and that is the name of the Messiah (as they were told to do by the Angel Messenger of Yahuah who announced the birth of the Messiah). Because as we will see, the name of the Messiah comes alive in the Torah/Prophets! Simply use the contraction Yahu'sha in replace of "Yahuah is salvation" or "Yahuah is my savior" or "salvation of Yahuah".

We know that with any contraction, you can replace the longer form in a sentence with the contraction; without changing the meaning of the sentence...

Example: *Don't*. The English word '*don't*' is a contraction of "do not". Whenever you see "do not" in a sentence, you can legally replace it with the contracted form "*don't*" without changing the meaning of the sentence.

Same is true in Hebrew. Let's do that in the scripture in question:

> **Isaiah 12:2**
> "Behold, Yahusha; I will trust, and will not be afraid; for Yahuah Elohim is my strength and my song, and he has become my salvation (by fulfilling His promise of a Messiah)." 3 With joy you will draw water from the wells of Yahusha.

You see, Yahusha knew that verse too, and he knew Isaiah was speaking of him. He also knew the Plan of Salvation foretold in the Book of the Mazzaroth, the Heavenly Scroll (it was passed down to him by the prophet Daniel), and that the fulfillment would come at the "end of the age". That is what Yahusha told his disciples:

> **Matthew 28:20**
> "and teaching them to obey everything I have commanded you. And surely I am with you always, to the very end of the age (of Pisces when he returns in the Age of Aquarius)."

We should never have expected Yahusha to return 'at any minute, or in a twinkling of an eye" because Ages are 2,000 years in duration!

We turned a deaf ear to the message proclaimed to all the Earth by the Zodiac (Psalms 19).

> **Psalm 19**
> 1 The heavens (stars and constellations) declare the glory of Yahuah; the skies proclaim the work of his hands. 2 Day after day they pour forth speech; night after night they reveal knowledge. 3 They have no speech, they use no words; no sound is heard from them. 4 Yet their voice goes out into all the earth, their words to the ends of the Age. In the heavens (among the Stars and Constellations) Yahuah has pitched a tent for the sun (the Zodiac). 5 It is like a bridegroom (Yahusha) coming out of his chamber (to wed the Bride, Remnant Israel), like a champion (Conquering King) rejoicing to run his course (through the ecliptic). 6 It rises at one end

of the heavens and makes its circuit (Zodiac means circuit of circle or path) to the other; nothing is deprived of its warmth. Yahusha, just like all the prophets, knew the Plan of Salvation written in the Stars and what the Age of Aquarius the Water Bearer really meant! That is why they celebrated the Festival of Water Libation on the last day of Sukkot by drawing living water out of a well and pouring out on the Altar. They just missed the physical to spiritual parallel, but it did not escape our Messiah! Nor does it escape me 2,000 years later. We need to have "eyes to see" the Mazzaroth, and "ears to hear" its message!

Yahusha knew the scriptures in Isaiah named him by name. He knew the Plan of Salvation in the Zodiac and the meaning of the Age of Aquarius the Water Bearer.

He knew what that Water Ceremony was all about and that is why he... stood and cried out, saying...

"If anyone is thirsty, let him come to me and drink!"

In front of the High Priest, all the Temple Priests, and all of Israel who were gathered on the Greatest Day of the Feast of Sukkot to draw living water from the well! Yahusha knew HE was "the water bearer of Aquarius" who would pour out living water and Mikveh Yahuah's creation and liberate it from sin/death at the beginning of the next "age"... That Age is Aquarius the Water Bearer.

Yahusha in Hebrew literally means "salvation of Yahuah"... so we draw water from the wells of Yahusha the living water.

> **Isaiah 12:3**
> 12 In that day you will say: "I will praise you, YAHUAH. Although you were angry with me, your anger has turned away and you have comforted me. ² Surely *Yahuah is my salvation* (Yahusha); I will trust and not be afraid. Yahuah himself, is my strength and my defense; He has become my salvation." ³ **With joy you will draw water from the wells of (Yahuah's) salvation (Yahu'sha)**. ⁴ In that day you will say: "Give praise to Yahuah, proclaim his name; make known among the nations what he has done, and proclaim that his name is exalted. ⁵ Sing to Yahuah, for he has done glorious things; let this be known to all the world. ⁶ Shout aloud and sing for joy, people of Zion, for great is the Holy One of Israel among you."

Why 12 constellations?

Now that we know who the author of the Zodiac is (Yahuah the Creator) it is very easy to understand why there are 12 constellations which are probably the most obvious symbolism of the Zodiac. The number 12 in Hebrew and Biblical numerology represents the number of Governmental Perfection. It can be found 187 times in scripture. There are 22 occurrences in the book of Revelation alone! From www.biblestudy.org - **Meaning of Numbers in the Bible** *The Number 12*:

> *"Twelve can be found in 187 places in God's word. Revelation alone has 22 occurrences of the number. The meaning of 12, which is considered a perfect number, is that it symbolizes God's power and authority, as well as serving as a perfect governmental foundation. It can also symbolize completeness or the nation of Israel as a whole."*

Many of the measurements of the Temple and other illustrations are multiples of 12, demonstrating perfection such as the numbers

144 and 144,000. Yahusha calling exactly 12 disciples as he came to "usher in the kingdom and governmental perfection".

Each of the 12 signs of the Zodiac are assigned to each of the 12 tribes of Israel. We see the physical to spiritual parallelism very prevalent in the 12 signs, they proclaim:

- 12 Tribes of Israel
- 12 brothers of Joseph
- 12 Judges of Israel
- 12 Great Patriarchs
- 12 OT Prophets
- 12 Kings of Israel
- 12 Princes of Israel
- Yahusha taught in the temple at age 12
- 12 disciples
- 12 in Biblical numerology is "placing things within perfect order or achieving governmental perfection."
- 12 months in a year

These attributes of the life of Yahusha were mimicked in all false solar god-men myths as I will show in this book series.

CHAPTER 11
WHEN WAS THE DEBAR FULFILLED IN THE FLESH

Chapter 11: *When was the Debar fulfilled in the flesh?*

When exactly was The Nazarene born in fulfillment of The Heavenly Scroll? According to The Heavenly Scroll, the Plan of Salvation through a mediating High Priest begins with his birth in the constellation Virgo.

> ***VIRGO***: A virgin will give birth to a beautiful glorious and righteous branch (Nazarene). The seed of the woman will be a man of humiliation to rise to be the desire of nations and will become exalted first as shepherd then as harvester.

There is nothing concerning the coming Branch before that point when he was born in his mother's womb. In the last chapter, I showed that Scripture declares the same thing.

> **Psalm 22:9-10**
> 9 But you took Me from My mother's womb, Yahuah! You made Me trust in You, even from My mother's breast. 10 <u>I was cast upon You from My birth</u>; from My mother's womb, You are My Strength.

There is no mention of Yahusha coming to Earth before he was created human anywhere in Scripture. He was not the reincarnated "the King of Salem", he was not the Archangel Michael, he was not in the lions den, did not wrestle with Jacob and so forth. Those are all implied lies under the Spirit of the False Messiah.

There is a great debate spanning 2000 years concerning the exact year The Nazarene was born to fulfill The Heavenly Scroll. The guesses by "experts" range from 12 BC through 4 AD. Every "guess" by humanity over this past 2000 years ignores the most telling factor in his birth. The Heavenly Scroll. We have denied Yahuah's witness of His Son found written in the stars. In this chapter, I am going to restore that vital piece of the puzzle, and identify the exact year of the coming of the branch.

Isaiah foretold the Messiah's birth to be on the cusp of Aries and Pisces... we just don't realize what Isaiah was looking at when he prophesied the birth of The Nazarene.

> Isaiah 7:14
> 14"Therefore Yahuah Himself will give you a sign ('sky' is Hebrew Shamayim or Heavens... stars are for signs not human women): Behold, a virgin (constellation Virgo) will be with child (the King Planet Jupiter will proceed out of Virgo's womb) and bear a son, and she will call His name (reputation) Immanuel (True and Faithful Witness).

This "sign in the sky" is laid out in detail in Revelation Chapter 12, as it is the sign of both the Messiah's first and second coming.

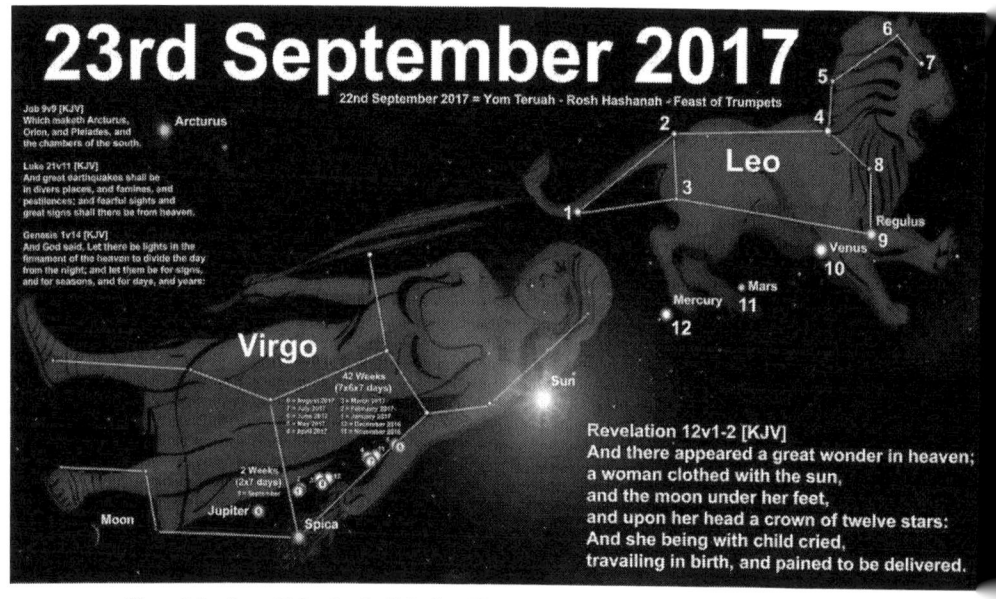

Sign of the Son of Man in the "sky" or Heaven. The sign of the transition of the Ages

The prophet Daniel accurately foretold the Messiah's birth down the timing of the Fall Feasts on the cusp of Aries/Pisces in the 70 Weeks Prophetic announcement. Daniel understood the timing as he "read The Heavenly Scroll".

Creation Cries Out!

The timeframe or Plan for Mankind is foretold reading clockwise from the "Living Creature" holding the Scroll just above the transition from Gemini to Taurus just above Adam and Eve.

The Plan of Salvation is told reading counter clockwise from Virgo to Leo. Simply line up the Messiah's birth (Virgo) with the timeframe and you land exactly on the cusp of Aries and Pisces 4,000 years into the Plan for Mankind.

Birth of Messiah foretold in The Heavenly Scroll

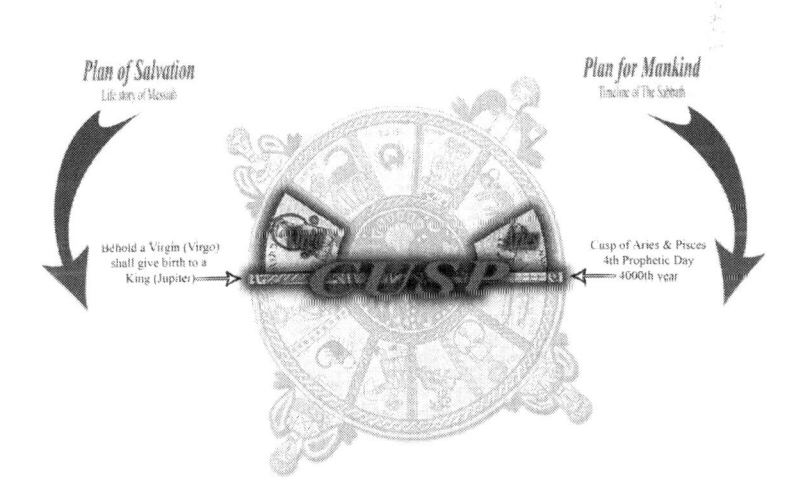

Plan of Salvation
Life story of Messiah

Behold a Virgin (Virgo) shall give birth to a King (Jupiter)

Plan for Mankind
Timeline of The Sabbath

Cusp of Aries & Pisces
4th Prophetic Day
4000th year

Rav Sha'ul

Daniel was the Chief Astrologer under 3 Kings and rose to prominence for his understanding of The Heavenly Scroll!

The Sabbath Covenant
Foretold in The Heavenly Scroll

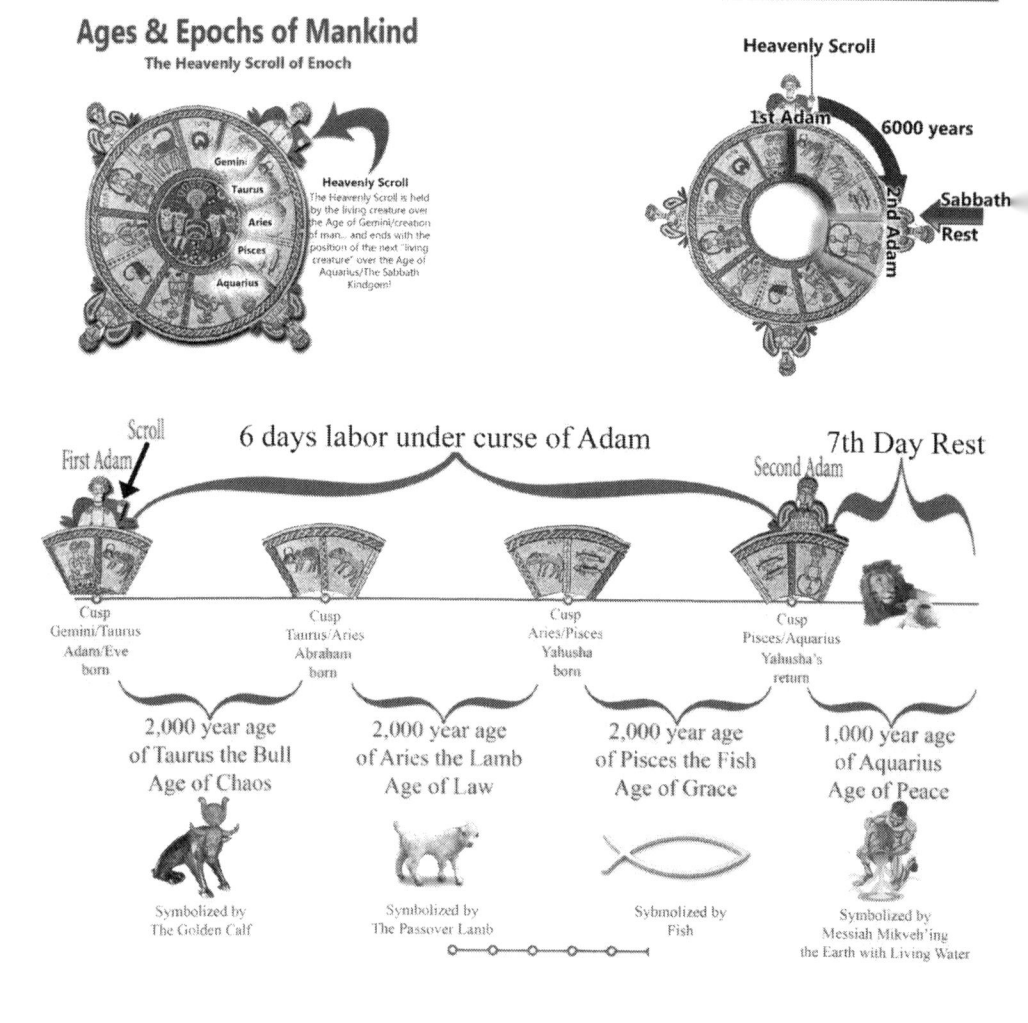

Ages & Epochs of Mankind
The Heavenly Scroll of Enoch

Heavenly Scroll
The Heavenly Scroll is held by the living creature over the Age of Gemini/creation of man... and ends with the position of the next "living creature" over the Age of Aquarius/The Sabbath Kindgom!

Heavenly Scroll

1st Adam — 6000 years
2nd Adam — Sabbath Rest

Scroll
First Adam — 6 days labor under curse of Adam — 7th Day Rest — Second Adam

| Cusp Gemini/Taurus Adam/Eve born | Cusp Taurus/Aries Abraham born | Cusp Aries/Pisces Yahusha born | Cusp Pisces/Aquarius Yahusha's return |

2,000 year age of Taurus the Bull
Age of Chaos
Symbolized by The Golden Calf

2,000 year age of Aries the Lamb
Age of Law
Symbolized by The Passover Lamb

2,000 year age of Pisces the Fish
Age of Grace
Symbolized by Fish

1,000 year age of Aquarius
Age of Peace
Symbolized by Messiah Mikveh'ing the Earth with Living Water

310

The Prophet Micah foretold the location...

Micah 5:2
"But you, Bethlehem Ephrathah, though you are small among the clans of Judah, out of you will come for me one who will be ruler over Israel, whose origins are (foretold) from of old (in The Heavenly Scroll), from ancient times (through the prophets Romans 1)."

Romans 1
2 concerning Yahusha, which Yahuah promised beforehand through His prophets in the holy Scriptures (both The Heavenly and Earthly Scrolls, he did not pre-exist), 3 concerning His Son, who was born of a descendant of David (through both parents) according to the flesh (Hebrew 'Sarki' meaning by human means ONLY, outside of ANY Divine intervention), 4 who was declared (Divine) the Son of Yahuah with power by the resurrection from the dead, according to the Spirit of holiness (Yahuah's Spiritual Seed is imparted upon resurrection NOT human birth), Yahusha the Messiah.

What year was the birth of the King?

When looking at dating Daniels 70 weeks prophecy there is the ongoing debate about when to begin the timing. Is it Cyrus' Decree which was postponed by resistance in the land or Artaxerxes Decree given to Nehemiah when the walls of Jerusalem began construction and then there are all the various human attempts at calculating dates and the difference between a 360 day "Jewish" year, or a 364 day Enoch Year, or a 365 day Julian year.
It is extremely inaccurate, to say the very least, and even more frustrating when trying to nail down a "timeline". Experts have been debating this for over a 1,000 years!

I have decided to do what no one else has done, and consult The Heavenly Scroll. The ONLY way history can be established, without a doubt, is by using creation and not human knowledge of ancient history when there was no calendar, as "signs" are in the stars and mankind cannot alter those signs. That is why Yahuah established The Heavenly Scroll to begin with.

7,000 Year Plan for Man
6 days and a 7th - The Sabbath Covenant foretold in The Heavnly Scroll

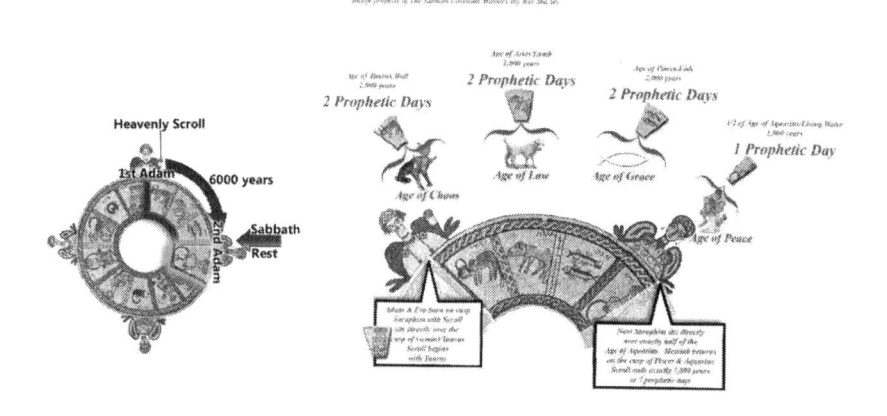

The only real date that can be established is the birth of the

Messiah as foretold in the stars. If we can determine that year/season, without a doubt, then every other "date" can be established with the various timeframes given in Daniel by working backward and forward from the Messiah's birth.

The Scriptural "clues"!

How do we determine the birth of the Messiah? That too has been the subject of many expert debates and ranges from 12 B.C. to 6 A.D.! No one has ever included The Heavenly Scroll in the calculation, which is why there has never been a solid date that is reliable. What we do know are "clues" that help us determine the date of Yahusha's birth:

> **Clue #1** - It was during the reign of Herod the Great
> **Clue #2** - It was during a Roman census year
> **Clue #3** - The Star of Bethlehem was over Jerusalem
> **Clue #4** - The Sign of the Son of Man was in the sky (per Isaiah)
> **Clue #5** - It was during the Fall Feasts

Armed with this data, I used Stellarium Software to search for the year that fit all 5 clues. If we can find a year with all 5 concurring witnesses... we have our rock solid "date" from which to build on. That year is 12 B.C.

The Evidence

During the Fall Feasts (September) in the year 12 B.C. we had:
Halley's Comet (Star of Bethlehem) over Jerusalem in the constellation Virgo during the Fall ...

> Professor Baratta, an astrophysicist at the Rome Observatory, said he had discovered new evidence after "many years of study", drawing on biblical sources, Roman history and astronomy. The most crucial errors had been made in the 6th century AD by the Scythian monk

Dionysius Exiguus, known in English as Denis The Little. Denis, an accomplished mathematician and astronomer, arrived in Rome after the death in AD 496 of Pope Gelasius the First, who had summoned him to re-organise the pontifical archives.

In AD 525 he drew up the calendar which became accepted throughout the West. But Denis, the professor says, failed to take into account the Year Zero - between 1BC and AD 1 - and also ignored the four-year period when the Roman Emperor Augustus was on the throne (31-27BC) under the name Octavian. Denis also omitted the first two years in which the Emperor Tiberius ruled after Augustus, his stepfather, died in AD 14.

This seven-year error would appear to support Kepler's theory, Professor Baratta says. On the other hand, Kepler's evidence rested mainly on his identification of the Star of Bethlehem as described by St Matthew. Kepler concluded, Professor Baratta says, that this referred to the conjunction of Jupiter and Saturn in 7BC.

But in following Kepler's calculations, the professor had discovered serious discrepancies. Professor Baratta's research pointed to 12BC, when an unusually bright and fiery "travelling star" had appeared between the constellations of Gemini and Leo. "It was in fact a comet, and was observed by the Chinese as well as by European astronomers of the time." Halley's Comet.

Source: http://www.datasync.com/~rsf1/fun/halley12.htm

Creation Cries Out!

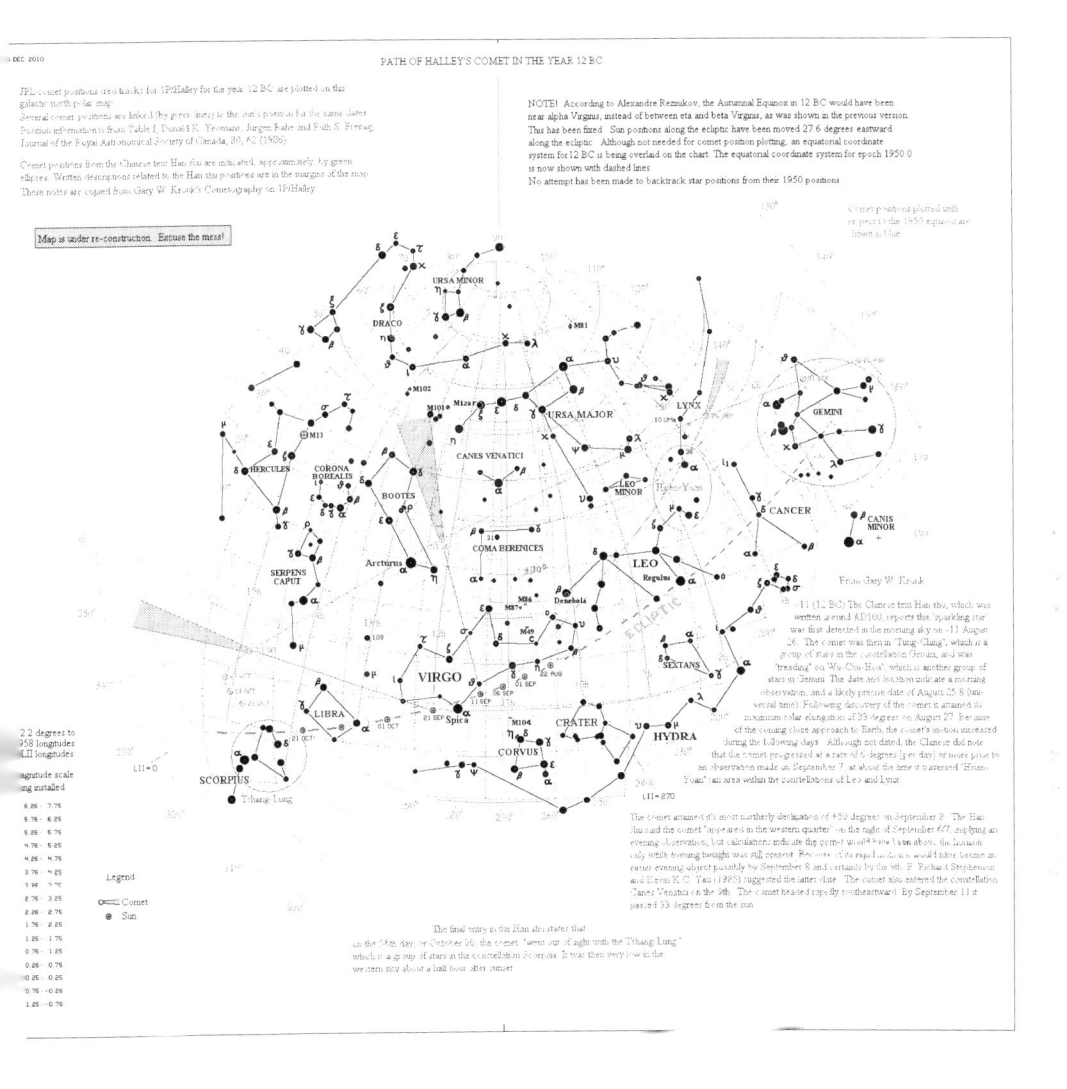

PATH OF HALLEY'S COMET IN THE YEAR 12 BC

JPL comet positions (red tracks) for 1P/Halley for the year 12 BC are plotted on this galactic north-polar map.

Several comet positions are linked (by green lines) to the sun's position for the same dates. Position information is from Table 1, Donald K. Yeomans, Jürgen Rahe and Ruth S. Freitag, Journal of the Royal Astronomical Society of Canada, 80, 62 (1986).

Comet positions from the Chinese text Han shu are indicated, approximately, by green ellipses. Written descriptions related to the Han shu positions are in the margins of the map. These notes are copied from Gary W. Kronk's Cometography on 1P/Halley.

NOTE! According to Alexandre Reznikov, the Autumnal Equinox in 12 BC would have been near alpha Virginis, instead of between eta and beta Virginis, as was shown in the previous version. This has been fixed. Sun positions along the ecliptic have been moved 27.6 degrees eastward along the ecliptic. Although not needed for comet position plotting, an equatorial coordinate system for 12 BC is being overlaid on the chart. The equatorial coordinate system for epoch 1950.0 is now shown with dashed lines.

No attempt has been made to backtrack star positions from their 1950 positions.

Map is under re-construction. Excuse the mess!

From Gary W. Kronk

11 (12 BC) The Chinese text Han shu, which was written around AD 100, reports that the "sparkling star" was first detected in the morning sky on -11 August 26. The comet was then in "Tung-Ching", which is a group of stars in the constellation Gemini, and was "treading" on Wu-Chu-Hou", which is another group of stars in Gemini. The date and location indicate a morning observation, and a likely precise date of August 25.8 (universal time). Following discovery of the comet it attained its maximum solar elongation of 93 degrees on August 27. Because of the evening close approach to Earth, the comet's motion increased during the following days. Although not dated, the Chinese did note that the comet progressed at a rate of 6 degrees (per day) or more prior to an observation made on September 7, at about the time it traversed "Hsuan-Yuan" (an area within the constellations of Leo and Lynx).

The comet attained it's most northerly declination of +50 degrees on September 8. The Han shu noted the comet "appeared in the western quarter" in the night of September 6/7, implying an evening observation, but calculations indicate the comet would have been above the horizon only while evening twilight was still present. Regardless, the comet would have become an easier evening object possibly by September 8 and certainly by the 9th. F. Richard Stephenson and Kevin K.C. Tau (1985) suggested the latter date. The comet also entered the constellation Canes Venatici on the 9th. The comet headed rapidly southeastward. By September 11 it passed 33 degrees from the sun.

The final entry in the Han shu states that on the 56th day, or October 20, the comet "went out of sight with the Tchang-Lung", which is a group of stars in the constellation Scorpius. It was then very low in the western sky about a half hour after sunset.

Legend
- Comet
- ● Sun

The Sun, and Jupiter in the Constellation Virgo which fulfills The Sign of the Son of Man during the Fall ...

It was during the reign of Herod the Great

> According to the historian Josephus, King Herod died in 4 B.C., so most scholars have placed Yahusha's birth in about that period. But Fleming, said Jerry Vardaman, director of archaeology at Mississippi State University, in a new unpublished work, describes finding tiny writing on Roman coins indicating an earlier census was made in 12 B.C.

It was a Roman census year

> Source: http://www.upi.com/Archives/1985/12/12/When-was-Jesus-born/8044503211600/
>
> Jerry Vardaman, director of archaeology at Mississippi State University, in a new unpublished work, describes

finding tiny writing on Roman coins indicating an earlier census was made in 12 B.C. The writing -- 'micro-graffiti,' Fleming calls it -- substantiates an inscription on a tablet found 300 years ago that referred to the same census. And, Fleming said, Halley's comet was visible twice in 12 B.C. This could have been the star that initially grabbed attention of the three Wise Men, and when it reappeared four months later led them to Bethlehem.

CHAPTER 12

THE BIBLE AND THE ZODIAC
TWO SCROLLS, ONE MESSAGE!

Chapter 12 – The Bible and The Zodiac: Two scrolls, one message

In the Bible there is one very well established reality: Yahuah has hidden Himself from the masses. He has *hidden things* of the Spiritual Realm and preserved them for His chosen sons and daughters. In other words, Yahuah does provide *Divine Counsel* (known as divination) to those whom He chooses and that is not forbidden. We see Rav Sha'ul, the Apostle, speak of these *hidden things* that were established and ordained <u>before the world was created as secret knowledge 'for our glory'</u>. That which was created before the world is the Original Revelation in the stars! What we call The Zodiac. It was the first and most complete Gospel of Yahusha the Messiah.

> **1 Corinthians 2**
> 4 And my speech and my preaching was not with enticing words of man's wisdom (Sha'ul or Yahusha did not speak in literal terms), but in the demonstration of the Spirit of Holiness and of power (which gives us understanding of hidden things): 5 That your faith should not stand in the (literal) wisdom of men (to be taken literally), but in the power of Yahuah (In a Mystery Language taught only by The Holy Spirit to a chosen few). 6 However we (Yahuah's Chosen Few) speak wisdom (Spiritual Understanding) among them that are perfect (perfected by The Spirit of Holiness): yet not the wisdom (literal / pagan / natural understanding) of this world, nor of the princes of this world, that come to nothing (they do not understand the Bible language nor the meaning of The Zodiac): 7 But we (Yahuah's Chosen Few) speak the wisdom of Yahuah in a mystery, even the hidden wisdom, which (these mysteries and hidden wisdom) Yahuah ordained before the world unto our glory.

As I have shown throughout this book, Yahuah has declared the Plan of Salvation was originally written in the stars (called Heaven) in what the Bible calls *The Mazzaroth*. We call it *the*

Zodiac which means (The Way). Yahusha is the fulfillment of the Plan of Salvation written in the Zodiac and he came to show us The Way by fulfilling the Heavenly Scroll.

These "hidden secret things" cannot be understood in the natural or literal sense; they are disclosed through physical shadows and metaphors much like that of the signs of the Zodiac. The sin in the Zodiac is <u>not trying to discern the divine message they contain</u> (righteous divination), but in understanding the Zodiac literally and worshipping the constellations, sun, moon, and stars.

> **Deuteronomy 3:19**
> When you look up to the sky (sky is Hebrew shamayim/Zodiac) and see the sun, moon, and stars (speaking of the Zodiac) — the whole heavenly (Mazzaroth/Zodiac) creation — you must not be seduced to worship and serve them (signs of the Zodiac), for Yahuah your Elohim has assigned them (the signs of the Zodiac) to all the people of the world (they were created by Yahuah to proclaim the coming Messiah Yahusha, see Psalm 19, they are not gods).

We see the Zodiac was assigned meaning and proclaims a message to all the people of the world.

*The signs (constellations) are **symbols with meaning** that shadow spiritual truths of the coming Messiah. Pictographs that tell a story; as the Sun travels through the constellations each year.*

Sha'ul continues:

> **1 Corinthians 2:4-15**
> 8 Which none of the princes of this world knew (speaking of the hidden mysteries): for had they known it (the true message contained in The Zodiac), they would not have crucified the King of glory (because the *'Lamb that would be slaughtered'* was foretold in the Zodiac *Revelation 13:8*). 9 But as it is written, (the natural) EYE (does not see Spiritual Truths and) hath not seen (the hidden mysteries), nor (the natural) EAR heard (the Spiritual Truth), neither have (these mysteries) entered into the (natural) HEART of (natural) man (humanity has been given over to a Spirit of Error and the mind has been depraved of Spiritual understanding *Romans 1*), the things which Yahuah hath prepared for them (the hidden mysteries prepared before the foundation of the world, written in the stars) that Love Him. 10 But Yahuah hath revealed them (the secret mysteries and hidden knowledge) unto us by His Spirit of Truth (righteous divination):

We see Sha'ul above in verse 10 say clearly that divination in the sense of seeking our Yahuah for direction through the Ruach is the only way to obtain the hidden mysteries. **Divination is seeking Divine Counsel**. Righteous divination is seeking that counsel from Yahuah through the Spirit (Ruach). We see an example of this in Genesis 30:27 "*27 But Laban said to him, "If I have found favor in your eyes, please stay. I have learned by divination that Yahuah has blessed me because of you*"…Unrighteous divination is seeking divine counsel through "another spirit".

> **1 John 4:1**
> Beloved, do not believe every spirit, but test the spirits to see whether they are from Yahuah, because many false prophets have gone out into the world.

Sha'ul's protégé, Timothy, also understood these things:

> **1 Timothy 3:9**
> 9 Holding the mystery (hidden or secret things: G3466) of the faith in a pure conscience.

Below is what the word "secret" or "hidden" means in Hebrew:

Hebrew Lexicon word H5641 – Secret is the word Cathar (saw-thar') which means:

    I. to hide, conceal

    A. (Niphal)

    i. to hide oneself

    ii. to be hidden, be concealed

    B. (Piel) to hide carefully

    C. (Pual) to be hidden carefully, be concealed

    D. (Hiphil) to conceal, hide

    E. (Hithpael) to hide oneself carefully

Yahuah has literally hidden Himself in plain sight! He has hidden Himself in His word and in His creation. We all have His Word, but only those who speak His Mystery Language (like Yahusha) understand what those words mean!

We see that all His prophets, through divination (Divine Counsel) were given this mystery language and understood the message contained in the stars:

Daniel 2
20 Daniel answered and said, Blessed be the name of God (Yahuah) for ever and ever: for wisdom and might are His: 21 And He changes the times and the seasons: He removes kings, and sets up kings: He gives (Spiritual) wisdom unto the (chosen) wise, and knowledge to them that know (Spiritual) understanding: 22 He reveals the deep and secret things!

Isaiah was eventually given this Mystery Language after many years of not understanding the Heavenly Scroll. Speaking of the message that is heard throughout all the Earth, written in the Zodiac:

> **Isaiah 48**
> 6 You have heard these things (the stars proclaim); look at them all (the constellations). Will you not admit them (they proclaim a message)? 'From now on I will tell you of new things (written in the stars), of hidden things unknown to you (mysteries preserved in the heavens). 7 They are created now, and not long ago; you have not heard of them before today. So you cannot say, "Yes, I knew of them." 8 You have neither heard nor understood (the Heavenly Scroll); from of old your ears have not been open (to hear its message).

Yahuah simply did not give The Spirit of Holiness to all of His Chosen that teaches us to know these hidden secret things <u>until The Yahushaic Covenant</u>.

Even then, Yahusha continued to veil these things behind parables and parallels so that only those so chosen could understand:

> **Matthew 13**
> 10 The disciples came to him and asked, 'Why do you speak to the people in parables?' 11 He replied, '**Because the knowledge of <u>the secrets of the kingdom of heaven</u> has been given to you, but not to them**. 12 Whoever has (the Spirit of Holiness) **will be given** (speaking of a future date when Yahuah pour out His Spirit) more (hidden knowledge), and they will have an abundance (of Spiritual understanding). Whoever does not have, even what they have will be taken from them. 13 This is why I speak to them in

parables: 'Though seeing (with their physical eyes), they do not see (the Spiritual parallel); though hearing (with their physical ear), they do not hear (the Spiritual Truth) or understand (the Spiritual meaning). 14 In them is fulfilled the prophecy of Isaiah:

"'You will be ever hearing but never understanding;
　you will be ever seeing but never perceiving.
15 For this people's heart has become calloused;
　they hardly hear with their ears,
　and they have closed their eyes.
Otherwise they might see with their eyes,
　hear with their ears,
　understand with their hearts
and turn, and I would heal them."

16 But blessed are your eyes because they see (the physical to Spiritual parallels), and your ears because they hear (the Truth). 17 For truly I tell you, many prophets and righteous people longed to see what you see but did not see it, and to hear what you hear but did not hear it (because it was not revealed until The Yahushaic Covenant and only then to a Chosen Few).

Matthew 13:35
That it might be fulfilled which was spoken by the prophet, saying, I will open my mouth in parables; I will utter things which have been kept secret from the foundation of the world.

Yes, Yahuah has hidden Himself in His Word and His creation in a Mystery Language that only the Chosen Few are ever given eyes to see and ears to hear and a mind to understand. You must have The Spirit of Holiness who teaches you this Mystery Language to understand the things of Yahuah.

That is how the Zodiac is properly understood, not in literal terms. The signs of the Zodiac are just that, "signs" created by Yahuah which are metaphors and allegories pertaining to the coming Messiah.

It is when we look up at the stars and constellation, interpret them literally, and worship them, and seek "their" counsel directly that divination is a sin we are in error.

> **1 Corinthians 14:2**
> ² For he that speaks in an unknown tongue (Mystery Metaphorical Language) speaks not unto (the physical things of) men, but unto (the hidden Spiritual things of) Yahuah: for no man understands him (they don't have eyes to see, ears to hear); however in the spirit (of Holiness) he speaks mysteries (of the Kingdom of Yahuah).

*This **Mystery Language** is spoken in allegorical terms through metaphors, idioms, similes, psalms/poetry, anthropomorphisms, physical to Spiritual parallels, proverbs, pictographs, numerology, etc. It is a <u>metaphorical language</u>.*

King Solomon was given the Mystery Language, the wisdom, and knowledge of understanding the Zodiac properly. It is said that "wisdom" is the anthropomorphism of "astrology" in the writings of Solomon. Astrologers in the Bible are called "wise men" and Solomon was the wisest man to have ever lived. Much of the misuse of Yahuah's creation into occult practices, witchcraft, unrighteous divination, corrupted astrology, and Jewish mysticism (Kabballah) are attributed to King Solomon today.

Jewish Virtual Library.org 'Ancient Jewish History: Astrology'

Genesis 24:1 is interpreted as the gift of astrology (Tosef., Kid. 5:17). Astrological consultation is one of the methods suggested by Jethro to Moses for governing the Children of Israel (Mekh., Amalek 2). Several instances are cited of astrologers whose predictions of future events came true (e.g., Shab. 119a). Gentile rulers were considered to have been especially well versed in astrology or to have consulted astrological experts; but knowledge of astrology was also attributed to King Solomon (Eccl. R. 7:23 no. 1). Nevertheless, the rabbis of the Talmud were skeptical of the astrologers' ability to interpret the stars correctly; they conceded the possibility that the astrologers might be able to predict the future by consulting the stars, but claimed that they err in understanding the contents of their forecasts. On the basis of the phrase in Isaiah 8:19, "the familiar spirits that chirp and mutter" (ha-mezafzefim ve-ha-mahgim), they developed the exegesis: "They gaze (zofin) and know not at what they gaze, they ponder (mehaggin) and know not what they ponder" (Sot. 12b).

We see above that it is possible to make future predictions using the stars (as did Yahuah's prophets), but the gentile astrologers did not know how to read the stars accurately as they did not possess the Spirit of Yahuah. We read in the Book of Wisdom, below, as Solomon describes the "wisdom of Yahuah" and how those who seek divine counsel (divination) apart from Yahuah will be deceived:

Wisdom 2
21 Such things they did imagine, and were deceived: for their own wickedness hath blinded them. 22 As for the mysteries of Yahuah, they knew them not

Wisdom 6:22
As for wisdom, what she is, and how she came up, I (Yahuah) will tell you (Solomon), and will not hide mysteries from you:

but will seek her out from the beginning of her nativity, and bring the knowledge of her into light, and will not pass over the truth.

Wisdom 8:4
For she (wisdom) is privy to the <u>mysteries of the knowledge of Yahuah</u>, and a lover of his works (creation, The Zodiac).

We read in The Book of Ben Sira (written by the Jewish scribe Shimon ben Yahusha ben Eliezer ben Sira of Jerusalem nearly 200 years before Yahusha lived which is considered the earliest witness to a canon of the books of the prophets):

Ben Sira 3
19 Many are in high place, and of renown: but mysteries are revealed unto the meek (righteous divination). 20 For the power of Yahuah is great, and He is honoured of the lowly. 21 Seek not out (divination, seeking Divine Counsel) things that are too hard for you, neither search the things that are above your strength. 22 But what is commanded of you, think upon with reverence, for you do not need to see with your (physical) eyes the things that are in secret.

Now, if you carefully read the verses above, you will now know and understand that the secret, hidden mysteries of Yahuah are told through parables (and parallels, shadow picture, and analogies) that not everyone is going to understand. That is specifically true of the Zodiac whose images are pictographs not gods. Only the humble and repentant heart (inner man, <u>the righteousness seeking mindset</u>) will perceive them. These things are understood in creation by means of a metaphorical language of physical to spiritual parallels. It is within this context the Zodiac is righteously interpreted.

Matthew 11:25
At that time Yahusha answered and said, I thank you, O Father, King of heaven (the place where the stars are located, i.e. The Mazzaroth/Zodiac) and earth, because you have hid these things (secrets preserved in the stars/heaven *Enoch 9:6*) from the wise and prudent, and have revealed them unto babes

"I will not yield my glory to another" ... *Yahuah Elohim*

We need to understand that much of what Yahuah forbids, is forbidden due to our "intention" of giving His Glory to another. We find anything that is done giving the Glory to Yahuah is considered a Righteous act. At the same time, those exact same things done in honor of another god... wicked acts. The difference is not in the act itself, but in the spirit or attitude in doing the act.

> **Isaiah 42:8**
> I am Yahuah; that is my name! I will not yield my glory to another or my praise to graven images

When we look at such things as astrology, divination, and the Zodiac; this same thing applies.

- We see that those who used the Zodiac as a function of Yahuah's creation and original revelation of the Plan of Salvation... called true *Prophets*. Where those who attempted to understand the Zodiac outside of Yahuah... called *Soothsayers*, *star gazers*, and *fools*.
- The *prophets* of Yahuah understood the Zodiac as a Divine Plan and discerned the Sun as a physical metaphor or shadow picture of the coming Messiah. Those not inspired by Yahuah saw the Sun as a god named Helios, Ba'al, Apollo, etc.
- The *prophets* who knew The Creator saw the signs of the Zodiac as divinely named and inspired shadows to proclaim the life of the coming Messiah as pictographs. Those not inspired by Yahuah saw the signs of the Zodiac as gods of the Pantheon or Olympus.

It is the age old battle between interpreting the heavens as a function of The Creator Yahuah vs. those who interpreted the heavens, the constellations, Sun, and Moon as gods. The Truth vs. Sun Worship.

The difference between true prophets and false prophets; righteous divination and sorcery...

is the Spirit behind these acts:

1 John 4:1
Beloved, do not believe every spirit, but test the spirits to see whether they are from Yahuah, for many false prophets have gone out into the world.

We see such things as omens, divination, and fortune telling forbidden by Yahuah. We then see Yahuah rise up His prophets to do that exact thing; interpret omens (casting lots, signs in the sky, dreams), employ divination (seek divine revelation), and tell the future (prophecy). Therefore, all instances where these things are forbidden is in the context of seeking divine counsel from other gods.

Daniel 2:27-28
Daniel answered the king and said, "No wise men, enchanters, magicians, or astrologers (under their own strength and wisdom) can show to the king the mystery that the king has asked, but there is a Elohim in heaven (the Zodiac) who reveals mysteries (through His Ruach to those whom He chooses), and he has made known (through righteous divination) to King Nebuchadnezzar what will be in the latter days (fortune telling, we call it prophecy)

We see Yahuah make such declarations as

Deuteronomy 18:9-12
"When you come into the land that Yahuah your Elohim is giving you, you shall not learn to follow the abominable practices of those nations (who seek divination from other

gods). There shall not be found among you anyone who burns his son or his daughter as an offering (to another god), anyone who practices divination (from another god), or tells fortunes (from another god) or interprets omens (from another god), or a sorcerer or a charmer or a medium or a necromancer or one who inquires of the dead, for whoever does these things (from another god) is an abomination to Yahuah. And because of these abominations Yahuah your Elohim is driving them out before you.

We need to put these restrictions in the proper context of '*from another god*' because then, we see the very same practices performed giving Yahuah the Glory and they are not an abomination; rather those men are His highest representatives i.e. prophets!

> *We see the practice of divination by interpreting omens, dreams, the Zodiac, casting of lots, and the use of Urim and Thummin to seek divine counsel from Yahuah as **righteously done by** 'prophets'.*

The very definition of Urim and Thummin is they are vessels used for divination. Remember, divination is a contraction 'divin'ation' of **Divine Revelation** and coming from Yahuah that is not only acceptable but the highest honor. Seeking it from anything other than Yahuah is an abomination, that is the context of Deuteronomy 18.

U·rim and Thum·mim
/ˈ(y)o͝orim, o͞oˈrēm and ˈTHəmim, to͞oˈmēm/

noun historical
noun: Thummim

two objects of a now unknown nature, possibly used for divination, worn on the breastplate of a Jewish high priest.

Translations, word origin, and more definitions

Divin'ation? Or Divine Revelation?

We read in the ***Jewish Encyclopedia*** concerning the practice of divination (seeking Divine Counsel) using this method, the Jewish Encyclopedia avoids the debate over divination by calling it "divine communication" which is exactly what divination is:

> I Sam. xxviii. 3-6 **mentions three methods of divine communication**: (1) the dream-oracle, of which frequent mention is made also in Assyrian and Babylonian literature; (2) the oracle by means of the Urim (here, undoubtedly, an abbreviation for "Urim and Thummim"); (3) the oracle by the word of the Prophets, found among all Semitic nations.
>
> The only other mention of actual consultation of Yhwh by means of the Urim and Thummim found in the Old Testament is in Num. xxvii. 21. Eleazar was then high priest, and Moses was permitted by the Lord to address Him directly. But Joshua and his successors could speak to the Lord only through the mediation of the high priest and by means of the Urim and Thummim. It cannot be inferred that answers were received at that time by means of them (V. Ryssel, in Kautzsch, "Apokryphen," p. 394).

The word translated as *divination* in scripture means *"witchcraft"* in context, and is defined in scripture as *"divination by consulting a familiar spirit"*. When we see the word *divination* in scripture it is referring to a specific form of divination not a blank statement against all divination but only from "familiar spirits" or other gods. This is because the people would seek knowledge from their dead relative which are 'familiar spirits'.

Notice in the definition of divination from the Brown-Driver-Briggs concordance, definition 3 is "in a good sense" demonstrating that there is actually righteous divination!

> **Brown-Driver-Briggs**
>
> קֶסֶם noun [masculine] **divination**; — absolute קֶ׳ Numbers 23:25+, קֶסֶם Ezekiel 21:26; construct קֶסֶם Ezekiel 13:6; plural קְסָמִים Deuteronomy 18:10 +; —
>
> **1 of the nations : Balaam**, Numbers 23:23 (poem in J E; ‴ נַחַשׁ; with בְּ against, as accusative of congnate meaning with verb לִקְאָסָם Ezekiel 21:26; קֶ׳ as instrument of divination בְּיָמִינוֹ Ezekiel 21:27; so of elders of Moab and Midian, קְסָמִים בְּיָדָם, Numbers 22:7(E). — Isaiah 2:6 see [קֶסֶם].
>
> **2 of false prophets** קָזַב קֶ׳ Ezekiel 13:6 (but see [קֶסֶם]); קֶ׳ as accusative of congnate meaning with verb Ezekiel 13:23 (Co Berthol Krae כָּזָב as Ezekiel 13:9; Ezekiel 21:34; Ezekiel 22:38); צְלִיל קֶ׳ (so Gf for ‴O וֶאֱלִיל Jeremiah 14:4 (all ‴ חֲזוֹן שָׁוְא or שֶׁקֶר קְסָמִים קֶסֶם); prohibited Deuteronomy 18:10; 2 Kings 17:17; reprobated 1 Samuel 15:23 (poem; ‴ תְּרָפִים).
>
> **3 in good sense** עַל שִׂפְתֵי ׳ק מֶלֶךְ Proverbs 16:10 (king's lips as oracle).

So at the heart of this matter is the *Spirit* behind the person/act. Do they represent Yahuah, or another god? Is the focus of their actions giving Glory to Yahuah as The Creator, to foretell His Will, or by a man who seeks his own personal gain?

With The Zodiac, it can be used both ways:

- It can be used by a Prophet... or a soothsayer/star gazer
- It can foretell the Plan of Salvation... or be used for horoscopes
- It can represent The Sun a metaphor for Yahuah/Yahusha... or be seen as a god (Helios, Ba'al)
- It can tell us of the coming Messiah (Yahusha)... or be the basis of a demi-god (Apollo, Horus, Jesus, Krishna)
- Stars and Consolations can be signs from Yahuah... or used as pagan Omens and made into 'gods'
- In the Zodiac we can see a Cherubim... or the Sphinx

Mankind has always erred in giving what is Yahuah's Glory to graven images, pagan gods, mythological figures, etc. When it comes to Creation, Yahuah alone reserves the Glory and He will not give it to anyone or anything else... that is why any act such as divination, fortune telling, sorcery, magic, witchcraft, etc. are strictly forbidden <u>in context of "familiar spirits'</u>; because those are the terms for using Creation improperly or seeking divine counsel outside of the Spirit of Yahuah!

> **Isaiah 45**
> 5 I am Yahuah, **and there is no other**; apart from me there is no God. 7 I form the light and create darkness, I bring prosperity and create disaster; I, **Yahuah, do all these things.** 12 It is I **who made the earth and created mankind upon it**. My own hands stretched out the heavens (stars); I marshaled their starry hosts (constellations).

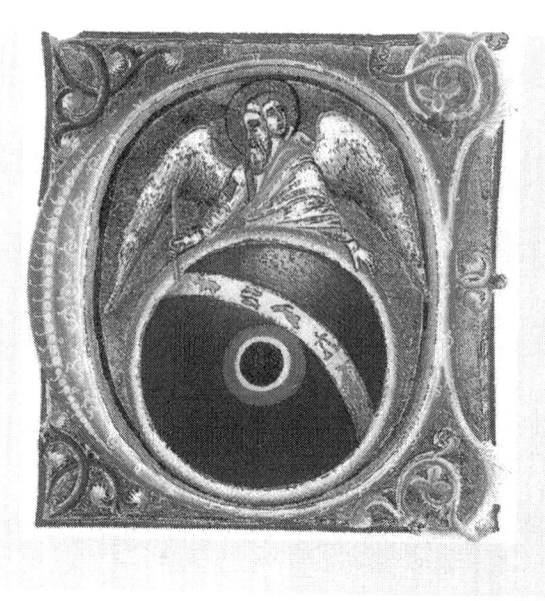

In every culture since the creation of man, "God" is seen as the author of The Zodiac. Above, notice "God" is authoring the Zodiac with his son "on his mind"

Isaiah 44
24 "This is what Yahuah says— your Redeemer, who formed you in the womb: I am Yahuah, the Maker of all things, who stretches out the heavens (to tell a story), who spreads out the earth by myself.

Isaiah 46
5 "To whom will you compare me or count me equal? To whom will you liken me that we may be compared? 8 "Remember this, fix it in mind, take it to heart, you rebels. 9 Remember the former things, those of long ago; I am God, and there is no other; I am God, and there is none like me. 10 I make known the end from the beginning (written in The Zodiac), from ancient times, what is still to come. I say: My purpose will stand, and I will do all that I please.

The bottom line is that Yahuah created the stars and the constellations, named them, gave them their meaning, proclaimed the Gospel in them, and <u>will not give that Glory to another</u>. So any use of the Zodiac outside of the Spirit of Yahuah is… sin.

> *We know that the heavens or Zodiac declare Yahuah's Glory which is Yahusha; not the glory of any other so called "gods" or "demi-gods". We know that Yahuah's Glory is Yahusha. Therefor the heavens or Zodiac declare Yahusha, not any other pagan demi-god.*

Therein lies the Battle of the Ages, the battle ground is the Zodiac, the Heavenly Scroll! Who is the Messiah who fulfills it? Pagan demi-god 'Christs', or Yahusha the Messiah? All pagan 'Christs' were assimilated into one demi-god at the Council of Nicaea named Hesus Horus Krishna. We know this false image today as Jesus H. Christ. The reason Jesus represents the sun rituals of Christmas, Easter, the Trinity, and so forth is because that image is based on the corrupted version of the Zodiac. See my book The Antichrist Revealed! For an in depth analysis of this false messianic image.

The Battle of the Ages has come down to **Jesus vs. Yahusha**; one is the fulfillment of the true message in the Zodiac, the other the twisted version of the Zodiac. Whom do you follow?

Could it be that the reason there are no real prophets left on Earth, like those of the likes of Moses, Jeremiah, Elijah, Daniel, Yahusha, and John the revelator; is because we have denied Yahuah the very basic foundation of all prophecy. The Zodiac? We have turned out back on any form of divination even when it is done seeking

Rav Sha'ul

counsel from Yahuah like all the aforementioned prophets?

The three-level world of astrology: the twelve mundane houses surrounding the twelve Zodiac signs and the seven planets (seals over the Heavenly Scroll), with the earth at the centre. The entire system is shown to be under God's control...
The British Library, C.4.c.9

Isaiah 42
⁵ This is what Yahuah says— **He** who created the heavens (the stars and constellations) and stretched them out (in order as the Sun moves through them to proclaim a message), who spread out the earth and all that comes out of it, who gives breath to its people, and life to those who walk on it:

We find that many things when done in context of giving Yahuah the Glory or Esteem, they are perfectly acceptable. For instance things like animal sacrifices and prayers. Both are performed by the people of Yahuah and by pagan religions.

> *It is a well-established fact, even scientific in nature, that the heavenly bodies in the Zodiac have some relationship to what happens here on Earth. It is the degree to which they either have influence or they are a reflection of what happens on Earth that is in question.*

For instance, the Moon impacts the tides in our oceans. It is proven the full moon has an impact on our psyche. But, do the stars and the constellations have any impact on each individual life on Earth? Or maybe they don't actually have an influence but Yahuah has encoded in them knowledge of every human He created? This subject is much the same as the Bible Code. Well, we know that the Zodiac foretells of at least one man's life, that of Yahusha! But do they somehow have a relationship to the lives of the rest of us? That is the age old question of Astrology. One that is not answered in scripture **nor is it forbidden to ask as long as it is Yahuah you are seeking those answers from**. Not familiar spirits or fallen angels or the spiritual remnant of the Nephilim known as demons.

There are those who believe the stars influence our daily lives, and therefore they consult their daily horoscopes which is the forbidden use of *divination*. There are those that believe that the stars provide valuable insight into the personalities of each person based on the alignment of the stars on the day of their birth called a Natal Chart (depending on who you give credit for this could be righteous or unrighteous divination). Then there are those who believe they can manipulate our reality by "telling the stars" through magic and witchcraft, obvious sin. Then there are those who say all of it is nonsense and trust only in scientific astronomy (deny Yahuah's mysterious hidden knowledge encoded in the stars) which is obvious sin. And, of course, then there are established religions of Christianity and most of Judaism that tells us it really doesn't matter because all of it is forbidden by Yahuah (not true… they sound bite scripture out of context as I have shown. They desire to control access to Yahuah and limit the masses from seeking divine counsel directly from the Creator so established religion forbids direct contact with the Creator to elevate its own priests/preachers over their followers) which is ignorance.

I want to address this issue and see if I can shed some light on all of it. I do not represent myself as an expert in any of these sacred disciplines studied by the greatest prophets of Yahuah such as Moses, Elijah, Jeremiah, Isaiah, Daniel, Yahusha, and John. I, like many of you, have steered clear of the entire issue all my life. I was taught it was a sin by my religion (I was also taught the Law, the Sabbath, Passover, and the entire original scriptures were sin too by that same religion). However, over the process of writing this book, I have come to see this subject in a new light; and come to understand the scriptures from a different perspective (just like I did when I realized the Law, Sabbath, Passover, and original scriptures were still in effect!).

I will do my best here to shed whatever light on this subject I can, given my lack of wisdom and knowledge into these things. To be clear, my definition of righteous astrology is to seek out the divine message behind it and to be vigilant to the "signs" in the stars as instructed in His word. It would seem that a basic personality profile is written in the stars based on the day you were born. It is only a guideline to your strengths and weaknesses to assist you in becoming all Yahuah has created you to be. Using the stars to predict your future, daily or long term is an abomination to Yahuah and an abuse of the Zodiac. It is in that sense that "astrology" is unrighteously used, as it becomes a source of "self" seeking instead of a righteous seeking mind set on Yahuah.

> *We are to see His will be done on Earth as it is in 'heaven' or written in the stars. We are not to seek to see our will be done as it is written in the stars. That is the defining line between righteous and unrighteousness.*

This book is written solely from the standpoint of seeking to understand the Gospel message authored into creation by the Creator. What we have done in this book would be considered righteous divination (seeking divine counsel) as we have acknowledged Yahuah in His creation and given to Him all Glory in the magnificence of the Zodiac and proclaimed His Glory (Yahusha) through the Heavenly Scroll. This is Astrology the way Yahuah intended.

Divine Corrections

If we look back over the progression of the Ages we find that as the age progresses in time, humanity falls away from the knowledge of Yahuah. Then we find that Yahuah steps into our realm and moves mightily to re-establish His Name and His Glory:

- *Age of Taurus* – After the fall of Adam, the intimate knowledge of Yahuah that Adam possessed, began to fade. Each successive generation became more and more wicked and lawless. Mankind eventually lost all knowledge of the Creator and sin dominated the hearts of man. Yahuah had to step in, destroy the surface of the Earth and everything on it and begin over with Noah. Yahuah revealed Himself in a personal way to Noah to re-establish His Name, His Laws and His Glory.

- *Age of Aries* – After Noah, mankind again drifted away from the Creator, losing knowledge of Yahuah and chasing after other "gods". Yahuah again stepped in and revealed Himself to Abraham in a personal way to re-establish His Name, His Laws, and His Glory. Over time the Israelites again began chasing after other "gods" and were taken into Egyptian captivity where they lost all knowledge of the Creator. Yahuah stepped in again, revealed Himself to Moses in a personal way to re-establish His Name, His Laws, and His Glory. Toward the end of the age, we became very legalistic and ritualistic doing things for the sake of doing them without love for our Creator. We removed the "reason" for the Laws and the rituals, and sought righteousness through works.

- *Age of Pisces* – Yahuah again stepped in and revealed Himself to Yahusha in a very personal way to re-establish His Name, His Laws, and His Glory. This time removing the enmity we felt toward our Creator because of the threat of death for disobedience. With the introduction of Yahuah's mercy and grace, the Law became a joy to us and we were able to be obedient out of love and respect for our Creator as our 'Abba' or Father. Over time, we lost sight of His Righteousness (Laws) and focused solely on His mercy forgetting His Laws and His Name. Toward the end of this age, we have come to do "whatever is right in our own eyes", forgetting His name for titles and for Ba'al worship.

- *Age of Aquarius* - The Messiah returns to reclaim the lost and re-unite the Household of Yahuah, destroy all sin and lawbreakers from the face of the Earth and setup the Kingdom of Yahuah on Earth. At the end of this age, the same thing happens yet again as "Satan" is loosed and mankind again falls into rebellion. Yahuah then destroys this Earth with fire.

The reason I point this process out here is this: we find ourselves again at the end of an age in need of a Divine Correction! Humanity has fallen so far from the knowledge of the Creator that it is about to take a major Divine act of correction to put us back on course again. Yahuah is moving on His elect and calling them out of the nations where they have been scattered. He is moving on us to go back to the beginning of this Age, just after His last Divine Correction, to seek out our faith. We are going back 2000 years and attempting to put ourselves back into that language/cultural matrix called the Hebraic Mindset.

We are looking back at the writings of that day, the historical documents, the religious texts, and piecing together "where it all went wrong". We are discovering, in the process, the fulfillment of the false religion and false messiah that has lead all humanity astray. We are now realizing the effects of Hellenism and syncretism. We can look back over the past 2000 years with "eyes to see" and discern how mankind gradually began to slip away from the Creator. Once again, we have fallen into a model of humanism, and this time a scientific dictatorship that denies The Creator completely.

With each successive generation, the mysteries of The Creator were gradually replaced with mythology, then philosophy, then humanism, and now science. The truth of Yahuah has been blended with paganism, mythology, sun worship, philosophy, and even pseudo-science (Christian Science movement and Scientology cults). With every step we take as a race on Earth, it is a step further away from the last Divine correction and one step closer to the next! So to reverse that path as individuals (we can't stop the coming Divine Correction), we must go back 2000 years (and beyond) to re-establish ***that faith***. The only thing we know for certain is that what we are being told from established religions today are all lies… and Yahusha is coming back to correct mankind yet again.

This is why I, Rav Sha'ul, test everything, and when *"religion"* tells me "**don't look at that!**"; I look ever harder to see what it is they don't want me to see.

One area that we are reluctant to investigate is the "supernatural" or mystical element of Yahuah; the realm of the Spirit and the ancient mysteries of how His creation works! Established religion has forbidden it as sin (an error of the Pope), and humanistic science has dismissed it as fables. Yet, when we look back 2000 years in the past just after the last Divine correction; **the Zodiac was a very prominent aspect of their faith: both Jewish and Christian**.

Many of the great prophets of Yahuah were astrologers! We simply will not admit this truth even though it is plainly stated in scripture. Astrology was the forefather of modern day astronomy something science refuses to admit! The difference is: we (who know our Creator) give Yahuah the Glory in astrology (seeking out the message of the Heavenly Scroll), where in modern day astronomy we deny Him altogether and deny Yahuah His Glory as Creator. In this chapter we are going to take a very hard look at scripture and be very honest with ourselves in what we read. We are not going to overlook anything, or read over it, and pretend we didn't see it.

- If Yahuah says He created and named the stars, *then so be*

- *it... HalleluYahuah!*
- If Yahuah said He created and named each constellation and gave them their meaning, *then so be it... HalleluYahuah!*
- If Yahuah said He set the path of the sun through the constellations as a message that goes out to all mankind, *then so be it... HalleluYahuah!*
- If Yahuah said he bound specific constellations together, then *then so be it... HalleluYahuah!*
- If, in His word, He declares the specific names of the signs of the Zodiac and says He was the author, *then so be it... HalleluYahuah!*
- If the prophets used the Zodiac as the foundation of their understanding, *then so be it... HalleluYahuah!*
- If Yahuah uses the Zodiac to witness to His chosen ones on earth, *then so be it... HalleluYahuah!*

- ***Far** be it* from me to not teach the Truth of His word to tickle the ears of the people. If people want to ignore me, judge me, and disown me, because I teach the Heavenly Scroll found in the Zodiac... *then so be it... HalleluYahuah!*

I am not going to deny Yahuah His glory simply because established religion is in open denial of the Truth. We, in this book, are not going to stick our head in the sand and pretend there is no positive mention of the Zodiac and signs of the Zodiac in scripture, when it is written all over the scriptures!

We are going to look at the role such things as the Zodiac and divination play in the Bible when done giving the Glory to Yahuah. We are going to define some terms, and come to a better understanding of things, not simply run from the word "Zodiac" because the enemy has perverted it (that is all the more reason to look into it further). As we have been doing in this book so far, we are going to remove the blinders placed over our eyes by Hellenizing words and concepts. We are not going to simply turned our backs on the mysteries of the Kingdom of Yahuah or deny our Creator His Glory in creation just because **the Pope said so**.

We are not going to just assume certain things are forbidden and a sin simply because **the Pharisees in Judaism told us so**. We are not going to sound-bite scripture to justify or current belief system. We are going to look at all things in full context. We are going to examine these things for ourselves, in other words!

Is the Zodiac a pagan symbol, or is it a Divine representation of the order of our cosmos given to us by the Creator? Are all forms of divination a sin, or like most everything else, can it be used both righteously and unrighteously based on context?

First we are going to look at the history of both Judaism and Christianity dating back to the first century, just after the last Divine Correction. Then we are going to closely inspect Yahuah's word to discern the truth behind divination. Are all forms of divination forbidden? If not, then why is divination even forbidden at all, and in what context is it Righteous in Yahuah's eyes? So let us begin there as we continue our journey to understand these *'hidden things'*.

Prophet or a Soothsayer?

Established religion is notorious for sound biting scripture and teaching false doctrines to the people. The sheeple are too lazy to do the research and study themselves. The leaders of the Church, most of the time, take the easy way out. Instead of properly teaching a subject (the people are too lazy to even pay attention that long), they just teach a very strict version of it. That way they are sure the people will not stumble getting lost in the fine print trying to do things on their own. *Divination* is one such area where Church leaders find it better to just "outlaw it" than try and explain the difference between its uses. Let us not fall into that trap in this book! Let us look closely at this word *divination*, define it, put some context around it... and understand it.

div·i·na·tion
/ˌdivəˈnāSH(ə)n/

noun
noun: **divination**; plural noun: **divinations**

> the practice of seeking knowledge of the future or the unknown by supernatural means.
> synonyms: fortune telling, divining, **prophecy**, prediction, soothsaying, augury, clairvoyance, second sight
> "he looked to divination for guidance"

Origin

LATIN	LATIN
divinare predict	divinatio

→ divination
late Middle English

ENGLISH
divine

late Middle English: from Latin *divinatio(n-)*, from *divinare* 'predict' (see divine²).

Divination, by definition, *is the act of seeking a divine prediction or divine counsel.* Divination is in effect a contraction of **DIVIN**e + revel**ATION**... Divin'ation. We see in the definition that *soothsaying* and *prophecy* are synonyms. Soothsaying being the forbidden use of divination and prophecy being the righteous act of divination. If we are to be very honest with ourselves, divination is not prohibited by Yahuah outright. In fact, <u>divination from Yahuah</u> is found practiced throughout the scriptures. Every mention of divination where it is prohibited should be taken in the proper context. It is speaking of those who seek 'divine predictions or counsel' from <u>any source other than Yahuah</u>.

True Prophets of Yahuah

Simply put, those who seek divine counsel from Yahuah, who understand the stars (The Zodiac) <u>as a divine message</u> (foretelling of the coming Messiah, Plan of Salvation, and divine clock of the Ages), men who have the Spirit of Yahuah guiding them; <u>are called true prophets and wise men in scripture</u>. All the prophets in scripture were, what we would consider today, '*astrologers*'; in as much as they consulted the stars to seek out Yahuah's plan of salvation and to foretell of the coming Messiah and other major events. *Wise men* are what Yahuah calls them, as "wisdom" seems to be directly related to the Heavenly Scroll.

Astrologers called "wise men" by Yahuah

It is interesting to note, that while all of Israel was expecting the Messiah's birth as foretold by Daniel; it was ONLY the wise men (Chaldean Astrologers) that actually found Yahusha, **no one else**. They used astrology, and the signs of the Zodiac to determine the time and location of the Messiah's birth as instructed by the prophet Daniel (a master astrologer)! In fact, Daniel was elevated in the courts of Babylon because of his expertise in using astrology and interpreting omens to seek out the knowledge of Yahuah (divination). Those who live at the end of the Age of Pisces, who look for the "*sign of the son of man*" in the sky (which is a sign in the constellation Virgo defined in Revelation Chapter 12) would be considered *astrologers* as well. Even Yahusha (who instructed us to seek out that sign) would be considered an *astrologer*. Yahusha made many references to the Sign and the Ages of the Zodiac.

False Prophets, soothsayers, and star gazers

Those who seek divine counsel (outside of Yahuah) from other 'gods', who see the Zodiac as means to foretell the fortunes of all men for money, as a tool for witchcraft and sorcery, who see the Zodiac signs, the Sun, and Moon as gods, and who are not guided by the Spirit of Yahuah; <u>are called false prophets, soothsayers, sorcerers, and star gazers</u>.

Does the Bible forbid the Zodiac, or the misuse of it?

Deuteronomy 3:19
When you look up to the sky (sky is Hebrew shamayim/Zodiac) and see the sun, moon, and stars (speaking of the Zodiac) — the whole heavenly (Mazzaroth/Zodiac) creation — you must not be seduced to worship and serve them (signs of the Zodiac), for Yahuah your Elohim has assigned them (the signs of the Zodiac) to all the people of the world (they were created by Yahuah to proclaim the coming Messiah Yahusha, see Psalm 19, they are not gods).

As we get further back in this Age, closer to the last Divine Correction we begin seeing the Zodiac come back into focus as <u>a centerpiece of their faith</u>. We see the Zodiac as the centerpiece of both Judaism and Christianity! Right after the last Divine Correction, mankind once again understood the message foretold in the "heavens", and gave glory to Yahuah as its author. In this chapter we will see the Zodiac was the foundation of both Judaism and Christianity until the Pope outlawed Yahuah's Original Revelation (just as he did The Law, the Sabbath, Passover, etc.).

Before we can rightfully discern what the Bible truly says about such things, let us define a few terms.

1. ***Astrology***: Astrology is the study of the positions of the planets in relationship to each other and the vibrational influences these relationships have upon humanity. It is the study of the names of the stars and grouping of stars into constellations in such a way as to tell a story. Astrology is both a science and an art. It is a science because constructing the chart is based upon exacting mathematical calculations of the planets' positions at the time of birth. It is an art because it depends upon the skill and metaphysical knowledge used in the interpretation of these planetary positions. The Wise Men

from the East, who came to pay homage to the baby Yahusha, were astrologers.... ***Webster's Ninth New Collegiate Dictionary.***

2. ***Magic/Sorcery***: Magic is an attempt by human beings to compel a divinity, by the use of physical means, to do what they wish that divinity to do. ***Stephen Benko, "Magic and Divination," Harper's Bible Dictionary, 1985 ed.***
As it is with anything else, there is a Righteous use and then there is an unrighteous use. Moses' staff is an example as Moses would use the staff to "compel Yahuah" to act by parting the Red Sea or making water flow from a rock. Or cast the staff down and turn it into a serpent and so forth. Moses' bronze serpent in the wilderness is an example of the use of magic. ***Numbers 21:4-9.*** This definition of magic also applies to the traditional interpretation of Yahusha's death on the cross. "And just as Moses lifted up the serpent in the wilderness, so must the Son of Man be lifted up, that whoever believes in him may have eternal life." ***John 3:14-15.*** The implication being that the lifting up of Yahusha on a stake, compels Yahuah to forgive and deliver those who believe. So by the strictest definition, that would be "magic".

3. ***Divination***: Divination is "Divine Revelation". It is an "attempt to secure information, also by the use of physical means, about matters and events that are currently hidden or that lie in the future from a divine source. With divination, in contrast to magic, one does not seek to alter the course of events, only to learn about them." ***Benko 594-595.***

As we have already discussed; the Bible depicts numerous avenues of divination. Among them are oracles, signs, calling up the dead, dream interpretation, casting of lots, visions, and the ephods. An ephod is a method of divination, used by the priests to determine Yahuah's response to a "yes" or "no" question asked by the leader of the people. These ephods are called Urim and Thummim. They are worn by the priest in a pouch over the heart." ***Jeremiah Unterman, "Urim and Thummim," Harper's Bible Dictionary, 1985 ed.***

An example of divination by the ephod may be found in Numbers below:

> **Numbers 27:21**
> "But he shall stand before Eleazar the priest, who shall inquire for him by the decision (seek a divine decision i.e. divination) of the Urim before Yahuah; at his word they shall go out, and at his word they shall come in, both he and all Israelites with him, the whole congregation."

As I have already explained in this chapter, scripture must be understood in "context" of how these things are used. Are they employed by "prophets" of Yahuah or by false prophets giving glory to other gods or accepting the glory themselves. Are they employed to Glorify Yahuah and seek out His will, or are they employed for personal gain or to gain advantage over others. The use of these things (astrology, magic, divination, sorcery) is forbidden when used outside of the Spirit of Yahuah for personal gain to make puppets out of others.

> **Isaiah 47:12-15**
> Stand fast in your enchantments and your many sorceries, with which you have labored from your youth; perhaps you may be able to succeed, perhaps you may inspire terror. You are wearied with your many consultations; let those who study the heavens (outside of Yahuah's Spirit) stand up and save you, those who gaze at the stars (as to worship them as idols), and at each new moon predict what shall befall you. See, they (who deny Yahuah His Glory in creation) are like stubble, the fire consumes them; they cannot deliver themselves from the power of the flame. No coal for warming oneself is this, no fire to sit before! Such to you are those with whom you have labored, who have trafficked with you from your youth; they all wander about in their own paths (self-seeking mindset); there is no one to save you."

Scripture presents 3 types of individuals who practice these ancient arts:

1. **_Righteous Level_** - The astrologers (or Wise Men of Matthew 2) and the Chaldeans, who have priestly functions, (of Daniel 1 and 2) rank on the highest level. Daniel is among those highest ranked ***Daniel 5:11. All of the prophets in***

scripture fall into this category.

2. *Unrighteous Level* - Below them we have sorcerers, enchanters, and charmers. Sorcerers use the power gained from the evil spirits the Bible calls "familiar spirits" to leverage the supernatural for personal gain or influence over others. ***Webster's Ninth New Collegiate Dictionary***. Revelation 21:8 and 22:15 include sorcerers in the list of those who will not enter the kingdom of Yahuah.

3. *Abomination Level* - On the lowest level we find those "sheep in wolf's clothing" who claim to represent Yahuah and serve His people. They, however, are imposters out to exploit the Household of Yahuah. For example, the "impostors" of II Timothy 3:13: "But wicked people and impostors will go from bad to worse, deceiving others and being deceived."23 The magician in Acts 13:6-11 is an example of the impostor. This would be your Christian Preachers, Priests, etc. They do not represent the interest of Yahuah, but their own financial interests and "tickle the ears" of those who pay them to lie.

To discern what the Bible teaches concerning astrology, divination, magic and so forth, it is not a cut and dried answer. We also must look at the character of those in question.

When considering "divination" and the Zodiac, we find those at the highest level (1) understand the physical to spiritual analogies behind the names of the stars/constellation. They seek out how these signs proclaim the ***Original Revelation*** of Yahuah concerning His Plan of Salvation through Yahusha. Men at mid-level (2 above) are your soothsayers, false prophets, and we find the Bible forbids their activities to fortune tell for a fee. Yahuah issued specific and definite restriction forbidding the activities of levels 2 and 3. These prohibitions are based on both the negative use of occult knowledge and the negative character of the practitioners. We are strictly forbidden to use these "arts" for personal gain or to influence others to achieve a desired outcome.

Again it is <u>worshipping the "starry hosts"</u> which are the constellations/signs of the Zodiac that is forbidden, NOT the Zodiac itself as it was created as a message to humanity. Yahuah hates the worship of the Sun (Ba'al worship), the worship of the signs of the Zodiac "starry hosts", those who swear by other gods, and those who use divination outside of seeking it from Yahuah:

<u>Zephaniah 1:1-6</u>
I will destroy every remnant of Baal worship in this place, the very names of the idolatrous priests— 5 those who bow down on the roofs to worship the starry host, those who bow down and swear by Yahuah and who also swear by Molek, 6 those who turn back from following Yahuah (and seek out other gods) and neither seek Yahuah nor inquire of him (righteous divination)."

<u>Deuteronomy 3:19</u>
When you look up to the sky (sky is Hebrew shamayim/Zodiac) and see the sun, moon, and stars (speaking of the Zodiac) — the whole heavenly (Mazzaroth/Zodiac) creation — you must not be seduced to worship and serve them (signs of the Zodiac), for Yahuah your Elohim has assigned them (the signs of the Zodiac) to all the people of the world (they were created by Yahuah to proclaim the coming Messiah Yahusha, see Psalm 19, they are not gods).

Seeking out Yahuah's *"hidden mysteries preserved in the heavens"* as the basic foundation of prophecy, the Plan of Salvation and the role of the Messiah is one thing… whereas worshipping the constellations and the Sun is quite another.

> *In our scientific mentality where it must be proven, seen, and proven again; we dismiss the mysteries of the Kingdom of Yahuah that our ancient ancestors cherished.*

We, today, scoff at the idea of a supernatural aspect to His Creation, yet all the men in the Bible proclaimed it. We love to say that Yahuah is the same yesterday, today, and forever; yet we box Him into "dispensations". We, in our own ignorance, say to ourselves "Yahuah doesn't speak to men today like He did in the "Old" Testament". Yes he does! He spoke to those prophets and mighty men of old through the Zodiac! He is still speaking to us today as that message is heard throughout the entire Earth as David proclaimed in Palms 19. <u>It is we who have stopped listening</u>. We just give lip service to "Yahuah is the Creator" then outright deny Him in His supernatural creation. The mere mention of the Zodiac sends us into a panic! Astrology has been given a bad name by the misuse and abuse of it. Make no mistake, however, is used in scripture as I have shown by all Yahuah's anointed prophets.

Do the stars have influence

The Age old question (during the Age of Pisces as we have fallen away from Yahuah over time, this was not even questioned in past Ages) is "do the stars have an influence over the events in individual lives on Earth?" Most of us say "no", that is ridiculous. Is it?

In my own search for Yahuah, I have an area of study I call "Rav Sha'ul's School of Theoretical Theology". There is one pupil in this school, and one teacher. This is where I take what humanity knows in the area of Theoretical Physics (the most advanced reaches of our most talented scientific minds) and I employ those ideas to what I know about Yahuah. My goal is to understand Yahuah's creation at the most fundamental levels.

The question of Astrology has been answered by Theoretical Physics at the quantum level (the smallest levels of physical reality). It has been proven that creation is linked in an inexplicable way! It is called "Quantum Entanglement". Below is the scientific definition:

> Quantum entanglement is a physical phenomenon that occurs when pairs or groups of particles are generated

or interact in ways such that the quantum state of each particle cannot be described independently — instead, <u>a quantum state may be given for the system as a whole</u>.

Measurements of physical properties such as position, momentum, spin, polarization, etc. performed on entangled particles are found to be appropriately correlated. For example, if a pair of particles is generated in such a way that their total spin is known to be zero, and one particle is found to have clockwise spin on a certain axis, then the spin of the other particle, measured on the same axis, will be found to be counterclockwise; because of the nature of quantum measurement. <u>**However, this behavior gives rise to effects that can appear paradoxical: any measurement of a property of a particle can be seen as acting on that particle (e.g. by collapsing a number of superposed states); and in the case of entangled particles, such action must be on the entangled system as a whole**. **It thus appears that one particle of an entangled pair "knows" what measurement has been performed on the other, and with what outcome, even though there is no known means for such information to be communicated between the particles, which at the time of measurement may be separated by arbitrarily large distances.**</u>

Ok, none of us are Quantum Physicist, so let me put this in layman's terms. Creation is linked together at the smallest levels, such that the entire physical "system" of creation is "linked together" as a whole! Distance is NOT a factor.

Whenever you change one particle in the system, the other particle somehow "knows" of this change and reacts accordingly... no matter how far away the two particles are from one another and with no means of communication! So the answer to the Age old question "can the stars have an impact on humans? Yes! They not only can, but they do. It is proven that creation is '*quantumly entangled*' together by some 'unknown' force! That 'unknown force' is Yahuah, the Creator, and His creation is linked together in a divine way that science is only now coming to realize. I'll leave this for another book. I just wanted to answer all those who, in their ignorance, make such declarations that Astrology is nonsense and deny Yahuah of His supernatural creation. There is a LOT MORE to creation that we have been told, taught, or experienced in our Scientific Dictatorship. Truths known by our ancient ancestors that we today deny. We would probably have more "divine experiences" like they did then, if we acknowledged Yahuah as they did in His creation.

Even though Yahuah outright declares it was He who named every star, and brought forth each constellation by name, and they proclaim a message that goes out unto all the Earth; <u>we dismiss the Zodiac as though it were a creation of the Greeks</u>. All the Greeks did was dream up a system of mythology around the Zodiac as to worship the creation over the Creator. Speaking to the Greeks in Rome, Sha'ul warned them against this very thing:

> **Romans 1**
> 18 The wrath of Yahuah is being revealed from heaven (the place where the stars are located i.e. The Zodiac) against all the godlessness and wickedness of people, who suppress the truth (of its message) by their wickedness (and worship the signs of the Zodiac, Sun, Moon, and stars), 19 since what may be known about Yahuah (the Plan of Salvation) is plain to them (is proclaimed in The Zodiac), because Yahuah has made it plain to them (this message goes out unto all the Earth *Psalms 19*, given to all mankind *Deuteronomy 3:19*). 20 For since the creation of the world (written in the stars at creation) Yahuah's invisible qualities—his eternal power and divine nature—have been clearly seen (in The Zodiac, as Yahuah witnessed the Gospel to Abraham *Genesis 15:5*), being understood (they are metaphors and analogies) from what has been made (in heaven: the Sun, Moon, stars, and constellations *Psalms 119*), so that people are without excuse. 21 For although they knew Yahuah (is The Creator), they neither glorified him as Elohim nor gave thanks to him (for the message proclaimed in the Zodiac), but their thinking

became futile (understanding the Zodiac literally as gods) and their foolish hearts were darkened (to worship the creation over The Creator). 22 Although they claimed to be wise (through philosophy and mythology), they became fools 23 and exchanged the glory of the immortal Elohim (the Glory of Yahuah is Yahusha *2 Corinthians 4:6*! So they exchanged Yahusha) for images made to look like a mortal human being (solar demi-gods) and birds and animals and reptiles (the signs of The Zodiac).

You see, the 'heavens" which is the Zodiac (stars and constellations) proclaim the Glory of Yahuah:

Psalms 19:1
The heavens (the Mazzaroth/Zodiac) declare the glory of Yahuah

That "glory of Yahuah" is that they proclaim the coming Messiah Yahusha as he is "the Glory of Yahuah" his father.

2 Corinthians 4:6 - 6
For it is Yahuah who once said (when creating the heavens), "Let light shine out of darkness," who has made his light shine in our hearts, *the light of the knowledge of Yahuah's glory shining in the face of the Messiah Yahusha.*

So in Romans 1, Sha'ul is explaining that the Greeks twisted the Zodiac and denied that it was proclaiming Yahusha! Instead they made up demi-gods and worshipped the sings of the Zodiac.

Even today, we deny Yahuah as the Creator of the Zodiac and turn over the **Original Revelation** to all mankind to the Greeks and give them credit for creating it. When we do so, we ignore historical facts. Our Western history books have hidden the history of astrology under the category of astronomy. The heavenly configurations have fascinated humanity from its earliest beginnings.

The information following is from the book ***Zohar, The History of Astrology*** (New York: Arco Publishing Co., Inc. 1972) which can be read online at Google Book.

> Astrology and astronomy were established as sciences around 5000 B.C.E. in Chaldea and Babylonia. Many of the great names in the history of our world civilization were astrologers. **Our Western history books simply call them philosophers, astronomers, doctors of medicine, theologians, politicians, mathematicians**—ignoring the fact that astrology played a major role in their lives and thinking.
>
> Born in 572 B.C.E., Pythagoras, as a result of his study of the heavenly configurations, knew the Earth is round. Many of our history books ignore this fact. Through his study of the stars and their relationship to humanity (the science of astrology), Pythagoras developed his doctrine of the harmony existing between the heavens and our planet Earth, the macrocosm of the universe and the microcosm of humanity. After his murder, Empedocles, Plato, Socrates, and Aristotle continued the study of this doctrine. Aristotle taught that our planet is inescapably linked to the motions of the cosmos of which it is a member.
>
> From the earliest times, doctors of medicine are fascinated by the science of astrology. Hippocrates, born around 460 B.C.E. and known as the "Father of Medicine," used astrology as the most scientific means of diagnosis available to the Greek physicians of his time. The Hippocratic School of Medicine focused on the study of the natal chart to determine the specific make-up of their parents.
>
> Galen, born in 30 C.E., is called the "Father of Experimental Physiology." His treatise Prognostication of Disease by Astrology resulted in widespread knowledge of astrological medicine. A synthesis of medical thought and astrological medical knowledge, Galen's books dominated the field of medicine for 1500 years.

Born around 100 C.E., Ptolemy had the reputation for being the greatest astrologer/astronomer of all times. During Ptolemy's day, "astrologia" and "astronomia" meant the same thing. His Tetrabiblos marked the culmination of astrological thought in the Graeco-Roman world. This book marked the end of the controversy concerning astrology. Tetrabiblos laid the foundation for the modern science of astrology. From that point on to the 17th century, astrology and medicine were allies.

The 13th century poet Dante taught that the primary moving force for both God and humanity is love. He believed the heavenly host of stars and planets turned under the radiating influence of love. For Dante, physical life is explained in terms of the spiritual.

Roger Bacon, born in 1214, taught the stars are regulated by angelic intelligences. An individual's personal nature is determined by the heavenly configurations at the time of birth. Medical astrology is valid because the functions of the physical body are determined by the influence of the stars.

Born around 1224, Thomas Aquinas is still considered to be one of the great Christian theologians. He placed importance upon the science of astrology in the study of natural science. According to Aquinas, God rules the inferior creatures—our earthly bodies—through superior creatures—the stars. Both Bacon and Aquinas believed the rational soul of humanity and the gift of freewill to be exempt from stellar influence.

Paracelsus was the most renowned and controversial advocate of astrology during the 15th century. Paracelsus taught that activity within the cosmos affects all else. Though he recognized the influence of the stars, he did not believe they completely controlled the destinies of humanity. Instead, he felt that humanity has the capacity to transcend the astrological influence of the stars. The means by which humanity can transcend the stellar influence is wisdom, acquired by the direct study of nature.

/ Jerome Cardan, born in 1501, was one of the best minds of his age. A great mathematician, physician, and astrologer, Cardan distinguished himself by the cautious way in which he approached his research, seeking to confirm his assertions with solid facts. Appointed professor of medicine at Pavia in 1547, his published works on algebra and astrology brought him fame throughout Europe.

In the late 15th century, the Roman church condemned astrology. Yet astrology continued to influence the greatest of minds. Among these is Nostradamus, a physician and astrologer born in 1503. Two great English scientists and astrologers were Edmond Halley, born in 1656, and Isaac Newton, born around 1642. Their laws of motion provided a firm foundation for astrological computation. Francis Bacon, born in 1561, recognized the connection between celestial and terrestrial phenomena; however, he opposed the natal chart and consulting astrology for predictions. He declared astrology to be filled with superstition in his De Augmentis Scientiarum.

The list of great minds continues. Shakespeare, an astrologer in addition to being a playwright, depicted his characters using astrology correctly. William Lilly, born in 1602, and Nicholas Culpepper, born in the early 1600's, were physicians who used medical astrology.

*Though modern astronomers seek to ignore the fact, Copernicus, Kepler (the "founder of modern astronomy and astrology"), and Galileo **were all astrologers**.*

Galileo's experience offers an excellent example of how the Church hierarchy has controlled the information available to the laity. Born in 1564, a great inventor, experimental philosopher, and astrologer, Galileo invented the telescope. As a result of the telescope, new scientific discoveries were made. Galileo attempted to reconcile these scientific discoveries with the Christian faith in a series of articles: "Letters of Sunspots," "Letter to Castelli," and "Letter to the Grand Duchess Christina." His work was to no avail. In 1615, a group of eleven theologians pronounced Galileo's belief in heliocentric theories absurd, heretical, and contrary to the Scriptures. In 1633, a papal court sentenced Galileo to prison. Galileo recanted belief in the Copernican theory that the Earth moves around the Sun and was placed under house arrest in the custody of a friend.

Born in 1596, Descartes believed it important to record the positions of the planets at the moment of birth because immediately after birth, the brain tissues set themselves and conserve throughout life the first impressions they received.

During the four hundred years since Descartes, the empirically based scientific community has sought to deny the validity of astrology. However, it has been unable to prove any falsehoods in astrological beliefs. Instead, an increasing number of scientists are actually studying the impact of the stars and planets upon humanity. They are even willing to speak out for astrology.42 In fact, scientific evidence now demonstrates that astrology works.

World renown psychiatrist Carl Jung believed that "synchronicity" explains how astrology works. Planets do not cause certain events. Instead, they are symbols of cosmic forces. The patterns they form synchronize with events on our planet Earth. In later life, Jung used the natal chart as a tool for working with his patients.

Additional examples of scientists investigating and verifying cosmic influences are available. RCA has determined that the positions of planets affect radio disturbances. Others have verified that planetary positions influence the occurrence of earthquakes; recorded the influence of particular planetary relationships upon incidences of road accidents; shown that the position of planets alters the biological clocks of humans, animals, and plants; and verified that the phases of the Moon influences human behavior.

That is quite a list of men whose minds changed the course of human history. Add to that list Adam, Enoch, Noah, Abraham, Moses, Elijah, Ezekiel, Jeremiah, Daniel, David, Yahusha, Sha'ul, and John the revelator; and that list becomes a who's who's list of the most amazing men who ever lived... all astrologers!

When you step outside of tradition and religion and seek Yahuah through His Word and His creation, you come to a very humbling reality: **The Zodiac is the Original Revelation from Yahuah to all mankind.**

Astrology was the foundation of prophecy used by all His prophets. The Zodiac was used to witness the Gospel to Abraham, to King David, and many others. Astrology is the foundation of modern day astronomy, medicine, and many other advances humanity now takes for granted.

There was a time when Yahuah was the source behind seeking out the stars and it was called Prophecy/Astrology. Now, Yahuah is outright denied existence, and it is called Astronomy. As science advances, astronomers are coming to the same conclusion, that the stars have an influence on the events here on Earth and the cosmos is a product of intelligent design. I mentioned Quantum Physics and how at that level it is proven His creation is supernaturally "linked together", the same conclusions are being drawn at the macro level of science... astronomy.

There is no explanation for what holds galaxies together, so man had to make up a word for the "force" that gives structure to the stars... we call it "dark matter'. There is no explanation for why the Universe does not collapse under the immense gravitational effects of this "dark matter", because instead of collapsing in on itself under the pressure, the Universe is actually expanding. A total contradiction of known "laws of physics". It is expanding at the "perfect rate" to allow for the existence of life. So what do we do, we make up a name for that force too, we call it "dark energy". We call these things "dark" because WE are in the dark as to what these things are! There is something out there holding this Universe together in perfect harmony. That same "something" holding together quantum particles, and there is communication in this creation that we cannot and do not understand. So before we write off Astrology, maybe we should instead just admit we are ignorant of the matter.

---

*The answer to our question "does the Bible forbid the use of The Zodiac?" The answer is a resounding "No!" It forbids the <u>**MISUSE**</u> of it.*

Humanity denies the Creator

Finally, in the waning moments of this Age, 1,500 years into this 2000-year Age, humanity had fallen so far from Yahuah that the false prophet Pope outlawed the Original Revelation and hid it from our sight! Just as he did The Law, The Sabbath, the Holy Days, etc. Only now is Yahuah moving again to restore this vital message among His chosen few.

We have fallen so far from Yahuah at this point that we actually think His Revelation in the Stars is "evil" and feel 'convicted' to even say the word "Zodiac"! We perceive it as 'pagan' when the word itself comes from a Hebrew origin "zodi" meaning "the way".

Yahusha came to show us "the Way" by living out the revelation of him in the stars and seeing to it that Yahuah's will be done on Earth as it is written in the stars in the Heavenly Scroll.

> **Matthew 6:10**
> Your kingdom come, your will be done, on earth as it is in 'heaven' (written in the Heavenly Scroll).

We are again in need of a Divine Correction. Twisting the Zodiac into a lie, Hellenizing words such as *'heaven'* to hide The Zodiac, abolishing everything Holy to Yahuah, the enemy has turned mankind against the Zodiac! Against the Heavenly Scroll! Against the very foundation from which prophecy is driven.

No wonder there are no real prophets on this Earth in these last days! This act to abolish the Heavenly Scroll was one of the last and greatest abominations of the Whore of Babylon, the Christian Church. Add that to all the other abominations of the "one who holds a cup FULL of abomination" and the act of totally abolishing the true word of Yahuah was complete.

Revelation 17:4 - *The woman was dressed in purple and scarlet, and was glittering with gold, precious stones and pearls. She held a golden cup in her hand, filled with abominable things and the filth of her adulteries*

Let's now take a journey back to the beginning of this Age, just after the last Divine Correction. We find the Zodiac the centerpiece of the faith as they knew it was speaking of The Plan of Salvation.

When we look back into the history of the faith, Judaism and Christianity you see the Zodiac is by far the most prevalent foundation glorified in floor mosaics, ceiling murals, paintings, and throughout scripture. That is because its author IS Yahuah, and it contains the most fundamental of all revelations.

CHAPTER 13
FOUNDATION OF ALL FAITHS

Chapter 13 – The Foundation of All Faiths

The Zodiac (from Hebrew word 'zodi' meaning 'the way') was given to Enoch, and passed down through the Ages:

- Yahuah proclaimed He created the Mazzaroth/Zodiac to Job
- Yahuah used it to proclaim the Gospel to Abraham who saw "Yahusha's day" viewing the Zodiac
- The 12 tribes of Israel each had an associated Zodiac Sign
- Every human Age/Epoch is defined by it, and properly uses its symbolism to represent the various Ages
- The Sabbath Covenant is accurately foretold by the Ages in the Zodiac "clock"
- The timing of the first and second advents of the Messiah are synchronized in both directions in the Zodiac "clock"
- The individual lifespan of mankind is established by the Zodiac "clock"
- The substitute of a Ram and the yearly sacrifice of a Lamb are prophesied within it
- The two comings of the "suffering servant" and the "conquering king" are proclaimed by it
- King David defined it and explained it's true meaning
- The wedding portrait of the Bridegroom and Bride is foretold by the Zodiac
- Ezekiel used it as a source of prophecy, "sees it" and describes it in great detail
- Daniel was a famous and devout Astrologer and used it as a means of prophecy, preserved it, and passed it down through the Chaldean Astrologers (Daniel 5:11)
- the Chaldean Astrologers known as very wise men used it to locate the young Messiah (no one else found him) and most probably passed its secrets down to Yahusha and John the Baptist
- The Nazarenes preserved it and its meaning
- Yahusha identifies himself as the fulfillment of it

- Sha'ul chastises the Galatians for not understanding it
- Yahuah gave it as a gift to all mankind, Sha'ul confirms humanity is without excuse because of it
- John, like Ezekiel and Daniel, prophecy by it and describe it in great detail in the book of Revelation!
- It is the Heavenly Scroll, and only the one who fulfills it is worthy to "read it" and break the seals over it

The reality is that the Heavenly Scroll was the original revelation to all mankind and the rest of scriptures are established in its foundation! The Book of Revelation literally describes the Zodiac and its fulfillment with Leo conquering the dragon and the rule of the Lion of the Tribe of Judah. Did it end there? Or is there evidence that the Zodiac continued to be the very foundation of the early Nazarene, Jewish, and Christian faiths?

In fact, the Zodiac was intimately related to Jewish worship for centuries to come and was the foundation of early Christianity! However, over time as this Age progresses we fell further and further away from the Creator until we had fallen so far we literally outlawed His original revelation to mankind found written in the stars! It was gradual but complete as we replaced Yahuah with pure science. Denying our roots, turning our back on the truths and hidden mysteries in the heavens; that are the foundation of modern medicine, astronomy, time keeping, and understanding the Will of the Creator.

The Zodiac – Foundation from which all faith was established

Remains of many Jewish synagogues dating back to the 1st century CE through the 6th century CE have been uncovered by archeologist to reveal the Zodiac as a major function of their religion. Many of them with elaborate mosaics of the Zodiac well preserved, alongside mosaics of Biblical stories. The 12 lunar Hebrew months of the year were closely associated with the 12 Zodiac signs and perservered in Hebrew writing on each corresponding Zodiac sign in these ancient synagogues. This demonstrates that if we look back in history at the last Divine Correction, we see the Zodiac and the Divine Clock were well understood and had a significant role in the places of worship.

Today, however, we are so arrogant as to believe "these early Jews had succumbed to Greek mythology!" No, they had come BACK to the truth of Yahuah following the last Divine Correction. The Zodiac was adopted by the Greeks FROM the Hebrews. It is we who, 2000 years later, have fallen from the truth of the Creator; not the other way around! The prevalence of the Zodiac and the prominence of these Zodiac mosaics in the Synagogues over the first 7 centuries dating all the way back to just before Yahusha came… speaks to the reality and importance of the message contained in the Zodiac.

Even the Talmud identified the 12 constellations of the Zodiac with the 12 months of the Hebrew calendar. The correspondence of the constellations with their names in Hebrew and the months is as follows:

1. Aries - Ṭaleh - Nisan
2. Taurus - Shor - Iyar
3. Gemini - Teomim - Sivan
4. Cancer - Sarṭon - Tammuz
5. Leo - Ari - Av
6. Virgo - Betulah - Elul
7. Libra - Moznayim - Tishrei

8. Scorpio - 'Aḵrab - Cheshvan
9. Sagittarius - Ḵasshat - Kislev
10. Capricorn - Gedi - Tevet
11. Aquarius - D'li - Shevat
12. Pisces - Dagim – Adar

We see these signs associated with Hebrew months on all Jewish Zodiacs in the first 7 centuries AD. **The implication of the Zodiac being so prominently displayed in synagogues going back to the 1st Century is astounding**.

Remember, John, Yahusha, Sha'ul, and all the men in the Renewed Covenant taught in the synagogues. It is possible some of these Zodiacs floor murals had the honor of the footprints of the Messiah; as the walked over them to speak to the people! Never once are they condemned in the New Testament writings or by the Messiah. These Zodiac mosaics were accepted right alongside mosaics of the Ark of the Covenant, Abraham sacrificing Isaac, Adam and Eve, and so on. They all were seen as "the story of salvation" proudly displayed in elaborate floor mosaics that survive today.

Below is from Harper Collins Bible Dictionary on the role of the Jewish Synagogue:

http://www.bibleodyssey.org/places/related-articles/first-century-synagogues.aspx

First Century Synagogues by *Chad Spigel*

According to the New Testament Gospels, Jesus often taught in synagogues, one of which was in Capernaum (Mark 1:21-28), in northern Israel. The book of Acts suggests that the apostle Sha'ul also taught in synagogues (Acts 17:1-2). But what exactly were synagogues in the first century C.E.? Were they different from modern synagogues? The answers to these questions not only illuminate stories in the New Testament, they also shed light on the early years of an important Jewish institution.

"Synagogue" is a Greek word that literally means a gathering of people but also refers to the place of assembly. Although the origin of the synagogue as a Jewish institution is unclear, by the first century C.E. they were found in both Palestine and the Diaspora, where they were used for a variety of communal needs:

- as schools (Josephus, Antiquities 16.43),
- or communal meals (Josephus, Antiquities 14.214-216),
- as hostels,
- as courts of Law (Acts 22:19),
- as a place to collect and distribute charity (Matt 6:2),
- and for political meetings (Josephus, Life 276-289).

Worship also took place in first-century synagogues, although this would not develop into something like modern Jewish synagogue worship until much later. Nonetheless, reading and interpreting the Torah and Prophets is well attested in first-century synagogues (Acts 15:21), and although scholars disagree about the extent of communal prayers, literary sources suggest that Jews prayed in at least some synagogues at this time (Matt 6:5, Josephus, Life 280-295).

In short, *the Synagogue was the focus and expression of Jewish faith.* Without a doubt, the most prominent feature of these ancient Jewish synagogues was… The Heavenly Scroll of Enoch's Zodiac! The Mazzaroth/Zodiac stood out as the foundation for Biblical stories that accompanied them and the Hebrew calendar (months associated with them). Given the Synagogue served the function of schools, legal courts, and politics; the prominent display of the Enoch Zodiac on the floors of these Jewish institutions speaks to reality that <u>they understood the Zodiac to have been created by Yahuah, given to all mankind, and containing the Plan of Salvation from which their entire religion was revealed</u>.

Astrology, the Zodiac and its associated meaning, had played a role in Hebrew history for at least the 2,000 years of the Age of Aries beginning with Yahuah proclaiming the Gospel to Abraham. As we have seen so far in this book, Yahuah took Abraham outside, under the canopy of stars, and instructed Abraham to look up and discern the meaning behind the Zodiac. But if legend and the book of Enoch is true, then the Zodiac came to mankind through Enoch. Then corrupted through the watchers.

As I have pointed out in this book, the Zodiac was literally the foundation from which the prophets of Yahuah made their predictions. They described the Zodiac perfectly, there is no doubt. The role of the Zodiac continued to play a major role during the current Age of Pisces at least for 6 maybe 7 Centuries if not all the way up to the 16th Century before the false prophet (Pope) abolished it. When you research into "what happened to Astrology" over the past several Centuries, Jewish and Christian authorities have a very difficult time explaining "why" the Enoch Zodiac (with all its meaning and implication) was removed from their religious traditions. <u>Yet, the fact that Astrology/Enoch Zodiac played a key and integral role in both religions is simply indisputable</u>. To deny the importance of the Heavenly Scroll (Zodiac), we would have to turn a blind eye to countless references to the Zodiac in both testaments, declarations made by Yahuah and Yahusha, all the prophets, and ignore the archeological evidence that all loudly proclaim… Yahuah is the author!

Rabbi Joel C. Dobin, *To Rule Both Day And Night: Astrology in the Bible, Midrash, & Talmud* explains:

> "***The basic philosophy of the astrologer is religious***, *regardless of the religious direction from which he seeks the truth. The basic philosophical thrust of astrology derives from the conviction that the human being, God, and the universe are in some way a unity; that man and universe, if you will, both swim in the sea of space-time whose substance is God."*

One of the most anointed and famous of all prophets of Yahuah, Daniel, was an astrologer! Daniel was "Chief Astrologer" under several kings and empires.

> **Daniel 5:11**
> "There is a man in your kingdom who is endowed with a spirit of the holy gods. In the days of your father he was found to have enlightenment, understanding, and wisdom like the wisdom of the gods. Your father, King Nebuchadnezzar, made him chief of the magicians, enchanters, Chaldeans, and diviners."

The proper use of astrology (discerning the Will of Yahuah in 'heaven' as to make it so on Earth) is still practiced today by many Rabbis. **Rabbi Joel C. Dobin** explains:

> *"That all-in-existence is subject to God's will is an essential beginning for the astrologer: 'One Creator, One Creation' should be the mantra for every astrologer! For, combining this latest statement with its forerunner—then man, God, and universe are an essential unity—allows the astrologer to seek in the Heavens for the evidence of God's will for mankind, which will help the individual person as well as the community realize and act on the basic religious statement: 'Make Thy will, my will.'"*

Rabbi Joel C. Dobin continues...

> *"Astrology revealed to me His order and His beauty, and His place for me in the Divine balance that links God, man, and universe into One Balanced Process which never ends in this or on other planes of awareness of life."*

This was the same desire of Yahusha the Messiah. That there is one Creator, one creation, and that he, and all the sons are to be one with the Father, and not his will but "thine be done". Yahusha's hope was that Yahuah's Will, as laid out and defined by Yahuah at creation and written in the stars, be done on this Earth.

Matthew 6:10
"your kingdom come, your will be done, on earth as it is in 'heaven/*shamayim* (where the stars are visible in the sky)"

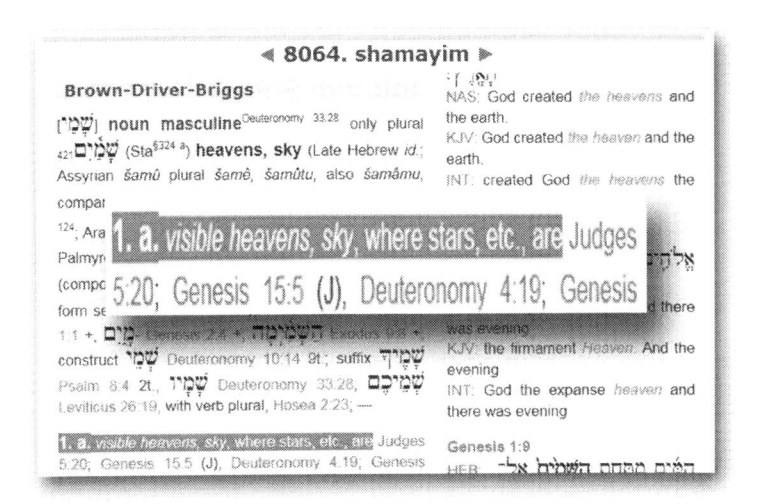

```
◀ 8064. shamayim ▶

Brown-Driver-Briggs

[שָׁמַי] noun masculine Deuteronomy 33:28 only plural
42: שָׁמַיִם (Sta§324 a) heavens, sky (Late Hebrew id.;
Assyrian šamû plural šamê, šamûtu, also šamâmu,
compa...
124, Ara             1. a. visible heavens, sky, where stars, etc., are Judges
Palmyr
(compa  5:20; Genesis 15:5 (J), Deuteronomy 4:19; Genesis
form se
1:1 +,
construct שְׁמֵי Deuteronomy 10:14 9t; suffix שָׁמַי
Psalm 8:4 2t., שָׁמֶיךָ Deuteronomy 33:28, שָׁמָיו
Leviticus 26:19, with verb plural, Hosea 2:23; —
1. a. visible heavens, sky, where stars, etc., are Judges
5:20; Genesis 15:5 (J), Deuteronomy 4:19; Genesis
```

We see in Psalms 11, King David proclaim that Yahuah's throne is in "heaven". What is David referring to? We already know in Psalms 19, David proclaimed the meaning of the Zodiac in great detail.

Psalms 11
4 Yahuah is in his holy temple; Yahuah's throne is in heaven (*shamayim*/Zodiac). His eyes watch; his eyes examine all people.

We also see Isaiah proclaim:

Isaiah 66:1
This is what Yahuah says: "Heaven (shamarym/Zodiac) is my throne, and the earth is my footstool. Where is the house you will build for me? Where will my resting place be?

We see Isaiah declare the exact same reality below. Remember "heavens" is actually specifically referring to *the place in the sky where the stars are*... i.e. the Zodiac. "Starry hosts" are the constellations that hosts the stars ...

> **Isaiah 40:26**
> Lift up your eyes and look to the heavens (the Zodiac): Who created all these? He who brings out the starry host (constellations) one by one and calls forth each (of the constellations) of them by name. Because of his great power and mighty strength, not one of them is missing (there are exactly 12 constellations in every culture dating back to the origin of man!).

Again we see David in Psalms 119 declare that Yahuah's "instructions" endure, they stand secure in heaven i.e. shamarym/Zodiac. The Mazzaroth/Zodiac is Yahuah's Original Revelation to all mankind, laying out His Plan for Man (the timeframe through 2000 year reverse Ages) and His Plan of Salvation through Yahusha the Messiah (as told by the 12 signs from Virgo-Leo). Let's shed the light of "context" on this passage with Psalm 19:

> **Psalm 19**
> 1 The heavens (stars and constellations) declare the glory of Yahuah; the skies proclaim the work of his hands. 2 Day after day they pour forth speech; night after night they reveal knowledge. 3 They have no speech, they use no words; no sound is heard from them. 4 Yet their voice goes out into all the earth, their words to the ends of the Age. In the heavens (among the Stars and Constellations) Yahuah has pitched a tent for the sun (the Zodiac). 5 It is like a bridegroom (Yahusha) coming out of his chamber (to wed the Bride, Remnant Israel), like a champion (Conquering King) rejoicing to run his course (through the ecliptic). 6 It rises at one end of the heavens and makes its circuit (Zodiac means circuit of circle or path) to the other; nothing is deprived of its warmth.

Rabbi Joel C. Dobin summarizes...

> *"Astrology helps man to understand God's will and to put himself in balance with Divine and universal forces, thus enriching his life and experience."*

Historical Evidence

The fundamental role played by the Zodiac throughout the Hebrew journey cannot be denied, and is evident in mosaics found across the region over several centuries. We simply can no longer ignore this overwhelming evidence and just "rationalize it away" simply because it no longer fits into our modern views. We must reclaim what is Yahuah's signature over His creation... the Zodiac ... and restore the message found in the Heavenly Scroll.

The ruins of the Hammath-Tiberias synagogue

The photos on the left reveal the ruins of the Hammath-Tiberias synagogue, used between the 3rd – 8th centuries. See that the floor of the synagogue was adorned with elaborate mosaics. The Ark of the Covenant, the Menorah, and other symbols sacred to the Hebrew religion in the top portion, the middle section containing the Enoch Zodiac in great detail, and the lower section a memorial to the founder of the synagogue. The Zodiac playing the most significant role in both size and as the centerpiece.

We see in this mosaic the Ark of the Covenant…

We see the Menorah along with the 'Lulav and Etrog' which are essential items for Sukkot, we see a Shofar and other items of the Hebrew faith:

And then, of course, even more prominently displayed as the centerpiece… Enoch's Zodiac in tremendous detail as the

Creation Cries Out!

Heavenly Scroll forms the foundation of the synagogue:

This mosaic is one of the most elaborate with careful detail paid to each sign of the Zodiac. The effort, time, and craftsmanship to produce such a mosaic is truly impressive. I can only image how colorful and exotic the sight of this mosaic would have been over a thousand years ago. It is impressive even today:

Mosaic of Zodiac on the floor of the synagogue at Zippori

In lower Galilee, there was discovered the ruins of the synagogue at Zippori (Sepphoris). Again, the Enoch Zodiac was the featured mosaic with the months of the Hebrew Lunar Calendar assigned to each sign of the Zodiac.

From https://en.wikipedia.org/wiki/Sepphoris

The remains of an ancient Tzippori Synagogue have been uncovered in the lower section of the city. It was built in the late 5th or early 6th century, at a time when the town's Christian population was increasing and the strength of the Jewish population was diminishing. Measuring 20.7 meters by 8 meters wide, it was located at the edge of the town.

The mosaic floor is divided into seven parts. Near the entrance there is a scene showing the angels visiting Sarah. The next section shows the binding of Isaac. There is a large Zodiac with the names of the months written in Hebrew as the centerpiece. The Messiah sits in the middle, in his sun chariot (Helios to the Greeks).

The last section shows two lions flanking a wreath, their paws resting on the head of an ox. The most interesting are the central sections of the mosaic. One shows the "tamid" sacrifice, the showbread, and the basket of first fruits form the Temple in Jerusalem. Also shown are a building facade, probably representing the Temple, incense shovels, shofars, and the seven-branched menorah from the Temple. Another section shows Aaron dressed in priestly robes preparing to offer sacrifices of oil, flour, a bull and a lamb.

Synagogue at Ein Gedi

Mosaic Floor of Synagogue at Ein Gedi lists all the signs of the Zodiac and identifies their corresponding months of the Hebrew calendar. Ein Gedi is an oasis located west of the Dead Sea

Mosaic of Zodiac at the Synagogue at Ein Harod

On the floor of the synagogue at Ein Harod, there is a massive Enoch Zodiac mosaic in the Valley Jezreel near Mt. Gilboa.

Mosaic of Zodiac at Synagogue Floor at Beit Alpha

Mosaic of Zodiac signs on the Synagogue Floor at Beit Alpha dating to the Byzantine Period – 6th Century – located at the foot of the northern slopes of Mount Gilboa. Again the centerpiece with the Ark of the Covenant in the upper portion and various pictorials of Biblical characters and stories surrounding and at the bottom portion.

Creation Cries Out!

This synagogue has one of the best preserved mosaics of the Zodiac:

Rabbi Joel C. Dobin...

"Astrology was so much part of Jewish life and experience and so well respected in our tradition and law that the abandonment of Astrology to follow the chimera of scientific linearality was one of the greatest religious tragedies that ever befell our people. For in so doing, we abandoned as well the mystical realities of our faith, our abilities to balance our lives and attain Unity, and we have created of our synagogues and temples arenas of contention for power and concern for financial sufficiency.... I write as an astrologer, seeking to turn all those whose various faiths have seemed to abandon them back to their own faith."

The Zodiac in the early Church

As the early church emerged out of Judaism, we see clear evidence that the Zodiac played a very key role. The early Popes (like all pagan kings/Queens) claimed the Zodiac as their Divine Right to Rule. Below we see the Pope enthroned under the banner of The Zodiac:

Not only did the Pope's reign by the "authority of The Zodiac", the image at the center of the Zodiac was drawn depicting by Jesus H. Christ. Now Christ sits on the throne surrounded by the four beasts described in Ezekiel's and John's visions.

The 4 wheels with a wheel are maintained. The underlying belief in the Zodiac as being the Original Revelation to all mankind was maintained going from Judaism to Christianity.

Creation Cries Out!

We see what appear to be a black rim, the Zodiac Signs, Angels, and then the center. Another mural image found in Catholicism:

387

Rav Sha'ul

Below we see Pope Gregory III attending a Zodiac lesson among his Bishops. Notice the subject being taught is the Zodiac as we see Scorpio and Libra.

We find Zodiac murals adorning ceilings in Catholic structures worldwide.

We see that Pisces became the symbol of "Christianity" and the Age of Pisces. Meeting places were adorned with the sign of Pisces…

If Astrology and the Zodiac was such a major factor in both Judaism and Christianity dating back to the Old Testament prophets, continuing through the first several centuries in the Common Era; what happened? Why are we deprived of the esoteric wisdom and knowledge contained within the very first revelation from Yahuah to humanity?

If the Zodiac was the source of inspiration used by Yahuah to witness the Gospel to Abraham, convey prophetic wisdom to Isaiah, Ezekiel, Daniel, John, and many others, what happened to this Original Revelation? The same thing that happened to the Law of Yahuah, the Feasts of Yahuah, the Name of Yahuah, and the Name of Yahusha!

More Abominations from the False Prophet

Daniel 7:25
He (the false prophet) shall speak words against the Most High, and shall wear out the saints of the Most High, and shall think to change the times and the law; and they shall be given into his hand for a time, times, and half a time.

The Pope is what happened. It was by Papal Decree that the Sabbath was done away with and Sunday worship was established. It was by Papal Decree that Yahuah became a Trinity. It was by Papal Decree that the Passover was changed to Easter. It was by Papal Decree that everything holy to Yahuah, all knowledge of the Creator was deemed "Old" and irrelevant and the original scriptures were labeled the Old Testament. It was by Papal Decree that the Law was deemed to be "done away with". And yes, that same system, the Beastly system prophesied to do all these things, is at the source once again of yet another abomination… outlawing the Zodiac, the Heavenly Scroll.

> In 1586, Pope Sixtus V issued papal bull Coeli et terras condemning judicial (mundane) astrology. This condemnation has deprived humanity (Catholic, Protestants, and all mankind) from the esoteric wisdom found in astrology to this day. Literally abolishing The Heavenly Scroll in the same way the Earthly Scroll (The Torah/Prophets) were abolished by the false prophet!

From this point forward humanity rushed headlong into a scientific dictatorship that denied the power and authority of The Creator. It is the age old battle that began with the "watchers" giving humanity advanced knowledge outside of the context of The Creator. Daniel Taylor in his article ***The Scientific Dictatorship Explained*** published in the **Old Thinker News** journal July, 26, 2011 made a very valid observation:

> *"The ideological roots of the Scientific Dictatorship can be traced to the works of Plato some 2,000 years ago. In truth, humanity has been battling the formation of this tyranny for much of known history."*

As humanity further distanced itself from the last Divine Correction over the past 2000 years we gradually moved toward a world defined by science outside of the knowledge of Yahuah. Yahuah was denied His Glory as Creator and theories such as the "Big Bang" and "Evolution" replace His creative acts. Humanity has fallen so far from Yahuah as the Creator, even Yahuah's Original Revelation to all humanity, written in the stars as illustrated by the Zodiac has been outlawed by the very institutions that claim to represent Him!

As I said earlier in this book "No wonder there are no real prophets on this Earth in these last days! This act to abolish the Heavenly Scroll was one of the last and greatest abominations of the Whore of Babylon, the Christian Church. Add that to all the other abominations of the "one who holds a cup FULL of abomination" and the act of totally abolishing the true word of Yahuah was complete."

Creation Cries Out!

Revelation 17:4 - *The woman was dressed in purple and scarlet, and was glittering with gold, precious stones and pearls. She held a golden cup in her hand, filled with abominable things and the filth of her adulteries*

CHAPTER 14
MESSIANIC SOLAR COUNTERFEITS

Chapter 14 – Messianic Solar Counterfeits

Many critics of the Hebrew Messiah Yahusha claim he never actually existed because it "appears" that his life is simply yet another "myth". They make this claim because there have been many Solar Christ incarnate god-men myths and legends throughout history with the same basic life story.

There are three reasons for these similarities between Christ myths and the true Messiah:

1. The message proclaimed in the heavens concerning the Messiah in the Zodiac was taught to mankind at the beginning of civilization

2. The Watchers taught the message in the Zodiac in a way to pervert the message into worshipping the stars

3. "Jesus" as he is taught actually is a composite "god" invented at the council of Nicaea and is not a true picture of Yahusha the Messiah. I go into this in great detail in this book series. Jesus is a "solar counterfeit"

Every culture throughout history has attempted to fulfill the message in the Zodiac by creating for themselves mythical demi-gods. As a result of these factors we have a false solar deity name Jesus H. Christ that is identical to every other mythical solar messiah all called "Christs" and all their followers called "Christians).

For instance, the Eastern Krishna (which means Christ) is one such counterfeit. Both Jesus and Krishna are often depicted as one or brothers or in identical fashion…

Krishna is depicted with 12 disciples:

All "solar Christ" myths are easily identified because they are depicted in most images with the Sun blazing behind their heads making the same gestures. Notice Krishna even has a "red dot" on his hand where Jesus has nail wounds and both with the blazing Sun behind them. "Jesus" with the equidistant cross of equinoxes identifying him as the fulfillment of the Zodiac:

Krishna is just one example; there actually are many examples of false solar deities throughout history as humanity read the message in the Zodiac and personified that message into counterfeit god-men to worship. We are going to examine the claim that all of them (including the Roman demi-god Jesus H. Christ or "I.H.S.") are all simply myths, one built upon the other.

As I mentioned earlier in this book, the "message" of the Zodiac was perverted into sun worship. Every culture had its own counterfeit messiah or Solar Christ based on the same message found written in the heavens (the Zodiac). Thus we find glaring examples of Yahuah's "revelation" plagiarized for demonic purposes. Research uncovered dozens of such examples and summarized them in the book "The Gods Who Walk Among Us."

Birthday's of the Savior God's worshiped on December 25th

Hermes	Buddha	Krishna	Horus	Hercules	Adonis
Greece	Nepal	India	Egypt	Greece	Phoenician
December 25th	December 25th	December 25th	December 25th	December 25th	December 25th
200 BC	563 BC	900 BC	3000 BC	800 BC	200 BC

Dionysus	Zarathustra	Jesus	Mithras	Tammuz
Greece	Greece	Rome	Persia	Babylon
December 25th	December 25th	December 25th	December 25th	December 25th
500 BC	1000 BC	3 BC	600 BC	400 BC

According to Scripture our Messiah Yahusha was born Feast of Trumpets (September) 3 BC

The worship of the Greek god Helios (the sun) by ancient Jews, for example, refers back to a time when ***Original Revelation*** was splintered and truth was fractured. Men "changed the truth of Yahuah into a lie, and worshipped and served the creature more than the Creator, who is blessed for ever." (Romans 1:25). We see this evident in the Bible:

> **2 Kings 23**
> 4 The king ordered Hilkiah the high priest, the priests next in rank and the doorkeepers to remove from the temple of Yahuah all the articles made *for Baal* (the Babylonian Sun God Nimrod) *and Asherah* (The Babylonian Queen of Heaven Ishtar/Semaramis) and all the starry hosts. He burned them outside Jerusalem in the fields of the Kidron Valley and took the ashes to Bethel. 5 He did away with the idolatrous priests appointed by the kings of Judah to burn incense on the high places of the towns of Judah and on those around Jerusalem—*those who burned incense to Baal, to the sun and moon, to the constellations and to all the starry hosts....* He removed from the entrance to the temple of Yahuah *the horses that the kings of Judah had dedicated to the sun.* They were in the court near the room of an official named Nathan-Melek. *Josiah then burned the chariots dedicated to the sun.*

Let us look at some of these "Solar Messiahs" that <u>were **myths made up by mankind**</u> as humanity tried to understand the message in the Zodiac and seek to fulfill that message. Mankind did not have "faith" in this message that it pointed to <u>a coming</u> Messiah so they created false messiahs along the way to worship. Humanity was intended to look to Yahuah for further revelation as to who this messiah would be and when that messiah would come. Instead, the ancients made up mythical messiah to worship, gave them names, made idols in their image and worshipped them. Not knowing Yahuah, the ancient civilizations were led astray by The Watchers to worship counterfeits.

Yahuah did, however, reveal to His prophets who the true Messiah would be. That Messiah was Yahusha; who did come exactly as foretold by His prophets who understood the Zodiac, and fulfilled exactly the message found written in the stars of him.

The Battle of the Ages

Humanity has been divided from the beginning in a battle to find Truth through the creation that surrounds them. That Truth of a creator is obviously found in creation in its mathematical complexity and precision alone. However, mankind has found it difficult to separate The Creator from His Creation and as a result has consistently fallen in idol worship of the creature above The Creator.

the Bible declares that the story of redemption is told in the Stars in the Heavens and that these celestial bodies were designed by The Creator to be used for signs, season, etc. From the very beginning of humanity, we have attempted to personify The Invisible Creator in the Stars above and in nature here on Earth creating "idols" to worship that represent Yahuah. Early in our development, humanity was clearly given advanced information concerning the workings of our solar system and as a result fell into idolatry by worshipping the Sun and the planets in our solar system. We then personified these "false deities" into Solar Messiahs giving them names and life stories found in the Zodiac.

Humanity has passed down this Sun Worship through many cultures and incorporated it into every religion including Christianity as I will demonstrate in this book series. Many of the very proofs we have that Yahuah exists and that Yahusha is truly the savior have been buried because the Zodiac has been corrupted for use in idolatry as this book has demonstrated. In fact, the Zodiac is not pagan idolatry in itself; it is only USED for purposes that are idolatrous in nature. It is used in ways it was not designed to be used as the message was corrupted by fallen angels as The Book of Enoch documents.

Attributes of all god-men throughout history

Most people know what "their" religion claims about "their" messiah or Christ, but few people realize one startling fact: they all have the same "life" story! Every significant "savior" or "messiah" or "Christ" has many things in common about the myths surrounding their lives. So much so; the question must be asked "are any of these saviors even real or are all of them simply based on the same myth?" Many college students raised "Christian" think they are solid in their faith until they take a course on comparative religions. They come out of this class on comparative religions as atheists because Christianity is a carbon copy of all pagan religions. How do we unravel this historical mystery? The earth has been deceived by Christianity thinking that the religion of Christianity is what is taught in the Bible. This is far from the truth. Christianity has no foundation at all in Biblical Truth as I will prove in this book series.

When looking back throughout history and cultures we see many of the "saviors" have the same basic life story:

- Born of a virgin
- Born on Dec. 25th
- Star in the east heralded their birth
- 3 Kings followed the Eastern Star to adorn "the son of God"
- They had 12 Disciples
- Teacher at 12
- Baptized at 30
- Hung on a cross
- Resurrected after 3 days

We must decipher this mystery once and for all because these traits are written in the stars and are the foundation of every culture's messiah or savior. This "story in the stars" was either written by an invisible Creator who wrote His Plan of Salvation through His handiwork… or ancient pagan civilizations literally combed the stars (with no telescope or technology or mathematical genius) and created an incredibly detailed scientific model of the workings of our solar system and applied that to a fantastically intricate mythical savior and then passed that down through all generations misleading the entire modern population 5,000 years later!

In other words, there is either a creator behind the story written in the stars (and that story was manipulated by fallen angels to lead humanity astray) or; there is no god and ancient man was clever and intelligent enough to understand advanced science and describe our solar system in such a way as to craft a solar messiah that to this day, is the foundation of every religion on earth.

God's Sun or the Sun of God

The race called The Nephilim ruled mankind and (together with The Watchers) provided humanity with advanced knowledge of how our solar system worked. Teaching "worthless knowledge" they promoted a "religion" around this knowledge that instead of giving The Creator glory for His handi-work, taught humanity to worship The Sun. That false religion survives today as Christianity which is a carbon copy of The Mystery Religion created in Babylon. Creating a false religion around the sun was not difficult for the fallen angels (if we put ourselves in the mindset of a culture living 5,000 years ago). The Sun was this amazing object that rose and fell every day. It was seen as a life giving entity and rightfully so. It was the Sun that Yahuah created or The Sun of God that was "the light of the world" and the "savior of mankind" as it rose and fell each day saving humanity from the predator filled darkness bringing life giving light to the world. It wasn't taught by The Watchers as a metaphor for the coming Messiah as it was created to be by Yahuah.

With the help of this advanced race that ruled over humanity, the Zodiac Chart was created to illustrate the movement of "the Sun of God" through the heavenly bodies. Mankind created all kinds of allegories of "how the sun traveled through the Zodiac". The constellations were anthropomorphized or "personified" into having human/creature traits and names that help associate them with the characteristics of the seasons on Earth when the sun passed through them. Humanity was "taught" by this advanced race Yahuah's Plan of Salvation but not in such a way as to point toward the True Messiah or even in a way that gave credit to Yahuah as The Creator. Rather, this plan written in the stars was taught to mankind in such a way as to dilute the significance of the events in the Messiah's Life as false god-men myths were created with these same attributes written of Yahusha in the stars.

The Watchers taught "solar messiahs". These "false Messiahs" have evolved into The False Messiah that is the "god" of the largest religion on Earth. They gave this pre-ordained plan to humanity outside of the will of Yahuah in order to confuse and distort this knowledge and corrupt the Zodiac. Mankind was taught the first "solar messiah" in Nimrod and his son Tammuz. Every messiah or Christ across time and various cultures share the exact same life experiences because they were in fact "written in the stars" concerning the true Messiah Yahusha.

While none of these solar messiahs actually lived as an actual human messiah, they were developed as myths passed on from culture to culture to dilute the importance of this heavenly prophecy concerning Yahusha. So humanity was taught false messiahs from the beginning and led to associate them with The Sun. Humanity personified "God" in the Sky as the Sun and the solar messiah his incarnate on Earth through myth.

The creation of these myths based on the message in the Zodiac is why all religions have the basic message and life story for their own false messiah.

These are the topics of my next two books in this series '***Mystery Babylon the Religion of the Beast***' and '***Christianity and the Great Deception***'. Available on Amazon books world-wide or at www.sabbathcovenant.com.

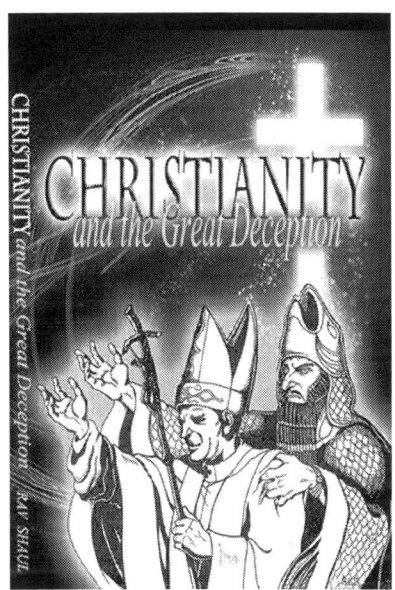

Why the cross is the universal symbol of ancient religions

The picture of the Zodiac was not just an artistic expression or tool to track the sun's movement; it was THE SYMBOL of sun worship and all "solar messiahs". The shorthand symbol of the cross was a cut-out of the center of the Zodiac or a cross with a sunburst behind it.

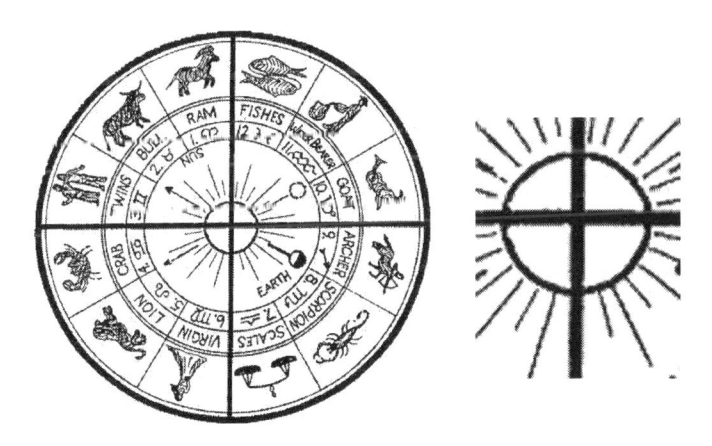

This short hand symbol of the Zodiac identifies the religions of sun worshippers adorned with its sign. Throughout each and every culture we find this symbol as THE symbol of their faith.

For instance, the ancient Babylonian "messiah" Tammuz (Jesus is the later incarnation of Tammuz). We see the cross was worn by his priests and was a symbol of the "T" or Tau the first letter of his name. These priests wore the cross around their neck and on their garments.

Tammuz was the second member of the Babylonian Trinity and regarded as the re-incarnated Nimrod or Ba'al the Sun god. He was "God in the flesh" or the incarnate god.

Creation Cries Out!

We also see this exact symbol, the center of the Zodiac, on Christian Churches around the world:

We see this cross and its association to sun worship many times as the cross is laid over "the sun":

405

Solar Messiahs

Below are a few of the "myths" of Solar Messiahs that were personified based on the message contained in the Zodiac.

> **Horus** – 3000 bc in Egypt. Horus had an enemy named Set. Horus, representing the Sun or Light, battled Set who represented the darkness, it was a metaphoric daily battle of Good vs. Evil as the sun rose and defeated Set then Set returned to defeat Horus/Sun and send the sun to the underworld.
>
> **Krishna of India** – 900 bc. Born of a virgin on December 25th, miracles, star in the east, resurrected
>
> **Dionysus** – Greek 500 bc, hung on a cross, the crucifix is his symbol, performed miracles such as turning water into wine, born of a virgin on Dec 25th, called The King of Kings, God's only begotten son, The Alpha and Omega, resurrected
>
> **Mithra of Persia** – 1200 bc – born of a virgin on December 25th, 12 disciples, miracles, the truth/light, Sunday worship, dead for 3 days, resurrected.

There are many "solar messiahs" in different cultures all subscribing to the same general characteristics because they are based on the message found in the Zodiac of Yahusha:

- Chrishna of Hindostan
- Buddha Sakai of India
- Salivahana of Bermuda
- Osiris and Orus of Egypt
- Odin of Scandinavia
- Crite of Chaldea
- Zoraster and Mithra of Persia
- Baal and Taut his only begotten son of God from Phoenecia

- Indra of Tibet
- Bali of Afghanistan
- Joa of Nepal
- Wittoba of Bilingonese
- Thammuz of Syria
- Atys of Phrygia
- Alcides of Thebes
- Beddru of Japan
- Hesus of the Druids
- Thor, son of Odin, of the Gauls
- And finally… Jesus H. Christ

All born of a virgin on December 25th, heralded by an eastern Star followed by 3 kings, child teacher at 12, at 30 baptized, hung on a cross, dead for 3 days, resurrected. The reason they all have these attributes is because this is the Gospel Message found written in the heavens concerning The Messiah. It is the message of the Zodiac which these ancient cultures were taught by The Watchers.

This is exactly why we must reclaim the Zodiac and its message because these Solar Messiah Myths are constantly used to discredit the true Messiah. We are told that Yahusha is just another myth based on these other mythical Solar Messiah's when it is the other way around. Yahusha was the fulfillment of the Message in the Stars and these other Solar Messiah's were myths based on the Message in the Stars. This was the purpose of corrupting the message so that when Yahusha came mankind would have already been indoctrinated into his life message as it was associated with all pagan god-men. Not realizing what happened we would think Yahusha is just another myth.

The birth sequence of The Messiah is written in the heavens. The star in the East is Sirius, the brightest star in the sky and on December 24th it aligns with the 3 brightest stars in Orion's Belt. These 3 stars are called the same thing today as they were in ancient times, the 3 Kings. These 3 Kings and Sirius all point or form a line directly to the sunrise on December 25th. That is "why" the 3 Kings "follow" the Star in the East to "locate" the rising sun or "birth of God's Sun". The "virgin Mary" is the constellation "Virgo" which in Latin means "Virgin". The ancient glif of Virgo is the altered "M". This is where we get the names for the virgin mothers such as Mary or Odonisis' mother Myrra, or Budha's mother Maya, all beginning with the letter "M". This constellation Virgo is also referred to as "The House of Bread" and the image is that of a virgin girl carrying a sheaf of wheat. This House of Bread represents August or September or the "time of harvest" which is the actual birth season of Yahusha the Messiah (not December 25th). In turn, the name Bethlehem literally translates into "House of Bread".

The Sun foretells of the death and resurrection

There is another very interesting phenomenon that occurs around December 25th or The Winter Solstice. From the Summer Solstice to the Winter Solstice the days become shorter and colder. From the perspective of the Northern Hemisphere the Sun appears to move further south and becomes smaller and smaller as it arcs shorter and shorter over the Southern Horizon. The shortening of the days and the death of the crops as it gets colder symbolize the process of death. It was the death of The Sun.

The sun rises above the horizon less each day as it "dies" until its demise is fully realized as it makes its lowest point in the sky after 6 months of moving south. The sun then STOPS MOVING SOUTH for 3 days. During these 3 days the Sun resides in the vicinity of the Southern Cross or Crux Constellation. After these 3 days on December 25th the Sun moves 1 degree North up from the horizon and thus "rises from the dead" foreshadowing longer days and the coming spring. Thus it is said *"the Sun dies on the cross for 3 days and then rises again"*. This is why Jesus H. Christ and many other sun gods share the crucifixion, 3 day death, and resurrection concept with the true Messiah Yahusha. It is the transition period before the progression of the sun back up from the Southern Hemisphere bringing warmth, longer lasting days, and salvation.

The Sun was a physical metaphor for The Son and foreshadowed his sacrifice. However, they did not celebrate the "resurrection" of the sun until the Spring Equinox or Easter when the sun officially overpowers the darkness (the light side of the Earth gets larger than the dark side) and daytime become longer in duration than nighttime. This led to the pagans celebrating Easter in honor of Tammuz. I explain all of this in this book series in great detail.

All these solar messiahs were "the sun of God", the "light of the world", who "comes again (daily) in the clouds", the Glory of God who defends against and casts off the "darkness" as he is born again every morning and can be seen again coming in the clouds up in heaven with his "crown of thorns" or sun rays. However, these mythical messiahs in ancient cultures were nothing more than man trying to fulfill the message foretold in the heavens before its time!

That message was fulfilled in The Messiah Yahusha in great detail.

CONCLUSION

Conclusion

The purpose of this first book, ***Creation Cries Out!*** is to firmly establish why so many ancient legends and "Christs" have the same basic life story. This is paramount in our search for The False Messiah and our search to understand the True Messiah. The difference between the true and false messiah is in how we understand the Zodiac. Because all false messiahs called Christs are based on the "other Gospel" as the watchers perverted the Heavenly Scroll.

Yahuah declares that He authored the Zodiac…

> **Isaiah 40:26**
> Lift up your eyes and look to the heavens (the Zodiac): Who created all these? He who brings out the starry host (constellations) one by one and calls forth each (of the constellations) of them by name. Because of his great power and mighty strength, not one of them is missing (there are exactly 12 constellations in every culture dating back to the origin of man!).

The Zodiac is His throne…

> **Psalms 11**
> 4 Yahuah is in his holy temple; Yahuah's throne is in heaven (shamayim/Zodiac). His eyes watch; his eyes examine all people.

> **Isaiah 66:1**
> This is what Yahuah says: "Heaven (shamayim/Zodiac) is my throne, and the earth is my footstool. Where is the house you will build for me? Where will my resting place be?

And His message is securely written in the Zodiac and endures for all mankind to "see"…

> **Psalms 119**
> O Yahuah, your instructions endure; they stand secure in heaven (originally written in the stars, untouched by human

hands).

That message is understood by the Zodiac; which is the path the Sun takes through the constellations each year...

> **Psalm 19**
> 1 The heavens (stars and constellations) declare the glory of Yahuah; the skies proclaim the work of his hands. 2 Day after day they pour forth speech; night after night they reveal knowledge. 3 They have no speech, they use no words; no sound is heard from them. 4 Yet their voice goes out into all the earth, their words to the ends of the Age. In the heavens (among the Stars and Constellations) Yahuah has pitched a tent for the sun (the Zodiac). 5 It is like a bridegroom (Yahusha) coming out of his chamber (to wed the Bride, Remnant Israel), like a champion (Conquering King) rejoicing to run his course (through the ecliptic). 6 It rises at one end of the heavens and makes its circuit (Zodiac means circuit of circle or path) to the other; nothing is deprived of its warmth.

The Zodiac is the gospel message of the coming Messiah Yahusha...

> **Genesis 15**
> 5 And he brought him forth abroad, and said, *Look now toward heaven, and tell (what the) the stars (proclaim)*, if thou be able to discern the order of them (the Zodiac): and he said unto him, So shall thy seed be (the Messiah proclaimed by the Zodiac)

It is Yahuah's will declared in the Zodiac that will be done on Earth...

> **Matthew 6:10**
> "your kingdom come, your will be done, on earth as it is (in Heaven) where the stars are visible in the sky (Mazzaroth)"

We are forbidden to misuse the Zodiac by creating images of the Zodiac Signs to worship...

> **Exodus 20**

Yahuah spoke all these words: 2 "I, Yahuah, am your Elohim, who brought you from the land of Egypt, from the house of slavery. 3 "You shall have no other gods before me (in My face). "You shall not make for yourself a carved image or any likeness of anything that is in heaven (shamayim i.e. the Mazzaroth) above or that is on the earth beneath or that is in the water below.

We are forbidden not to worship the signs of the Zodiac, they are not gods but a message to all mankind...

Deuteronomy 3:19
When you look up to the sky (sky is Hebrew shamayim/Zodiac) and see the sun, moon, and stars (speaking of the Zodiac) — the whole heavenly (Mazzaroth/Zodiac) creation — you must not be seduced to worship and serve them (signs of the Zodiac), for Yahuah your Elohim has assigned them (the signs of the Zodiac) to all the people of the world (they were created by Yahuah to proclaim the coming Messiah Yahusha, see Psalm 19, they are not gods).

The Zodiac reveals Yahuah's wrath upon all those who take it literally and worship the Zodiac instead of understanding it as physical to Spiritual parallels, metaphors, and analogies.

Romans 1
18 The wrath of Yahuah is being revealed from heaven (the place where the stars are located i.e. The Zodiac) against all the godlessness and wickedness of people, who suppress the truth (of its message) by their wickedness (and worship the signs of the Zodiac, Sun, Moon, and stars *Deuteronomy 3:19*), 19 since what may be known about Yahuah (the Plan of Salvation) is plain to them (proclaimed in The Zodiac), because Yahuah has made it plain to them (this message goes out unto all the Earth *Psalms 19*, given to all mankind *Deuteronomy 3:19*). 20 For since the creation of the world (written in the stars at creation *Rev. 13:8, 1 Peter 1:20*) Yahuah's invisible qualities—his eternal power and divine nature—have been clearly seen (in The Zodiac *Galatians 3:1*, as Yahuah witnessed the Gospel to Abraham *Genesis 15:5*), being understood (they are metaphors and analogies) from what has been made (in heaven: the Sun, Moon, stars, and

constellations *Psalms 119*), so that people are without excuse. 21 For although they knew Yahuah (is The Creator), they neither glorified him as Elohim nor gave thanks to him (for the message proclaimed in the Zodiac), but their thinking became futile (understanding the Zodiac literally as gods) and their foolish hearts were darkened (to worship the creation over The Creator). 22 Although they claimed to be wise (through philosophy and mythology), they became fools (*1 Cor. 1:25*) 23 and exchanged the glory of the immortal Elohim (the Glory of Yahuah is Yahshua *2 Corinthians 4:6*! So they exchanged Yahusha) for images made to look like a mortal human being (solar demi-gods) and birds and animals and reptiles (the signs of The Zodiac).

What Sha'ul was telling the Greco-Roman people is to look at the very Zodiac they corrupted into mythology. That very Zodiac condemns them being revealed from (the place in the sky where the stars are located) heaven for their literal interpretation. They fail to see the Spiritual message behind it. This is the story of the battle of the Ages in the Bible.

It is the battle between the Truth and Sun Worship. This battle has raged since the creation of man. Yahuah created The Zodiac as a witness to all mankind of His Plan of Salvation through a human messiah. The watchers (fallen angels) perverted that message and revealed to mankind the "secrets preserved in the heavens" but in such a way as to cause mankind to worship the Sun, Moon, Stars, and Constellations. They viewed the Sun as the supreme deity. They then created for themselves Solar Messiahs to fulfill the message in the Zodiac (pagan demi-god Christs from Tammuz to Jesus).

This twisted version of the Zodiac was formulated into a religion in Babylon. This religion of sun worship was then dispersed throughout the Earth when the languages were confused at the Tower of Babel. Every pagan religion on Earth is an incarnation of the religion of sun worship in Babylon which was based on the corrupt message of the Zodiac. The message in the Zodiac is universal (being authored by the Creator) that is why every pagan solar messiah or 'Christ' is a demi-god member of a Trinity with the same basic life story. These demi-gods, beginning with the Babylonian Tammuz, were all human attempts at fulfilling the Heavenly Scroll.

The Zodiac (the path the sun takes through the constellations), the names and meanings of each constellation, and the names and meanings of the stars that make them up are all divinely inspired and created by Yahuah. The images that are associated with the Zodiac are simply pictographs that represent the meaning of the constellation.

The sons of Yahuah have passed down the proper meaning of the Zodiac from Seth to Enoch to Noah to Abraham to Daniel to Yahusha who fulfilled its message, to the Nazarenes to me, Rav Sha'ul to you today. The pagans have passed down the twisted version of the Zodiac which idolizes the Sun and the signs of the Zodiac as to worship them.

In conclusion, what we have today is the true Zodiac passed down by Seth to Enoch to Noah to Abraham to Daniel to Yahusha to the Nazarenes represented by the Enoch Zodiac.

Then we have the pagan Zodiac, which perverted the Enoch Zodiac into mythical 'gods' and worshipped the sun and signs of the Zodiac. All the "signs" went from being pictographs to Greek 'gods'...

Creation Cries Out!

And finally, we have the Christian (Christopagan) Zodiac which, through syncretism, merged the true Zodiac with the pagan Zodiac

We see the center throne described by all the prophets changed to the image of "Jesus" making the sign 666 with cryptic hand gestures, the mark of the beast Xi, Psi, Sigma (see my book *The Antichrist Revealed!*), the 4 beasts removed along with his throne, the sun symbol of the equidistant cross added behind his head in replace of the crown of Glory. We have Chinese, Babylonian, Sumerian, and many others cultural Zodiacs. Every culture since the creation of man was given this divine revelation and either interpreted it righteously by the Ruach, or misinterpreted it completely into a symbol of idolatry (mostly the latter).

The 'Battle of the Ages' continues…

This is "the Battle of the Ages" in Scripture; the battle for the message contained in the "Zodiac" … ***The Heavenly Scroll***:
- Jerusalem vs. Rome/Babylon
- Yahuah vs. Sol Invictus/Ba'al
- The Shema vs. Incarnation
- Yahusha vs. Jesus/Tammuz
- The son of God vs. God the Son
- The Sabbath vs. Dias Solis/Sunday
- The Passover Lamb vs. Easter/The Ishtar Pig
- The Holy Days vs. Holidays
- The Law vs. Lawlessness
- The Spirit of Truth/Torah vs. The Spirit of Error/Law abolished
- The Spirit of Yahuah vs. the Spirit of the False Messiah/Incarnation
- The Nazarene vs. Christianity/Christopaganism found in all pagan religions whose roots go back to Babylon.

In my book series, I established that there was ***Original Revelation*** to man from Yahuah that was corrupted into Sun Worship. I then begin to define ***The Mystery Religion of Babylon***. It is important we understand exactly what religion evolved out of Babylon because it is that religion that is condemned in the Bible as the religion that leads humanity astray at the end. It is THE religion that The Messiah returns to destroy with his testimony.

The Babylonian religion is the formal religion built around the "other Gospel" of the corrupted Zodiac as taught by the watchers. The religion that evolved out of Babylon was dispersed throughout the Earth when Yahuah scattered humanity and confused the languages at The Tower of Babel. That Mystery Religion was Sun Worship, and it was passed down from Babylon to Egypt to Rome and survives even today. Christianity is identical to the Mystery Religion of Babylon which is proven in my book series.

Book 1: Creation Cries Out!

In this book I trace the great deception back to its origin and explain how the "Gospel message in the stars" was corrupted into another gospel. I re-establish the message contained in the Heavenly Scroll and give Yahuah the Glory He deserves as the Creator of all things. In this book, the original revelation found written in the stars is broken down, defined, and glorified. I explain how the watchers corrupted the true message and taught mankind to worship the creation over the Creator. Creation Cries Out! Reveals the secrets preserved in the Heavens, and provides clear instruction so that the Great Seal over the Bible and the books of prophecy can be opened. Every prophet of Yahuah based their predictions on the Heavenly Scroll and described it in great detail.

Book 2: Mystery Babylon the Religion of the Beast

In this book I explain how that corrupted message was formulated into a formal religion in Babylon and define that religion as it existed then. We will go back to the very beginning of "paganism" and examine the gods and rituals that define this false religion. We will trace this religion, show how it evolved, who created it, and how it came to dominate all mankind. This information is vital as there is prophesied to be, at the end, a religion on Earth based on Mystery Babylon that deceives all humanity. The only way to properly identify that religion today that has fulfilled this prophecy is to fully understand Mystery Babylon.

Book 3: 'Christianity and the Great Deception'

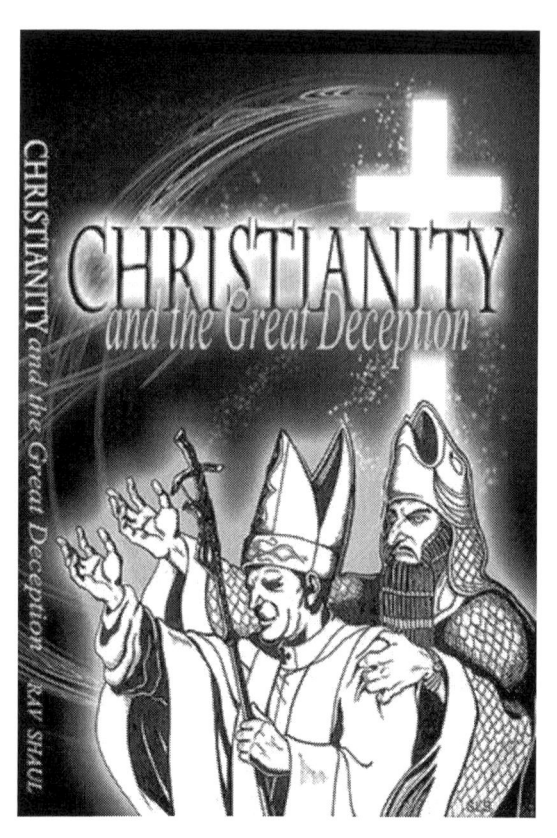

I compare Christianity to Mystery Babylon and prove that it is a carbon copy and is the prophesied false religion. Every description of "God" is taken directly from Babylon. From the Trinity to calling the Creator "The LORD" are all based on sun worship. I explain where Jesus H. Christ came from, who created that false image, and how that false messiah is a carbon copy of the second member of the Babylonian Trinity named Tammuz. From the false sacrifice of a pig on Easter, to Sunday worship, to Christmas... every aspect of the Christian Religion is a carbon copy of Mystery Babylon! I document everything carefully from historical sources, the Catholic Church documents, and the Bible. No one who has read this book has remained a "Christian" after finishing it.

Book 4: 'The Antichrist Revealed!'

In this book I prove that Jesus H. Christ is the false image of the true messiah, and I demonstrate how he meets every prophecy of the "Antichrist". I define in great detail such things as the Abomination of Desolation, the Spirit of the Antichrist, the Spirit of Error, the other Gospel, and much more. In this book, I demonstrate through Biblical prophecy that the false messiah is an "image" of the true Messiah not an actual person. This book is 500 pages of solid proof that the "god" of this Earth, Jesus Christ is the "Abominable Beast" foretold by name, sacrifice, and rituals. I prove that "Jesus" is not the name of the Messiah in any language much less Hebrew. We dissect that name and prove how the name of the Messiah was intentionally altered to give glory to Zeus over Yahuah. The true name of the Messiah is Yahusha.

Book 5: 'The Kingdom'

With the false religion, the false messiah, the false sacrifice, the false rituals clearly defined in the first 4 books, I begin to relay a firm foundation in what is true. In this book I define The Kingdom of Yahuah in great detail. I explain how all previous 6 covenants were transposed into the final 7th Covenant of Yahusha. I breakdown every aspect of the Kingdom using physical to spiritual parallels of a kingdom on Earth. What is this Kingdom, what is its purpose, what is its domain, who is its King, what is its constitution, who are its citizens, and what responsibility to the citizens who gain citizenship? All answered in this book.

Book 6: 'The Yahushaic Covenant Volume 1 - The Mediator'

In this book I break down The New Covenant and explain who Yahusha is in relation to Yahuah, what our roles are in the covenant of Yahusha, and much more. The Yahushaic Covenant is the "Salvation of Yahuah Covenant". I explain the role the Law plays in our lives under covenant with Yahusha. I explain the effects of Hellenism and blending the truth with paganism. I breakdown the scripture in context, shedding light on the writings in the Renewed Covenant with the original scriptures (Old Testament if you must). I re-teach the scriptures in light of the ancient language and cultural matrix of the 1st Century people of Yahuah living in the land of Israel.

Book 7: 'The Yahushaic Covenant Volume 2 - The Law and the Sha'uline Doctrine'

In this book, I explain the role the Law plays in our lives and re-teach Sha'ul's writings from the standpoint of intent. I overcome the Christian lie that Sha'ul taught against the Torah. We go in and take a hard look at how Sha'ul's writing were translated and "twisted" by the Greeks into another Gospel called The Pauline Doctrine. In this book, I introduce us all to Rav Sha'ul the leader of the Nazarenes! What does that mean, and what does that one fact say about the way his writings have been translated today? I explain the various aspects of The Law, how it was transposed over time from the Mind of Yahuah, to written in the stars at creation, to given orally, to written in stone, to finally written on our hearts. I explain the various jurisdictional aspects of the Law, look at the Law from the standpoint of intent, and provide solid instruction to the Nazarene today in how to approach the Law of Yahuah.

Book 8: 'The Yahushaic Covenant Volume 3 - Melchizedek and the Passover Lamb'

What does Melchizedek really mean? In this book I explain how Yahusha became the King of Kings and the Eternal High Priest by blood lineage to King David and the ordained Zadok Priesthood. We travel back 2,000 years to the time of the Messiah's birth to fully understand the mindset of that time. A time of great expectation toward the coming Messiah. We look back into historical documents surrounding that time period to identify the lineage of Yahusha. Lineage that was lost to antiquity when Rome burned the original manuscripts. Who were Yahusha's "other grandparents" that contributed equally to his bloodline, we have just never been introduce to? How is Yahusha "King of Israel". How is Yahusha the "High Priest of Israel". The Bible declares Yahusha inherited those titles. If so, how and from whom? This book is a must read and introduction to the REAL Messiah in a way you have never known him.

Book 9: 'The Narrow Gate'

In this book I explain how keeping the Feasts of Yahuah properly is a pre-requisite of entering the Kingdom. The Feast Cycle is the "Narrow Gate" of a wedding and we must rehearse these events from the standpoint of "a Bride". What is the true meaning of the feasts, what are they rehearsing, how do we keep them? All these questions are answered and more in the final book in this series, The Narrow Gate.

Book 10: The Mistranslated Book of Galatians

The letter to the Galatians is one of the most mistranslated (purposely) books in the Bible. The Greeks twisted the words of Sha'ul into a lie to abolish the Law. In this book, I go verse by verse showing were and how the words were twisted, showing the proper translation, and then using all of Sha'ul's writing to shed light on what Sha'ul was talking about in this letter. The resulting translation is the first of its kind! The real letter to the Galatians says the exact opposite of what you read in your English Bibles. The basic foundation of the Christian Church is found to be a lie and the truth revealed in this book about what Sha'ul actually taught concerning The Law, Circumcision, and many other things.

Book 11: The Nazarene

The true Messiah was a Nazarene. What does that mean exactly? Who were The Nazarenes, what did they believe, and what happened to them? What does it mean to be a Nazarene today? This book will change the way you see Yahusha the Nazarene. I go into depth about who Yahusha was defining his humanity vs his divinity. This book is an all out assault on the Spirit of the False Messiah! Each page will have you putting the book down to just say "Wow!". I explain how Yahusha serves as Eternal High Priest and by what authority. How Yahusha is the King of Kings and what they means. The Nazarene is 600 pages of truth and history hidden from us all for 2,000 years by tradition and religion and a "must have"! It will change your life.

All Glory belongs to Yahuah. He is our Creator, Author of the Heavenly Scroll, and Father of the called out ones (Nazarenes). And to Yahusha the Nazarene, the Messiah and Royal High Priest of Israel, I say…

"WORTHY IS THE LAMB! TO RECEIVE HONOR, AND GLORY, AND POWER, AND PRAISE"

HALLELUYAHUAH

LET IS BE SO DONE, ON EARTH AS IT IS WRITTEN IN THE HEAVENLY SCROLL.

Kingdom blessings, and much love…

Rav Sha'ul

If this book has been a blessing to you, please support this ministry. Click on the donate button at www.sabbathcovenant.com

Made in the USA
Middletown, DE
05 June 2017